SO-ECM-895

Lingua TOEFL® CBT
Test Book II

Practice Test 7, 8, 9, 10, 11, and 12

LinguaForum

TOEFL® and TWE® are registered trademarks of Educational Testing Service. This publication is neither endorsed nor reviewed by ETS.

JUN 1 4 2003

Lingua TOEFL® CBT: Test Book II

Practice Test 7, 8, 9, 10, 11, and 12

Prior editions Copyright © 2000, 2001 by Lingua Forum, Inc.

Published by Lingua Forum, Inc.
Copyright © 2002 by Lingua Forum, Inc.
All rights reserved.

No part of this book may be reproduced or transmitted
in any form or by any means, electronic or mechanical,
including photocopying, recording, or by any information storage
and retrieval system without the written permission of the publisher.

Printed with corrections, October 2002

ISBN: 89-89260-20-5 94740

TOEFL® is a registered trademark of Educational Testing Service.
This book has been neither reviewed nor endorsed by ETS.
Printed in the Republic of Korea

Reference Number: 10210015/02080115/01310240/10250250

Contents

What is the TOEFL?

The Test of English as a Foreign Language (TOEFL) is a vital measure of proficiency in English. TOEFL covers the essentials of English, including grammar, listening, and reading. TOEFL focuses on the basic principles of English. TOEFL assists English study by promoting mastery of basic principles. These principles are essential and cannot be overemphasized. Mastering essentials is the key to success in TOEFL. TOEFL requires strong basic skills in English. Mastering those skills is a must. TOEFL therefore leads to the right direction in English study because it requires thorough grasp of the basic principles of English.

TOEFL and ETS (Educational Testing Service)

Since 1963, the TOEFL has been used by scholarship selection committees of governments, universities, and agencies such as Fulbright, the Agency for International Development, AMIDEAST, the Latin American Scholarship Program, and many others as a standard measure to evaluate the English proficiency of candidates whose native language is not English. Also, most admissions committees at colleges and universities in the United States and Canada refer to TOEFL test scores. They require foreign applicants to submit TOEFL scores along with transcripts to be considered for admission.

The Educational Testing Service (ETS), based in Princeton, New Jersey, U.S.A., administers the test under the general direction of the College Board and the Graduate Record Examinations Board. Sylvan Learning Systems Inc. administers the computer-based TOEFL test at Sylvan Technology Centers in various locations. ETS also administers English proficiency tests such as TOEIC and most of the entrance exams. Other tests include SAT, GRE, GMAT, and LSAT. Because there are no passing or failing scores on tests administered by ETS, each institution applies its own standards.

TOEFL Scoring

TOEFL is a test to assess foreigners' proficiency in English. For this reason, it is used not only for university and college admissions, but also for middle/high school transfer admissions. To be admitted to a university in North America, where the acceptable score range differs from one school and major to another, a score of PBT 500 to 630 (CBT 173 to 267) is the average requirement for an established institution. A few schools will consider scores as low as PBT 450 (CBT 133), but the quality of education at such institutions should be regarded with skepticism.

The highest possible score on TOEFL is PBT 677 (CBT 300). Scores always end with 0, 3, or 7 as the final digit. Therefore, a score such as 555 cannot be a valid one supplied by ETS, and claims to have received "the highest score in the world" are fictitious. Moreover, ETS does not report scores in percentage terms, because TOEFL evaluates an individual's linguistic competency. That is why the percentage concept, which promotes comparison of scores, should not be applied to TOEFL.

Characteristics of CBT (Computer-Based TOEFL)

CBT TOEFL was introduced in 1998 in many parts of the world and has been administered in eastern Asia since October 2000. This change of methods is not limited to using a computer in place of paper and pencil. Question types and passages also have been modified greatly, and new material has been added.

Because length and contents were altered, previous PBT-style questions are no longer appropriate for the new CBT TOEFL. Also, TOEFL's switch to CAT means that unlike PBT, where all students received the same contents, the test will present students with questions on different levels.

The Listening and Structure sections are CAT, and other sections are computer-linear. The number of questions and the time allotted are not identical for all TOEFL tests. Total test time (answering + directions + tutorials) differs from one examinee to another.

If one does not know how to use a computer, one needs to spend some time on tutorials before starting the test. A test-taker who already knows how to use a computer, on the other hand, will save time by skipping the tutorials.

Time management is up to the individual. If one finishes the Listening section before the allotted time is up, then one can proceed to the next section and thereby finish the entire test before other examinees.

Below is a comparison of number of questions and time allotted for PBT and CBT.

	LISTENING		STRUCTURE		READING		WRITING	
	PBT	CBT	PBT	CBT	PBT	CBT	PBT	CBT
Number of Question	50	30~49/50	40	20~25	50	44~55	1 (Optional)	1 (Mandatory)
Time (min.)	30~40	40~60	25	15~20	55	70~90	30	30

- **Listening: Focus on campus-related topics; de-emphasis on idioms**

  (1) Unlike the PBT, which had Parts A, B, and C, CBT is composed of Part A and Part B.
  (2) Also unlike the PBT, where two speakers had only one turn each to speak, the CBT gives each speaker either one or two turns.
  (3) Part B involves Casual Conversation, Academic Discussion/Seminar, and Short and Long Lecture.
  (4) Casual Conversation in CBT Part B might be longer than in the PBT.
  (5) Academic Discussion/Seminar involves two to five speakers.
  (6) Short and Long Lectures are on academic topics exclusively.
  (7) Two-answer questions, Matching questions, Ordering questions, and Graphic questions are newly added to the CBT TOEFL.

- **Structure: Less than half of the Structure-Writing section**

  (1) The separate portions of the Structure and Written section on the PBT have been combined into a Structure section on the CBT.
  (2) The number of questions has been lowered from 40 in PBT to 20 to 25 in CBT. In the scoring system, unlike PBT, the score from the Structure section and Writing section is calculated together in CBT. In other words, the Structure-Writing section consists of one-third of the total score (300 points). However, it is known that Structure is less than half of the Structure-Writing section. Although the Structure section has been de-emphasized, Structure remains vital, because grammar is still the foundation of English studies.

- **Reading: Introduction of Antonyms**

  (1) Extended readings
  (2) Graphic-related questions
  (3) Introduction of new Insertion question
  (4) Antonym questions have been seen only rarely since May 2000.

- **Characteristics of CAT**

  (1) Questions in CAT sections are categorized by difficulty and content, and are chosen by the computer according to how one answered previous questions. The individual student's performance determines which questions are asked.
  (2) CBT TOEFL Structure and Listening sections are tested as CAT, and therefore the first three to five questions influence the section score greatly. In the Reading section following the PBT, all students are presented with similarly advanced material.

- **Directions**

  (1) Be able to use CBT TOEFL icons on screen before the actual test.
  (2) Because Structure and Listening sections are CAT, skipping questions is not allowed.
  (3) In the Structure and Listening sections, after clicking on the answer, the next question will not appear unless the Answer Confirm icon is clicked. Once the Answer Confirm icon is clicked, previous questions cannot be viewed again.
  (4) Because the Reading section is not CAT, but linear as in PBT, students may proceed to the next question without answering and may return to review previously presented material.
  (5) In all sections, remaining time is indicated on the monitor. Examinees therefore should think carefully about time management.

● Effects of Changes in CBT

With the change to CBT, TOEFL became EASIER to score up to CBT 230, and became HARDER to score for CBT 270 and above. The reasons for ease of scoring are: (1) The Reading section, which was one of the most difficult parts of the PBT TOEFL, became much easier because of time allotted. (2) Generally, the Writing section is often considered the most difficult part. However, with a mediocre writing skill, 3.0~3.5 can be easily obtained, and with just 2~3 weeks of preparation, scoring 4.5 can be easy. (3) In the CBT Listening section, the next stimulus can be heard only after choosing an answer and confirming it. The test-takers are not limited to 12 seconds between questions as in a PBT test, and may take as much time as needed to select an answer. (4) Idiomatic expressions are rarely asked any more, reducing the number of things to memorize for the Listening section.

The reasons for increased difficulty are: (1) Most of the TOEFL test-takers are not yet accustomed to the computer testing style and automatically assume CBT is difficult. For example, examinees need to roll down the scroll bar on screen to read the entire script in the Reading section. However, if reading in that fashion is not familiar, the test-taker can feel uncomfortable during the test. For all sections, only one question appears on the computer screen. However, examinees might feel they want to choose the order in which they answer questions. Test-takers need to make themselves familiar and comfortable with the CBT TOEFL before the actual test begins. (2) Each stimulus is followed by questions and the questions can only be known after the stimulus is presented. Therefore, the strategy for choosing an answer by looking at the answer choices while listening cannot be applied to CBT TOEFL. (3) The Listening section's Long Lectures can be up to 300~400 words in length. Therefore, test-takers need practice with Long Lectures. For examinees who want to score CBT 270 or above, more exercise for listening is required than in the PBT. (4) Scoring high in the Writing section can be challenging for some.

● Concordance Table ●

Total Score Comparison

Paper-Based Total	Computer-Based Total	Paper-Based Total	Computer-Based Total
677	300	447	130
673	297	443	127
670	293	440	123
667	290	437	123
663	287	433	120
660	287	430	117
657	283	427	113
653	280	423	113
650	280	420	110
647	277	417	107
643	273	413	103
640	273	410	103
637	270	407	100
633	267	403	97
630	267	400	97
627	263	397	93
623	263	393	90
620	260	390	90
617	260	387	87
613	257	383	83
610	253	380	83
607	253	377	80
603	250	373	77
600	250	370	77
597	247	367	73
593	243	363	73
590	243	360	70
587	240	357	70
583	237	353	67
580	237	350	63
577	233	347	63
573	230	343	60
570	230	340	60
567	227	337	57
563	223	333	57
560	220	330	53
557	220	327	50
553	217	323	50
550	213	320	47
547	210	317	47
543	207	313	43
540	207	310	40
537	203		
533	200		
530	197		
527	197		
523	193		
520	190		
517	187		
513	183		
510	180		
507	180		
503	177		
500	173		
497	170		
493	167		
490	163		
487	163		
483	160		
480	157		
477	153		
473	150		
470	150		
467	147		
463	143		
460	140		
457	137		
453	133		
450	133		

Range Comparison

Paper-Based Total	Computer-Based Total
660-677	287-300
640-657	273-283
620-637	260-270
600-617	250-260
580-597	237-247
560-577	220-233
540-557	207-220
520-537	190-203
500-517	173-187
480-497	157-170
460-477	140-153
440-457	123-137
420-437	110-123
400-417	97-107
380-397	83-93
360-377	70-80
340-357	60-70
320-337	47-57
310-317	40-47

Section Scaled Score Comparison

Listening		Structure / Writing		Reading	
Score-to-Score		**Score-to-Score**		**Score-to-Score**	
Paper-Based Listening Comprehension	Computer-Based Listening	Paper-Based Structure and Written Expression	Computer-Based Structure/Writing	Paper-Based Reading Comprehension	Computer-Based Reading
68	30	68	30	67	30
67	30	67	29	66	29
66	29	66	28	65	28
65	28	65	28	64	28
64	27	64	27	63	27
63	27	63	27	62	26
62	26	62	26	61	26
61	25	61	26	60	25
60	25	60	25	59	25
59	24	59	25	58	24
58	23	58	24	57	23
57	22	57	23	56	22
56	22	56	23	55	21
55	21	55	22	54	21
54	20	54	21	53	20
53	19	53	20	52	19
52	18	52	20	51	18
51	17	51	19	50	17
50	16	50	18	49	16
49	15	49	17	48	16
48	14	48	17	47	15
47	13	47	16	46	14
46	12	46	15	45	13
45	11	45	14	44	13
44	10	44	14	43	12
43	9	43	13	42	11
42	9	42	12	41	11
41	8	41	11	40	10
40	7	40	11	39	9
39	6	39	10	38	9
38	6	38	9	37	8
37	5	37	9	36	8
36	5	36	8	35	7
35	4	35	8	34	7
34	4	34	7	33	6
33	3	33	7	32	6
32	3	32	6	31	5
31	2	31	6		
Range-to-Range		**Range-to-Range**		**Range-to-Range**	
Paper-Based Listening Comprehension	Computer-Based Listening	Paper-Based Structure and Written Expression	Computer-Based Structure/Writing	Paper-Based Reading Comprehension	Computer-Based Reading
64-68	27-30	64-68	27-30	64-67	28-30
59-63	24-27	59-63	25-27	59-63	25-27
54-58	20-23	54-58	21-24	54-58	21-24
49-53	15-19	49-53	17-20	49-53	16-20
44-48	10-14	44-48	14-17	44-48	13-16
39-43	6-9	39-43	10-13	39-43	9-12
34-38	4-6	34-38	7-9	34-38	7-9
31-33	2-3	31-33	6-7	31-33	5-6

Practice Test 7

Listening: 60 Minutes (including listening time)
Structure: 15 Minutes
Reading: 70 Minutes
Writing: 30 Minutes

Suggested Total Time: 175 Minutes

ANSWER SHEET

Lingua TOEFL® CBT Test Book II
PRACTICE TEST 7

Name	
Sex	☐ male ☐ female
E-mail address	
Telephone No.	

No. of Correct Answers/Converted Score		
Listening		
Structure		
Reading		
Writing		
TOTAL		

Section 1: Listening		Section 2: Structure	Section 3: Reading	
1 Ⓐ Ⓑ Ⓒ Ⓓ	40	1 Ⓐ Ⓑ Ⓒ Ⓓ	1 Ⓐ Ⓑ Ⓒ Ⓓ	31 Ⓐ Ⓑ Ⓒ Ⓓ
2 Ⓐ Ⓑ Ⓒ Ⓓ		2 Ⓐ Ⓑ Ⓒ Ⓓ	2 Ⓐ Ⓑ Ⓒ Ⓓ	32 Ⓐ Ⓑ Ⓒ Ⓓ
3 Ⓐ Ⓑ Ⓒ Ⓓ		3 Ⓐ Ⓑ Ⓒ Ⓓ	3 Ⓐ Ⓑ Ⓒ Ⓓ	33 Ⓐ Ⓑ Ⓒ Ⓓ
4 Ⓐ Ⓑ Ⓒ Ⓓ		4 Ⓐ Ⓑ Ⓒ Ⓓ	4 Ⓐ Ⓑ Ⓒ Ⓓ	34 Ⓐ Ⓑ Ⓒ Ⓓ
5 Ⓐ Ⓑ Ⓒ Ⓓ	41 Ⓐ Ⓑ Ⓒ Ⓓ	5 Ⓐ Ⓑ Ⓒ Ⓓ	5	35 Ⓐ Ⓑ Ⓒ Ⓓ
6 Ⓐ Ⓑ Ⓒ Ⓓ	42 Ⓐ Ⓑ Ⓒ Ⓓ	6 Ⓐ Ⓑ Ⓒ Ⓓ	6 Ⓐ Ⓑ Ⓒ Ⓓ	36
7 Ⓐ Ⓑ Ⓒ Ⓓ	43 Ⓐ Ⓑ Ⓒ Ⓓ	7 Ⓐ Ⓑ Ⓒ Ⓓ	7 Ⓐ Ⓑ Ⓒ Ⓓ	37 Ⓐ Ⓑ Ⓒ Ⓓ
8 Ⓐ Ⓑ Ⓒ Ⓓ	44 Ⓐ Ⓑ Ⓒ Ⓓ	8 Ⓐ Ⓑ Ⓒ Ⓓ	8 Ⓐ Ⓑ Ⓒ Ⓓ	38 Ⓐ Ⓑ Ⓒ Ⓓ
9 Ⓐ Ⓑ Ⓒ Ⓓ	45 Ⓐ Ⓑ Ⓒ Ⓓ	9 Ⓐ Ⓑ Ⓒ Ⓓ	9 Ⓐ Ⓑ Ⓒ Ⓓ	39
10 Ⓐ Ⓑ Ⓒ Ⓓ	46	10 Ⓐ Ⓑ Ⓒ Ⓓ	10 Ⓐ Ⓑ Ⓒ Ⓓ	40 Ⓐ Ⓑ Ⓒ Ⓓ
11 Ⓐ Ⓑ Ⓒ Ⓓ		11 Ⓐ Ⓑ Ⓒ Ⓓ	11	41 Ⓐ Ⓑ Ⓒ Ⓓ
12 Ⓐ Ⓑ Ⓒ Ⓓ		12 Ⓐ Ⓑ Ⓒ Ⓓ	12 Ⓐ Ⓑ Ⓒ Ⓓ	42 Ⓐ Ⓑ Ⓒ Ⓓ
13 Ⓐ Ⓑ Ⓒ Ⓓ		13 Ⓐ Ⓑ Ⓒ Ⓓ	13 Ⓐ Ⓑ Ⓒ Ⓓ	43 Ⓐ Ⓑ Ⓒ Ⓓ
14 Ⓐ Ⓑ Ⓒ Ⓓ	47 Ⓐ Ⓑ Ⓒ Ⓓ	14 Ⓐ Ⓑ Ⓒ Ⓓ	14 Ⓐ Ⓑ Ⓒ Ⓓ	44 Ⓐ Ⓑ Ⓒ Ⓓ
15 Ⓐ Ⓑ Ⓒ Ⓓ	48 Ⓐ Ⓑ Ⓒ Ⓓ	15 Ⓐ Ⓑ Ⓒ Ⓓ	15 Ⓐ Ⓑ Ⓒ Ⓓ	
16 Ⓐ Ⓑ Ⓒ Ⓓ	49 Ⓐ Ⓑ Ⓒ Ⓓ	16 Ⓐ Ⓑ Ⓒ Ⓓ	16	
17 Ⓐ Ⓑ Ⓒ Ⓓ	50 Ⓐ Ⓑ Ⓒ Ⓓ	17 Ⓐ Ⓑ Ⓒ Ⓓ	17 Ⓐ Ⓑ Ⓒ Ⓓ	
18 Ⓐ Ⓑ Ⓒ Ⓓ		18 Ⓐ Ⓑ Ⓒ Ⓓ	18	
19		19 Ⓐ Ⓑ Ⓒ Ⓓ	19 Ⓐ Ⓑ Ⓒ Ⓓ	
		20 Ⓐ Ⓑ Ⓒ Ⓓ	20 Ⓐ Ⓑ Ⓒ Ⓓ	
			21 Ⓐ Ⓑ Ⓒ Ⓓ	
			22 Ⓐ Ⓑ Ⓒ Ⓓ	
20 Ⓐ Ⓑ Ⓒ Ⓓ			23 Ⓐ Ⓑ Ⓒ Ⓓ	
21 Ⓐ Ⓑ Ⓒ Ⓓ			24	
22 Ⓐ Ⓑ Ⓒ Ⓓ			25 Ⓐ Ⓑ Ⓒ Ⓓ	
23 Feudalism –			26 Ⓐ Ⓑ Ⓒ Ⓓ	
Empire –			27 Ⓐ Ⓑ Ⓒ Ⓓ	
International relations –			28 Ⓐ Ⓑ Ⓒ Ⓓ	
24 Ⓐ Ⓑ Ⓒ Ⓓ			29	
25 Ⓐ Ⓑ Ⓒ Ⓓ			30 Ⓐ Ⓑ Ⓒ Ⓓ	
26 Ⓐ Ⓑ Ⓒ Ⓓ				
27 Ⓐ Ⓑ Ⓒ Ⓓ				
28 Ⓐ Ⓑ Ⓒ Ⓓ				
29 Ⓐ Ⓑ Ⓒ Ⓓ				
30 Ⓐ Ⓑ Ⓒ Ⓓ				
31 Ⓐ Ⓑ Ⓒ Ⓓ				
32 Ⓐ Ⓑ Ⓒ Ⓓ				
33 Ⓐ Ⓑ Ⓒ Ⓓ				
34 Ⓐ Ⓑ Ⓒ Ⓓ				
35 Ⓐ Ⓑ Ⓒ Ⓓ				
36 Ⓐ Ⓑ Ⓒ Ⓓ				
37 Ⓐ Ⓑ Ⓒ Ⓓ				
38 Ⓐ Ⓑ Ⓒ Ⓓ				
39 Ⓐ Ⓑ Ⓒ Ⓓ				

■ **Have you taken the official TOEFL Test?**

☐ Yes   if any →
☐ No

PBT Score	
Listening	
Structure	
Reading	
Writing	
TOTAL	

CBT Score	
Listening	
Structure	
Reading	
Writing	
TOTAL	

■ **Educational background**

☐ middle/high school   ☐ undergraduate   ☐ graduate

SIGNED: _____
(SIGN YOUR NAME AS IF SIGNING A BUSINESS LETTER.)

DATE: ____ / ____ / ____
MO.   DAY   YEAR

Cut here.

LinguaForum

Copyright © 2002 by Lingua Forum, Inc. All rights reserved.

ANSWER SHEET

Lingua TOEFL® CBT Test Book II
PRACTICE TEST 7

Read the topic below and then make any notes that will help you plan your response. Begin typing your response in the box at the bottom of the screen, or write your answer on the answer sheet provided to you.

Imagine that a university intends to start a new research institution in your country, for research in either business or farming. Which of these purposes would you favor, and why? Provide specific reasons for your choice.

Cut

Paste

Undo

Time

LinguaForum

Help   Confirm   Next

?   Answer

LinguaForum
Copyright © 2002 by Lingua Forum, Inc. All rights reserved.

Test

7

SECTION 1
LISTENING
Suggested Time: 25 Minutes

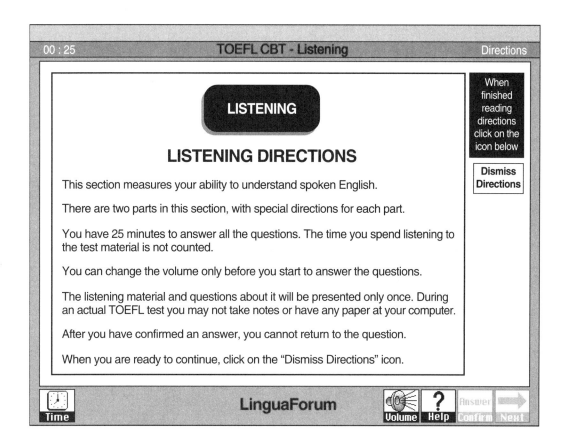

| 00 : 25 | TOEFL CBT - Listening | Directions |

LISTENING

LISTENING DIRECTIONS

This section measures your ability to understand spoken English.

There are two parts in this section, with special directions for each part.

You have 25 minutes to answer all the questions. The time you spend listening to the test material is not counted.

You can change the volume only before you start to answer the questions.

The listening material and questions about it will be presented only once. During an actual TOEFL test you may not take notes or have any paper at your computer.

After you have confirmed an answer, you cannot return to the question.

When you are ready to continue, click on the "Dismiss Directions" icon.

When finished reading directions click on the icon below

Dismiss Directions

Time

LinguaForum

Volume **Help** Answer Confirm Next

Test
7

SECTION 1
LISTENING

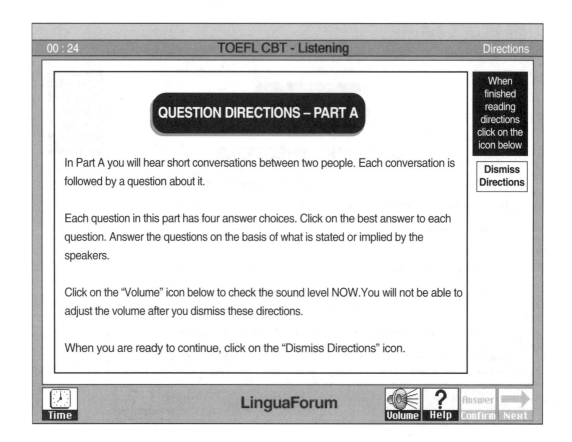

| 00 : 24 | TOEFL CBT - Listening | Directions |

QUESTION DIRECTIONS – PART A

In Part A you will hear short conversations between two people. Each conversation is followed by a question about it.

Each question in this part has four answer choices. Click on the best answer to each question. Answer the questions on the basis of what is stated or implied by the speakers.

Click on the "Volume" icon below to check the sound level NOW. You will not be able to adjust the volume after you dismiss these directions.

When you are ready to continue, click on the "Dismiss Directions" icon.

When finished reading directions click on the icon below

Dismiss Directions

Time

LinguaForum

Volume Help Answer Confirm Next

Listening

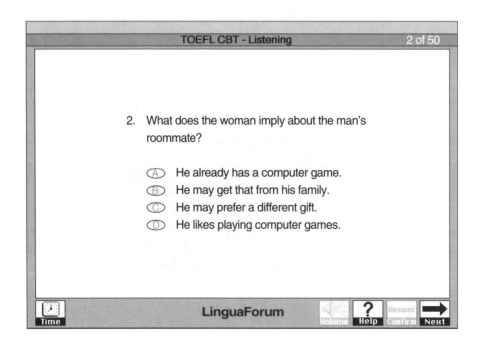

1. What does the man mean?

   Ⓐ He is not going to take a full load of courses.
   Ⓑ His roommate got the assistantship.
   Ⓒ Teaching is more difficult than studying.
   Ⓓ The woman is correct.

Time   **LinguaForum**   Volume   ? Help   Answer Confirm   Next

2. What does the woman imply about the man's roommate?

   Ⓐ He already has a computer game.
   Ⓑ He may get that from his family.
   Ⓒ He may prefer a different gift.
   Ⓓ He likes playing computer games.

Time   **LinguaForum**   Volume   ? Help   Answer Confirm   Next

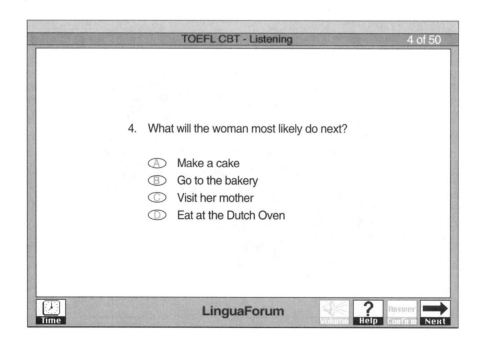

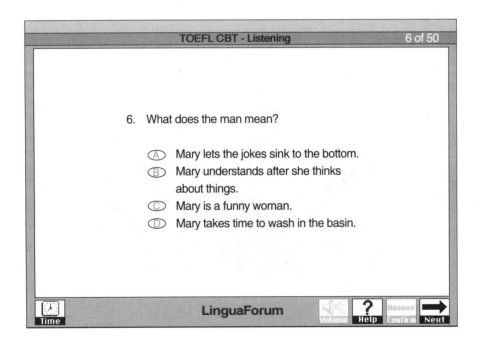

TOEFL CBT - Listening   5 of 50

5.   What does the woman suggest?

     Ⓐ   Wear a nicotine patch
     Ⓑ   Use will power
     Ⓒ   Join a support group
     Ⓓ   Chew gum

LinguaForum

Time   Volume Help Answer Confirm Next

TOEFL CBT - Listening   6 of 50

6.   What does the man mean?

     Ⓐ   Mary lets the jokes sink to the bottom.
     Ⓑ   Mary understands after she thinks
          about things.
     Ⓒ   Mary is a funny woman.
     Ⓓ   Mary takes time to wash in the basin.

LinguaForum

Time   Volume Help Answer Confirm Next

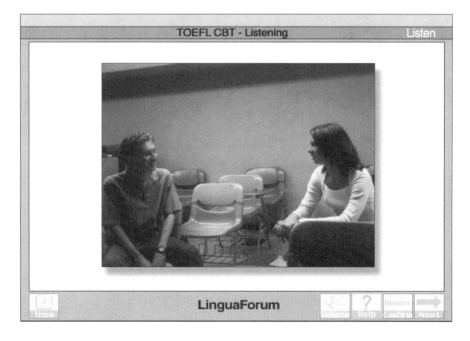

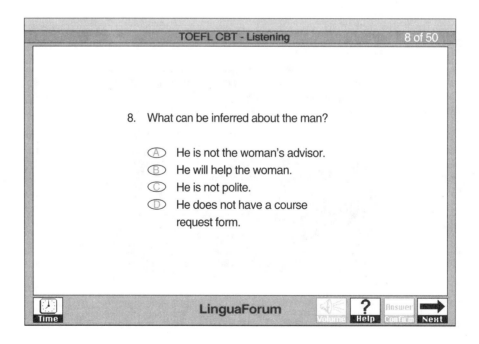

Listening

9. How much did the two bags cost?

     Ⓐ $20.95
     Ⓑ $19.88
     Ⓒ $29.95
     Ⓓ $59.90

LinguaForum   Volume | ? Help | Answer Confirm | Next

Time

10. What can we say about the man?

     Ⓐ   He left the pizza out.
     Ⓑ   He got sick.
     Ⓒ   He does not like cold pizza.
     Ⓓ   He forgot where he put the pizza.

LinguaForum   Volume | ? Help | Answer Confirm | Next

Time

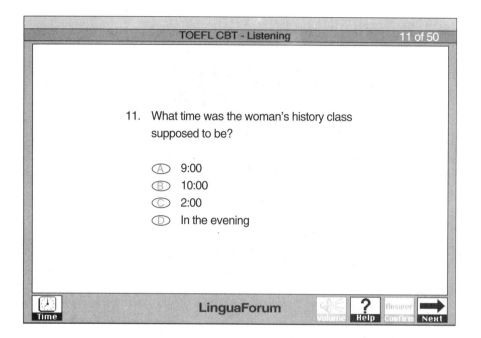

11. What time was the woman's history class supposed to be?

Ⓐ 9:00
Ⓑ 10:00
Ⓒ 2:00
Ⓓ In the evening

LinguaForum

Time   Volume Help Confirm Next

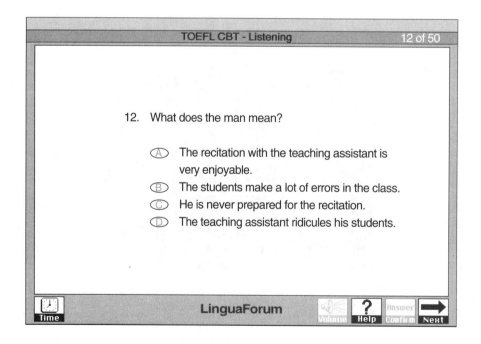

12. What does the man mean?

Ⓐ The recitation with the teaching assistant is very enjoyable.
Ⓑ The students make a lot of errors in the class.
Ⓒ He is never prepared for the recitation.
Ⓓ The teaching assistant ridicules his students.

LinguaForum

Time   Volume Help Confirm Next

Listening

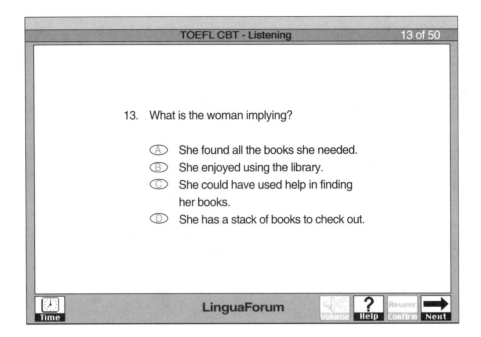

13. What is the woman implying?

   Ⓐ   She found all the books she needed.
   Ⓑ   She enjoyed using the library.
   Ⓒ   She could have used help in finding
        her books.
   Ⓓ   She has a stack of books to check out.

LinguaForum

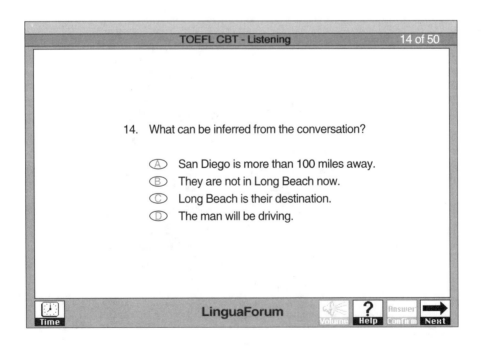

14. What can be inferred from the conversation?

   Ⓐ   San Diego is more than 100 miles away.
   Ⓑ   They are not in Long Beach now.
   Ⓒ   Long Beach is their destination.
   Ⓓ   The man will be driving.

LinguaForum

Listening

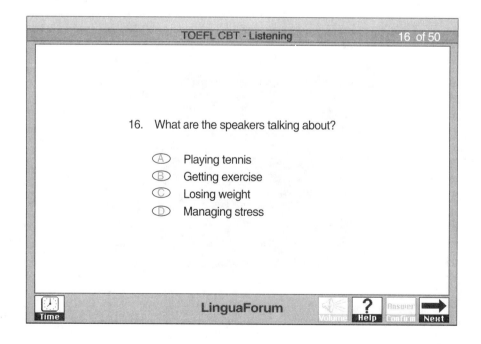

15. How much are the tickets the woman decides to buy?

    Ⓐ $15
    Ⓑ $35
    Ⓒ $45
    Ⓓ $60

LinguaForum

16. What are the speakers talking about?

    Ⓐ   Playing tennis
    Ⓑ   Getting exercise
    Ⓒ   Losing weight
    Ⓓ   Managing stress

LinguaForum

Listening

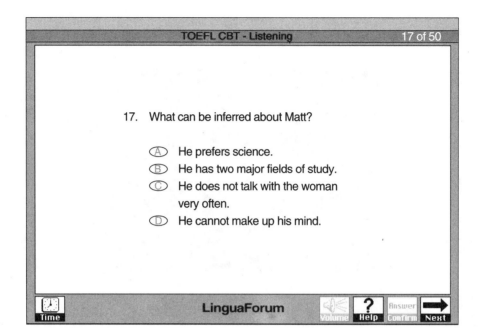

Test
7

SECTION 1
LISTENING

TOEFL CBT - Listening   Directions

QUESTION DIRECTIONS – PART B

When finished reading directions click on the icon below

Dismiss Directions

In Part B there are several talks and conversations. Each talk or conversation is followed by several questions.

The conversations and talks are about a variety of topics. You do not need special knowledge of the topics to answer the questions correctly. You should answer each question on the basis of what is stated or implied by the speakers.

Click on the "Volume" icon below to check the sound level NOW. You will not be able to adjust the volume after you dismiss these directions.

When you are ready to continue, click on the "Dismiss Directions" icon.

Time   **LinguaForum**   Volume Help Answer Confirm Next

Listening

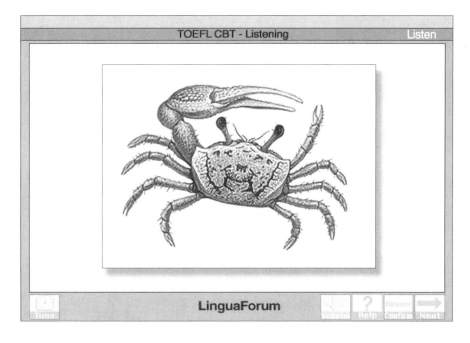

Questions 18-21

TOEFL CBT - Listening   18 of 50

18. Which best describes the habitat of fiddler crabs?

   Ⓐ Tropical and sub-tropical oceans
   Ⓑ Southern California and Boston Harbor
   Ⓒ Mud flats in tropical estuaries and sheltered coasts
   Ⓓ Sand and mud flats around the world

LinguaForum   Volume   **?** Help   Answer Confirm   ➡ Next

Time

TOEFL CBT - Listening   19 of 50

19. The professor describes the following steps of how the fiddler crab eats. Put them into the proper order.

> Click on a sentence. Then click on the space where it belongs. Use each sentence only once.

The clean mud is spat out.
It scoops mud up into its mouth.
The detritus is swallowed.
Water is pumped in to separate detritus from the mud.

1. [   ]   3. [   ]

2. [   ]   4. [   ]

LinguaForum   Volume   **?** Help   Answer Confirm   ➡ Next

Time

PRACTICE TEST 7

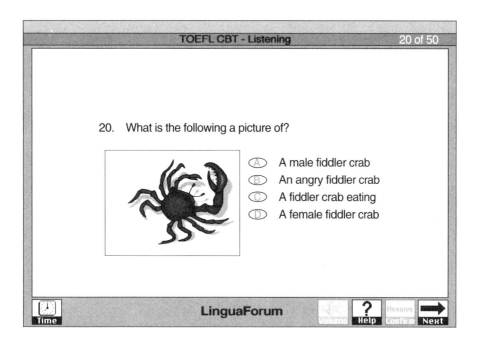

TOEFL CBT - Listening   20 of 50

20.   What is the following a picture of?

Ⓐ   A male fiddler crab
Ⓑ   An angry fiddler crab
Ⓒ   A fiddler crab eating
Ⓓ   A female fiddler crab

LinguaForum

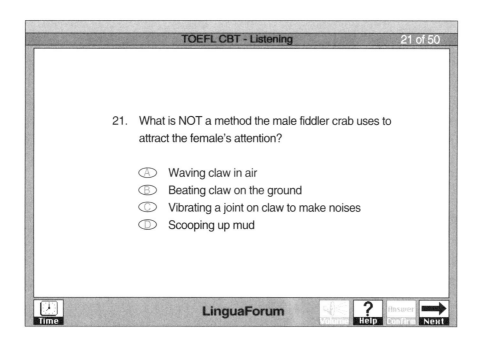

TOEFL CBT - Listening   21 of 50

21.   What is NOT a method the male fiddler crab uses to
        attract the female's attention?

Ⓐ   Waving claw in air
Ⓑ   Beating claw on the ground
Ⓒ   Vibrating a joint on claw to make noises
Ⓓ   Scooping up mud

LinguaForum

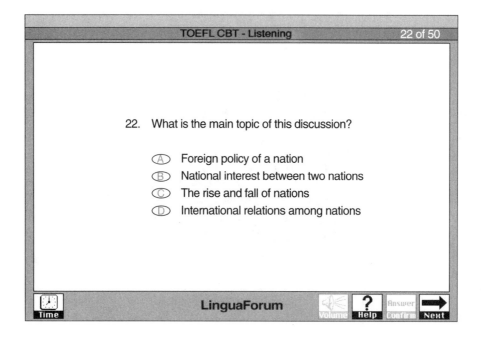

22. What is the main topic of this discussion?

     A Foreign policy of a nation
     B National interest between two nations
     C The rise and fall of nations
     D International relations among nations

LinguaForum

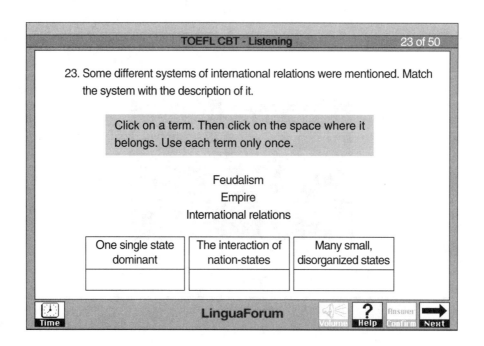

23. Some different systems of international relations were mentioned. Match the system with the description of it.

> Click on a term. Then click on the space where it belongs. Use each term only once.

Feudalism
Empire
International relations

One single state dominant	The interaction of nation-states	Many small, disorganized states

LinguaForum

Listening

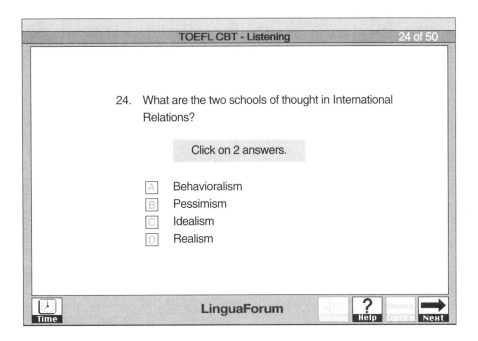

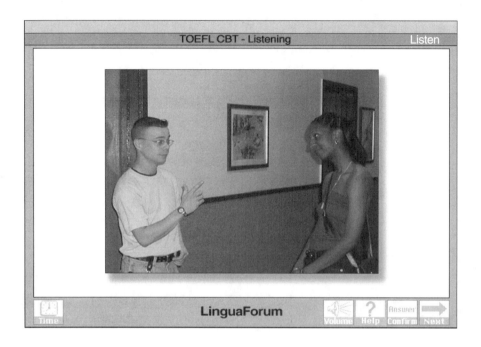

Listening

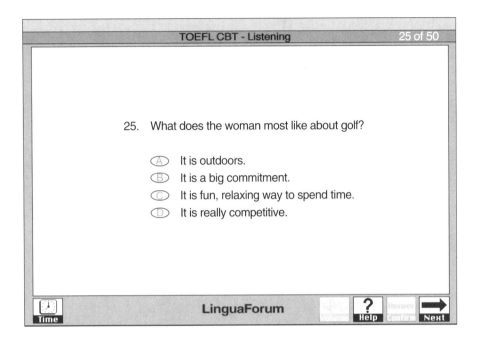

TOEFL CBT - Listening   25 of 50

25. What does the woman most like about golf?

   Ⓐ   It is outdoors.
   Ⓑ   It is a big commitment.
   Ⓒ   It is fun, relaxing way to spend time.
   Ⓓ   It is really competitive.

LinguaForum

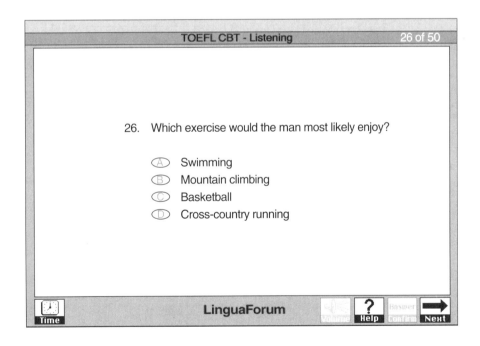

TOEFL CBT - Listening   26 of 50

26. Which exercise would the man most likely enjoy?

   Ⓐ   Swimming
   Ⓑ   Mountain climbing
   Ⓒ   Basketball
   Ⓓ   Cross-country running

LinguaForum

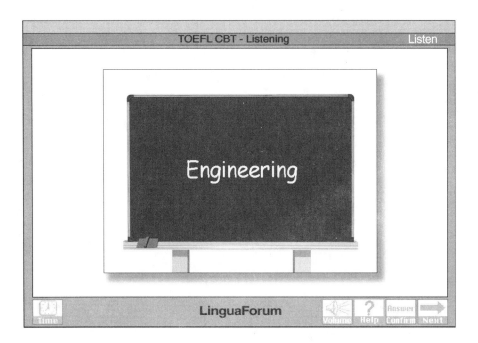

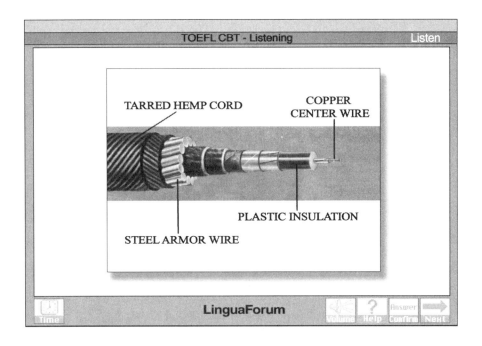

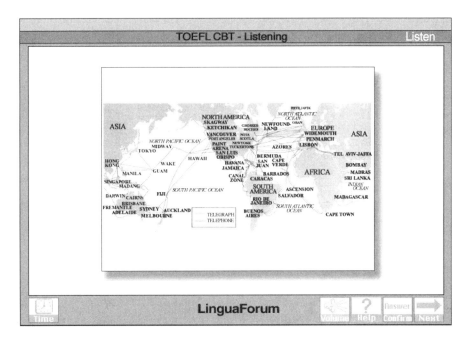

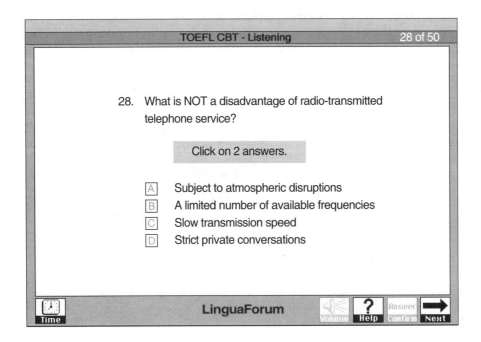

27. What is the main topic of this lecture?

    (A)   Global communications
    (B)   Deep ocean cables
    (C)   Trans-Atlantic telephone lines
    (D)   Cable television

LinguaForum

Time   Volume   Help   Answer Confirm   Next

28. What is NOT a disadvantage of radio-transmitted telephone service?

    Click on 2 answers.

    [A]   Subject to atmospheric disruptions
    [B]   A limited number of available frequencies
    [C]   Slow transmission speed
    [D]   Strict private conversations

LinguaForum

Time   Volume   Help   Answer Confirm   Next

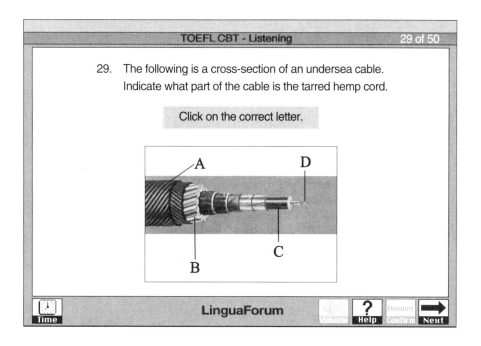

29. The following is a cross-section of an undersea cable. Indicate what part of the cable is the tarred hemp cord.

Click on the correct letter.

A   D

B   C

Time   LinguaForum   Volume Help Confirm Next

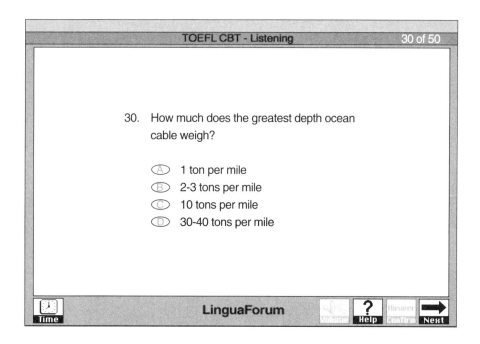

30. How much does the greatest depth ocean cable weigh?

(A) 1 ton per mile
(B) 2-3 tons per mile
(C) 10 tons per mile
(D) 30-40 tons per mile

Time   LinguaForum   Volume Help Confirm Next

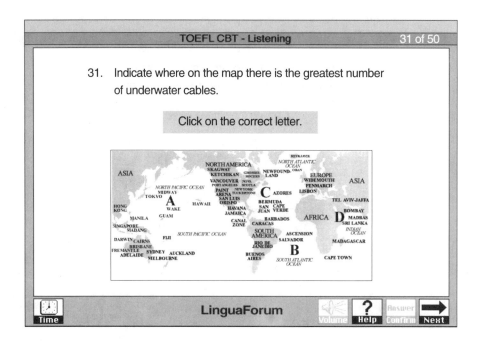

Listening

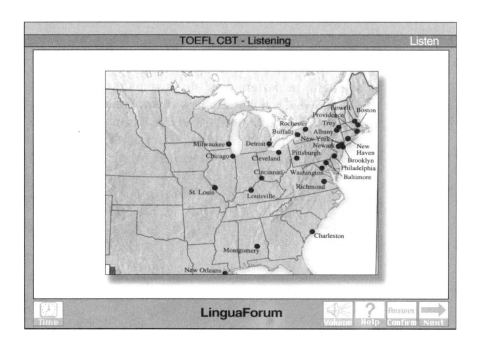

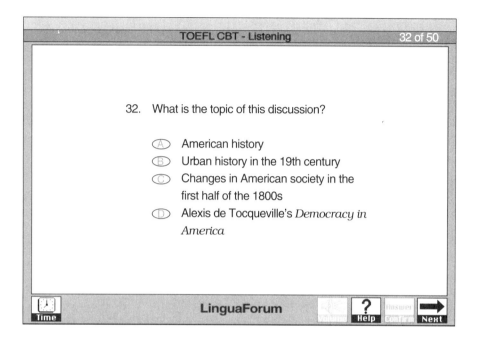

32. What is the topic of this discussion?

     Ⓐ   American history
     Ⓑ   Urban history in the 19th century
     Ⓒ   Changes in American society in the
          first half of the 1800s
     Ⓓ   Alexis de Tocqueville's *Democracy in
          America*

LinguaForum   Volume   ? Help   Answer Confirm   Next

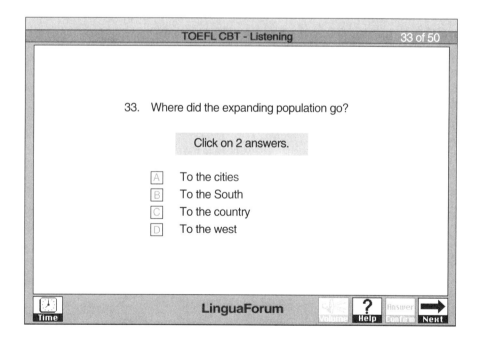

33. Where did the expanding population go?

        Click on 2 answers.

     A   To the cities
     B   To the South
     C   To the country
     D   To the west

LinguaForum   Volume   ? Help   Answer Confirm   Next

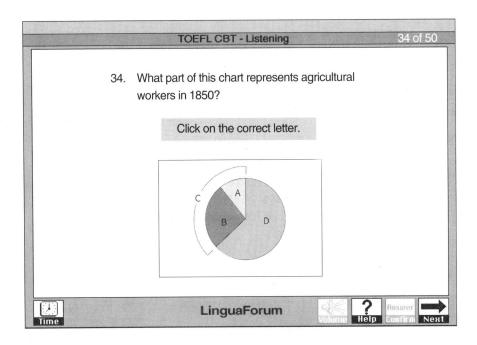

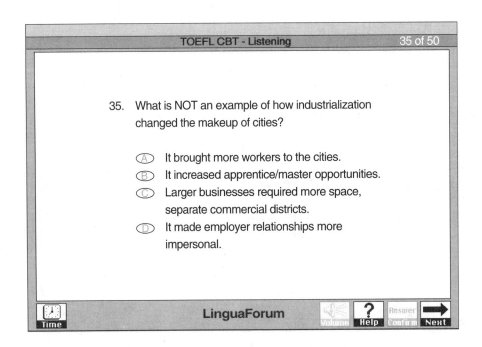

Questions 36-38

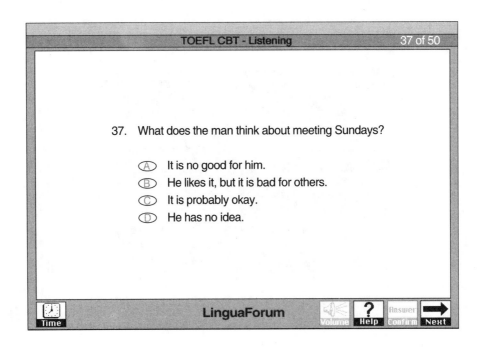

36. What is the main topic of this discussion?

   (A) Forming a study group
   (B) How to study for Psychology
   (C) The difficulty of Psychology
   (D) Organizing students on weekends

LinguaForum

37. What does the man think about meeting Sundays?

   (A) It is no good for him.
   (B) He likes it, but it is bad for others.
   (C) It is probably okay.
   (D) He has no idea.

LinguaForum

Listening

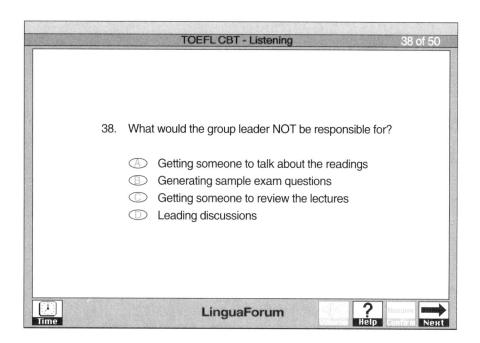

38. What would the group leader NOT be responsible for?

    Ⓐ Getting someone to talk about the readings
    Ⓑ Generating sample exam questions
    Ⓒ Getting someone to review the lectures
    Ⓓ Leading discussions

LinguaForum   Help   Next

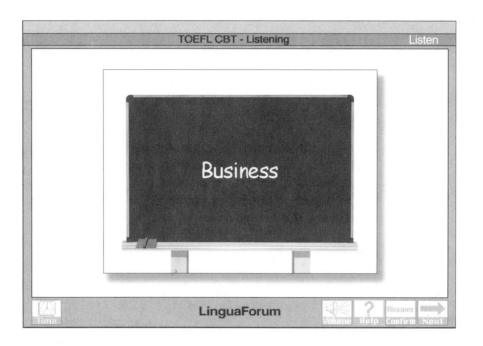

Listening

39. What is the speaker's opinion of insurance?

(A) It is the best way to protect people from danger.
(B) It is very risky.
(C) It is an essential part of society.
(D) It is a costly business expense.

LinguaForum

40. The speaker described the history of insurance. Summarize by placing the following events into the correct order.

Click on an expression. Then click on the space where it belongs. Use each expression only once.

The first insurance in America
The first life insurance
King Hammurabi's Code
The first fire insurance

1. ___ 3. ___
2. ___ 4. ___

LinguaForum

Listening

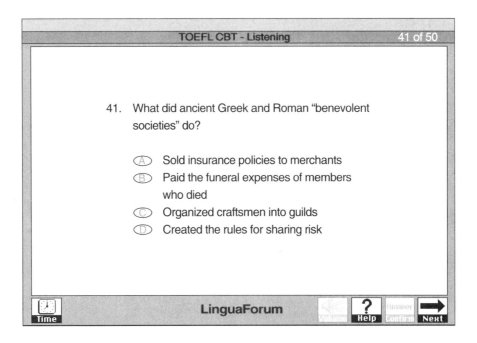

TOEFL CBT - Listening   41 of 50

41. What did ancient Greek and Roman "benevolent societies" do?

    Ⓐ   Sold insurance policies to merchants
    Ⓑ   Paid the funeral expenses of members who died
    Ⓒ   Organized craftsmen into guilds
    Ⓓ   Created the rules for sharing risk

LinguaForum

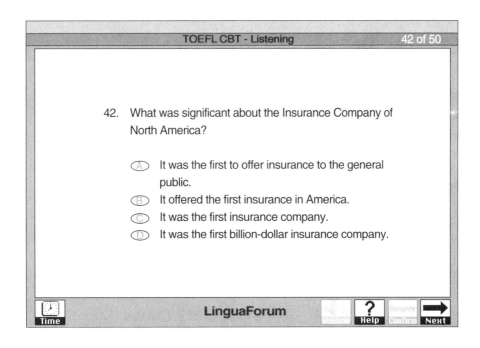

TOEFL CBT - Listening   42 of 50

42. What was significant about the Insurance Company of North America?

    Ⓐ   It was the first to offer insurance to the general public.
    Ⓑ   It offered the first insurance in America.
    Ⓒ   It was the first insurance company.
    Ⓓ   It was the first billion-dollar insurance company.

LinguaForum

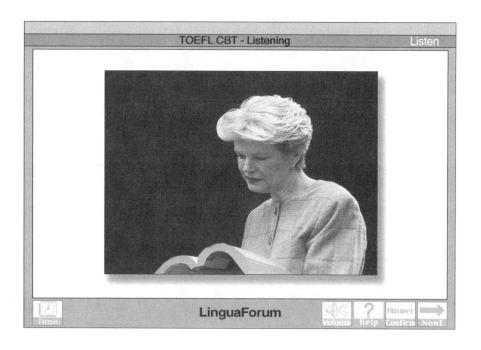

Listening

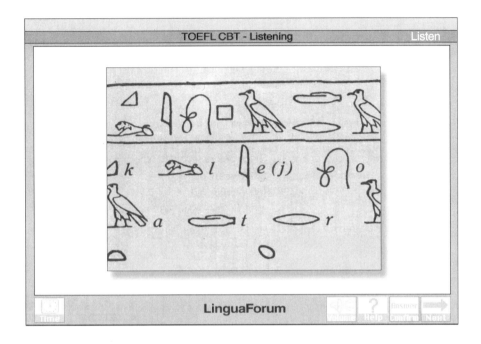

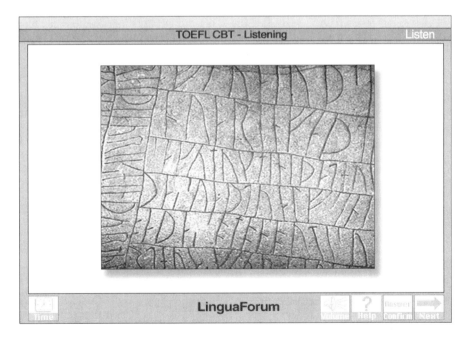

Questions 43-47

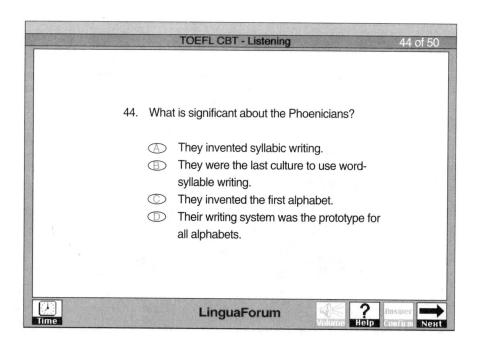

43. How old is writing?

- Ⓐ Since before recorded time
- Ⓑ 5,000 years old
- Ⓒ 2,000 years old
- Ⓓ 1,000-1,500 years old

LinguaForum

44. What is significant about the Phoenicians?

- Ⓐ They invented syllabic writing.
- Ⓑ They were the last culture to use word-syllable writing.
- Ⓒ They invented the first alphabet.
- Ⓓ Their writing system was the prototype for all alphabets.

LinguaForum

Listening

PRACTICE
TEST 7

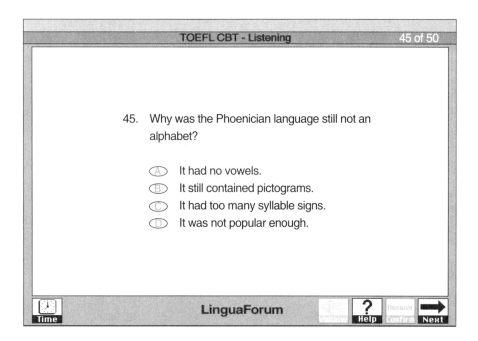

TOEFL CBT - Listening — 45 of 50

45. Why was the Phoenician language still not an alphabet?

   Ⓐ It had no vowels.
   Ⓑ It still contained pictograms.
   Ⓒ It had too many syllable signs.
   Ⓓ It was not popular enough.

LinguaForum

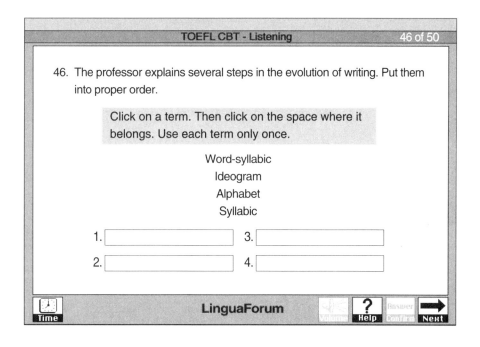

TOEFL CBT - Listening — 46 of 50

46. The professor explains several steps in the evolution of writing. Put them into proper order.

> Click on a term. Then click on the space where it belongs. Use each term only once.

Word-syllabic
Ideogram
Alphabet
Syllabic

1. [   ]   3. [   ]

2. [   ]   4. [   ]

LinguaForum

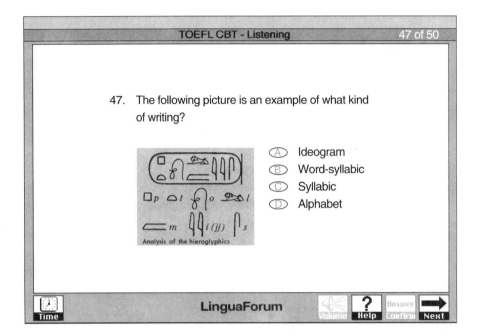

Questions 48-50

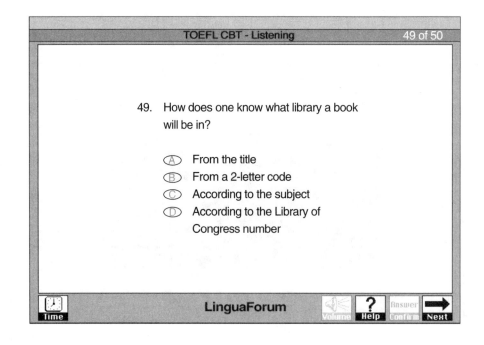

48. What is the man looking for?

    (A) A new book about art
    (B) A book about famous artists
    (C) An art book about a particular period of art
    (D) His friend, Irving, who has his book

LinguaForum

49. How does one know what library a book
     will be in?

    (A) From the title
    (B) From a 2-letter code
    (C) According to the subject
    (D) According to the Library of
        Congress number

LinguaForum

Listening

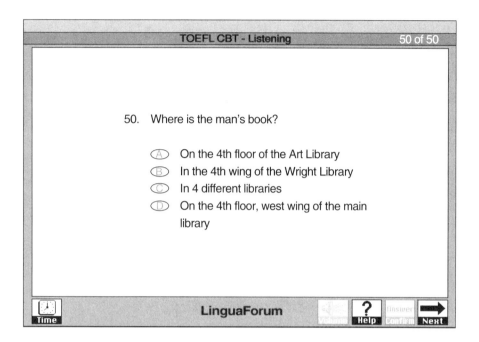

TOEFL CBT - Listening   50 of 50

50.   Where is the man's book?

   Ⓐ   On the 4th floor of the Art Library
   Ⓑ   In the 4th wing of the Wright Library
   Ⓒ   In 4 different libraries
   Ⓓ   On the 4th floor, west wing of the main
      library

Time   LinguaForum   Help   Confirm   Next

Test
7

SECTION 2
STRUCTURE

Suggested Time: 15 Minutes

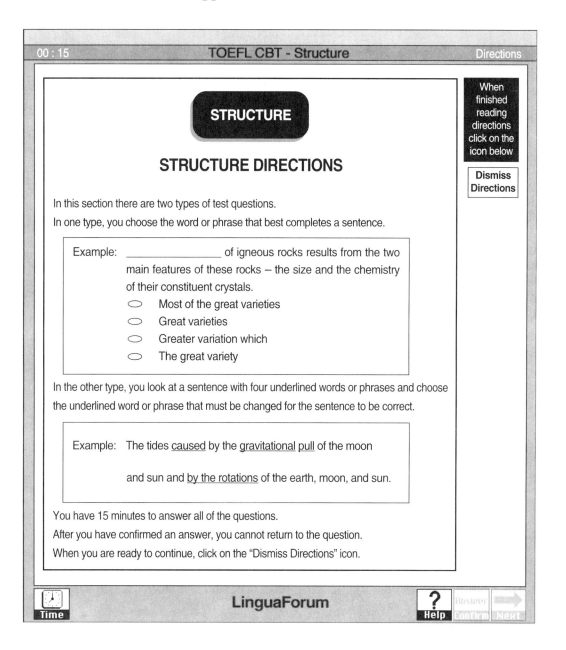

00 : 15 TOEFL CBT - Structure Directions

When finished reading directions click on the icon below

Dismiss Directions

STRUCTURE

STRUCTURE DIRECTIONS

In this section there are two types of test questions.

In one type, you choose the word or phrase that best completes a sentence.

> Example: _____ of igneous rocks results from the two
> main features of these rocks – the size and the chemistry
> of their constituent crystals.
> ○   Most of the great varieties
> ○   Great varieties
> ○   Greater variation which
> ○   The great variety

In the other type, you look at a sentence with four underlined words or phrases and choose the underlined word or phrase that must be changed for the sentence to be correct.

> Example: The tides caused by the gravitational pull of the moon
>
> and sun and by the rotations of the earth, moon, and sun.

You have 15 minutes to answer all of the questions.

After you have confirmed an answer, you cannot return to the question.

When you are ready to continue, click on the "Dismiss Directions" icon.

Time

LinguaForum

?
Help   Answer Confirm Next

71

Structure

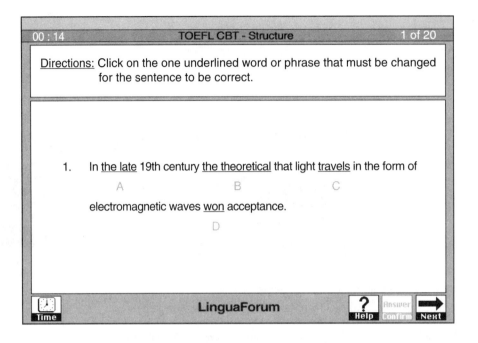

Directions: Click on the one underlined word or phrase that must be changed
for the sentence to be correct.

1.   In the late 19th century the theoretical that light travels in the form of
         A   B   C

electromagnetic waves won acceptance.
                      D

LinguaForum

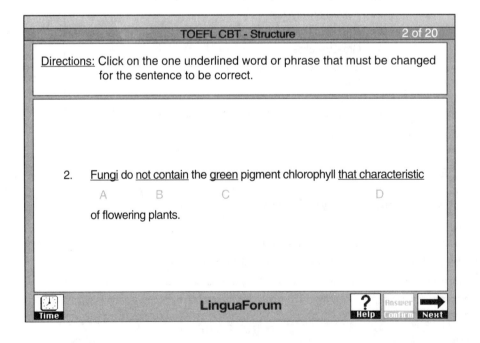

Directions: Click on the one underlined word or phrase that must be changed
for the sentence to be correct.

2.   Fungi do not contain the green pigment chlorophyll that characteristic
         A   B   C   D

of flowering plants.

LinguaForum

Structure

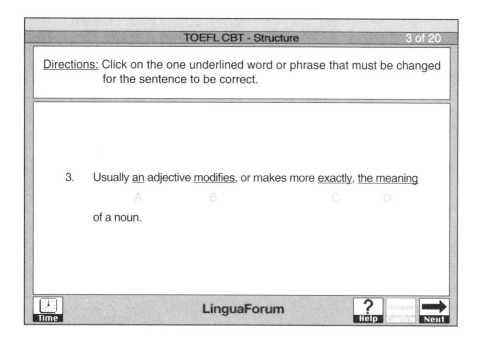

TOEFL CBT - Structure   3 of 20

<u>Directions:</u> Click on the one underlined word or phrase that must be changed for the sentence to be correct.

3.   Usually <u>an</u> adjective <u>modifies</u>, or makes more <u>exactly</u>, <u>the meaning</u>
                A   B   C   D

      of a noun.

LinguaForum

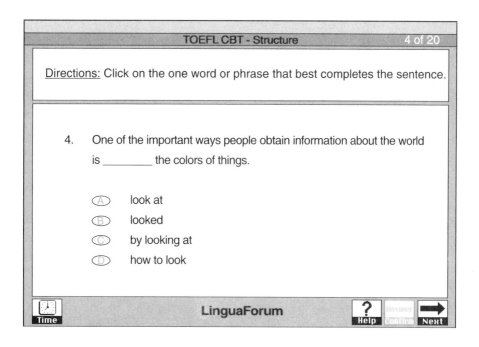

TOEFL CBT - Structure   4 of 20

<u>Directions:</u> Click on the one word or phrase that best completes the sentence.

4.   One of the important ways people obtain information about the world
      is _____ the colors of things.

     (A)   look at
     (B)   looked
     (C)   by looking at
     (D)   how to look

LinguaForum

Structure

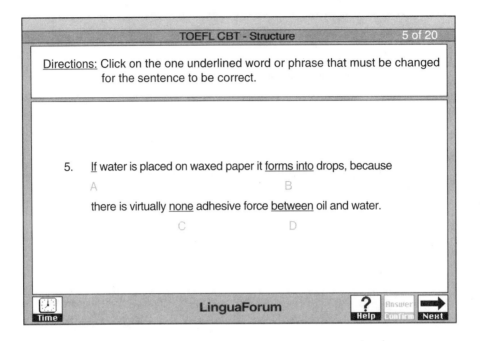

Directions: Click on the one underlined word or phrase that must be changed for the sentence to be correct.

5.   If water is placed on waxed paper it forms into drops, because
     A   B
     there is virtually none adhesive force between oil and water.
                       C   D

LinguaForum

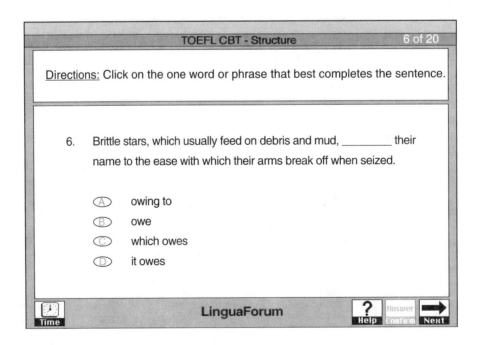

Directions: Click on the one word or phrase that best completes the sentence.

6.   Brittle stars, which usually feed on debris and mud, _____ their
     name to the ease with which their arms break off when seized.

     (A)   owing to
     (B)   owe
     (C)   which owes
     (D)   it owes

LinguaForum

Structure

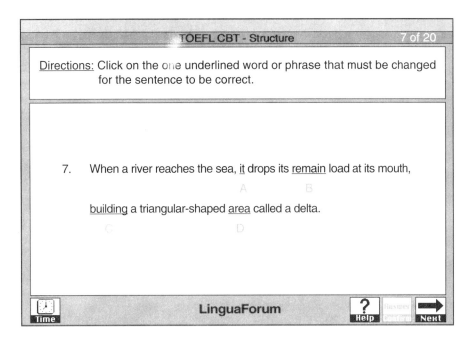

Directions: Click on the one underlined word or phrase that must be changed for the sentence to be correct.

7.   When a river reaches the sea, it drops its remain load at its mouth,
                                    A   B

building a triangular-shaped area called a delta.
    C   D

LinguaForum   ? Answer →
                   Help Confirm Next

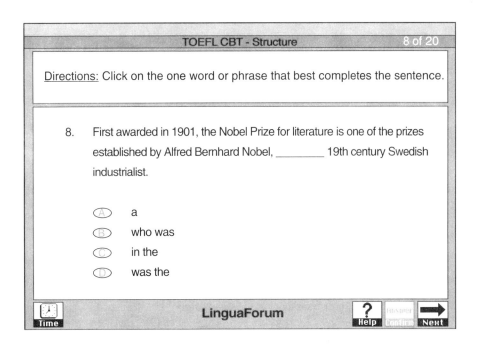

Directions: Click on the one word or phrase that best completes the sentence.

8.   First awarded in 1901, the Nobel Prize for literature is one of the prizes
      established by Alfred Bernhard Nobel, _____ 19th century Swedish
      industrialist.

      (A)   a
      (B)   who was
      (C)   in the
      (D)   was the

LinguaForum   ? Answer →
                   Help Confirm Next

Directions: Click on the one underlined word or phrase that must be changed for the sentence to be correct.

9.   The London Company had the colonists they make experiments in
                                                    A

      growing a variety of crops - grapevines, flax, oranges, tobacco, and
         B   C   D

      mulberry trees to feed silkworms.

Directions: Click on the one word or phrase that best completes the sentence.

10.   A morpheme can be _____ a word, or it can be a piece of a word.

      Ⓐ   is called
      Ⓑ   we call it
      Ⓒ   calling what we
      Ⓓ   what we call

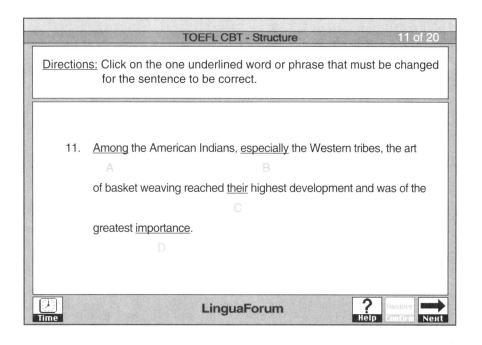

Directions: Click on the one underlined word or phrase that must be changed for the sentence to be correct.

11.   <u>Among</u> the American Indians, <u>especially</u> the Western tribes, the art
      A   B

of basket weaving reached <u>their</u> highest development and was of the
                    C

greatest <u>importance</u>.
       D

LinguaForum

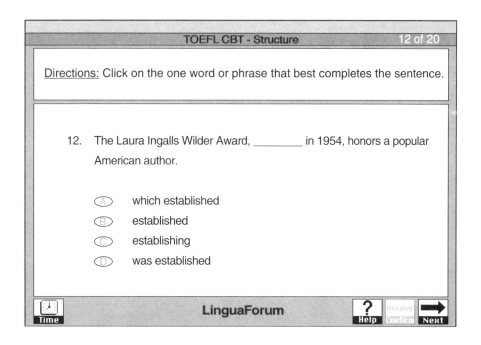

Directions: Click on the one word or phrase that best completes the sentence.

12.   The Laura Ingalls Wilder Award, _____ in 1954, honors a popular American author.

    (A)   which established
    (B)   established
    (C)   establishing
    (D)   was established

LinguaForum

Structure

Directions: Click on the one underlined word or phrase that must be changed for the sentence to be correct.

13. A new <u>photographic</u> technique called holography <u>which uses</u> laser

                  A   B

light <u>to produce</u> a three- dimensional <u>image</u> of a subject.

            C   D

LinguaForum   ? Help   Answer Confirm   Next

Time

Directions: Click on the one word or phrase that best completes the sentence.

14. In most cases _____ emits light when it is stimulated by radiation or by emission such as cathode rays or X rays.

     Ⓐ   a material is luminescent
     Ⓑ   a luminescent material is
     Ⓒ   what a luminescent material
     Ⓓ   a luminescent material

LinguaForum   ? Help   Answer Confirm   Next

Time

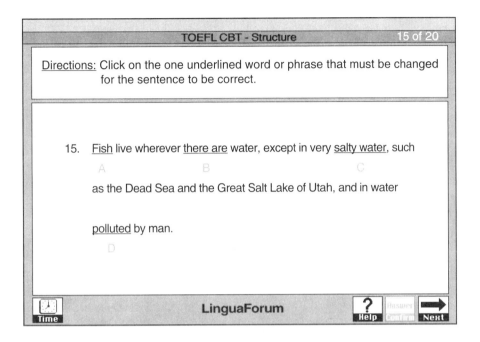

Directions: Click on the one underlined word or phrase that must be changed
for the sentence to be correct.

15. Fish live wherever there are water, except in very salty water, such
          A   B   C

as the Dead Sea and the Great Salt Lake of Utah, and in water

polluted by man.
     D

LinguaForum

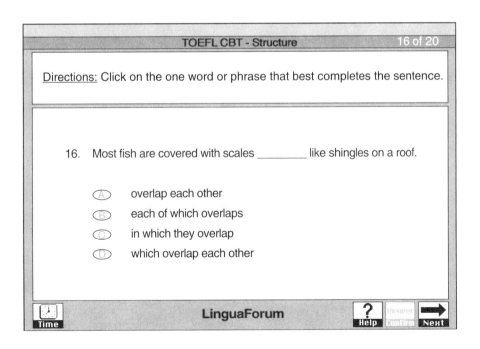

Directions: Click on the one word or phrase that best completes the sentence.

16. Most fish are covered with scales _____ like shingles on a roof.

     Ⓐ   overlap each other
     Ⓑ   each of which overlaps
     Ⓒ   in which they overlap
     Ⓓ   which overlap each other

LinguaForum

Directions: Click on the one underlined word or phrase that must be changed
for the sentence to be correct.

17.   Isotopes play a role in the treatment of many forms of cancer, and
                    A   B

they also have a number of diagnostic use in medicine.
      C   D

Time   **LinguaForum**   ? Answer ➡
                                              Help Confirm Next

---

Directions: Click on the one word or phrase that best completes the sentence.

18.   The skin of a toad is usually dry to the touch, _____ rough and
      covered with prominent warts.

      Ⓐ   and its
      Ⓑ   whose
      Ⓒ   and it is
      Ⓓ   where it is

Time   **LinguaForum**   ? Answer ➡
                                              Help Confirm Next

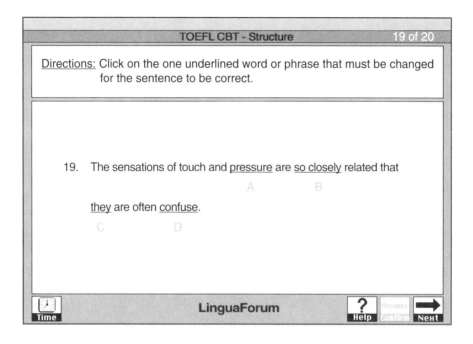

TOEFL CBT - Structure   19 of 20

Directions: Click on the one underlined word or phrase that must be changed for the sentence to be correct.

19.   The sensations of touch and pressure are so closely related that
                                         A   B

they are often confuse.
 C   D

LinguaForum

? Help   Answer Confirm   Next
Time

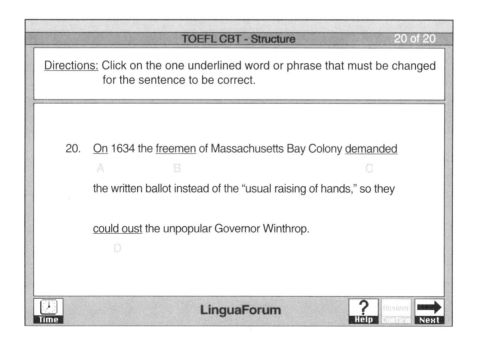

TOEFL CBT - Structure   20 of 20

Directions: Click on the one underlined word or phrase that must be changed for the sentence to be correct.

20.   On 1634 the freemen of Massachusetts Bay Colony demanded
         A   B   C

the written ballot instead of the "usual raising of hands," so they

could oust the unpopular Governor Winthrop.
 D

LinguaForum

? Help   Answer Confirm   Next
Time

Test
7

SECTION 3
READING

Suggested Time: 70 Minutes

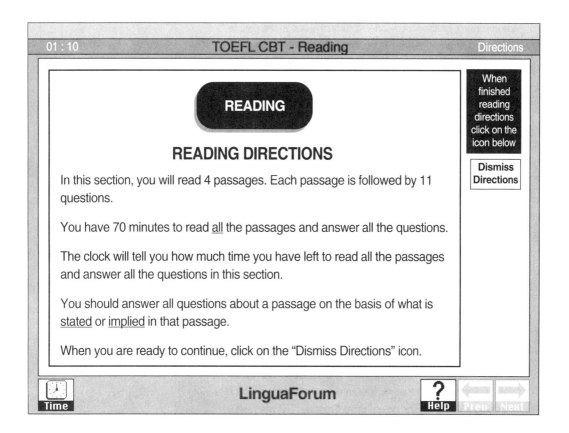

| 01 : 10 | TOEFL CBT - Reading | Directions |

When finished reading directions click on the icon below

Dismiss Directions

READING

READING DIRECTIONS

In this section, you will read 4 passages. Each passage is followed by 11 questions.

You have 70 minutes to read <u>all</u> the passages and answer all the questions.

The clock will tell you how much time you have left to read all the passages and answer all the questions in this section.

You should answer all questions about a passage on the basis of what is <u>stated</u> or <u>implied</u> in that passage.

When you are ready to continue, click on the "Dismiss Directions" icon.

Time

LinguaForum

? Help   Prev   Next

Reading

Beginning

When finished reading the passage click on the icon below

Proceed

Several events further eroded the fragile relationship between the American colonies and England. Lord North had promised to heal the breach that had been developing between the colonies and the mother country, but he soon provided the colonists with the occasion to bring resentment from a simmer to a boil.

In 1773, the only duty remaining from the Townsend Acts, one that was established to raise revenue in the colonies, was the tax on tea. North's scheme was a clever contrivance designed to bail out the East India Company, which was nearly bankrupt. To save the company, parliament decided to drop the tax on tea paid in England but kept the import tax on tea in the colonies. Under the Tea Act of 1773, the government would refund the British duty of twelve pence per pound on all that was shipped to the colonies and collect only the existing threepence duty payable at the colonial port. By this arrangement colonists could get tea more cheaply than English buyers could. North's clever plan misfired when he allowed the company to sell tea directly to retailers, bypassing the wholesalers, at a set price rather than at public auction.

Colonial merchants saw these actions as arbitrary. They believed that with no public auction to set the price of tea, the company had in essence been given a monopoly. Reaction was immediate. In December 1773, when the Governor of Massachusetts refused to send recently arrived tea ships back to England, men dressed as Indians boarded the ships and dumped 342 chests of tea into the harbor.

The English in turn reacted strongly with a series of Coercive Acts referred by the colonists as the Intolerable Acts of 1774. They were meant to punish the Bostonians for their "Tea Party." One act, the Boston Port Bill, closed the port of Boston by forbidding the unloading of all ships in the harbor. The Quebec Act set up a permanent, highly centralized government for Canada in which parliament was given the power to tax Quebec. The colonists

LinguaForum

? Help   Prev   Next

Time

Passage 1

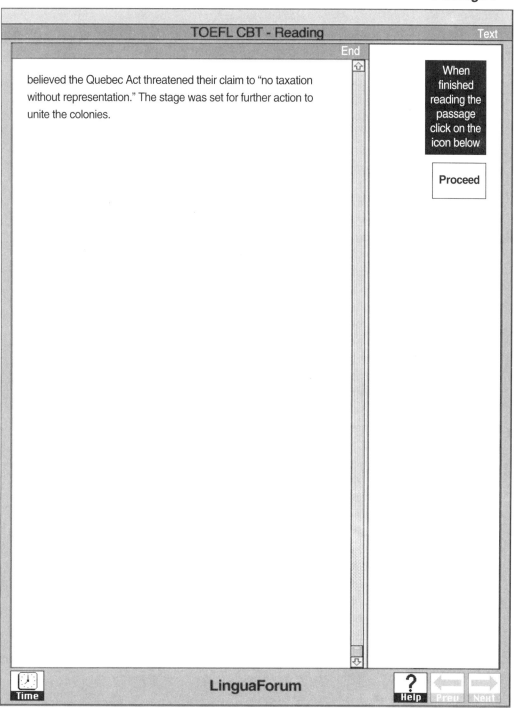

believed the Quebec Act threatened their claim to "no taxation without representation." The stage was set for further action to unite the colonies.

Reading

Several events further eroded the fragile relationship between the American colonies and England. Lord North had promised to heal the breach that had been developing between the colonies and the mother country, but he soon provided the colonists with the occasion to bring resentment from a simmer to a boil.

In 1773, the only duty remaining from the Townsend Acts, one that was established to raise revenue in the colonies, was the tax on tea. North's scheme was a clever contrivance designed to bail out the East India Company, which was nearly bankrupt. To save the company, parliament decided to drop the tax on tea paid in England but kept the import tax on tea in the colonies. Under the Tea Act of 1773, the government would refund the British duty of twelve pence per pound on all that was shipped to the colonies and collect only the existing threepence duty payable at the colonial port. By this arrangement colonists could get tea more cheaply than English buyers could. North's clever plan misfired when he allowed the company to sell tea directly to retailers, bypassing the wholesalers, at a set price rather than at public auction.

Colonial merchants saw these actions as arbitrary. They believed that with no public auction to set the price of tea, the company had in essence been given a monopoly. Reaction was immediate. In December 1773, when the Governor of Massachusetts refused to send recently arrived tea ships back to England, men dressed as Indians boarded the ships and dumped 342 chests of tea into the harbor.

The English in turn reacted strongly with a series of Coercive Acts referred by the colonists as the Intolerable Acts of 1774. They were meant to punish the Bostonians for their "Tea Party." One act, the Boston Port Bill, closed the port of Boston by forbidding the unloading of all ships in the harbor. The Quebec Act set up a permanent, highly centralized government for Canada in which parliament was given the power to tax Quebec. The colonists believed the Quebec Act threatened their claim to "no taxation

1. The purpose of the passage is to

(A) introduce the colonial history of America

(B) analyze the causes behind the American Revolution

(C) describe the tyrannical behavior of the British toward their American colonies

(D) discuss the economic embargo imposed by England on American colonies

LinguaForum

? Help   ← Prev   → Next

Time

Reading

Passage 1

TOEFL CBT - Reading   1 of 44

Questions 1 to 11   End

without representation." The stage was set for further action to
unite the colonies.

LinguaForum   Help   Preu   Next

Time

Several events further eroded the fragile relationship between the American colonies and England. Lord North had promised to heal the breach that had been developing between the colonies and the mother country, but he soon provided the colonists with the occasion to bring resentment from a simmer to a boil.

In 1773, the only duty remaining from the Townsend Acts, one that was established to raise revenue in the colonies, was the tax on tea. North's scheme was a clever contrivance designed to bail out the East India Company, which was nearly bankrupt. To save the company, parliament decided to drop the tax on tea paid in England but kept the import tax on tea in the colonies. Under the Tea Act of 1773, the government would refund the British duty of twelve pence per pound on all that was shipped to the colonies and collect only the existing threepence duty payable at the colonial port. By this arrangement colonists could get tea more cheaply than English buyers could. North's clever plan misfired when he allowed the company to sell tea directly to retailers, bypassing the wholesalers, at a set price rather than at public auction.

Colonial merchants saw these actions as arbitrary. They believed that with no public auction to set the price of tea, the company had in essence been given a monopoly. Reaction was immediate. In December 1773, when the Governor of Massachusetts refused to send recently arrived tea ships back to England, men dressed as Indians boarded the ships and dumped 342 chests of tea into the harbor.

The English in turn reacted strongly with a series of Coercive Acts referred by the colonists as the Intolerable Acts of 1774. They were meant to punish the Bostonians for their "Tea Party." One act, the Boston Port Bill, closed the port of Boston by forbidding the unloading of all ships in the harbor. The Quebec Act set up a permanent, highly centralized government for Canada in which parliament was given the power to tax Quebec. The colonists believed the Quebec Act threatened their claim to "no taxation

---

2. The word eroded in the passage is closest in meaning to

Ⓐ wasted
Ⓑ widened
Ⓒ decayed
Ⓓ corroded

3. The analogy used to describe the colonists' resentment in the first paragraph, from a simmer to a boil, means

Ⓐ tepid to freezing
Ⓑ warming to cooling
Ⓒ warming to hot
Ⓓ frozen to freezing

4. The Townsend Acts were designed to

Ⓐ impose taxes
Ⓑ establish order
Ⓒ strengthen British rule
Ⓓ raise profits

Reading

Passage 1

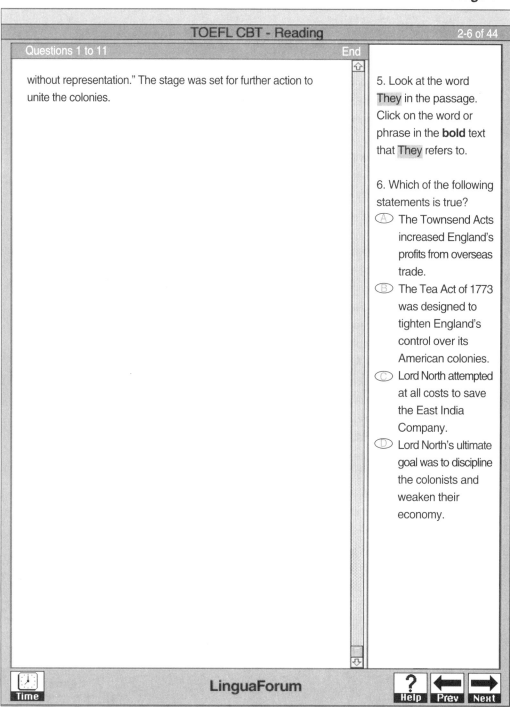

Questions 1 to 11   End

without representation." The stage was set for further action to unite the colonies.

5. Look at the word They in the passage. Click on the word or phrase in the **bold** text that They refers to.

6. Which of the following statements is true?

Ⓐ The Townsend Acts increased England's profits from overseas trade.

Ⓑ The Tea Act of 1773 was designed to tighten England's control over its American colonies.

Ⓒ Lord North attempted at all costs to save the East India Company.

Ⓓ Lord North's ultimate goal was to discipline the colonists and weaken their economy.

Time   LinguaForum   ? Help   ← Prev   → Next

Reading

Several events further eroded the fragile relationship between the American colonies and England. Lord North had promised to heal the breach that had been developing between the colonies and the mother country, but he soon provided the colonists with the occasion to bring resentment from a simmer to a boil.

In 1773, the only duty remaining from the Townsend Acts, one that was established to raise revenue in the colonies, was the tax on tea. North's scheme was a clever contrivance designed to bail out the East India Company, which was nearly bankrupt. To save the company, parliament decided to drop the tax on tea paid in England but kept the import tax on tea in the colonies. Under the Tea Act of 1773, the government would refund the British duty of twelve pence per pound on all that was shipped to the colonies and collect only the existing threepence duty payable at the colonial port. By this arrangement colonists could get tea more cheaply than English buyers could. North's clever plan misfired when he allowed the company to sell tea directly to retailers, bypassing the wholesalers, at a set price rather than at public auction.

➡ Colonial merchants saw these actions as arbitrary. ■ They believed that with no public auction to set the price of tea, the company had in essence been given a monopoly. ■ Reaction was immediate. In December 1773, when the Governor of Massachusetts refused to send recently arrived tea ships back to England, men dressed as Indians boarded the ships and dumped 342 chests of tea into the harbor. ■

➡ The English in turn reacted strongly with a series of Coercive Acts referred by the colonists as the Intolerable Acts of 1774. ■ They were meant to punish the Bostonians for their "Tea Party."

■ One act, the Boston Port Bill, closed the port of Boston by forbidding the unloading of all ships in the harbor. ■ The Quebec

---

7. Lord North had miscalculated
- (A) in believing that he could save the East India Company
- (B) in assuming that he could satisfy colonists with cheap prices
- (C) in assuming that he could tighten control over the colonies
- (D) in assuming that he could raise revenues in the colonies

8. The word arbitrary in the passage could best be replaced by
- (A) motivated
- (B) intentional
- (C) despotic
- (D) random

9. The colonists' decision to dress as Indians for the Boston Tea Party was NOT
- (A) unconventional
- (B) theatrical
- (C) rational
- (D) aggressive

Time   LinguaForum   **Help** **Prev** **Next**

Reading

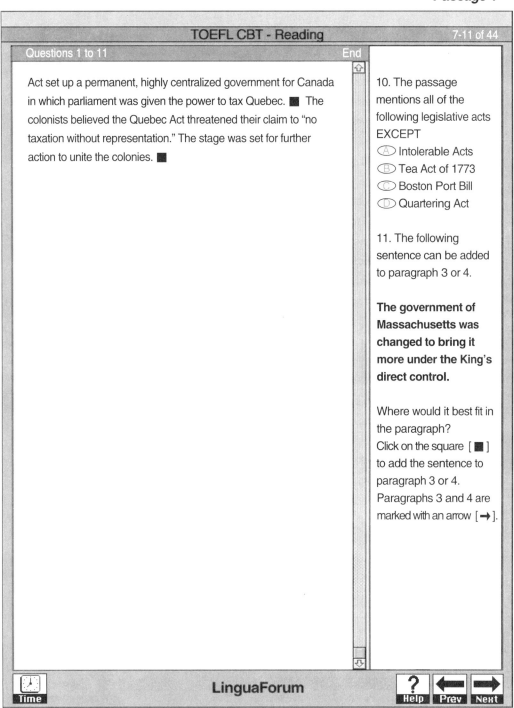

Questions 1 to 11 End

Act set up a permanent, highly centralized government for Canada in which parliament was given the power to tax Quebec. ■ The colonists believed the Quebec Act threatened their claim to "no taxation without representation." The stage was set for further action to unite the colonies. ■

10. The passage mentions all of the following legislative acts EXCEPT
ⓐ Intolerable Acts
ⓑ Tea Act of 1773
ⓒ Boston Port Bill
ⓓ Quartering Act

11. The following sentence can be added to paragraph 3 or 4.

The government of Massachusetts was changed to bring it more under the King's direct control.

Where would it best fit in the paragraph?
Click on the square [■] to add the sentence to paragraph 3 or 4. Paragraphs 3 and 4 are marked with an arrow [→].

Time

LinguaForum

? Help Prev Next

→ Many fishes form well-developed groups or schools. ■ Some, including herrings, sardines, mullets and some mackerels, school throughout their lives. Others are part-time schoolers, especially as juveniles or during feeding. ■ Most cartilaginous fishes are solitary, but a few, such as hammerhead sharks, mantas, and other rays, sometimes travel in schools. ■ It has been estimated that around 4,000 species, including both marine and freshwater species, school as adults. Schools can be huge, as large as 4,580 million m³ in the Atlantic herring. ■

→ **Schools function as well-coordinated units, though they appear to have no leaders. ■ The individual fishes tend to keep a constant distance between themselves, turning, stopping, and starting in near perfect** unison. **■ Vision has been found to play an important role in the orientation of individuals within a school. In some species, though, blind fish can school in a coordinated way. ■** These **probably use the lateral line, olfaction and sound they emit to keep track of each other. ■**

There is much debate about why fishes school. One explanation is that schooling offers protection against predation. Predators may be confused if the school circles the predator or splits into several groups. It is also difficult for a predator to aim for just one fish in a cloud of shifting, darting individuals. On the other hand, some predators, such as jacks or Caranx, are more efficient when they attack schools of prey rather than individuals. It has also been suggested that schooling increases the swimming efficiency of the fish because the fish in front form an eddy that reduces water resistance for those behind. There is experimental evidence, however, that this is not always the case and that fish do not always align in a hydrodynamically efficient way. In at least some fishes, schooling is advantageous in feeding or mating. There is probably no single reason that fishes school, and the reasons probably vary from species to species.

LinguaForum

Reading

12. The main topic of the passage is
    - Ⓐ survival methods of fishes
    - Ⓑ group survival of fishes
    - Ⓒ group formation of fishes
    - Ⓓ collective survival of fishes

13. All of the following school EXCEPT
    - Ⓐ freshwater species
    - Ⓑ mullets
    - Ⓒ jacks
    - Ⓓ sardines

14. Which of the following is NOT a cartilaginous fish?
    - Ⓐ herrings
    - Ⓑ mantas
    - Ⓒ hammerhead sharks
    - Ⓓ rays

15. The word unison in the passage is closest in meaning to
    - Ⓐ movement
    - Ⓑ coordination
    - Ⓒ behavior
    - Ⓓ understanding

16. Look at the word These in the passage. Click on the word or phrase in the **bold** text that These refers to.

17. Blind fish use all of the following for orientation within a school EXCEPT
    - Ⓐ lateral line
    - Ⓑ touch
    - Ⓒ sound
    - Ⓓ smell

18. The following sentence can be added to paragraph 1 or 2.

    The tight coordination of schooling fishes may break down when they are feeding or attacked by a predator.

    Where would it best fit in the paragraph?
    Click on the square [■] to add the sentence to paragraph 1 or 2.
    Paragraphs 1 and 2 are marked with an arrow [➡].

19. Click on the drawing that does NOT represent the behavior, movement or reaction described in the third paragraph.

    Click on a picture.

    Ⓐ   Ⓑ

    Ⓒ   Ⓓ

20. The word darting in the passage is closest in meaning to
    - Ⓐ rushing
    - Ⓑ fleeing
    - Ⓒ sprinting
    - Ⓓ scattering

21. All of the following are reasons given for schooling EXCEPT
    - Ⓐ safety
    - Ⓑ feeding
    - Ⓒ survival
    - Ⓓ traveling

22. How is the information in the passage organized?
    - Ⓐ It states the thesis, argues for the thesis and further develops the thesis.
    - Ⓑ It states a general idea, discusses it more specifically and concludes with a thesis.
    - Ⓒ It states the main idea, further develops it and explains the argument behind the main idea.
    - Ⓓ It presents the main idea, argues favorably and provides evidence in support of the main idea.

Reading

The first successful photograph was made in 1826 by Nicephore Niepce, a French lithographer. Ten years later Jacques Daguerre was experimenting with the process that bears his name. In 1888, George Eastman introduced the famous box camera, with its handy roll of negative film and with the promise of cheap and widely available film processing. Since then, photography has become the art form of the masses.

The introduction of photography revolutionized the arts of drawing and painting. It also altered the way we perceive the world. When viewers examined Daguerre's first productions, they were astonished to observe details that they had never noticed in the original scene.

→ William H. F. Talbot, the inventor of the negative-positive system now in use, commented in the 1840s that "it frequently happens ... and this is one of the charms of photography – that the operator himself discovers ... that he has depicted many things he had no intention of at the time."

■ Here, apparently, is another class of invisible entities, which we do not see when we look at a scene, but which the camera sees and tells us exist. ■ "The camera does not lie," it is said. Do our eyes lie, then? ■ Why do we select part of a scene for conscious awareness and ignore others? Is the camera's view of things the true one if it is something we cannot or do not see with our own eyes? ■

→ Before the invention of photography the great majority of painted images were portraits, small enough to be carried in a locket for remembrance. ■ Suddenly, painting was relieved of the necessity of "communicating" in this pedestrian way. ■ The result, was an explosion of new styles and methods. ■ Impressionism was the crowning glory of those times. ■ It was followed by cubism, dadaism, surrealism and abstract expressionism, as well as other movements in art of our time, including photorealism, in which the painter paints an image that, from a distance, is indistinguishable from a photograph. ■

LinguaForum

Time Help Prev Next

Reading

23. The best title for this passage is
    - (A) Inventors of Photography
    - (B) Art and its Revolution
    - (C) New Ways of Seeing
    - (D) Technological Advances of the Nineteenth Century

24. Look at the word **its** in the passage. Click on the word or phrase in the **bold** text that **its** refers to.

25. The first paragraph implies that
    - (A) before the arrival of photography, the general public did not have a shared art form
    - (B) before Eastman's invention, photography was a luxury item
    - (C) before Eastman's invention, people used positive film
    - (D) before the invention of photography, people did not have access to art

26. The passage supports all of the following EXCEPT that
    - (A) we do not perceive all visible matter in the world
    - (B) Talbot perfected Eastman's invention
    - (C) Eastman invented the camera
    - (D) the camera changed the way we see the world

27. According to the passage, the camera has all of the following characteristics EXCEPT that
    - (A) it is perfect
    - (B) it is honest
    - (C) it is neutral
    - (D) it is objective

28. The passage suggests that our perception depends on
    - (A) our eyesight
    - (B) our environment
    - (C) our consciousness
    - (D) our objectives

29. The following sentence can be added to paragraph 3 or 4.

    What is truth, that we cannot know it?

    Where would it best fit in the paragraph?
    Click on the square [■] to add the sentence to paragraph 3 or 4.
    Paragraphs 3 and 4 are marked with an arrow [➡].

30. Before the invention of photography, art
    - (A) was widely practiced
    - (B) served a practical purpose
    - (C) was experimental
    - (D) was not as perfect as photography

31. The word **pedestrian** in the passage is closest in meaning to
    - (A) normal
    - (B) predictable
    - (C) common
    - (D) expected

32. With the invention of photography, art transformed its
    - (A) subject matter
    - (B) form
    - (C) industry
    - (D) patronage

33. The word **crowning** in the passage is closest in meaning to
    - (A) noble
    - (B) royal
    - (C) greatest
    - (D) dramatic

Reading

The Aristotelian ideal of the educated person, "critical" in all or almost all branches of knowledge, survived for centuries as the aim of a liberal education. **Originally, the student would be taught seven arts or skills, consisting of the trivium, grammar, rhetoric and logic, and the quadrivium, arithmetic, geometry, astronomy and music. The arts or skills were "liberal" because they were liberating. That is, they freed their possessor from the ignorance that bound the uneducated.**

➡ The twentieth century has seen radical change in this traditional scheme of education. ■ The failure of the Renaissance to produce successful "Renaissance men" did not go unnoticed. If such men as Leonardo, Pico, Bacon, and many others almost as famous could not succeed in their presumed dream of knowing all there was to know about everything, then lesser men should not presume to try. ■ The alternative became self-evident: achieve expertise in one field while others attained expertise in theirs. ■ Much easier to accomplish, this course led to a more comfortable academic community. ■

➡ The convenient device for accomplishing the change consisted of a divided and subdivided university, with separate departments, like armed feudalities, facing one another across a gulf of ignorance. ■ The remaining competition involved the use of university funds, which were distributed according to principles that had little to do with academic values or knowledge as such. ■ The original belief that an educated person should be "critical" in more fields than his own no longer existed. ■ The "uni" in the university also became meaningless as the institution, possessing more and more power as government funds were pumped into it for research, turned into a loose confederation of disconnected mini-states, instead of an organization devoted to the joint research for knowledge and truth. ■

All that remained was the sometimes admiring, sometimes ironic, and sometimes contemptuous phrase "Renaissance man," which was applied to almost anyone who manifested an ability to do more than one thing well. Even then, the phrase was never used in its original, Aristotelian sense. That ideal and idea have been lost completely.

LinguaForum

? Help   ← Prev   → Next

Reading

34. The main topic of the passage is
    - Ⓐ the development of the educational system
    - Ⓑ the idea of liberal education
    - Ⓒ the concept of the "Renaissance Man"
    - Ⓓ the Aristotelian notion of education

35. The word critical in the passage is closest in meaning to
    - Ⓐ judgmental
    - Ⓑ rational
    - Ⓒ careful
    - Ⓓ discerning

36. Look at the word they in the passage. Click on the word or phrase in the **bold** text that they refers to.

37. The passage suggests that the Aristotelian ideal of an educated person was
    - Ⓐ pragmatic and reasonable
    - Ⓑ arrogant and ambitious
    - Ⓒ noble and unrealistic
    - Ⓓ irrational and arrogant

38. The author suggests that Leonardo and others cited as examples of "Renaissance men"
    - Ⓐ are not the most perfect geniuses
    - Ⓑ are not to be surpassed by others in terms of intelligence
    - Ⓒ are by far the best examples of the well-rounded scholar
    - Ⓓ are the prime examples of the Aristotelian ideal

39. The following sentence can be added to paragraph 2 or 3.

    Now an authority in one field need compete only with experts in his field.

    Where would it best fit in the paragraph?
    Click on the square [■] to add the sentence to paragraph 2 or 3.
    Paragraphs 2 and 3 are marked with an arrow [➡].

40. Which of the following could best replace the word presume in the passage?
    - Ⓐ Dare
    - Ⓑ Assume
    - Ⓒ Attempt
    - Ⓓ Expect

41. The modern response to the Aristotelian ideal was
    - Ⓐ a radical change in the educational system
    - Ⓑ foundation of the university
    - Ⓒ establishment of vocational schools
    - Ⓓ emphasis on professionalism

42. The author considers the usage of "uni" to be ironic because
    - Ⓐ institutions are no longer committed to learning
    - Ⓑ institutions are no longer united in their commitment to learning
    - Ⓒ institutions are no longer dispersed into disparate units
    - Ⓓ institutions are isolated in their respective areas of expertise

43. The author sees the university as being
    - Ⓐ useless
    - Ⓑ materialistic
    - Ⓒ idealistic
    - Ⓓ isolated

44. The tone of the author is
    - Ⓐ optimistic
    - Ⓑ ironic
    - Ⓒ discouraged
    - Ⓓ contemptuous

Test
7

SECTION 4
WRITING

Suggested Time: 30 Minutes

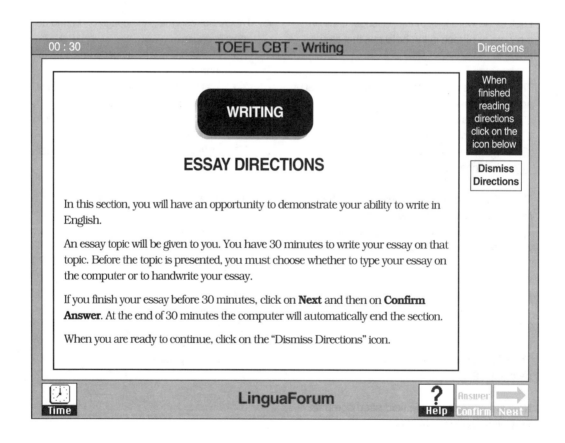

Writing

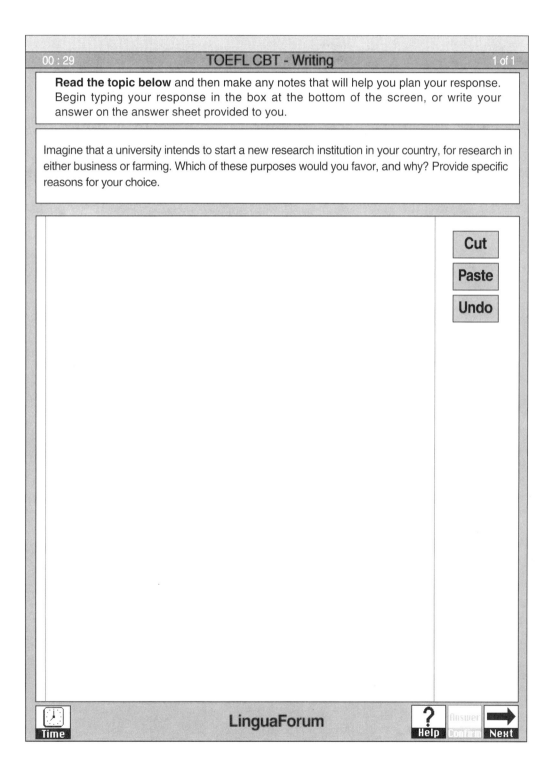

Practice Test 8

Listening: 40 Minutes (including listening time)
Structure: 20 Minutes
Reading: 90 Minutes
Writing: 30 Minutes

Suggested Total Time: 180 Minutes

ANSWER SHEET

Lingua TOEFL® CBT Test Book II
PRACTICE TEST 8

Name	
Sex	☐ male ☐ female
E-mail address	
Telephone No.	

No. of Correct Answers/Converted Score		
Listening		
Structure		
Reading		
Writing		
TOTAL		

Section 1: Listening

1. Ⓐ Ⓑ Ⓒ Ⓓ
2. Ⓐ Ⓑ Ⓒ Ⓓ
3. Ⓐ Ⓑ Ⓒ Ⓓ
4. Ⓐ Ⓑ Ⓒ Ⓓ
5. Ⓐ Ⓑ Ⓒ Ⓓ
6. Ⓐ Ⓑ Ⓒ Ⓓ
7. Ⓐ Ⓑ Ⓒ Ⓓ
8. Ⓐ Ⓑ Ⓒ Ⓓ
9. Ⓐ Ⓑ Ⓒ Ⓓ
10. Ⓐ Ⓑ Ⓒ Ⓓ
11. Ⓐ Ⓑ Ⓒ Ⓓ
12. Ⓐ Ⓑ Ⓒ Ⓓ
13. Ⓐ Ⓑ Ⓒ Ⓓ
14. Star Wars –
    Star Trek –
    2001 : A Space Odyssey –
15. Ⓐ Ⓑ Ⓒ Ⓓ
16. Ⓐ Ⓑ Ⓒ Ⓓ
17. Ⓐ Ⓑ Ⓒ Ⓓ
18. Painting –
    Etching –
    Drawing –
19. Ⓐ Ⓑ Ⓒ Ⓓ
20. Ⓐ Ⓑ Ⓒ Ⓓ
21. Ⓐ Ⓑ Ⓒ Ⓓ
22. Ⓐ Ⓑ Ⓒ Ⓓ
23. The Sovereingn –
    The Great Republic –
    The Oriental –
24. Ⓐ Ⓑ Ⓒ Ⓓ
25. Ⓐ Ⓑ Ⓒ Ⓓ
26. Ⓐ Ⓑ Ⓒ Ⓓ
27. Moved to Copenhagen
28. Ⓐ Ⓑ Ⓒ Ⓓ
29. Ⓐ Ⓑ Ⓒ Ⓓ
30. Ⓐ Ⓑ Ⓒ Ⓓ

Section 2: Structure

1. Ⓐ Ⓑ Ⓒ Ⓓ
2. Ⓐ Ⓑ Ⓒ Ⓓ
3. Ⓐ Ⓑ Ⓒ Ⓓ
4. Ⓐ Ⓑ Ⓒ Ⓓ
5. Ⓐ Ⓑ Ⓒ Ⓓ
6. Ⓐ Ⓑ Ⓒ Ⓓ
7. Ⓐ Ⓑ Ⓒ Ⓓ
8. Ⓐ Ⓑ Ⓒ Ⓓ
9. Ⓐ Ⓑ Ⓒ Ⓓ
10. Ⓐ Ⓑ Ⓒ Ⓓ
11. Ⓐ Ⓑ Ⓒ Ⓓ
12. Ⓐ Ⓑ Ⓒ Ⓓ
13. Ⓐ Ⓑ Ⓒ Ⓓ
14. Ⓐ Ⓑ Ⓒ Ⓓ
15. Ⓐ Ⓑ Ⓒ Ⓓ
16. Ⓐ Ⓑ Ⓒ Ⓓ
17. Ⓐ Ⓑ Ⓒ Ⓓ
18. Ⓐ Ⓑ Ⓒ Ⓓ
19. Ⓐ Ⓑ Ⓒ Ⓓ
20. Ⓐ Ⓑ Ⓒ Ⓓ
21. Ⓐ Ⓑ Ⓒ Ⓓ
22. Ⓐ Ⓑ Ⓒ Ⓓ
23. Ⓐ Ⓑ Ⓒ Ⓓ
24. Ⓐ Ⓑ Ⓒ Ⓓ
25. Ⓐ Ⓑ Ⓒ Ⓓ

Section 3: Reading

1. Ⓐ Ⓑ Ⓒ Ⓓ
2.
3. Ⓐ Ⓑ Ⓒ Ⓓ
4. Ⓐ Ⓑ Ⓒ Ⓓ
5.
6. Ⓐ Ⓑ Ⓒ Ⓓ
7. Ⓐ Ⓑ Ⓒ Ⓓ
8.
9. Ⓐ Ⓑ Ⓒ Ⓓ
10. Ⓐ Ⓑ Ⓒ Ⓓ
11. Ⓐ Ⓑ Ⓒ Ⓓ
12. Ⓐ Ⓑ Ⓒ Ⓓ
13.
14. Ⓐ Ⓑ Ⓒ Ⓓ
15. Ⓐ Ⓑ Ⓒ Ⓓ
16.
17. Ⓐ Ⓑ Ⓒ Ⓓ
18. Ⓐ Ⓑ Ⓒ Ⓓ
19.
20.
21. Ⓐ Ⓑ Ⓒ Ⓓ
22. Ⓐ Ⓑ Ⓒ Ⓓ
23. Ⓐ Ⓑ Ⓒ Ⓓ
24.
25.
26. Ⓐ Ⓑ Ⓒ Ⓓ
27. Ⓐ Ⓑ Ⓒ Ⓓ
28. Ⓐ Ⓑ Ⓒ Ⓓ
29. Ⓐ Ⓑ Ⓒ Ⓓ
30. Ⓐ Ⓑ Ⓒ Ⓓ

31. Ⓐ Ⓑ Ⓒ Ⓓ
32.
33.
34. Ⓐ Ⓑ Ⓒ Ⓓ
35.
36.
37. Ⓐ Ⓑ Ⓒ Ⓓ
38.
39. Ⓐ Ⓑ Ⓒ Ⓓ
40. Ⓐ Ⓑ Ⓒ Ⓓ
41. Ⓐ Ⓑ Ⓒ Ⓓ
42. Ⓐ Ⓑ Ⓒ Ⓓ
43. Ⓐ Ⓑ Ⓒ Ⓓ
44. Ⓐ Ⓑ Ⓒ Ⓓ
45. Ⓐ Ⓑ Ⓒ Ⓓ
46.
47. Ⓐ Ⓑ Ⓒ Ⓓ
48. Ⓐ Ⓑ Ⓒ Ⓓ
49. Ⓐ Ⓑ Ⓒ Ⓓ
50. Ⓐ Ⓑ Ⓒ Ⓓ
51.
52. Ⓐ Ⓑ Ⓒ Ⓓ
53. Ⓐ Ⓑ Ⓒ Ⓓ
54.
55.

■ Have you taken the official **TOEFL Test?**

☐ Yes → if any
☐ No

PBT Score	
Listening	
Structure	
Reading	
Writing	
TOTAL	

CBT Score	
Listening	
Structure	
Reading	
Writing	
TOTAL	

■ **Educational background**

☐ middle/high school ☐ undergraduate ☐ graduate

SIGNED: _____
(SIGN YOUR NAME AS IF SIGNING A BUSINESS LETTER.)

DATE: ___ / ___ / ___
MO.   DAY   YEAR

Cut here.

LinguaForum
Copyright © 2002 by Lingua Forum, Inc. All rights reserved.

ANSWER SHEET

Lingua TOEFL® CBT Test Book II
PRACTICE TEST 8

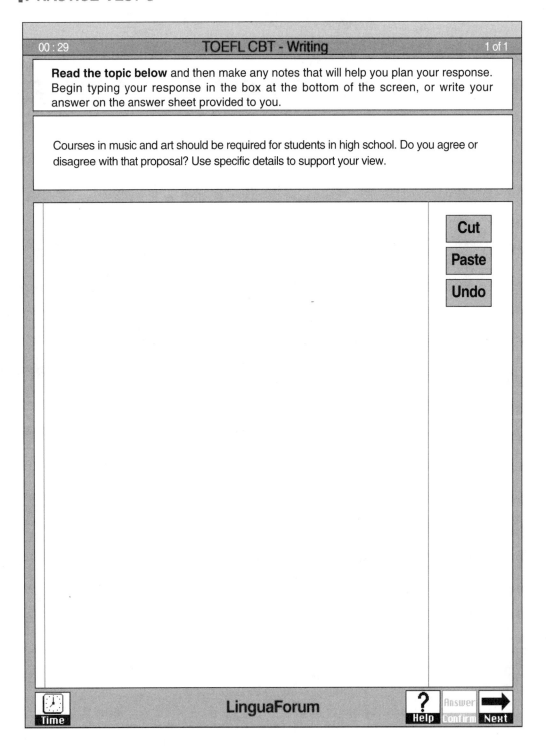

Read the topic below and then make any notes that will help you plan your response. Begin typing your response in the box at the bottom of the screen, or write your answer on the answer sheet provided to you.

Courses in music and art should be required for students in high school. Do you agree or disagree with that proposal? Use specific details to support your view.

Cut

Paste

Undo

Time   LinguaForum   ? Help   Answer Confirm   Next

LinguaForum

Copyright © 2002 by Lingua Forum, Inc. All rights reserved.

Test
8

SECTION 1
LISTENING
Suggested Time: 15 Minutes

PRACTICE
TEST 8

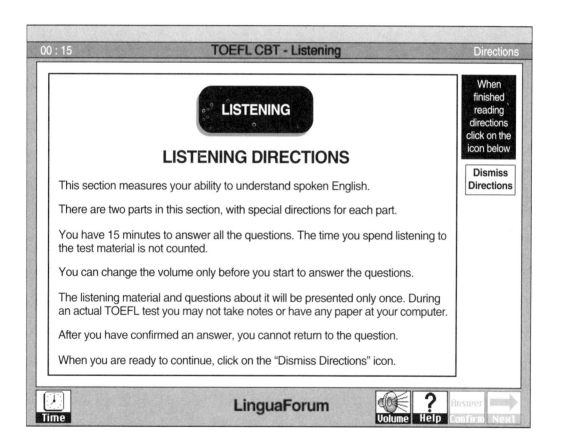

Test
8

SECTION 1
LISTENING

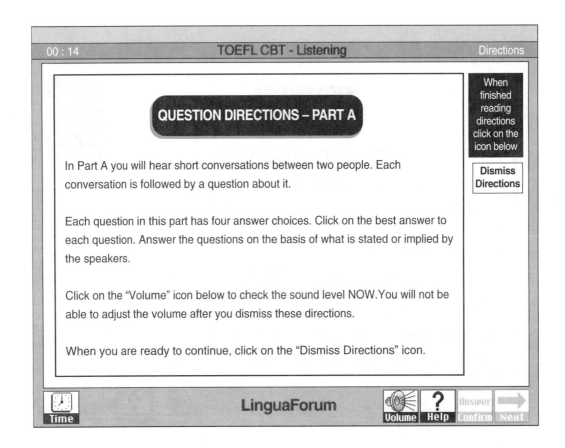

00 : 14   TOEFL CBT - Listening   Directions

When
finished
reading
directions
click on the
icon below

**Dismiss
Directions**

QUESTION DIRECTIONS – PART A

In Part A you will hear short conversations between two people. Each
conversation is followed by a question about it.

Each question in this part has four answer choices. Click on the best answer to
each question. Answer the questions on the basis of what is stated or implied by
the speakers.

Click on the "Volume" icon below to check the sound level NOW. You will not be
able to adjust the volume after you dismiss these directions.

When you are ready to continue, click on the "Dismiss Directions" icon.

LinguaForum

Time   Volume   Help   Answer Confirm   Next

106

PRACTICE
TEST 8

Test 8

1. What does the woman mean?

   (A) Dave will win because he's trying his best.
   (B) Although Dave is working very hard, he will not win the award.
   (C) Dave will not become the mayor.
   (D) Dave has the best chance of winning the scholarship.

LinguaForum   Volume   Help   Confirm   Next

Time

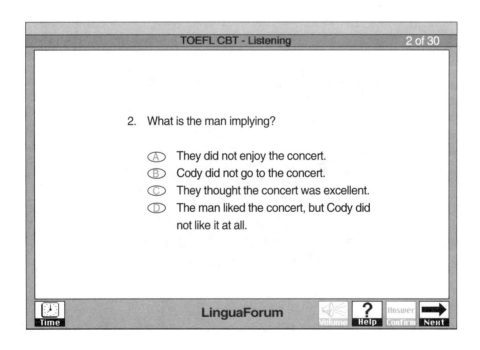

2. What is the man implying?

   (A) They did not enjoy the concert.
   (B) Cody did not go to the concert.
   (C) They thought the concert was excellent.
   (D) The man liked the concert, but Cody did not like it at all.

LinguaForum   Volume   Help   Confirm   Next

Time

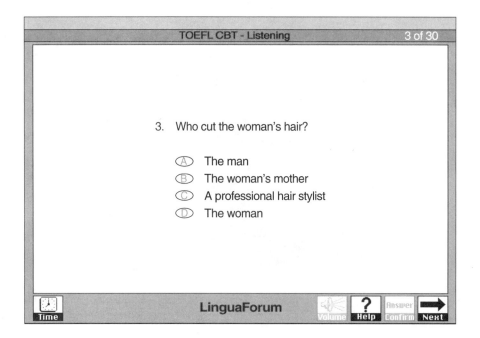

TOEFL CBT - Listening   3 of 30

3. Who cut the woman's hair?

    Ⓐ The man
    Ⓑ The woman's mother
    Ⓒ A professional hair stylist
    Ⓓ The woman

LinguaForum

Time   Volume Help Confirm Next

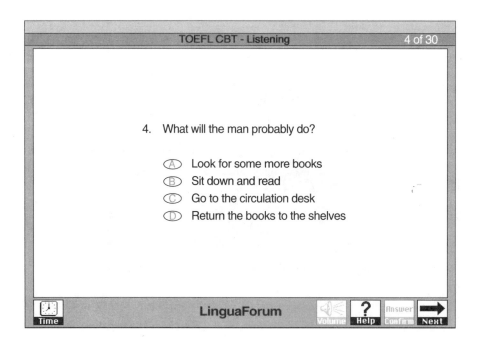

TOEFL CBT - Listening   4 of 30

4. What will the man probably do?

    Ⓐ Look for some more books
    Ⓑ Sit down and read
    Ⓒ Go to the circulation desk
    Ⓓ Return the books to the shelves

LinguaForum

Time   Volume Help Confirm Next

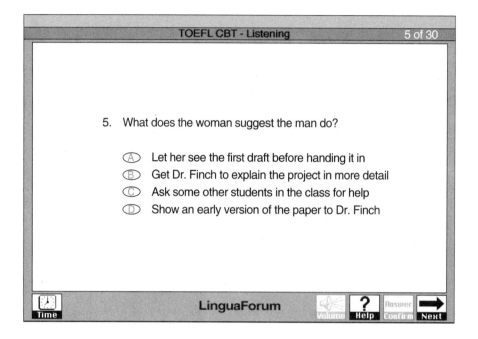

5. What does the woman suggest the man do?

    Ⓐ Let her see the first draft before handing it in
    Ⓑ Get Dr. Finch to explain the project in more detail
    Ⓒ Ask some other students in the class for help
    Ⓓ Show an early version of the paper to Dr. Finch

LinguaForum

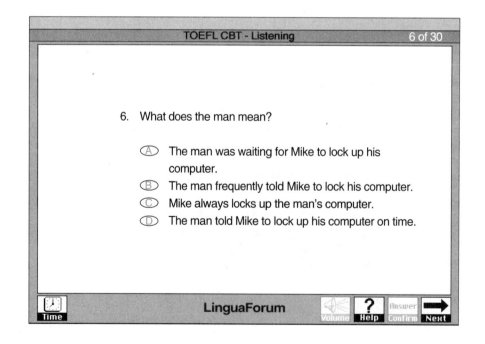

6. What does the man mean?

    Ⓐ The man was waiting for Mike to lock up his computer.
    Ⓑ The man frequently told Mike to lock his computer.
    Ⓒ Mike always locks up the man's computer.
    Ⓓ The man told Mike to lock up his computer on time.

LinguaForum

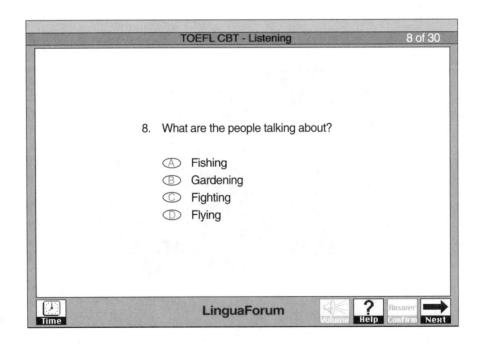

7. What did the man assume about the woman?

    Ⓐ   She was Tanya Lords.
    Ⓑ   She was Tanya Lords' cousin.
    Ⓒ   She was Tanya Lords' sister.
    Ⓓ   She was Tanya Lords' friend.

LinguaForum

Time   Volume   Help   Confirm   Next

8. What are the people talking about?

    Ⓐ   Fishing
    Ⓑ   Gardening
    Ⓒ   Fighting
    Ⓓ   Flying

LinguaForum

Time   Volume   Help   Confirm   Next

PRACTICE
TEST 8

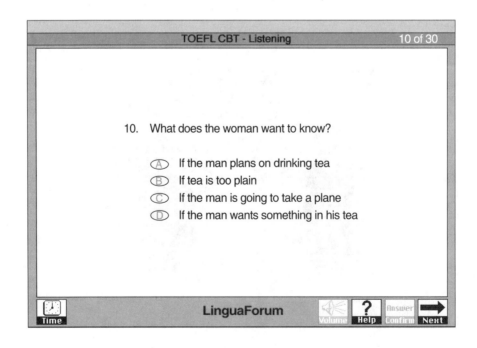

9. Where will the woman have a picnic?

Ⓐ New Hampshire
Ⓑ Maine
Ⓒ Boston
Ⓓ Along the interstate

LinguaForum

10. What does the woman want to know?

Ⓐ If the man plans on drinking tea
Ⓑ If tea is too plain
Ⓒ If the man is going to take a plane
Ⓓ If the man wants something in his tea

LinguaForum

Specialist Solutions for TOEFL® CBT

PRACTICE
TEST 8

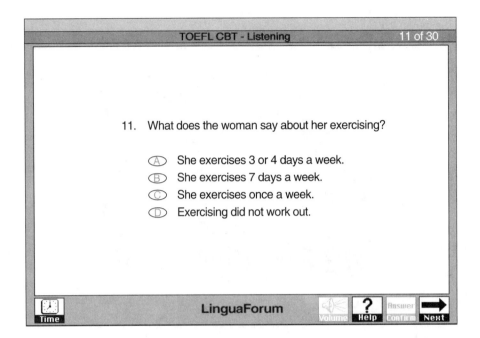

Test
8

SECTION 1
LISTENING

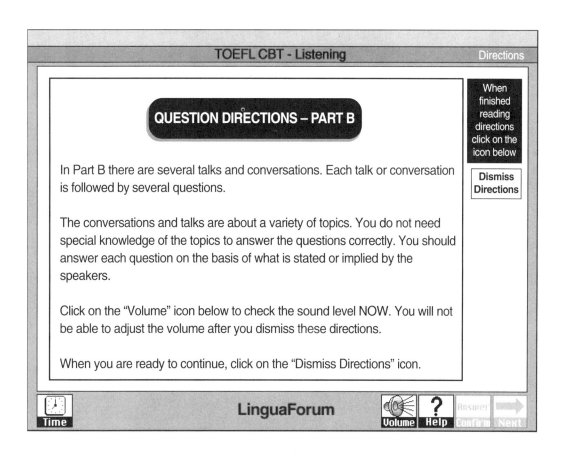

TOEFL CBT - Listening   Directions

When
finished
reading
directions
click on the
icon below

QUESTION DIRECTIONS – PART B

Dismiss
Directions

In Part B there are several talks and conversations. Each talk or conversation
is followed by several questions.

The conversations and talks are about a variety of topics. You do not need
special knowledge of the topics to answer the questions correctly. You should
answer each question on the basis of what is stated or implied by the
speakers.

Click on the "Volume" icon below to check the sound level NOW. You will not
be able to adjust the volume after you dismiss these directions.

When you are ready to continue, click on the "Dismiss Directions" icon.

Time   **LinguaForum**   Volume Help Answer
                                                            Confirm Next

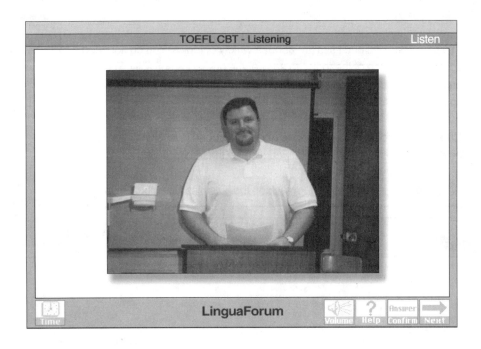

Listening

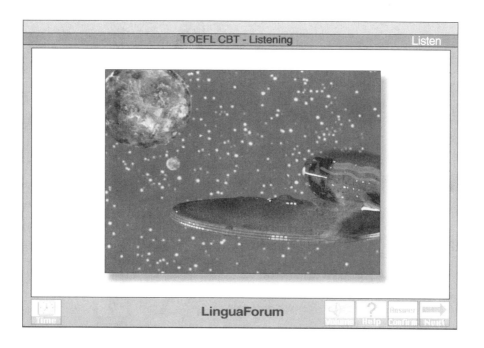

Questions 12-15

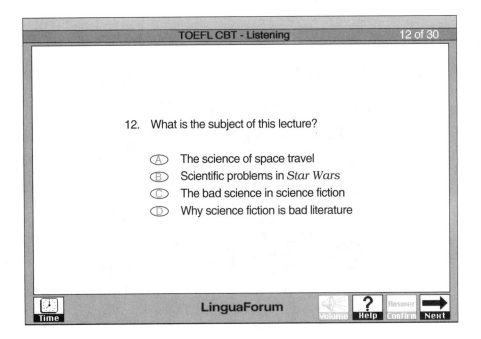

TOEFL CBT - Listening — 12 of 30

12. What is the subject of this lecture?

- Ⓐ The science of space travel
- Ⓑ Scientific problems in *Star Wars*
- Ⓒ The bad science in science fiction
- Ⓓ Why science fiction is bad literature

LinguaForum

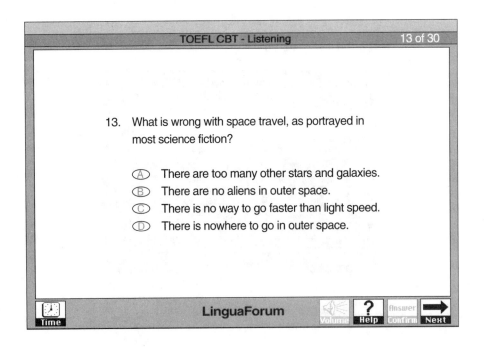

TOEFL CBT - Listening — 13 of 30

13. What is wrong with space travel, as portrayed in most science fiction?

- Ⓐ There are too many other stars and galaxies.
- Ⓑ There are no aliens in outer space.
- Ⓒ There is no way to go faster than light speed.
- Ⓓ There is nowhere to go in outer space.

LinguaForum

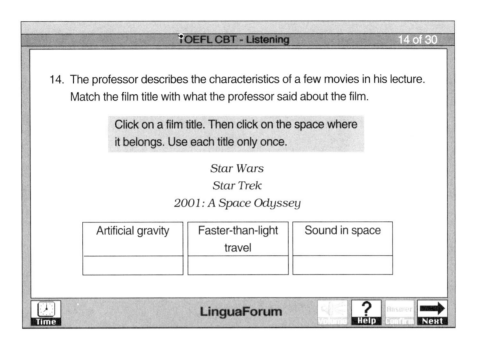

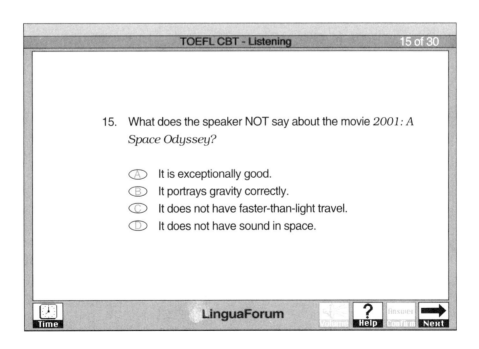

PRACTICE
TEST 8

PRACTICE
TEST 8

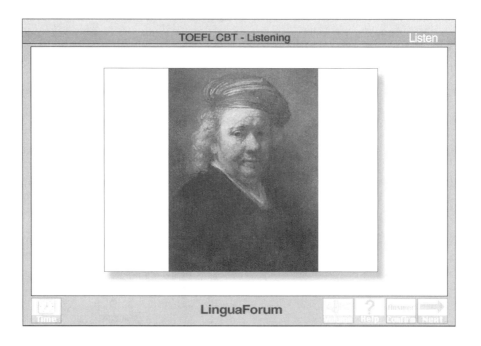

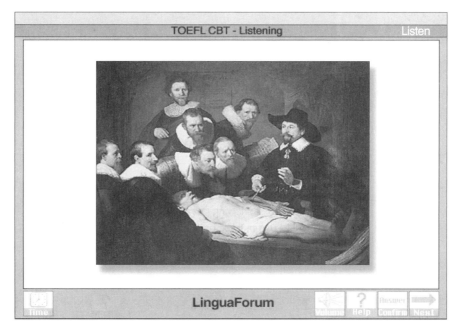

Questions 16-18

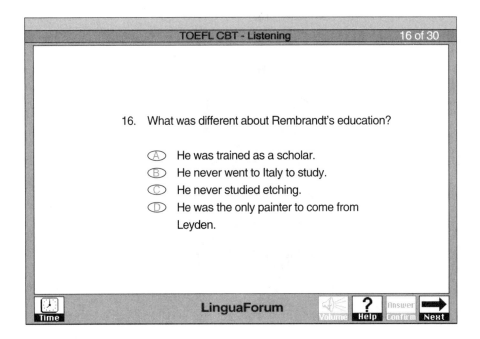

16. What was different about Rembrandt's education?

    (A) He was trained as a scholar.
    (B) He never went to Italy to study.
    (C) He never studied etching.
    (D) He was the only painter to come from Leyden.

LinguaForum

Time   Volume   Help   Confirm   Next

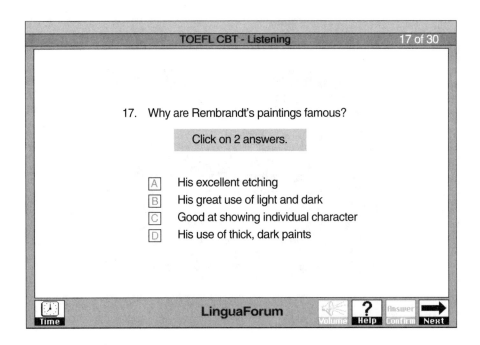

17. Why are Rembrandt's paintings famous?

Click on 2 answers.

    [A] His excellent etching
    [B] His great use of light and dark
    [C] Good at showing individual character
    [D] His use of thick, dark paints

LinguaForum

Time   Volume   Help   Confirm   Next

Specialist Solutions for TOEFL® CBT

Listening

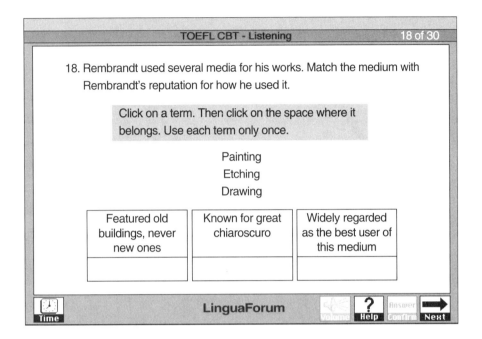

18. Rembrandt used several media for his works. Match the medium with Rembrandt's reputation for how he used it.

Click on a term. Then click on the space where it belongs. Use each term only once.

Painting
Etching
Drawing

Featured old buildings, never new ones	Known for great chiaroscuro	Widely regarded as the best user of this medium

LinguaForum

Time   Volume   Help   Confirm   Next

PRACTICE
TEST 8

128

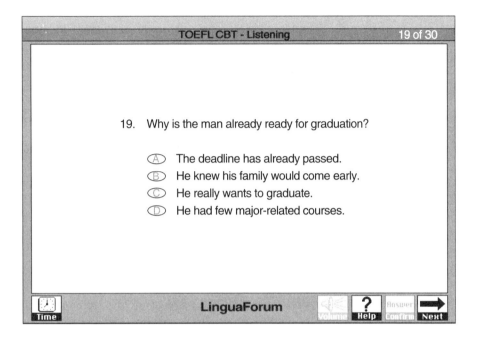

19. Why is the man already ready for graduation?

    Ⓐ The deadline has already passed.
    Ⓑ He knew his family would come early.
    Ⓒ He really wants to graduate.
    Ⓓ He had few major-related courses.

LinguaForum

Time | Volume | Help | Answer Confirm | Next

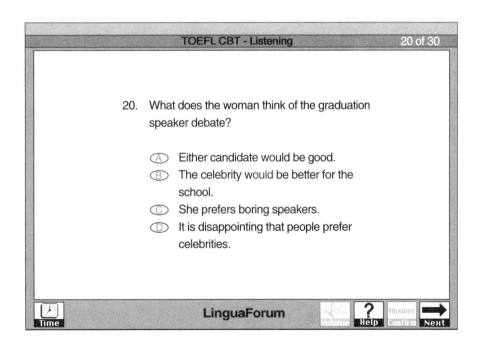

20. What does the woman think of the graduation
     speaker debate?

    Ⓐ Either candidate would be good.
    Ⓑ The celebrity would be better for the
       school.
    Ⓒ She prefers boring speakers.
    Ⓓ It is disappointing that people prefer
       celebrities.

LinguaForum

Time | Volume | Help | Answer Confirm | Next

PRACTICE
TEST 8

Listening

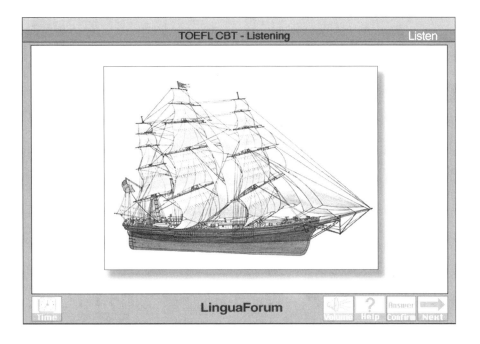

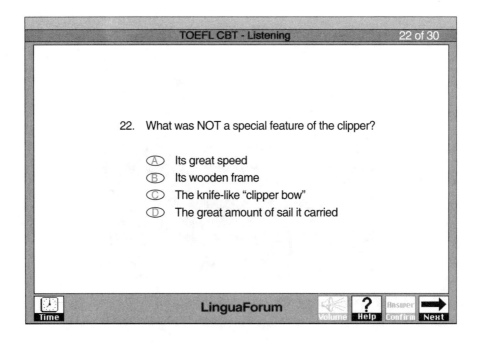

Listening

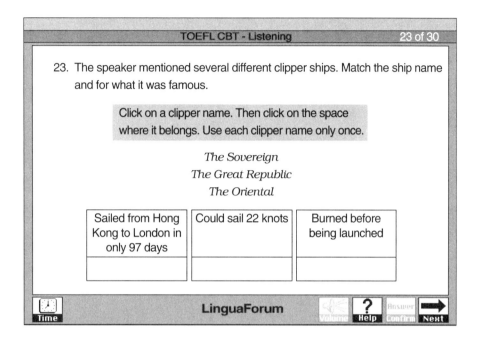

23. The speaker mentioned several different clipper ships. Match the ship name and for what it was famous.

Click on a clipper name. Then click on the space where it belongs. Use each clipper name only once.

The Sovereign
The Great Republic
The Oriental

Sailed from Hong Kong to London in only 97 days	Could sail 22 knots	Burned before being launched

LinguaForum

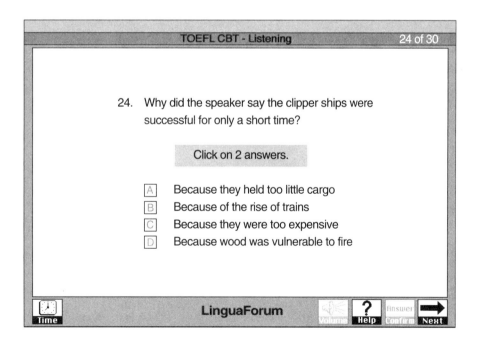

24. Why did the speaker say the clipper ships were successful for only a short time?

Click on 2 answers.

A   Because they held too little cargo
B   Because of the rise of trains
C   Because they were too expensive
D   Because wood was vulnerable to fire

LinguaForum

PRACTICE TEST 8

PRACTICE
TEST 8

Questions 25-28

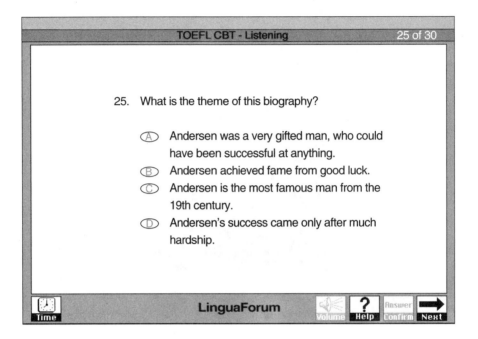

25. What is the theme of this biography?

   Ⓐ Andersen was a very gifted man, who could have been successful at anything.

   Ⓑ Andersen achieved fame from good luck.

   Ⓒ Andersen is the most famous man from the 19th century.

   Ⓓ Andersen's success came only after much hardship.

LinguaForum

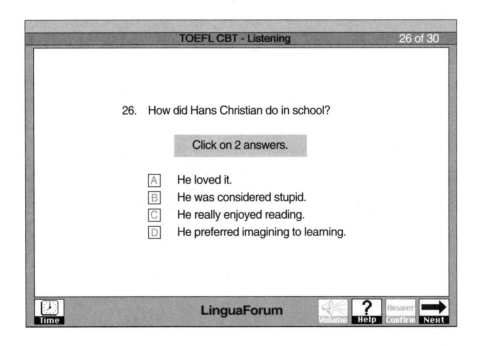

26. How did Hans Christian do in school?

Click on 2 answers.

   A He loved it.

   B He was considered stupid.

   C He really enjoyed reading.

   D He preferred imagining to learning.

LinguaForum

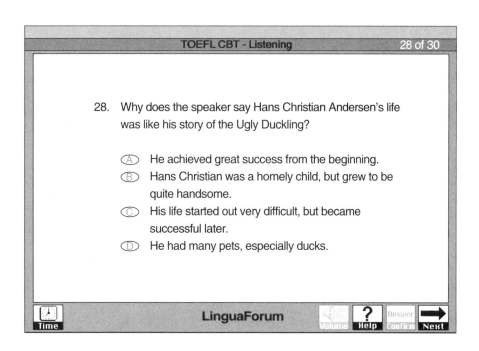

TOEFL CBT - Listening   27 of 30

27. The professor explains a series of events of Hans Christian Andersen's life. Put them into chronological order.

> Click on an expression. Then click on the space where it belongs. Use each expression only once.

Moved to Copenhagen
Honored by Denmark in a festival
Published his first fairy tale
Entered university
First published his poems

1. **Moved to Copenhagen**
2.
3.
4.
5.

Time   **LinguaForum**   Volume   Help   Confirm   Next

TOEFL CBT - Listening   28 of 30

28. Why does the speaker say Hans Christian Andersen's life was like his story of the Ugly Duckling?

  Ⓐ He achieved great success from the beginning.
  Ⓑ Hans Christian was a homely child, but grew to be quite handsome.
  Ⓒ His life started out very difficult, but became successful later.
  Ⓓ He had many pets, especially ducks.

Time   **LinguaForum**   Volume   Help   Confirm   Next

138

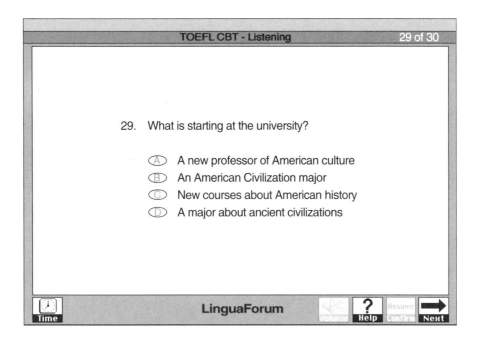

29. What is starting at the university?

  Ⓐ   A new professor of American culture
  Ⓑ   An American Civilization major
  Ⓒ   New courses about American history
  Ⓓ   A major about ancient civilizations

LinguaForum

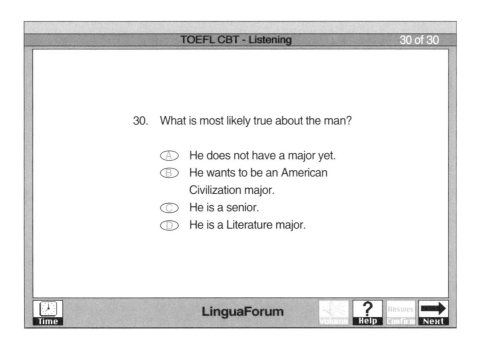

30. What is most likely true about the man?

  Ⓐ   He does not have a major yet.
  Ⓑ   He wants to be an American
        Civilization major.
  Ⓒ   He is a senior.
  Ⓓ   He is a Literature major.

LinguaForum

PRACTICE
TEST 8

Test
8

SECTION 2
STRUCTURE
Suggested Time: 19 Minutes

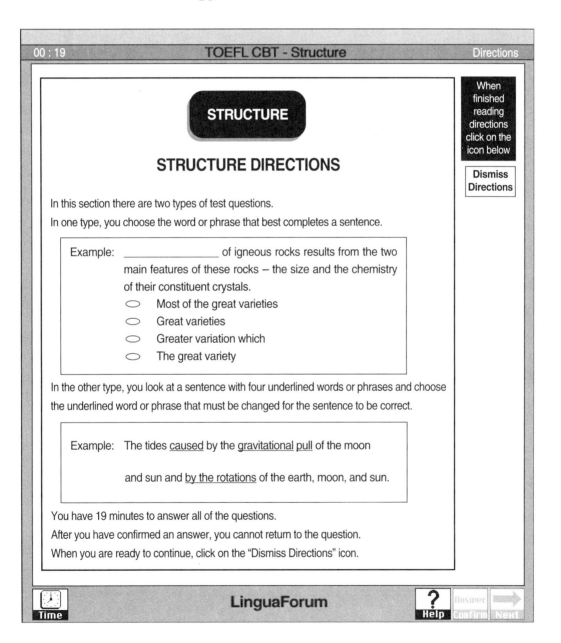

00 : 19   TOEFL CBT - Structure   Directions

When finished reading directions click on the icon below

Dismiss Directions

STRUCTURE

STRUCTURE DIRECTIONS

In this section there are two types of test questions.

In one type, you choose the word or phrase that best completes a sentence.

> Example: _____ of igneous rocks results from the two
> main features of these rocks – the size and the chemistry
> of their constituent crystals.
> ○ Most of the great varieties
> ○ Great varieties
> ○ Greater variation which
> ○ The great variety

In the other type, you look at a sentence with four underlined words or phrases and choose the underlined word or phrase that must be changed for the sentence to be correct.

> Example: The tides <u>caused</u> by the <u>gravitational</u> <u>pull</u> of the moon
>
> and sun and <u>by the rotations</u> of the earth, moon, and sun.

You have 19 minutes to answer all of the questions.

After you have confirmed an answer, you cannot return to the question.

When you are ready to continue, click on the "Dismiss Directions" icon.

Time   **LinguaForum**   ? Help   Answer   Confirm   Next

Structure

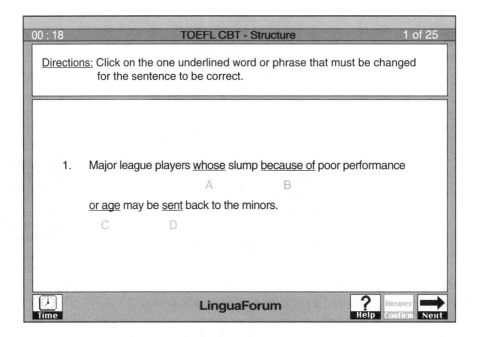

Directions: Click on the one underlined word or phrase that must be changed for the sentence to be correct.

1. Major league players <u>whose</u> slump <u>because of</u> poor performance
         A   B

   <u>or age</u> may be <u>sent</u> back to the minors.
      C   D

LinguaForum

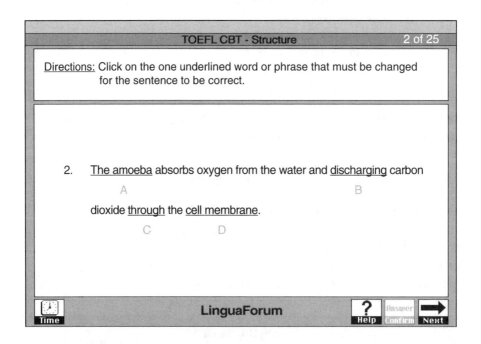

Directions: Click on the one underlined word or phrase that must be changed for the sentence to be correct.

2. <u>The amoeba</u> absorbs oxygen from the water and <u>discharging</u> carbon
      A   B

   dioxide <u>through</u> the <u>cell membrane</u>.
              C   D

LinguaForum

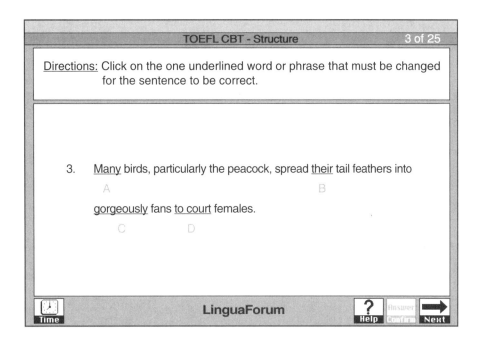

Directions: Click on the one underlined word or phrase that must be changed for the sentence to be correct.

3.   Many birds, particularly the peacock, spread their tail feathers into
      A   B

   gorgeously fans to court females.
       C   D

LinguaForum

PRACTICE TEST 8

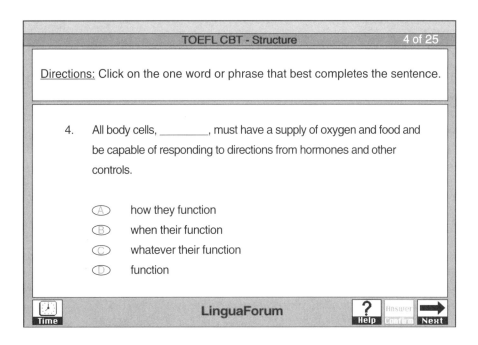

Directions: Click on the one word or phrase that best completes the sentence.

4.   All body cells, _____, must have a supply of oxygen and food and be capable of responding to directions from hormones and other controls.

     Ⓐ   how they function
     Ⓑ   when their function
     Ⓒ   whatever their function
     Ⓓ   function

LinguaForum

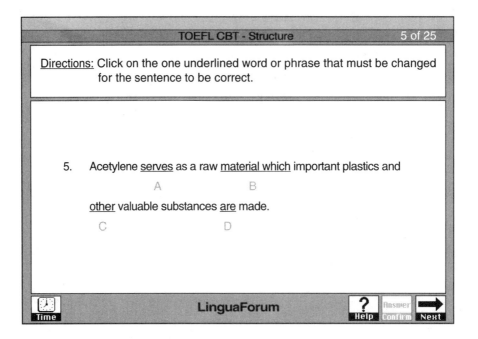

Directions: Click on the one underlined word or phrase that must be changed for the sentence to be correct.

5.   Acetylene <u>serves</u> as a raw <u>material which</u> important plastics and
                      A   B

<u>other</u> valuable substances <u>are</u> made.
        C   D

LinguaForum

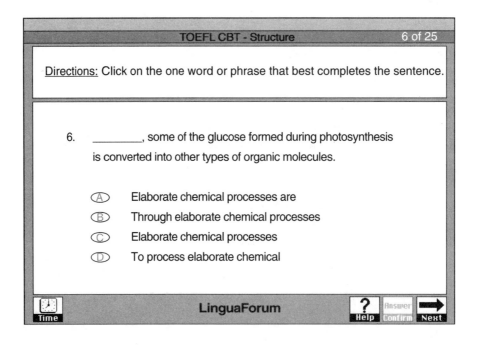

Directions: Click on the one word or phrase that best completes the sentence.

6.   _____, some of the glucose formed during photosynthesis
      is converted into other types of organic molecules.

      (A)   Elaborate chemical processes are
      (B)   Through elaborate chemical processes
      (C)   Elaborate chemical processes
      (D)   To process elaborate chemical

LinguaForum

PRACTICE
TEST 8

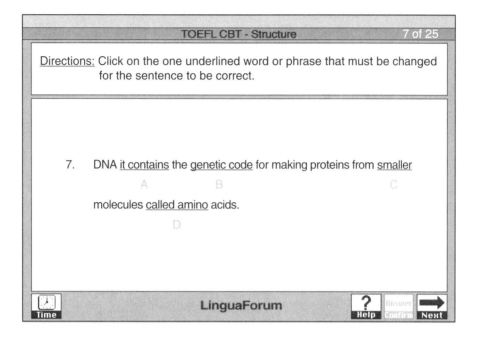

Directions: Click on the one underlined word or phrase that must be changed
                 for the sentence to be correct.

7.   DNA it contains the genetic code for making proteins from smaller
                      A   B   C

       molecules called amino acids.
                            D

Time   LinguaForum   ? Answer ➡
                                     Help Confirm Next

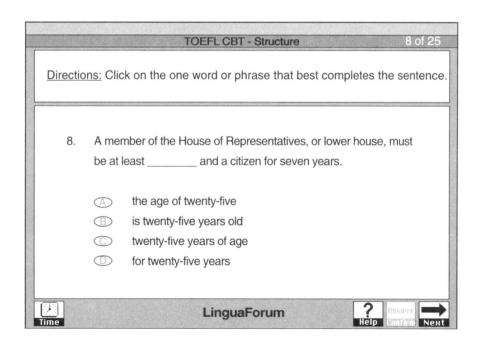

Directions: Click on the one word or phrase that best completes the sentence.

8.   A member of the House of Representatives, or lower house, must
       be at least _____ and a citizen for seven years.

       Ⓐ   the age of twenty-five
       Ⓑ   is twenty-five years old
       Ⓒ   twenty-five years of age
       Ⓓ   for twenty-five years

Time   LinguaForum   ? Answer ➡
                                     Help Confirm Next

145

Structure

Directions: Click on the one underlined word or phrase that must be changed for the sentence to be correct.

9. Heat <u>felt is</u> because the hot water <u>stimulates</u> <u>certain</u> special nerve
           A   B   C

    endings <u>contained</u> in the skin of the hand.
                  D

Directions: Click on the one word or phrase that best completes the sentence.

10. Coffee, especially if consumed in the evening, tends to make some
     persons sleepless; _____ no difficulty in getting to sleep.

     (A)   but others experiencing
     (B)   others experience
     (C)   while experiencing
     (D)   to experience others

Structure

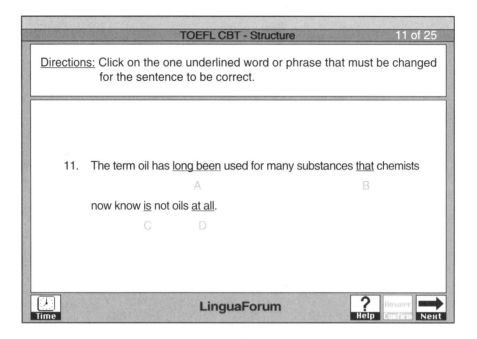

TOEFL CBT - Structure   11 of 25

Directions: Click on the one underlined word or phrase that must be changed
for the sentence to be correct.

11.   The term oil has <u>long been</u> used for many substances <u>that</u> chemists

                                         A   B

now know <u>is</u> not oils <u>at all</u>.

                    C   D

LinguaForum

Time   ? Help   Answer Confirm   Next

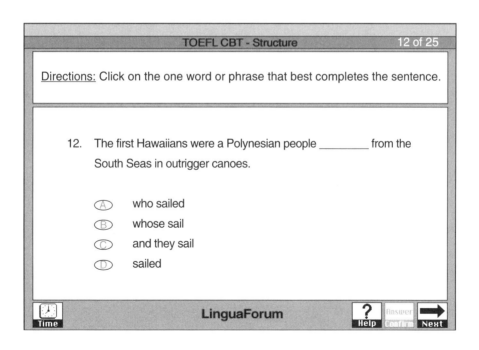

TOEFL CBT - Structure   12 of 25

Directions: Click on the one word or phrase that best completes the sentence.

12.   The first Hawaiians were a Polynesian people _____ from the
South Seas in outrigger canoes.

      Ⓐ   who sailed

      Ⓑ   whose sail

      Ⓒ   and they sail

      Ⓓ   sailed

LinguaForum

Time   ? Help   Answer Confirm   Next

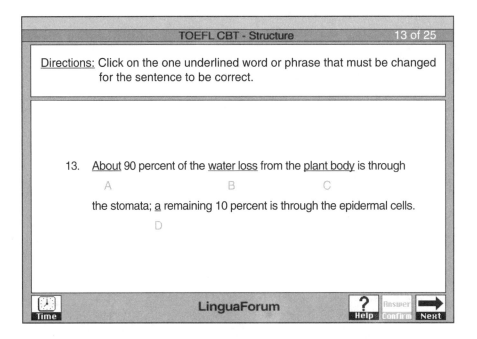

Directions: Click on the one underlined word or phrase that must be changed for the sentence to be correct.

13. About 90 percent of the water loss from the plant body is through
    A   B   C

the stomata; a remaining 10 percent is through the epidermal cells.
                 D

LinguaForum

Time   Help Answer Confirm Next

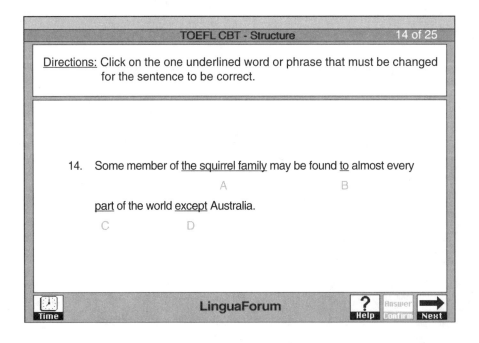

Directions: Click on the one underlined word or phrase that must be changed for the sentence to be correct.

14. Some member of the squirrel family may be found to almost every
                            A   B

part of the world except Australia.
  C   D

LinguaForum

Time   Help Answer Confirm Next

Structure

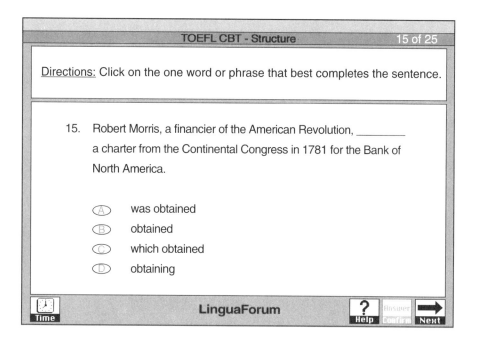

Directions: Click on the one word or phrase that best completes the sentence.

15. Robert Morris, a financier of the American Revolution, _____ a charter from the Continental Congress in 1781 for the Bank of North America.

    (A) was obtained
    (B) obtained
    (C) which obtained
    (D) obtaining

Time   LinguaForum   ? Help Answer Confirm Next

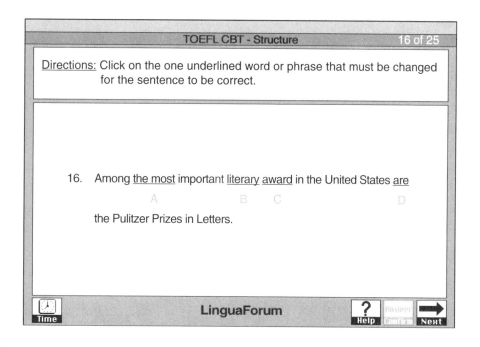

Directions: Click on the one underlined word or phrase that must be changed for the sentence to be correct.

16. Among the most important literary award in the United States are
           A   B C   D

the Pulitzer Prizes in Letters.

Time   LinguaForum   ? Help Answer Confirm Next

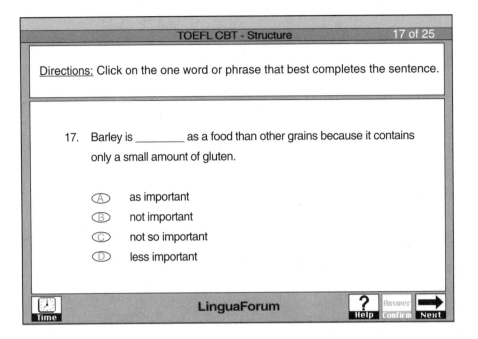

Directions: Click on the one word or phrase that best completes the sentence.

17.   Barley is _____ as a food than other grains because it contains only a small amount of gluten.

    (A)   as important
    (B)   not important
    (C)   not so important
    (D)   less important

LinguaForum

? Help   Answer Confirm   Next

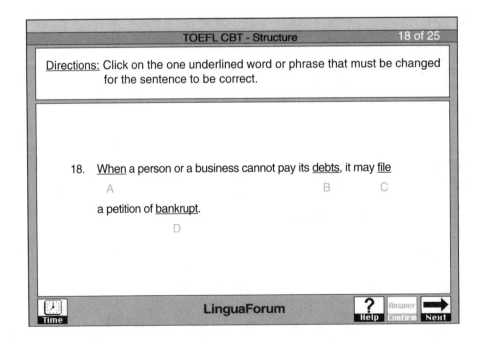

Directions: Click on the one underlined word or phrase that must be changed for the sentence to be correct.

18.   When a person or a business cannot pay its debts, it may file
    A   B   C
    a petition of bankrupt.
             D

LinguaForum

? Help   Answer Confirm   Next

Structure

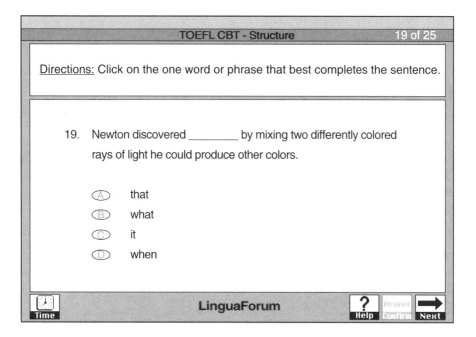

Directions: Click on the one word or phrase that best completes the sentence.

19. Newton discovered _____ by mixing two differently colored
rays of light he could produce other colors.

     Ⓐ   that
     Ⓑ   what
     Ⓒ   it
     Ⓓ   when

LinguaForum   ? Help   Answer Confirm   Next   Time

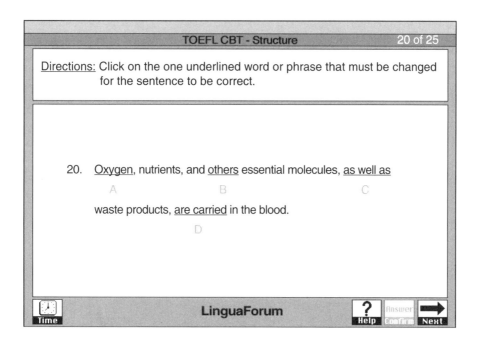

Directions: Click on the one underlined word or phrase that must be changed
for the sentence to be correct.

20. <u>Oxygen</u>, nutrients, and <u>others</u> essential molecules, <u>as well as</u>
     A   B   C

waste products, <u>are carried</u> in the blood.
            D

LinguaForum   ? Help   Answer Confirm   Next   Time

Structure

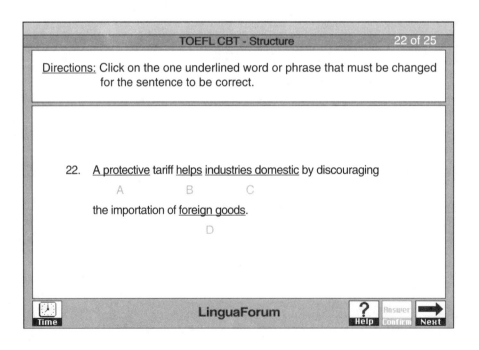

Directions: Click on the one word or phrase that best completes the sentence.

21. In 1681 William Penn persuaded the King of England _____
land for a Quaker colony in America, to be named Pennsylvania.

   (A)   grant him
   (B)   he granted
   (C)   that granting
   (D)   to grant him

LinguaForum

? Help   Answer Confirm   → Next

Directions: Click on the one underlined word or phrase that must be changed
for the sentence to be correct.

22. A protective tariff helps industries domestic by discouraging
    A   B   C

the importation of foreign goods.
               D

LinguaForum

? Help   Answer Confirm   → Next

Structure

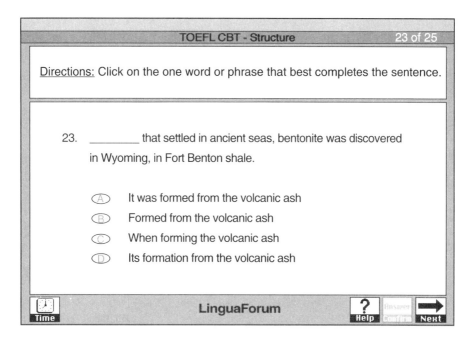

Directions: Click on the one word or phrase that best completes the sentence.

23. _____ that settled in ancient seas, bentonite was discovered in Wyoming, in Fort Benton shale.

    (A)   It was formed from the volcanic ash

    (B)   Formed from the volcanic ash

    (C)   When forming the volcanic ash

    (D)   Its formation from the volcanic ash

LinguaForum   Time   Help   Answer Confirm   Next

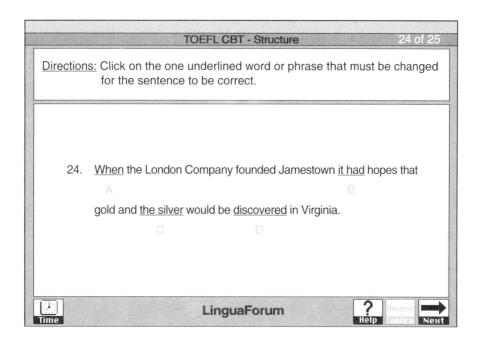

Directions: Click on the one underlined word or phrase that must be changed for the sentence to be correct.

24. When the London Company founded Jamestown it had hopes that
     A   B

gold and the silver would be discovered in Virginia.
        C   D

LinguaForum   Time   Help   Answer Confirm   Next

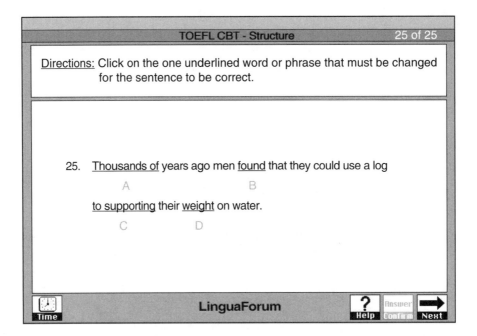

Directions: Click on the one underlined word or phrase that must be changed
for the sentence to be correct.

25. <u>Thousands of</u> years ago men <u>found</u> that they could use a log
     A   B

<u>to supporting</u> their <u>weight</u> on water.
  C   D

LinguaForum

? Help Answer Confirm Next

PRACTICE
TEST 8

SECTION 3
READING
Suggested Time: 90 Minutes

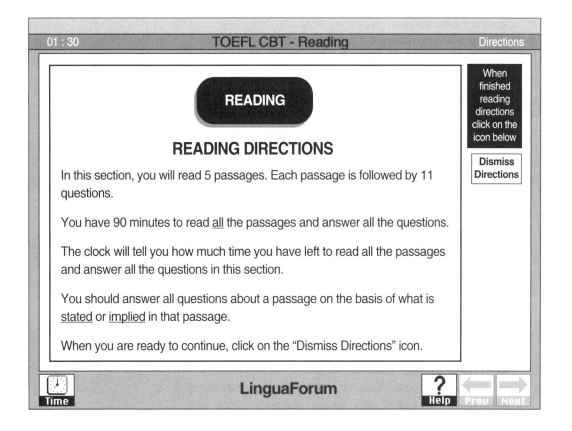

01 : 30   TOEFL CBT - Reading   Directions

READING

READING DIRECTIONS

When finished reading directions click on the icon below

Dismiss Directions

In this section, you will read 5 passages. Each passage is followed by 11 questions.

You have 90 minutes to read <u>all</u> the passages and answer all the questions.

The clock will tell you how much time you have left to read all the passages and answer all the questions in this section.

You should answer all questions about a passage on the basis of what is <u>stated</u> or <u>implied</u> in that passage.

When you are ready to continue, click on the "Dismiss Directions" icon.

Time   **LinguaForum**   ? Help   Preu Next

Passage 1

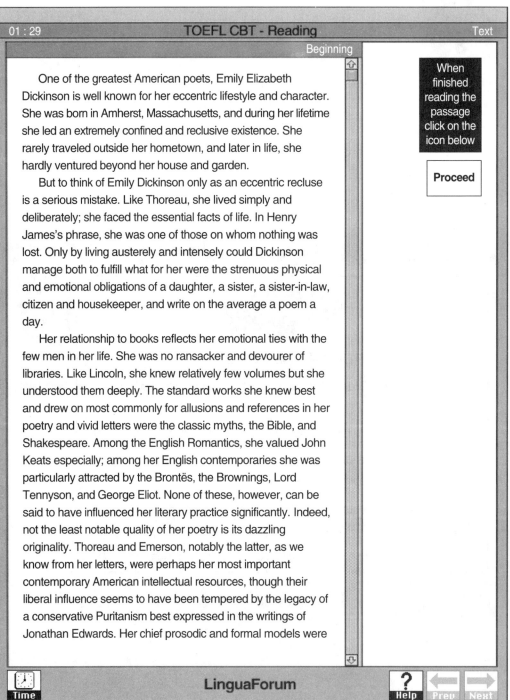

Passage 1

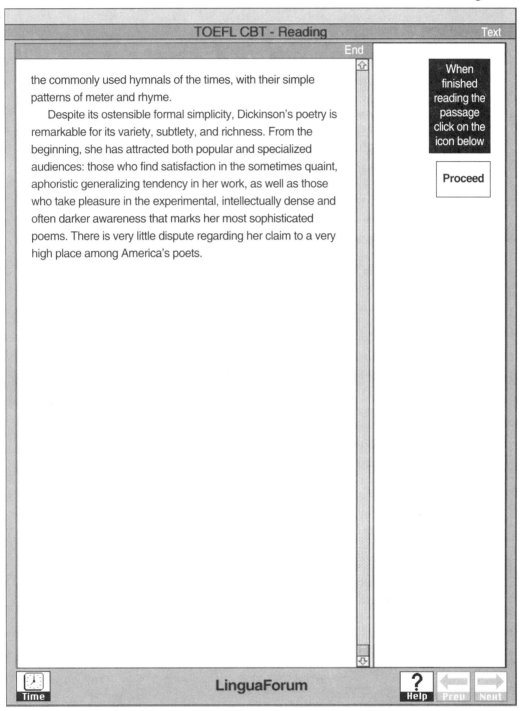

the commonly used hymnals of the times, with their simple patterns of meter and rhyme.

Despite its ostensible formal simplicity, Dickinson's poetry is remarkable for its variety, subtlety, and richness. From the beginning, she has attracted both popular and specialized audiences: those who find satisfaction in the sometimes quaint, aphoristic generalizing tendency in her work, as well as those who take pleasure in the experimental, intellectually dense and often darker awareness that marks her most sophisticated poems. There is very little dispute regarding her claim to a very high place among America's poets.

When finished reading the passage click on the icon below

Proceed

PRACTICE
TEST 8

Time

LinguaForum

Help Prev Next

One of the greatest American poets, Emily Elizabeth Dickinson is well known for her eccentric lifestyle and character. She was born in Amherst, Massachusetts, and during her lifetime she led an extremely confined and reclusive existence. She rarely traveled outside her hometown, and later in life, she hardly ventured beyond her house and garden.

But to think of Emily Dickinson only as an eccentric recluse is a serious mistake. Like Thoreau, she lived simply and deliberately; she faced the essential facts of life. In Henry James's phrase, she was one of those on whom nothing was lost. Only by living austerely and intensely could Dickinson manage both to fulfill what for her were the strenuous physical and emotional obligations of a daughter, a sister, a sister-in-law, citizen and housekeeper, and write on the average a poem a day.

Her relationship to books reflects her emotional ties with the few men in her life. She was no ransacker and devourer of libraries. Like Lincoln, she knew relatively few volumes but she understood them deeply. The standard works she knew best and drew on most commonly for allusions and references in her poetry and vivid letters were the classic myths, the Bible, and Shakespeare. Among the English Romantics, she valued John Keats especially; among her English contemporaries she was particularly attracted by the Brontës, the Brownings, Lord Tennyson, and George Eliot. None of these, however, can be said to have influenced her literary practice significantly. Indeed, not the least notable quality of her poetry is its dazzling originality. Thoreau and Emerson, notably the latter, as we know from her letters, were perhaps her most important contemporary American intellectual resources, though their liberal influence seems to have been tempered by the legacy of a conservative Puritanism best expressed in the writings of Jonathan Edwards. Her chief prosodic and formal models were

1. The purpose of the passage is

  Ⓐ to trace the sources of Dickinson's poetry

  Ⓑ to introduce the strange life of Dickinson

  Ⓒ to evaluate the work of Dickinson

  Ⓓ to introduce the life and works of Dickinson

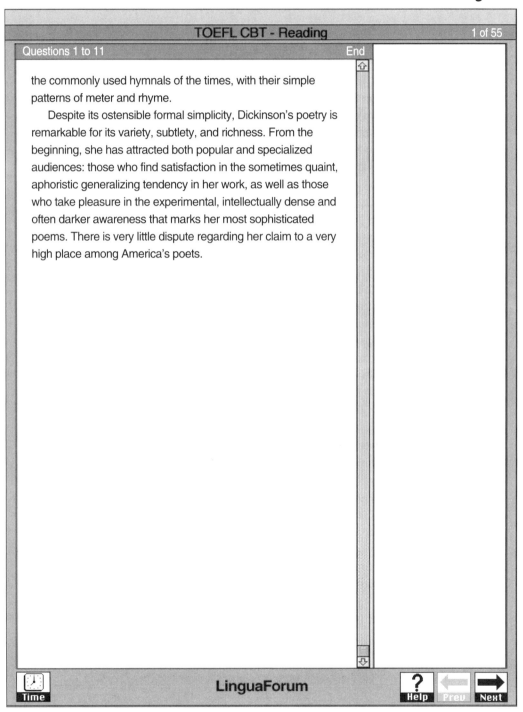

TOEFL CBT - Reading   1 of 55

Questions 1 to 11   End

the commonly used hymnals of the times, with their simple patterns of meter and rhyme.

Despite its ostensible formal simplicity, Dickinson's poetry is remarkable for its variety, subtlety, and richness. From the beginning, she has attracted both popular and specialized audiences: those who find satisfaction in the sometimes quaint, aphoristic generalizing tendency in her work, as well as those who take pleasure in the experimental, intellectually dense and often darker awareness that marks her most sophisticated poems. There is very little dispute regarding her claim to a very high place among America's poets.

LinguaForum

Time   Help   Prev   Next

PRACTICE
TEST 8

One of the greatest American poets, Emily Elizabeth **Dickinson is well known for her eccentric lifestyle and character. She was born in Amherst, Massachusetts, and during her lifetime she led an extremely confined and reclusive existence. She** rarely **traveled outside her hometown, and later in life, she hardly ventured beyond her house and garden.**

But to think of Emily Dickinson only as an eccentric recluse is a serious mistake. Like Thoreau, she lived simply and deliberately; she faced the essential facts of life. **In Henry James's phrase, she was one of those on whom nothing was lost. Only by living austerely and intensely could Dickinson manage both to fulfill what for** her **were the strenuous physical and emotional obligations of a daughter, a sister, a sister-in-law, citizen and housekeeper, and write on the average a poem a day.**

Her relationship to books reflects her emotional ties with the few men in her life. She was no ransacker and devourer of libraries. Like Lincoln, she knew relatively few volumes but she understood them deeply. The standard works she knew best and drew on most commonly for allusions and references in her poetry and vivid letters were the classic myths, the Bible, and Shakespeare. Among the English Romantics, she valued John Keats especially; among her English contemporaries she was particularly attracted by the Brontës, the Brownings, Lord Tennyson, and George Eliot. None of these, however, can be said to have influenced her literary practice significantly. Indeed, not the least notable quality of her poetry is its dazzling originality. Thoreau and Emerson, notably the latter, as we know from her letters, were perhaps her most important contemporary American intellectual resources, though their liberal influence seems to have been tempered by the legacy of

2. Look at the word rarely in the passage. Click on the word or phrase in the **bold** text that best replaces rarely.

3. Emily Dickinson stands out among American literary figures for her
- (A) eccentricity
- (B) silence
- (C) complexity
- (D) simplicity

4. Contrary to popular belief, Dickinson
- (A) did not do much besides write poetry
- (B) was very much tied to various responsibilities
- (C) had no family obligations to carry out
- (D) was too busy to lead her own personal life

Reading

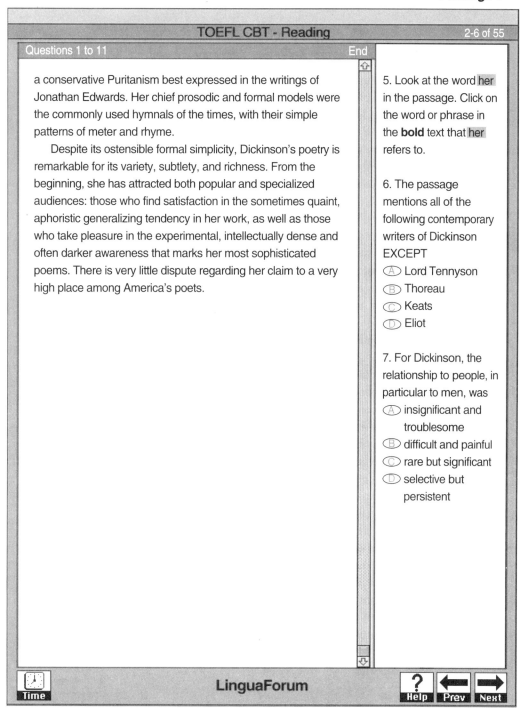

Questions 1 to 11 — End

a conservative Puritanism best expressed in the writings of Jonathan Edwards. Her chief prosodic and formal models were the commonly used hymnals of the times, with their simple patterns of meter and rhyme.

Despite its ostensible formal simplicity, Dickinson's poetry is remarkable for its variety, subtlety, and richness. From the beginning, she has attracted both popular and specialized audiences: those who find satisfaction in the sometimes quaint, aphoristic generalizing tendency in her work, as well as those who take pleasure in the experimental, intellectually dense and often darker awareness that marks her most sophisticated poems. There is very little dispute regarding her claim to a very high place among America's poets.

5. Look at the word **her** in the passage. Click on the word or phrase in the **bold** text that **her** refers to.

6. The passage mentions all of the following contemporary writers of Dickinson EXCEPT
(A) Lord Tennyson
(B) Thoreau
(C) Keats
(D) Eliot

7. For Dickinson, the relationship to people, in particular to men, was
(A) insignificant and troublesome
(B) difficult and painful
(C) rare but significant
(D) selective but persistent

Time — LinguaForum — Help — Prev — Next

PRACTICE TEST 8

Reading

Passage 1

Questions 1 to 11   Beginning

One of the greatest American poets, Emily Elizabeth Dickinson is well known for her eccentric lifestyle and character. She was born in Amherst, Massachusetts, and during her lifetime she led an extremely confined and reclusive existence. She rarely traveled outside her hometown, and later in life, she hardly ventured beyond her house and garden.

But to think of Emily Dickinson only as an eccentric recluse is a serious mistake. Like Thoreau, she lived simply and deliberately; she faced the essential facts of life. In Henry James's phrase, she was one of those on whom nothing was lost. Only by living austerely and intensely could Dickinson manage both to fulfill what for her were the strenuous physical and emotional obligations of a daughter, a sister, a sister-in-law, citizen and housekeeper, and write on the average a poem a day.

→ Her relationship to books reflects her emotional ties with the few men in her life. ■ She was no ransacker and devourer of libraries. ■ Like Lincoln, she knew relatively few volumes but she understood them deeply. ■ The standard works she knew best and drew on most commonly for allusions and references in her poetry and vivid letters were the classic myths, the Bible, and Shakespeare. ■ Among the English Romantics, she valued John Keats especially; among her English contemporaries she was particularly attracted by the Brontës, the Brownings, Lord Tennyson, and George Eliot. None of these, however, can be said to have influenced her literary practice significantly. ■ Indeed, not the least notable quality of her poetry is its dazzling originality. ■ Thoreau and Emerson, notably the latter, as we know from her letters, were perhaps her most important contemporary American intellectual resources, though their liberal influence seems to have been tempered by the legacy of a conservative Puritanism best expressed in the writings of Jonathan Edwards. ■ Her chief

8. The following sentence can be added to paragraph 3 or 4.

As a girl she attended Amherst Academy and also Mount Holyoke Female Seminary, but school gave her neither intellectual nor social satisfactions to compensate for the reassuring intimacy of home and family she keenly missed.

Where would it best fit in the paragraph? Click on the square [■] to add the sentence to paragraph 3 or 4. Paragraphs 3 and 4 are marked with an arrow [→].

9. Despite the literary allusions and references, Dickinson's poetry is notable for its
Ⓐ imitation
Ⓑ originality
Ⓒ universality
Ⓓ difficulty

Time

LinguaForum

Help Prev Next

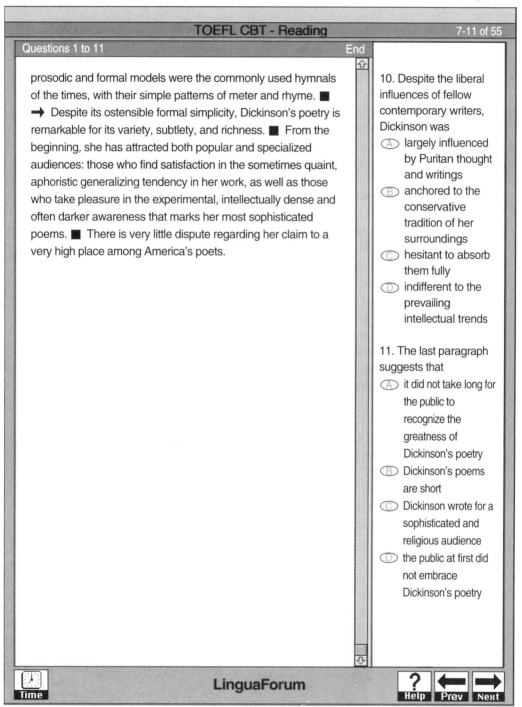

Questions 1 to 11   End

prosodic and formal models were the commonly used hymnals of the times, with their simple patterns of meter and rhyme. ■
➡ Despite its ostensible formal simplicity, Dickinson's poetry is remarkable for its variety, subtlety, and richness. ■ From the beginning, she has attracted both popular and specialized audiences: those who find satisfaction in the sometimes quaint, aphoristic generalizing tendency in her work, as well as those who take pleasure in the experimental, intellectually dense and often darker awareness that marks her most sophisticated poems. ■ There is very little dispute regarding her claim to a very high place among America's poets.

10. Despite the liberal influences of fellow contemporary writers, Dickinson was

Ⓐ largely influenced by Puritan thought and writings

Ⓑ anchored to the conservative tradition of her surroundings

Ⓒ hesitant to absorb them fully

Ⓓ indifferent to the prevailing intellectual trends

11. The last paragraph suggests that

Ⓐ it did not take long for the public to recognize the greatness of Dickinson's poetry

Ⓑ Dickinson's poems are short

Ⓒ Dickinson wrote for a sophisticated and religious audience

Ⓓ the public at first did not embrace Dickinson's poetry

Time   **LinguaForum**   ? Help   ← Prev   → Next

Passage 2

Darwin was an assiduous and voracious reader. Not long after his return from his South American voyage, he came across a short but much talked-about sociological treatise by the Reverend Thomas Malthus that had first appeared in 1798. In this essay, Malthus warned, as economists have warned ever since, that the human population was increasing so rapidly that it would soon be impossible to feed all the earth's inhabitants. Darwin saw that Malthus' conclusion – that food supply and other factors hold populations in check – is true for all species, not just the human one. Darwin calculated that a single breeding pair of elephants would, if all their progeny lived and reproduced the normal number of offspring over a normal life span, produce a standing population of 19 million elephants in 750 years, yet the average number of elephants generally remains the same over the years. Although a single breeding pair could have produced 19 million descendants, it did produce an average of only two. But why these particular two? Darwin gave birth to the theory of natural selection by answering the question.

→ Natural selection was a process analogous to the type of selection exercised by breeders of cattle, horses or dogs. ■ In artificial selection, humans choose individual specimens of plants or animals for breeding on the basis of characteristics that seem desirable. ■ In natural selection, the environment takes the place of human choice. ■ As individuals with certain hereditary characteristics survive and reproduce, and individuals with other hereditary specificities are eliminated, the population will slowly change. ■

→ According to Darwin, inherited variations among individuals are a matter of chance. ■ They are not produced by the environment, by a "creative force" or by the unconscious striving of the organism. ■ In themselves, they have no goal or direction, but they often have positive or negative values; that is, they may be more or less useful to an organism as measured by its survival and reproduction. ■ It is the operation of natural selection – the interaction of individual organisms with their environment – over a series of generation that gives direction to evolution. ■

The essential difference between Darwin's formulation and that of any of his predecessors is the central role he gave to variation. Others had thought of variations as mere disturbances in the overall design, whereas Darwin saw that variations among individuals are the real fabric of the evolutionary process. Species arise, he proposed, when differences among individuals within a group are gradually converted into differences between groups as the groups become separated in space and time.

LinguaForum

Reading

12. The passage discusses mainly
    - Ⓐ the intellectual background of Darwin
    - Ⓑ Darwin's theory of natural selection
    - Ⓒ differences between artificial and natural selection
    - Ⓓ the significance of Darwin's theory

13. Look at the word treatise in the passage. Click on the word or phrase in the **bold** text that is closest in meaning to treatise.

14. The first paragraph suggests all of the following EXCEPT that
    - Ⓐ Darwin based his studies mainly on observations
    - Ⓑ in addition to observations, Darwin based his work on the ideas of other scientists
    - Ⓒ Malthus was a church official
    - Ⓓ Malthus and Darwin were contemporaries

15. Malthus' work led Darwin to conclude all of the following EXCEPT that
    - Ⓐ the supply of food is one of the key factors that affect heredity
    - Ⓑ the ability to acquire food determines the species' survival rate
    - Ⓒ the supply of food would outlast the increasing rate of human population growth
    - Ⓓ the supply of food affects the hereditary characteristics of other living creatures

16. Look at the word progeny in the passage. Click on the word or phrase in the **bold** text that is closest in meaning to progeny.

17. The example of the elephants serves to
    - Ⓐ illustrate that Darwin based his studies on elephants
    - Ⓑ show that life on earth evolved through natural selection
    - Ⓒ prove that natural selection was more influential than artificial selection
    - Ⓓ provide an example of artificial selection

18. Humans : artificial selection is analogous to
    - Ⓐ environment : natural selection
    - Ⓑ breeders : dogs
    - Ⓒ cattle : horses
    - Ⓓ dogs : cats

19. Look at the word characteristics in the passage. Click on the word or phrase in the **bold** text that is closest in meaning to characteristics.

20. The following sentence can be added to paragraph 2 or 3.

    A variation that gives an organism even a slight advantage makes that organism more likely to leave more surviving offspring.

    Where would it best fit in the paragraph?
    Click on the square [■] to add the sentence to paragraph 2 or 3.
    Paragraphs 2 and 3 are marked with an arrow [→].

21. The word they in the passage most likely refers to
    - Ⓐ organisms
    - Ⓑ individuals
    - Ⓒ values
    - Ⓓ variations

22. Darwin considered variation to be
    - Ⓐ disturbances in the evolutionary process
    - Ⓑ rare among life on earth
    - Ⓒ the key to understanding evolution
    - Ⓓ as significant as natural selection

➡ There is more to chimpanzee society than power take-overs. ■ The picture that I have drawn so far is completely one-sided, in the sense that it only deals with the hard, opportunistic aspect of colony life. ■ It is the impressive charging displays and noisy conflicts between the males which demand immediate attention. ■ However, while the social hierarchy is stable, it is possible to look at a host of other, no less fascinating elements of chimpanzee life, such as the formation of social ties, the different ways in which females bring up their children, reassuring and reconciliatory behavior, sexual intercourse, and adolescence. ■

➡ The classical lens through which Western research workers have tended to study the social behavior of animals has resulted in a sharp focus on competition, territorialism and dominance. ■ Ever since the discovery of the pecking order among hens by the Norwegian Schjelderup-Ebbe in 1922, the status hierarchy has been seen as the main form of social organization. ■ The study of monkeys and apes was for years dominated by attempts to rank individuals on a vertical scale, from high to low. ■ There was, however, an exception: within the Japanese school of primatology, research workers were more interested in kinship and friendships. They classified individuals horizontally, representing them in a web of social connections. A distinction was made between central positions in the web and – in concentric circles around the heart of the group – increasingly peripheral positions. ■ They were interested in the extent to which the other members of the group accepted an individual and which kinship group he or she belonged to. ■

Broadly speaking, whereas the Western view sought to describe primate society in terms of a ladder, the Japanese were thinking in terms of a network. If we regard these two methods of approach as complementary, it becomes clear why stable dominance relationships only partially ensure peace in the social system. "Horizontal" developments – in which children grow up and social ties are established, neglected or broken – inevitably affect the temporarily fixed "vertical" component, the hierarchy.

LinguaForum   ? ← →
                               Help Prev Next

Reading

23. The author mainly discusses
    - Ⓐ the social organization of chimpanzees
    - Ⓑ the different views on the social organization of chimpanzees and of primates
    - Ⓒ the distinction between Western and Japanese understanding of social organizations
    - Ⓓ the advantages and disadvantages of social organization of primates

24. The following sentence can be added to paragraph 1 or 2.

    Each element represents another angle from which the life of the group as a whole can be studied.

    Where would it best fit in the paragraph?
    Click on the square [■] to add the sentence to paragraph 1 or 2.
    Paragraphs 1 and 2 are marked with an arrow [➡].

25. Look at the word conflicts in the passage. Click on the word or phrase in the **bold** text that best replaces conflicts.

26. The passage preceding this one is most likely to discuss
    - Ⓐ the different types of chimpanzee society
    - Ⓑ the power struggle among chimpanzees
    - Ⓒ the significance of role-taking among chimpanzees
    - Ⓓ the requirements for leadership in chimpanzee society

27. The first paragraph suggests that
    - Ⓐ the chimpanzee society is patriarchal
    - Ⓑ female chimpanzees do not participate in openly hostile fights as much as the male chimpanzees
    - Ⓒ male chimpanzees are less cooperative than female chimpanzees
    - Ⓓ there is continuous power struggle in chimpanzee society

28. All of the following describes the Western view on primate social organization EXCEPT
    - Ⓐ hierarchical
    - Ⓑ competitive
    - Ⓒ kinship
    - Ⓓ vertical

29. Whcih of the following does the word They in the passage refer to?
    - Ⓐ Peripheral positions
    - Ⓑ Members
    - Ⓒ Individuals
    - Ⓓ Research workers

30. The Japanese understanding of primate social relations is concerned less with
    - Ⓐ power struggle
    - Ⓑ cooperation
    - Ⓒ cohabitation
    - Ⓓ collective identity

31. Horizontal and vertical social relations are analogous to
    - Ⓐ circle : periphery
    - Ⓑ high : low
    - Ⓒ network : ladder
    - Ⓓ straight : bent

32. Look at the word central in the passage. Click on the word or phrase in the **bold** text that is OPPOSITE in meaning to central.

33. Look at the word established in the passage. Click on the word or phrase in the **bold** text that is closest in meaning to established.

→ In 1976, a combination of several pieces of evidence fell into place. ■ They confirmed climatologists' understanding of the basic cause of the rhythmic ebb and flow of the glaciers that have characterized the more recent series of ice ages on Earth. ■ The greatest significance of the breakthrough in understanding ice ages is that it provided a firm prediction of how the natural course of events will develop – if undisturbed by our activities – over the next few thousand years. ■ We can say unequivocally that the warmest period of the present "interglacial" is over, and that from here on we can expect a cooling-off. ■ Within about ten thousand years the world will be in grip of another full ice age. ■

→ Depending on your point of view, that is either worrying or reassuring. ■ The prophets of doom, comparing the prospect of another ice age with the very long history of the Earth, argue that by those standards the next ice age is "just around the corner." ■ On the other hand, optimists such as myself argue that the evidence shows that we do not have to worry about the ice for a couple of thousand years yet. ■ If we survive that long, we should be able to do something about preventing the spread of ice. ■

The astronomical theory of ice ages that makes these predictions possible is generally called the "Milankovitch model," after Milutin Milankovitch of Yugoslavia, who spelled out details of the idea more than half a century ago. The basis of the idea is much older, and among those who supported it even before Milankovitch was Alfred Wegener, better known today as one of the originators of the concept of continental drift. Like that theory, the Milankovitch model of ice ages survived for decades before at last being proved basically correct.

Standard textbooks have long acknowledged the existence of the Milankovitch model and explained the details of its basic mechanism. Three separate, cyclic changes in the Earth's movements through space combine to produce the overall changes in the solar radiation falling on the Earth and are the key to the theory.

34. The author discusses primarily
    - Ⓐ the Milankovitch model
    - Ⓑ the understanding of glaciers
    - Ⓒ the theory of ice ages
    - Ⓓ the cause of ice ages

35. Look at the word it in the passage. Click on the word or phrase in the **bold** text that it refers to.

36. The following sentence can be added to paragraph 1 or 2.

    Probably the same processes also affected the changing climate during the previous ice epochs, hundreds of millions of years ago.

    Where would it best fit in the paragraph? Click on the square [■] to add the sentence to paragraph 1 or 2.
    Paragraphs 1 and 2 are marked with an arrow [➡].

37. The phrase fell into place in paragraph 1 means that
    - Ⓐ the evidence fell into its appropriate place
    - Ⓑ the evidence was correct
    - Ⓒ the evidence helped to support the understanding of glaciers
    - Ⓓ the evidence finally accomplished its objectives

38. Look at the phrase warmest period in the passage. Click on the word or phrase in the **bold** text that is OPPOSITE in meaning to warmest period.

39. The understanding of the ice ages is important because
    - Ⓐ scientists can predict the movement of glaciers for the next thousand years
    - Ⓑ scientists can trace the climate changes of the past thousand years
    - Ⓒ scientists can offer a reliable prediction on the formation of the next ice age
    - Ⓓ scientists can predict the drift of the Earth for the next thousand years

40. The first paragraph suggests that
    - Ⓐ human interference such as nuclear wars will affect the course of events
    - Ⓑ theories by nature are unpredictable
    - Ⓒ the immediate danger of freezing to death is over
    - Ⓓ with advanced technology, it is fairly easy to predict nature's course of events

41. According to the passage, until now the Earth has been
    - Ⓐ cool
    - Ⓑ warm
    - Ⓒ hot
    - Ⓓ melting

42. The prophets of doom worry that the next ice age is "just around the corner," meaning that
    - Ⓐ it is located very close
    - Ⓑ it will take place at the North Pole
    - Ⓒ it will take place sooner than most people think
    - Ⓓ it will take place as predicted previously

43. The author is not worried because
    - Ⓐ he has faith in nature
    - Ⓑ he believes in the accuracy of the theory
    - Ⓒ he believes that human intelligence will save us
    - Ⓓ he thinks that climate change is not too dangerous

44. It can be inferred from the third paragraph that
    - Ⓐ the theory of continental drift is quite old
    - Ⓑ scientists did not accept the theory of continental drift for a long time
    - Ⓒ the theory of continental drift was revolutionary
    - Ⓓ the Milankovitch model is as controversial as the theory of continental drift

PRACTICE TEST 8

Reading

Passage 5

→ **The epic story of Professor Ray Davis and his search for solar neutrinos has become part of modern scientific folklore. ■ The idea of burrowing into the ground to build a detector designed to study the interior of the Sun is curious enough. ■ Even more intriguing is the recent revelation that the underground detector may be telling us as much about the origins and fate of the whole universe as it does about the Sun. ■ It takes a mind like that of the mythical Sherlock Holmes to unravel all the twists of logical argument in the tale and show how what happens in Davis's tank of cleaning fluid really does suggest that the Universe is not destined to expand forever, but may one day collapse back into a fireball reminiscent of the Big Bang of creation. ■**

→ All good stories have a beginning, a middle and an end. ■ Here and now, "The Case of the Missing Neutrinos" has only a beginning and a middle: the end is yet to be written. ■ But what we have is intriguing enough. ■

The beginning came with the prediction that the nuclear reactions in the Sun ought to be producing vast quantities of fundamental particles known as neutrinos, and with the efforts of Davis and his team to detect them. These efforts have met with partial success – Davis indeed found some neutrinos, but not as many as the theories predict. This is in a way worse than finding none at all. **If the detector detected nothing, the explanation might be that the detector did not work. The fact that some solar neutrinos are spotted suggests that the detector does work, but that we don't understand what is going on as well as we thought we did. This has led to the middle of our story – a variety of bizarre speculations offered up to explain the gap between observation and theory. The most outrageous of these was surely the suggestion that the Sun has "gone out" in the center, with nuclear fusion reactions temporarily turned off.**

LinguaForum

Reading

45. The author discusses primarily
    - (A) the process of writing good stories
    - (B) the composition of neutrinos
    - (C) the theory of the collapsing Universe
    - (D) the saga for the search of the missing neutrinos

46. The following sentence can be added to paragraph 1 or 2.

    But it has to be admitted that there is also a touch of Carrollian absurdity about the whole business – if not the hunting of the Snark, then certainly Alice in Wonderland.

    Where would it best fit in the paragraph? Click on the square [■] to add the sentence to paragraph 1 or 2.
    Paragraphs 1 and 2 are marked with an arrow [➡].

47. Look at the word curious in the passage. Click on the word or phrase in the **bold** text that best replaces curious.

48. Professor Davis's search for neutrinos is described as folklore due to its
    - (A) improbability
    - (B) eccentricity
    - (C) legendary significance
    - (D) originality

49. Professor Davis's research method was seen as "curious" because
    - (A) it was unexpected
    - (B) it was insane
    - (C) it was too risky
    - (D) it was dangerous

50. The first paragraph suggests that
    - (A) in order to learn more about the sun, people expected scientists to study the sun and not the earth
    - (B) in order to learn more about the sun, it was much safer to study the interior of the earth than the sun
    - (C) people thought that the interior of the earth was useless
    - (D) people thought that it was impossible to penetrate deep into the earth

51. Look at the word expand in the passage. Click on the word or phrase in the **bold** text that is OPPOSITE in meaning to expand.

52. Neutrinos are
    - (A) mysterious elements of the Sun
    - (B) unknown elements of the Sun
    - (C) missing elements of the Sun
    - (D) fundamental elements of the Sun

53. The discovery of neutrinos caused
    - (A) a great sensation
    - (B) much disappointment
    - (C) more confusion
    - (D) partial success

54. Look at the word detected in the passage. Click on the word or phrase in the **bold** text that is closest in meaning to detected.

55. Look at the word these in the passage. Click on the word or phrase in the **bold** text that these refers to.

PRACTICE TEST 8

SECTION 4
WRITING
Suggested Time: 30 Minutes

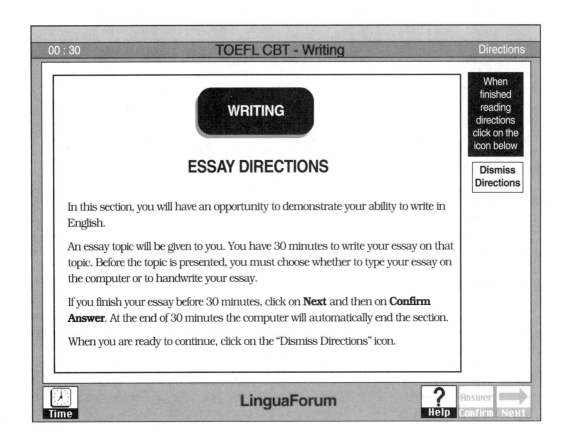

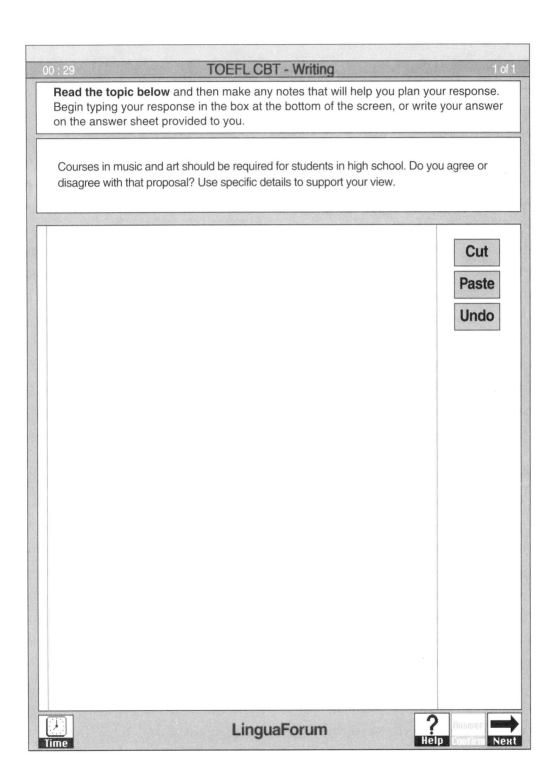

Practice Test 9

Listening: 60 Minutes (including listening time)
Structure: 15 Minutes
Reading: 70 Minutes
Writing: 30 Minutes

Suggested Total Time: 175 Minutes

ANSWER SHEET

Lingua TOEFL® CBT Test Book II
PRACTICE TEST 9

Name	
Sex	☐ male ☐ female
E-mail address	
Telephone No.	

No. of Correct Answers/Converted Score		
Listening		
Structure		
Reading		
Writing		
TOTAL		

Section 1: Listening

1 Ⓐ Ⓑ Ⓒ Ⓓ
2 Ⓐ Ⓑ Ⓒ Ⓓ
3 Ⓐ Ⓑ Ⓒ Ⓓ
4 Ⓐ Ⓑ Ⓒ Ⓓ
5 Ⓐ Ⓑ Ⓒ Ⓓ
6 Ⓐ Ⓑ Ⓒ Ⓓ
7 Ⓐ Ⓑ Ⓒ Ⓓ
8 Ⓐ Ⓑ Ⓒ Ⓓ
9 Ⓐ Ⓑ Ⓒ Ⓓ
10 Ⓐ Ⓑ Ⓒ Ⓓ
11 Ⓐ Ⓑ Ⓒ Ⓓ
12 Ⓐ Ⓑ Ⓒ Ⓓ
13 Ⓐ Ⓑ Ⓒ Ⓓ
14 Ⓐ Ⓑ Ⓒ Ⓓ
15 Ⓐ Ⓑ Ⓒ Ⓓ
16 Ⓐ Ⓑ Ⓒ Ⓓ
17 Ⓐ Ⓑ Ⓒ Ⓓ
18 Ⓐ Ⓑ Ⓒ Ⓓ
19 Ⓐ Ⓑ Ⓒ Ⓓ
20 Geologists –
   Environmentalists –
   Meteorologists –
21 Ⓐ Ⓑ Ⓒ Ⓓ
22 Ⓐ Ⓑ Ⓒ Ⓓ
23 Ⓐ Ⓑ Ⓒ Ⓓ
24 Ⓐ Ⓑ Ⓒ Ⓓ
25 Orthographic projection –
   Mercator projection –
   Goode's Homolosine ... –
26 Ⓐ Ⓑ Ⓒ Ⓓ
27 Ⓐ Ⓑ Ⓒ Ⓓ
28 Ⓐ Ⓑ Ⓒ Ⓓ
29 Radio –
   Television –
   Film –
30 Ⓐ Ⓑ Ⓒ Ⓓ
31 Ⓐ Ⓑ Ⓒ Ⓓ
32 Ⓐ Ⓑ Ⓒ Ⓓ
33 Ⓐ Ⓑ Ⓒ Ⓓ
34
35 Ⓐ Ⓑ Ⓒ Ⓓ

36 Ⓐ Ⓑ Ⓒ Ⓓ
37 Ⓐ Ⓑ Ⓒ Ⓓ
38 Ⓐ Ⓑ Ⓒ Ⓓ
39 Ⓐ Ⓑ Ⓒ Ⓓ
40
41 Ⓐ Ⓑ Ⓒ Ⓓ
42 Paleolithic –
   Mesolithic –
   Neolithic –
43 Ⓐ Ⓑ Ⓒ Ⓓ
44 Ⓐ Ⓑ Ⓒ Ⓓ
45 Ⓐ Ⓑ Ⓒ Ⓓ
46
47 Ⓐ Ⓑ Ⓒ Ⓓ
48 Ⓐ Ⓑ Ⓒ Ⓓ
49 Ⓐ Ⓑ Ⓒ Ⓓ
50 Ⓐ Ⓑ Ⓒ Ⓓ

Section 2: Structure

1 Ⓐ Ⓑ Ⓒ Ⓓ
2 Ⓐ Ⓑ Ⓒ Ⓓ
3 Ⓐ Ⓑ Ⓒ Ⓓ
4 Ⓐ Ⓑ Ⓒ Ⓓ
5 Ⓐ Ⓑ Ⓒ Ⓓ
6 Ⓐ Ⓑ Ⓒ Ⓓ
7 Ⓐ Ⓑ Ⓒ Ⓓ
8 Ⓐ Ⓑ Ⓒ Ⓓ
9 Ⓐ Ⓑ Ⓒ Ⓓ
10 Ⓐ Ⓑ Ⓒ Ⓓ
11 Ⓐ Ⓑ Ⓒ Ⓓ
12 Ⓐ Ⓑ Ⓒ Ⓓ
13 Ⓐ Ⓑ Ⓒ Ⓓ
14 Ⓐ Ⓑ Ⓒ Ⓓ
15 Ⓐ Ⓑ Ⓒ Ⓓ
16 Ⓐ Ⓑ Ⓒ Ⓓ
17 Ⓐ Ⓑ Ⓒ Ⓓ
18 Ⓐ Ⓑ Ⓒ Ⓓ
19 Ⓐ Ⓑ Ⓒ Ⓓ
20 Ⓐ Ⓑ Ⓒ Ⓓ

Section 3: Reading

1 Ⓐ Ⓑ Ⓒ Ⓓ
2
3 Ⓐ Ⓑ Ⓒ Ⓓ
4 Ⓐ Ⓑ Ⓒ Ⓓ
5 Ⓐ Ⓑ Ⓒ Ⓓ
6 Ⓐ Ⓑ Ⓒ Ⓓ
7 Ⓐ Ⓑ Ⓒ Ⓓ
8 Ⓐ Ⓑ Ⓒ Ⓓ
9
10 Ⓐ Ⓑ Ⓒ Ⓓ
11
12 Ⓐ Ⓑ Ⓒ Ⓓ
13
14 Ⓐ Ⓑ Ⓒ Ⓓ
15 Ⓐ Ⓑ Ⓒ Ⓓ
16 Ⓐ Ⓑ Ⓒ Ⓓ
17 Ⓐ Ⓑ Ⓒ Ⓓ
18 Ⓐ Ⓑ Ⓒ Ⓓ
19 Ⓐ Ⓑ Ⓒ Ⓓ
20 Ⓐ Ⓑ Ⓒ Ⓓ
21
22 Ⓐ Ⓑ Ⓒ Ⓓ
23 Ⓐ Ⓑ Ⓒ Ⓓ
24 Ⓐ Ⓑ Ⓒ Ⓓ
25 Ⓐ Ⓑ Ⓒ Ⓓ
26 Ⓐ Ⓑ Ⓒ Ⓓ
27
28 Ⓐ Ⓑ Ⓒ Ⓓ
29 Ⓐ Ⓑ Ⓒ Ⓓ
30 Ⓐ Ⓑ Ⓒ Ⓓ

31
32 Ⓐ Ⓑ Ⓒ Ⓓ
33 Ⓐ Ⓑ Ⓒ Ⓓ
34 Ⓐ Ⓑ Ⓒ Ⓓ
35 Ⓐ Ⓑ Ⓒ Ⓓ
36 Ⓐ Ⓑ Ⓒ Ⓓ
37
38 Ⓐ Ⓑ Ⓒ Ⓓ
39 Ⓐ Ⓑ Ⓒ Ⓓ
40 Ⓐ Ⓑ Ⓒ Ⓓ
41 Ⓐ Ⓑ Ⓒ Ⓓ
42 Ⓐ Ⓑ Ⓒ Ⓓ
43
44 Ⓐ Ⓑ Ⓒ Ⓓ

■ **Have you taken the official TOEFL Test?**

☐ Yes → if any
☐ No

PBT Score	
Listening	
Structure	
Reading	
Writing	
TOTAL	

CBT Score	
Listening	
Structure	
Reading	
Writing	
TOTAL	

■ **Educational background**

☐ middle/high school ☐ undergraduate ☐ graduate

SIGNED: _____
(SIGN YOUR NAME AS IF SIGNING A BUSINESS LETTER.)

DATE: ___ / ___ / ___
         MO.   DAY   YEAR

Cut here.

LynguaForum
Copyright © 2002 by Lingua Forum, Inc. All rights reserved.

ANSWER SHEET

Lingua TOEFL® CBT Test Book II
PRACTICE TEST 9

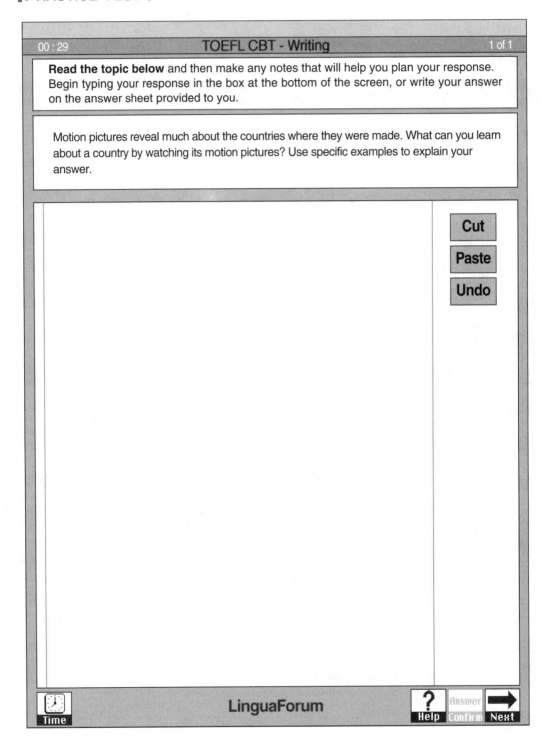

00 : 29   TOEFL CBT - Writing   1 of 1

Read the topic below and then make any notes that will help you plan your response. Begin typing your response in the box at the bottom of the screen, or write your answer on the answer sheet provided to you.

Motion pictures reveal much about the countries where they were made. What can you learn about a country by watching its motion pictures? Use specific examples to explain your answer.

Cut

Paste

Undo

Time   LinguaForum   Help   Confirm   Next

LinguaForum
Copyright © 2002 by Lingua Forum, Inc. All rights reserved.

Test
9

SECTION 1
LISTENING
Suggested Time: 25 Minutes

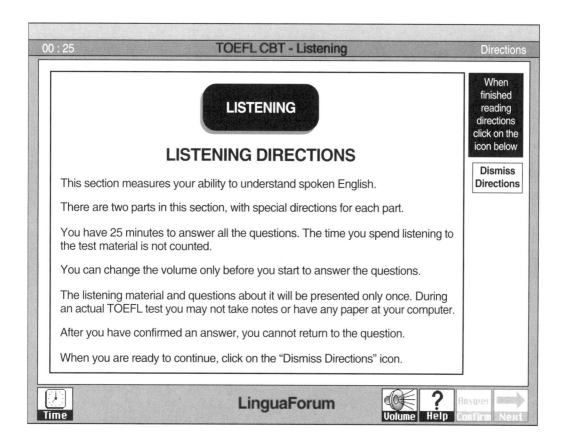

00 : 25   TOEFL CBT - Listening   Directions

LISTENING

When finished reading directions click on the icon below

Dismiss Directions

LISTENING DIRECTIONS

This section measures your ability to understand spoken English.

There are two parts in this section, with special directions for each part.

You have 25 minutes to answer all the questions. The time you spend listening to the test material is not counted.

You can change the volume only before you start to answer the questions.

The listening material and questions about it will be presented only once. During an actual TOEFL test you may not take notes or have any paper at your computer.

After you have confirmed an answer, you cannot return to the question.

When you are ready to continue, click on the "Dismiss Directions" icon.

Time   **LinguaForum**   Volume   Help   Answer Confirm   Next

Test
9

SECTION 1
LISTENING

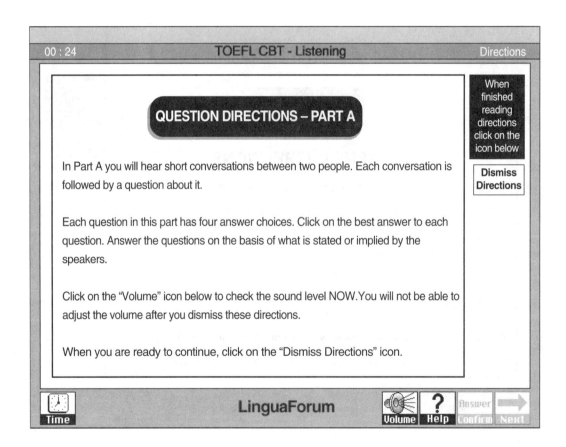

TOEFL CBT - Listening

00 : 24   Directions

When finished reading directions click on the icon below

Dismiss Directions

QUESTION DIRECTIONS – PART A

In Part A you will hear short conversations between two people. Each conversation is followed by a question about it.

Each question in this part has four answer choices. Click on the best answer to each question. Answer the questions on the basis of what is stated or implied by the speakers.

Click on the "Volume" icon below to check the sound level NOW. You will not be able to adjust the volume after you dismiss these directions.

When you are ready to continue, click on the "Dismiss Directions" icon.

LinguaForum

Time   Volume   Help   Answer Confirm   Next

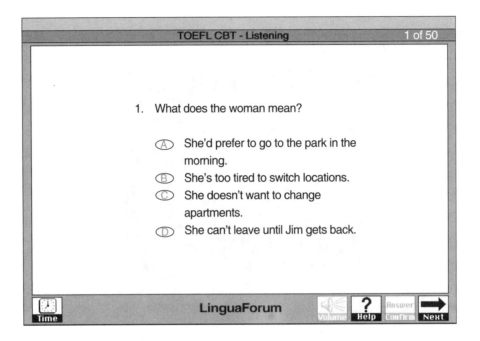

1. What does the woman mean?

Ⓐ She'd prefer to go to the park in the morning.

Ⓑ She's too tired to switch locations.

Ⓒ She doesn't want to change apartments.

Ⓓ She can't leave until Jim gets back.

LinguaForum

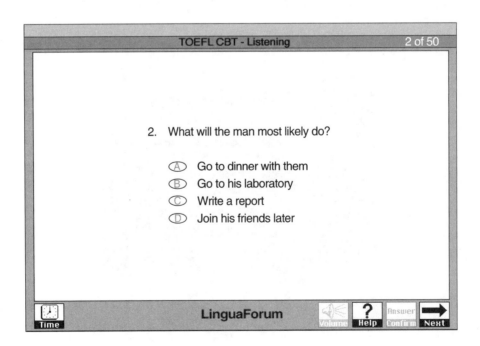

2. What will the man most likely do?

Ⓐ Go to dinner with them

Ⓑ Go to his laboratory

Ⓒ Write a report

Ⓓ Join his friends later

LinguaForum

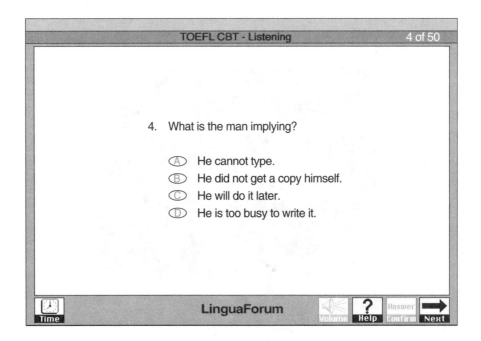

3. Who fixed Alex's computer?

    Ⓐ   Bernie
    Ⓑ   Alex
    Ⓒ   Bernie's friend
    Ⓓ   A computer technician

LinguaForum

Time   Volume   Help   Confirm   Next

4. What is the man implying?

    Ⓐ   He cannot type.
    Ⓑ   He did not get a copy himself.
    Ⓒ   He will do it later.
    Ⓓ   He is too busy to write it.

LinguaForum

Time   Volume   Help   Confirm   Next

185

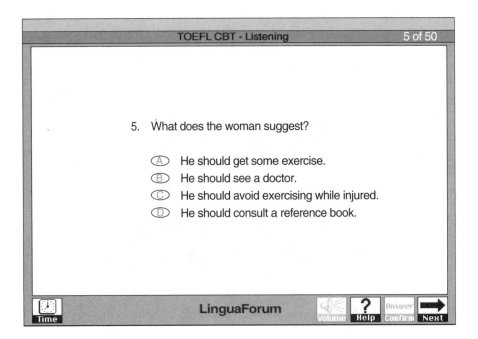

5.   What does the woman suggest?

     (A) He should get some exercise.
     (B) He should see a doctor.
     (C) He should avoid exercising while injured.
     (D) He should consult a reference book.

LinguaForum

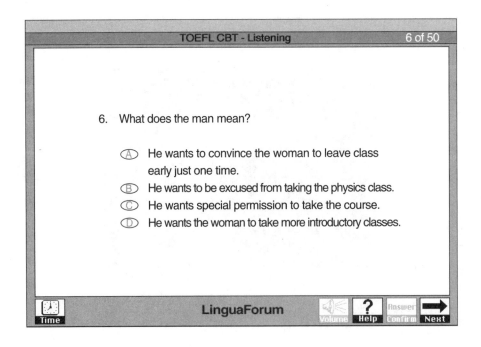

6.   What does the man mean?

     (A) He wants to convince the woman to leave class
          early just one time.
     (B) He wants to be excused from taking the physics class.
     (C) He wants special permission to take the course.
     (D) He wants the woman to take more introductory classes.

LinguaForum

Listening

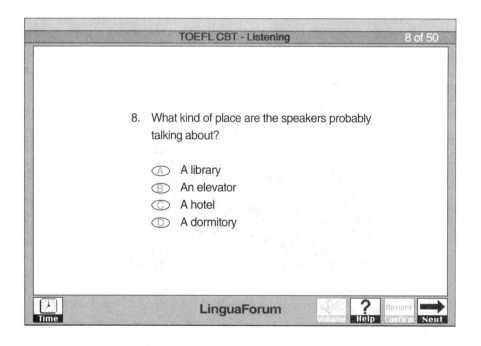

7. What is the woman assuming?

   Ⓐ Ken did not enter the science fair.
   Ⓑ The science fair would not be held.
   Ⓒ Ken would win an award.
   Ⓓ The science fair was not very important.

LinguaForum

8. What kind of place are the speakers probably talking about?

   Ⓐ A library
   Ⓑ An elevator
   Ⓒ A hotel
   Ⓓ A dormitory

LinguaForum

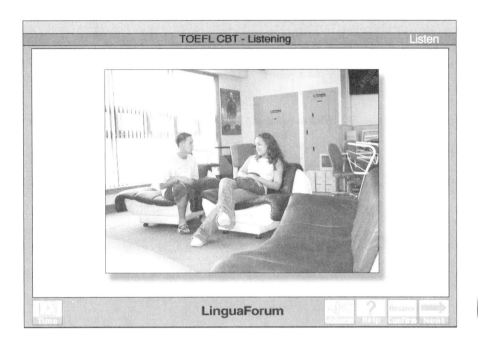

PRACTICE
TEST 9

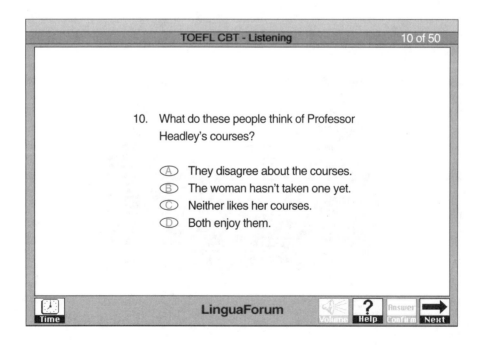

9. What is true about the Columbia River area?

    Ⓐ It is famous for its lottery system.
    Ⓑ The first claim to the river was the right one.
    Ⓒ Many ancient pots have been found there.
    Ⓓ It contains the essential ingredient for
        pottery making.

LinguaForum

10. What do these people think of Professor
     Headley's courses?

    Ⓐ They disagree about the courses.
    Ⓑ The woman hasn't taken one yet.
    Ⓒ Neither likes her courses.
    Ⓓ Both enjoy them.

LinguaForum

Listening

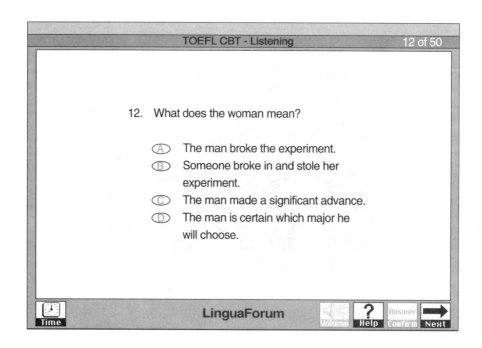

11. When will the man and woman meet?

   Ⓐ During the movies
   Ⓑ Some time next week
   Ⓒ When the man returns from the movies
   Ⓓ In the early evening

LinguaForum

Time   Volume   Help   Confirm   Next

12. What does the woman mean?

   Ⓐ The man broke the experiment.
   Ⓑ Someone broke in and stole her
       experiment.
   Ⓒ The man made a significant advance.
   Ⓓ The man is certain which major he
       will choose.

LinguaForum

Time   Volume   Help   Confirm   Next

Listening

TOEFL CBT - Listening | Listen

LinguaForum

Time | Volume Help Confirm Next

PRACTICE
TEST 9

Question 13

TOEFL CBT - Listening | Listen

LinguaForum

Time | Volume Help Confirm Next

Question 14

193

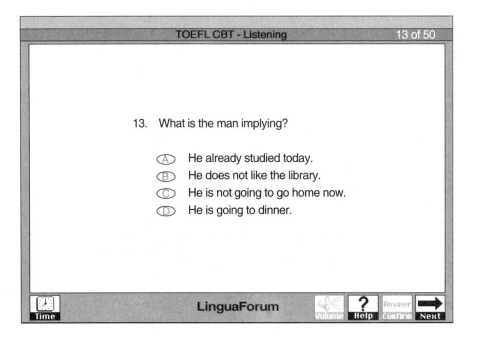

TOEFL CBT - Listening

13 of 50

13.   What is the man implying?

(A)   He already studied today.
(B)   He does not like the library.
(C)   He is not going to go home now.
(D)   He is going to dinner.

LinguaForum

Time   Volume   Help   Confirm   Next

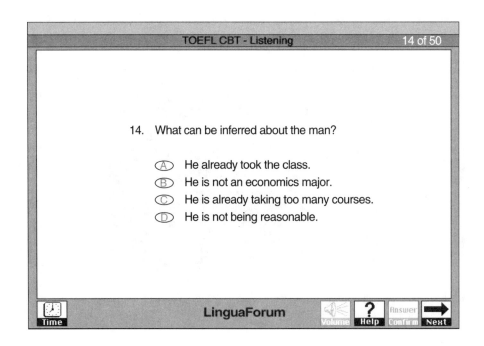

TOEFL CBT - Listening

14 of 50

14.   What can be inferred about the man?

(A)   He already took the class.
(B)   He is not an economics major.
(C)   He is already taking too many courses.
(D)   He is not being reasonable.

LinguaForum

Time   Volume   Help   Confirm   Next

Listening

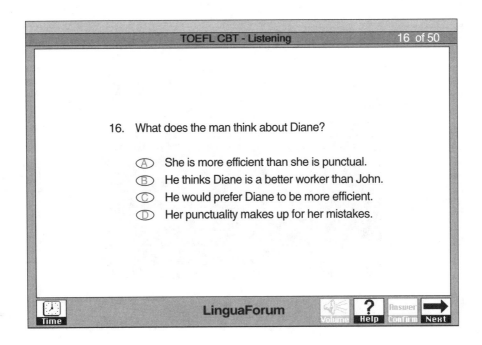

15. How long has the man attended the university?

     Ⓐ   2 years
     Ⓑ   4 years
     Ⓒ   6 years
     Ⓓ   7 years

LinguaForum

16. What does the man think about Diane?

     Ⓐ   She is more efficient than she is punctual.
     Ⓑ   He thinks Diane is a better worker than John.
     Ⓒ   He would prefer Diane to be more efficient.
     Ⓓ   Her punctuality makes up for her mistakes.

LinguaForum

PRACTICE TEST 9

197

17.   What can be inferred about the woman?

  Ⓐ She does not like the certificate.
  Ⓑ She is Dr. Reynolds' teaching assistant.
  Ⓒ She was not able to attend the party.
  Ⓓ She is an honors student.

LinguaForum

Time   Volume   Help   Answer Confirm   Next

Test
9

SECTION 1
LISTENING

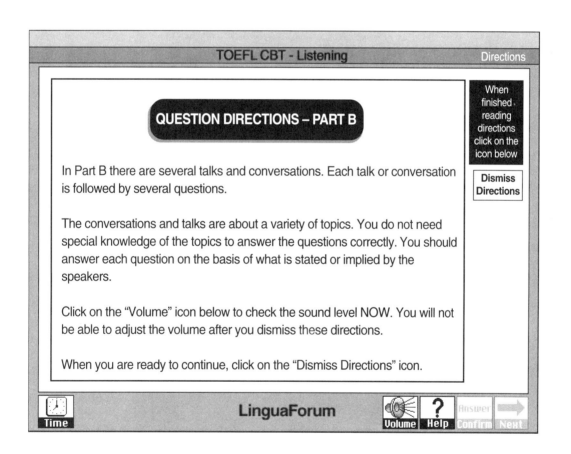

TOEFL CBT - Listening   Directions

When
finished
reading
directions
click on the
icon below

QUESTION DIRECTIONS – PART B

Dismiss
Directions

In Part B there are several talks and conversations. Each talk or conversation
is followed by several questions.

The conversations and talks are about a variety of topics. You do not need
special knowledge of the topics to answer the questions correctly. You should
answer each question on the basis of what is stated or implied by the
speakers.

Click on the "Volume" icon below to check the sound level NOW. You will not
be able to adjust the volume after you dismiss these directions.

When you are ready to continue, click on the "Dismiss Directions" icon.

Time   **LinguaForum**   Volume Help Confirm Next Answer

Listening

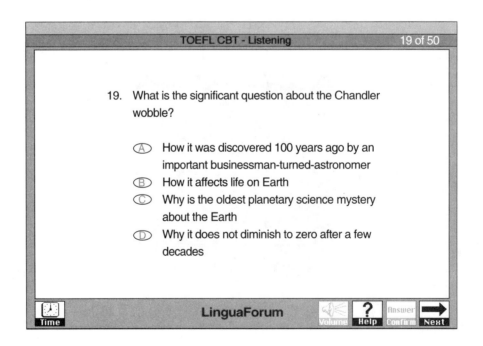

18. What is this lecture about?

   (A) How new data and research methods are improving our understanding of our planet

   (B) The American astronomer Seth Carlo Chandler

   (C) How ocean pressure and the atmosphere affect the Earth

   (D) Why the Earth wobbles

LinguaForum

19. What is the significant question about the Chandler wobble?

   (A) How it was discovered 100 years ago by an important businessman-turned-astronomer

   (B) How it affects life on Earth

   (C) Why is the oldest planetary science mystery about the Earth

   (D) Why it does not diminish to zero after a few decades

LinguaForum

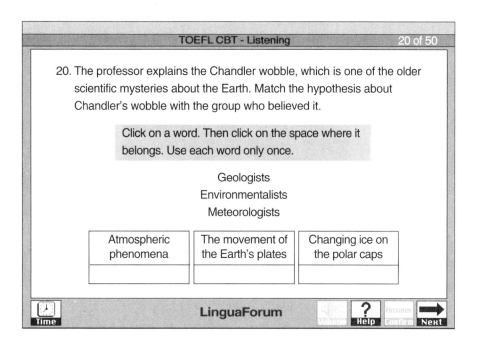

20. The professor explains the Chandler wobble, which is one of the older scientific mysteries about the Earth. Match the hypothesis about Chandler's wobble with the group who believed it.

Click on a word. Then click on the space where it belongs. Use each word only once.

Geologists

Environmentalists

Meteorologists

Atmospheric phenomena	The movement of the Earth's plates	Changing ice on the polar caps

LinguaForum

Time   Help   Next

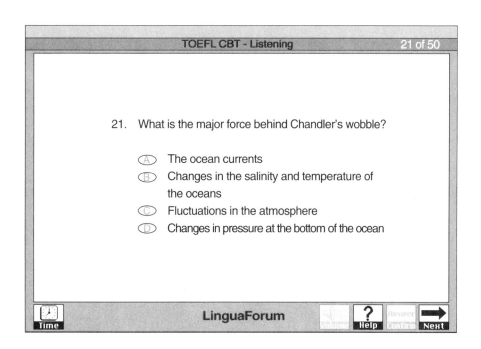

21.   What is the major force behind Chandler's wobble?

Ⓐ   The ocean currents

Ⓑ   Changes in the salinity and temperature of the oceans

Ⓒ   Fluctuations in the atmosphere

Ⓓ   Changes in pressure at the bottom of the ocean

LinguaForum

Time   Help   Next

PRACTICE TEST 9

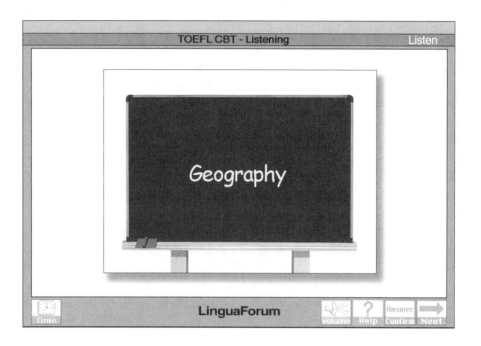

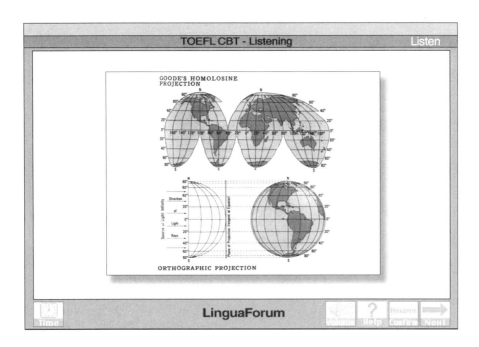

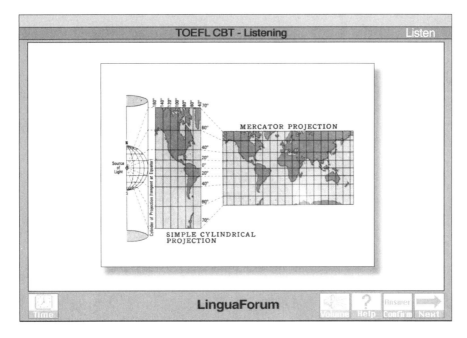

Questions 22-25

PRACTICE
TEST 9

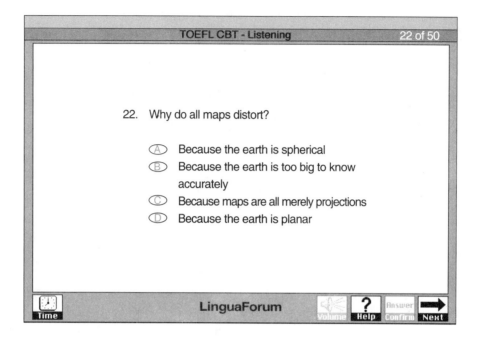

22. Why do all maps distort?

  A Because the earth is spherical
  B Because the earth is too big to know accurately
  C Because maps are all merely projections
  D Because the earth is planar

LinguaForum

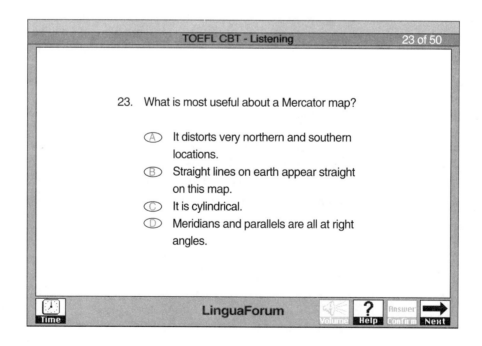

23. What is most useful about a Mercator map?

  A It distorts very northern and southern locations.
  B Straight lines on earth appear straight on this map.
  C It is cylindrical.
  D Meridians and parallels are all at right angles.

LinguaForum

Listening

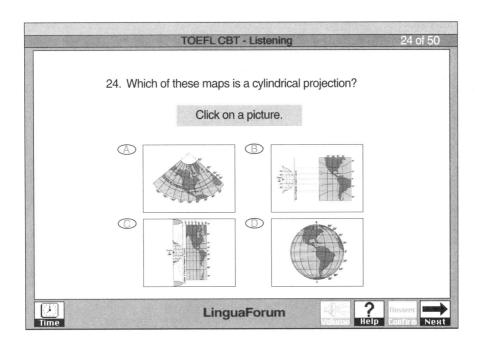

PRACTICE TEST 9

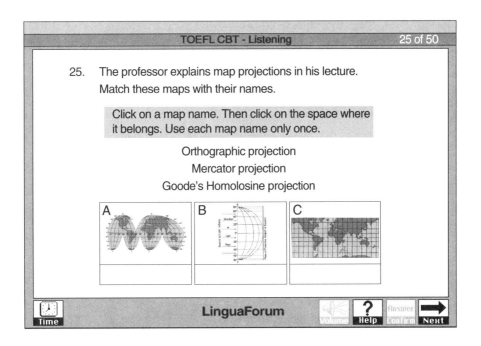

 Questions 26-27

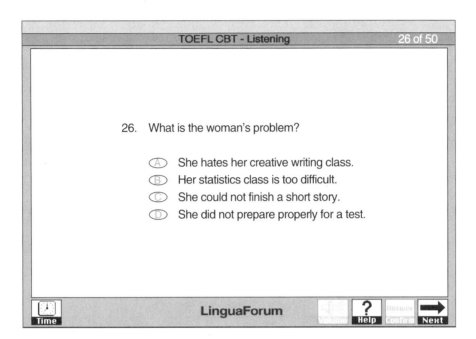

26. What is the woman's problem?

    Ⓐ She hates her creative writing class.
    Ⓑ Her statistics class is too difficult.
    Ⓒ She could not finish a short story.
    Ⓓ She did not prepare properly for a test.

LinguaForum

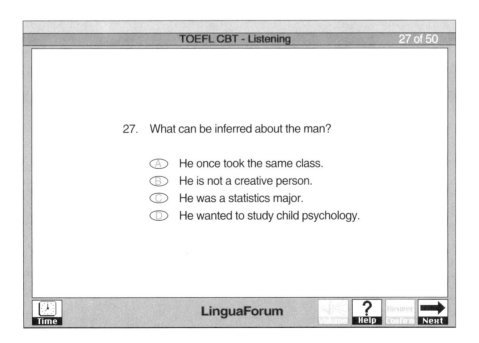

27. What can be inferred about the man?

    Ⓐ He once took the same class.
    Ⓑ He is not a creative person.
    Ⓒ He was a statistics major.
    Ⓓ He wanted to study child psychology.

LinguaForum

PRACTICE TEST 9

Listening

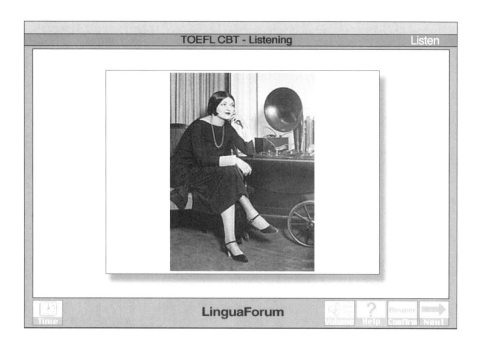

Questions 28-31

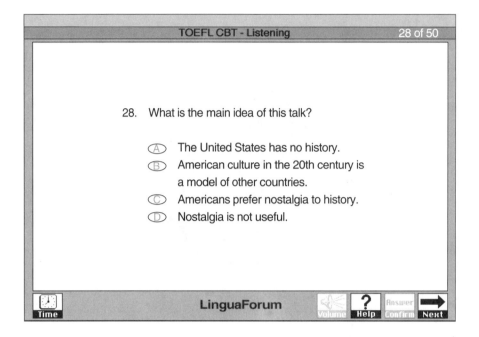

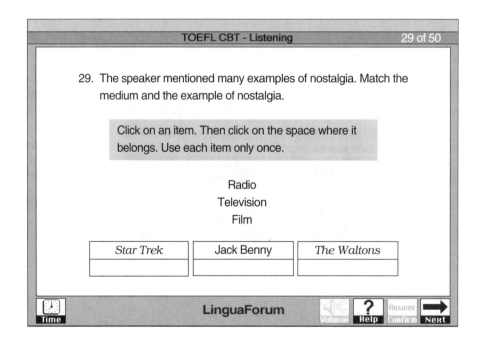

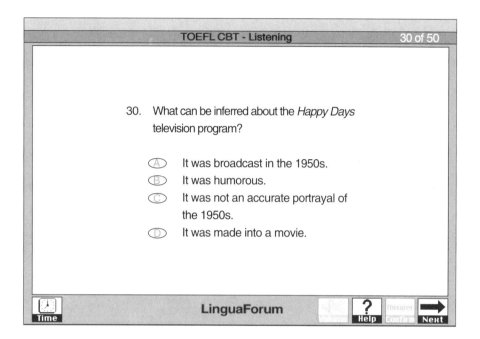

30. What can be inferred about the *Happy Days* television program?

- Ⓐ It was broadcast in the 1950s.
- Ⓑ It was humorous.
- Ⓒ It was not an accurate portrayal of the 1950s.
- Ⓓ It was made into a movie.

LinguaForum

Time | Volume | Help | Answer Confirm | Next

PRACTICE
TEST 9

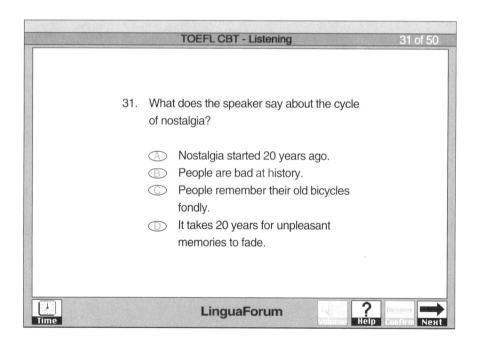

31. What does the speaker say about the cycle of nostalgia?

- Ⓐ Nostalgia started 20 years ago.
- Ⓑ People are bad at history.
- Ⓒ People remember their old bicycles fondly.
- Ⓓ It takes 20 years for unpleasant memories to fade.

LinguaForum

Time | Volume | Help | Answer Confirm | Next

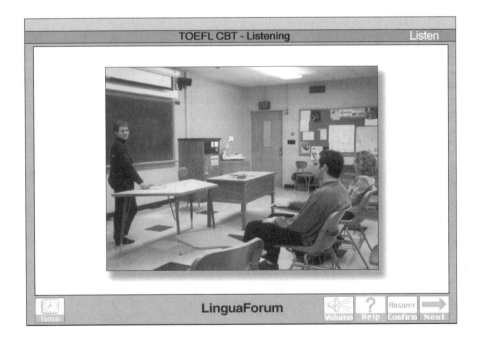

Listening

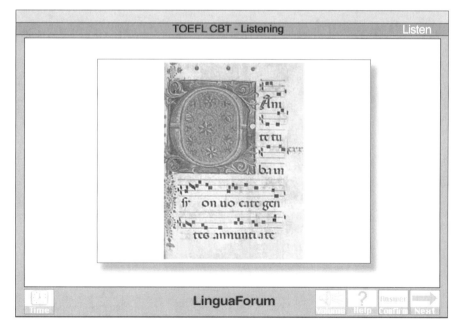

215

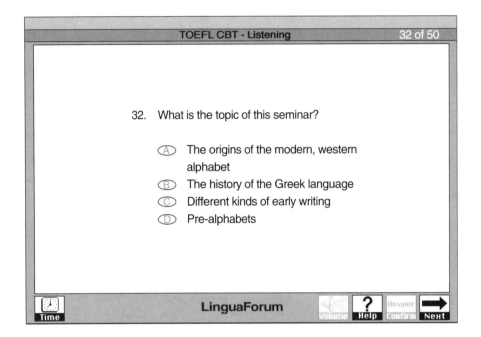

32. What is the topic of this seminar?

    Ⓐ   The origins of the modern, western alphabet

    Ⓑ   The history of the Greek language

    Ⓒ   Different kinds of early writing

    Ⓓ   Pre-alphabets

LinguaForum

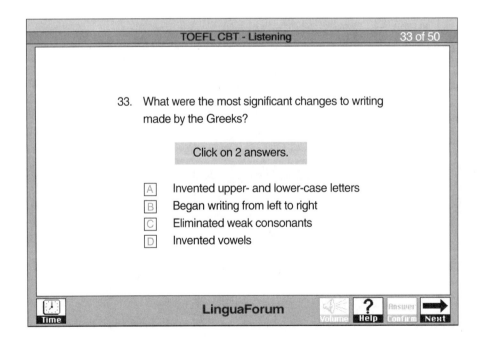

33. What were the most significant changes to writing made by the Greeks?

> Click on 2 answers.

    A   Invented upper- and lower-case letters

    B   Began writing from left to right

    C   Eliminated weak consonants

    D   Invented vowels

LinguaForum

Listening

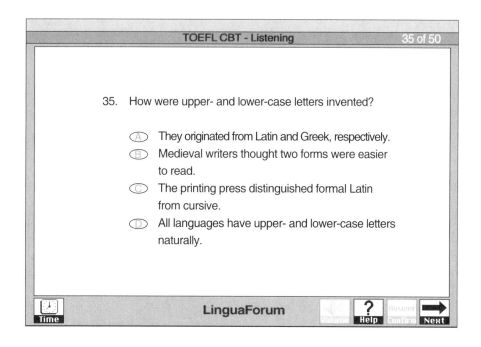

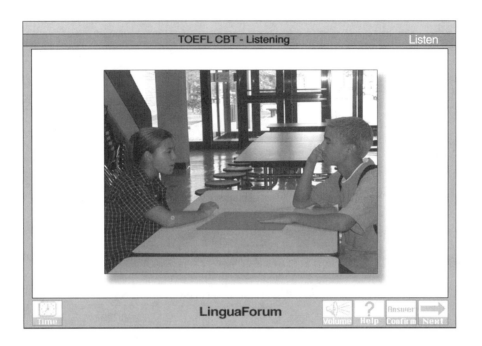

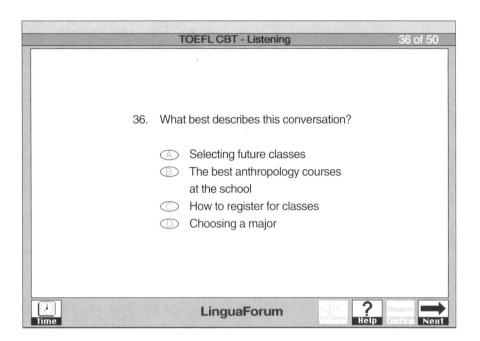

36. What best describes this conversation?

    (A) Selecting future classes
    (B) The best anthropology courses
        at the school
    (C) How to register for classes
    (D) Choosing a major

LinguaForum

Time   Help   Next

PRACTICE
TEST 9

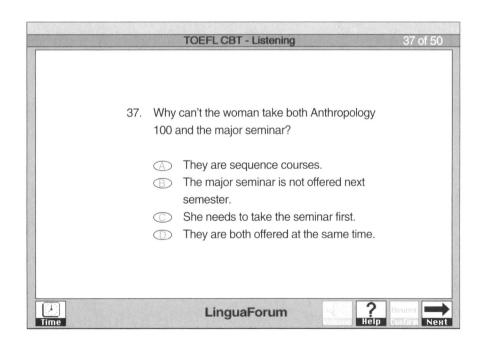

37. Why can't the woman take both Anthropology
100 and the major seminar?

    (A) They are sequence courses.
    (B) The major seminar is not offered next
        semester.
    (C) She needs to take the seminar first.
    (D) They are both offered at the same time.

LinguaForum

Time   Help   Next

TOEFL CBT - Listening
38 of 50

38. What course does the man NOT describe
as major-related?

- Ⓐ Statistics
- Ⓑ Economics
- Ⓒ Computer science
- Ⓓ Biology

Time
LinguaForum
Volume Help Confirm Next

PRACTICE TEST 9

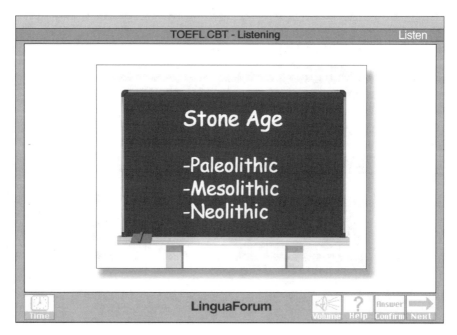

Questions 39-42

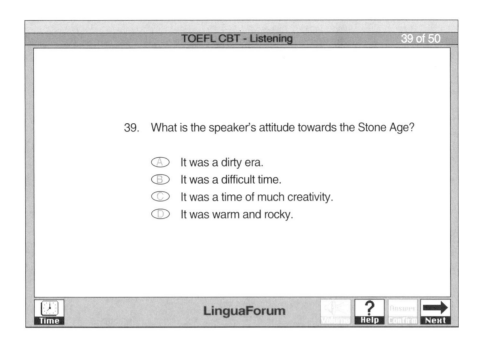

39. What is the speaker's attitude towards the Stone Age?

(A) It was a dirty era.
(B) It was a difficult time.
(C) It was a time of much creativity.
(D) It was warm and rocky.

LinguaForum

Time   Volume   Help   Answer Confirm   Next

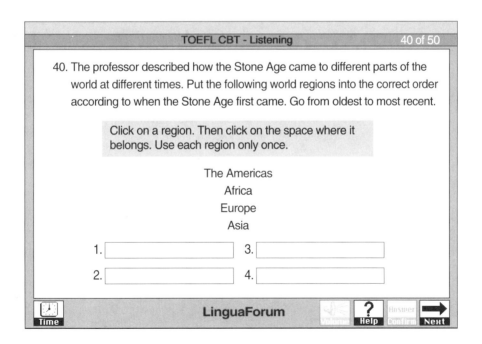

40. The professor described how the Stone Age came to different parts of the world at different times. Put the following world regions into the correct order according to when the Stone Age first came. Go from oldest to most recent.

Click on a region. Then click on the space where it belongs. Use each region only once.

The Americas
Africa
Europe
Asia

1. [   ]   3. [   ]

2. [   ]   4. [   ]

LinguaForum

Time   Volume   Help   Answer Confirm   Next

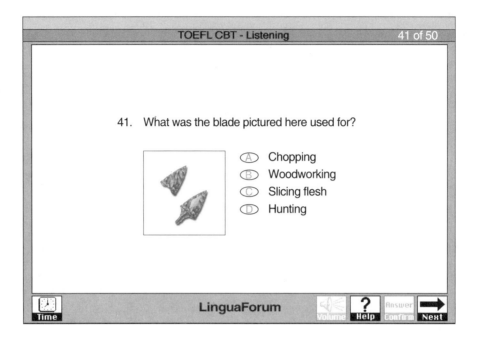

41. What was the blade pictured here used for?

ⓐ Chopping
ⓑ Woodworking
ⓒ Slicing flesh
ⓓ Hunting

LinguaForum

Time   Volume Help Confirm Next

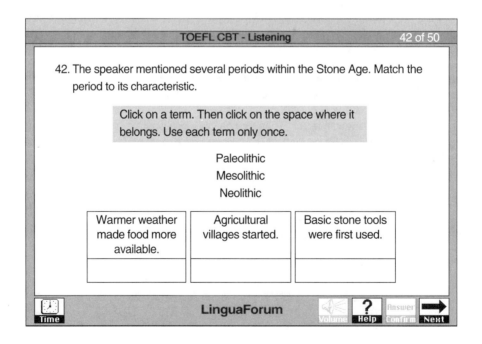

42. The speaker mentioned several periods within the Stone Age. Match the period to its characteristic.

Click on a term. Then click on the space where it belongs. Use each term only once.

Paleolithic
Mesolithic
Neolithic

Warmer weather made food more available.	Agricultural villages started.	Basic stone tools were first used.

LinguaForum

Time   Volume Help Confirm Next

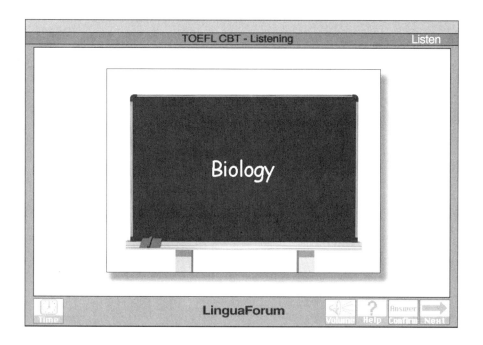

**PRACTICE
TEST 9**

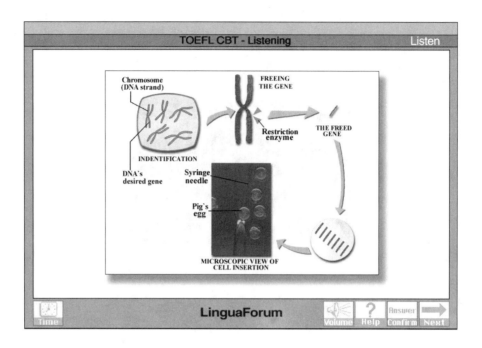

Listening

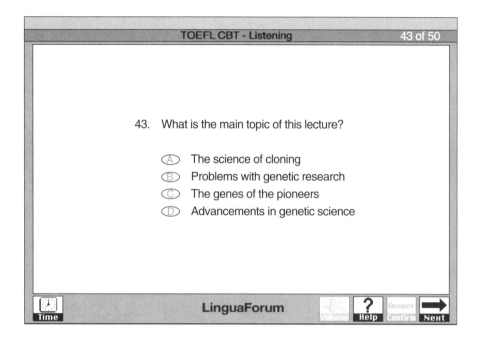

43. What is the main topic of this lecture?

    Ⓐ   The science of cloning
    Ⓑ   Problems with genetic research
    Ⓒ   The genes of the pioneers
    Ⓓ   Advancements in genetic science

LinguaForum

Time   Volume   Help   Confirm   Next

PRACTICE TEST 9

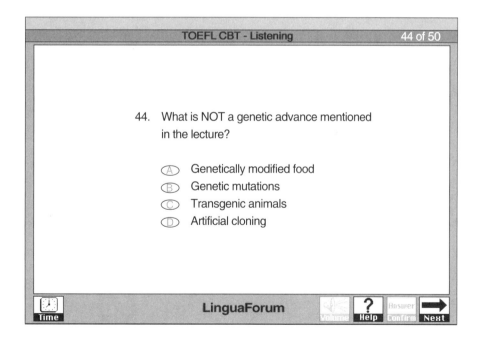

44. What is NOT a genetic advance mentioned
     in the lecture?

    Ⓐ   Genetically modified food
    Ⓑ   Genetic mutations
    Ⓒ   Transgenic animals
    Ⓓ   Artificial cloning

LinguaForum

Time   Volume   Help   Confirm   Next

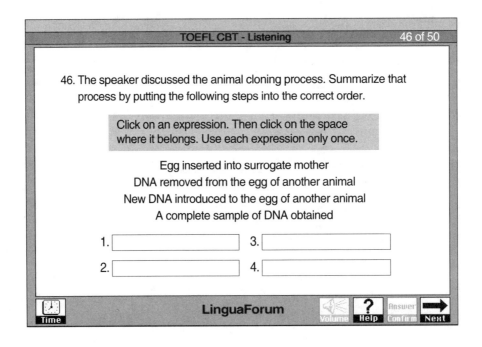

45. What is an example of a clone?

Click on 2 answers.

A Identical twins
B A polymerase chain reaction
C Genetically modified foods
D Most bacteria

LinguaForum

46. The speaker discussed the animal cloning process. Summarize that process by putting the following steps into the correct order.

Click on an expression. Then click on the space where it belongs. Use each expression only once.

Egg inserted into surrogate mother
DNA removed from the egg of another animal
New DNA introduced to the egg of another animal
A complete sample of DNA obtained

1. [   ]   3. [   ]

2. [   ]   4. [   ]

LinguaForum

Listening

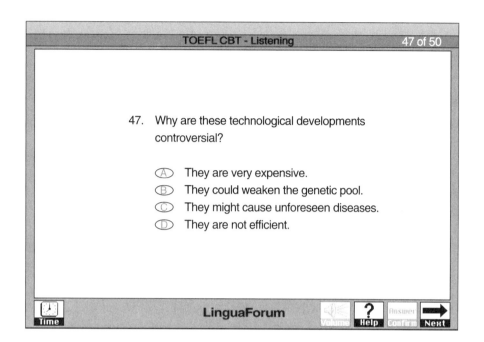

Listening

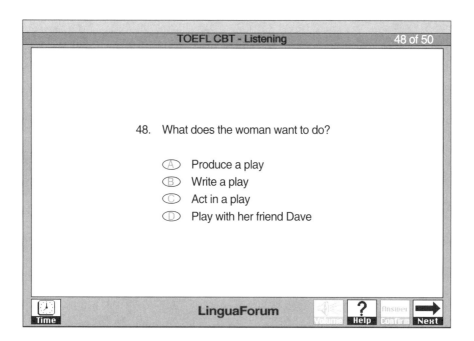

TOEFL CBT - Listening   48 of 50

48. What does the woman want to do?

   Ⓐ Produce a play
   Ⓑ Write a play
   Ⓒ Act in a play
   Ⓓ Play with her friend Dave

LinguaForum

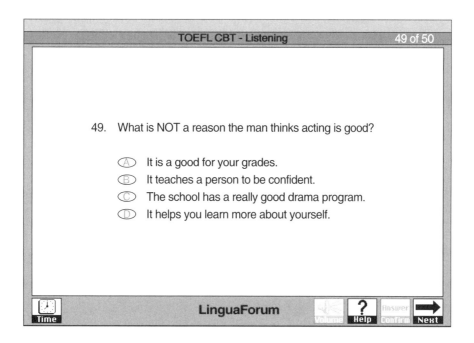

TOEFL CBT - Listening   49 of 50

49. What is NOT a reason the man thinks acting is good?

   Ⓐ It is a good for your grades.
   Ⓑ It teaches a person to be confident.
   Ⓒ The school has a really good drama program.
   Ⓓ It helps you learn more about yourself.

LinguaForum

PRACTICE TEST 9

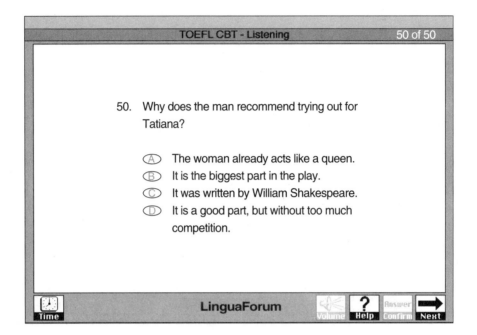

Test
9

SECTION 2
STRUCTURE

Suggested Time: 15 Minutes

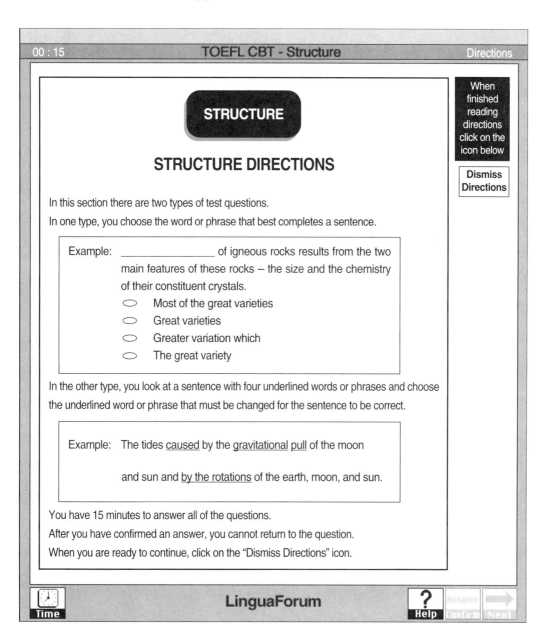

When finished reading directions click on the icon below

Dismiss Directions

STRUCTURE

STRUCTURE DIRECTIONS

In this section there are two types of test questions.

In one type, you choose the word or phrase that best completes a sentence.

Example: _____ of igneous rocks results from the two main features of these rocks – the size and the chemistry of their constituent crystals.

- ⬭ Most of the great varieties
- ⬭ Great varieties
- ⬭ Greater variation which
- ⬭ The great variety

In the other type, you look at a sentence with four underlined words or phrases and choose the underlined word or phrase that must be changed for the sentence to be correct.

Example: The tides <u>caused</u> by the <u>gravitational</u> <u>pull</u> of the moon

and sun and <u>by the rotations</u> of the earth, moon, and sun.

You have 15 minutes to answer all of the questions.

After you have confirmed an answer, you cannot return to the question.

When you are ready to continue, click on the "Dismiss Directions" icon.

Time   **LinguaForum**   ? Help Answer Confirm Next

PRACTICE
TEST 9

Structure

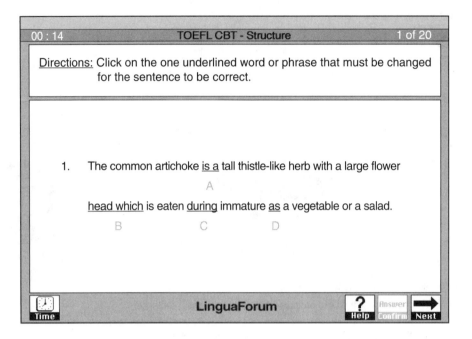

Directions: Click on the one underlined word or phrase that must be changed for the sentence to be correct.

1.　　The common artichoke <u>is a</u> tall thistle-like herb with a large flower
　　　　　　　　　　　　　　A

　　　<u>head which</u> is eaten <u>during</u> immature <u>as</u> a vegetable or a salad.
　　　　　B　　　　　　　　　C　　　　　　D

Time　　　　　　　　　LinguaForum　　　　　？　Answer　➡
　　　　　　　　　　　　　　　　　　　　　　Help　Confirm　Next

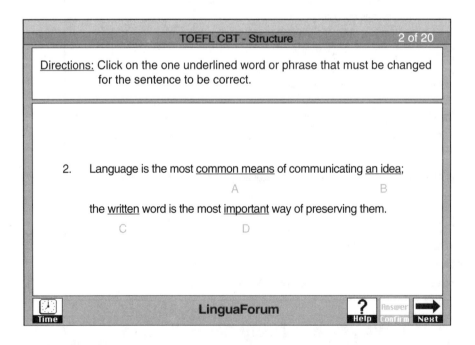

Directions: Click on the one underlined word or phrase that must be changed for the sentence to be correct.

2.　　Language is the most <u>common means</u> of communicating <u>an idea</u>;
　　　　　　　　　　　　　　　　A　　　　　　　　　　　　　　　B

　　　the <u>written</u> word is the most <u>important</u> way of preserving them.
　　　　　　C　　　　　　　　　　D

Time　　　　　　　　　LinguaForum　　　　　？　Answer　➡
　　　　　　　　　　　　　　　　　　　　　　Help　Confirm　Next

Specialist Solutions for TOEFL® CBT

Structure

Directions: Click on the one underlined word or phrase that must be changed for the sentence to be correct.

3. <u>Instant</u> coffees, from <u>them</u> a beverage is <u>made by</u> dissolving a

      A   B   C

powder in hot water, were invented in <u>the early</u> 1900s.

                                   D

LinguaForum

Time   Help   Answer Confirm   Next

Directions: Click on the one word or phrase that best completes the sentence.

4. An artist is a highly sensitive person, especially aware of _____.

   (A)   which surround him

   (B)   the things which surrounding him

   (C)   the things his surroundings

   (D)   the things that surround him

LinguaForum

Time   Help   Answer Confirm   Next

PRACTICE TEST 9

Directions: Click on the one underlined word or phrase that must be changed
for the sentence to be correct.

5. <u>There were</u> different <u>kinds</u> of arrows, depending upon the use to which
        A   B

    they <u>put</u> and the place <u>where</u> they were made.
        C   D

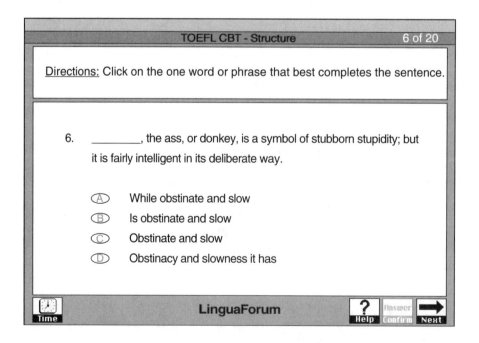

LinguaForum

Time | ? Help | Answer Confirm | ➡ Next

Directions: Click on the one word or phrase that best completes the sentence.

6. _____, the ass, or donkey, is a symbol of stubborn stupidity; but
    it is fairly intelligent in its deliberate way.

    Ⓐ   While obstinate and slow
    Ⓑ   Is obstinate and slow
    Ⓒ   Obstinate and slow
    Ⓓ   Obstinacy and slowness it has

LinguaForum

Time | ? Help | Answer Confirm | ➡ Next

Specialist Solutions for TOEFL® CBT

Structure

Directions: Click on the one underlined word or phrase that must be changed
for the sentence to be correct.

7.   In America billiards <u>is played</u> on a table usually <u>ten feet long</u> and half
                        A   B

    as wide, <u>having</u> a very smooth and <u>surface level</u> of slate covered with
                 C   D

    green baize.

LinguaForum

PRACTICE TEST 9

Directions: Click on the one word or phrase that best completes the sentence.

8.   An Autogiro cannot fly sideways, backward, _____, but its large
       rotor makes it very maneuverable at all speeds.

    Ⓐ   or vertical flight
    Ⓑ   or vertically
    Ⓒ   to fly vertically
    Ⓓ   and be vertical

LinguaForum

Structure

Directions: Click on the one underlined word or phrase that must be changed for the sentence to be correct.

9. Unable <u>finding</u> a <u>publisher</u> for <u>his</u> *Birds of America* in the United States,
         A   B   C

    John James Audubon <u>went</u> to England.
                             D

LinguaForum

Time | Help | Answer Confirm | Next

Directions: Click on the one word or phrase that best completes the sentence.

10. The United States had _____ of soil conservation until the
    economic depression and drought of the early 1930s.

    Ⓐ   not programed national
    Ⓑ   national program which none
    Ⓒ   not any national program
    Ⓓ   no national program

LinguaForum

Time | Help | Answer Confirm | Next

238

Structure

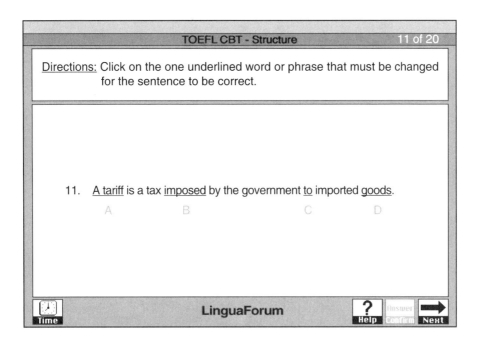

Directions: Click on the one underlined word or phrase that must be changed for the sentence to be correct.

11. A tariff is a tax imposed by the government to imported goods.
A   B   C   D

LinguaForum

Time   Help   Confirm   Next

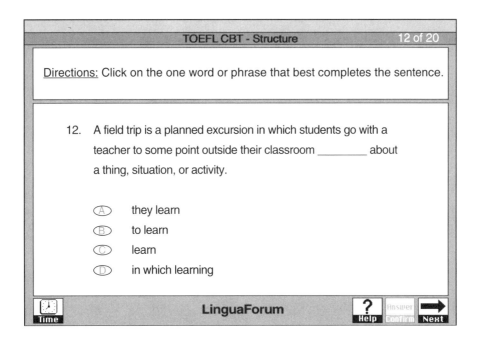

Directions: Click on the one word or phrase that best completes the sentence.

12. A field trip is a planned excursion in which students go with a teacher to some point outside their classroom _____ about a thing, situation, or activity.

(A) they learn
(B) to learn
(C) learn
(D) in which learning

LinguaForum

Time   Help   Confirm   Next

Structure

Directions: Click on the one underlined word or phrase that must be changed for the sentence to be correct.

13. An <u>autobiographer</u> differs from a biography, <u>which is</u> a life story
                    A   B

      <u>written</u> by someone <u>other</u> than the subject.
        C   D

LinguaForum

Time   **?** Help   Answer Confirm   Next

Directions: Click on the one word or phrase that best completes the sentence.

14. When a well is sunk deep in the earth, water _____ up naturally, as it does from a spring.

     (A)   sometimes flows
     (B)   some flows
     (C)   it sometimes flows
     (D)   its flow

LinguaForum

Time   **?** Help   Answer Confirm   Next

Structure

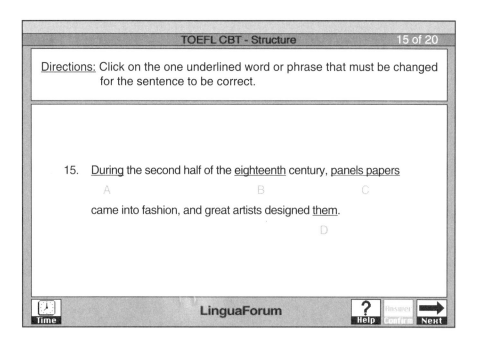

TOEFL CBT - Structure | 15 of 20

Directions: Click on the one underlined word or phrase that must be changed for the sentence to be correct.

15. <u>During</u> the second half of the <u>eighteenth</u> century, <u>panels papers</u>
    A   B   C

came into fashion, and great artists designed <u>them</u>.
                                                D

LinguaForum

Time   Help   Confirm   Next

PRACTICE
TEST 9

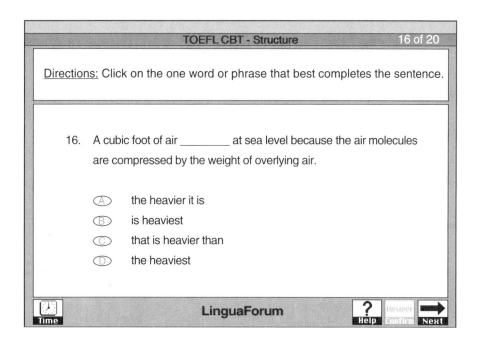

TOEFL CBT - Structure | 16 of 20

Directions: Click on the one word or phrase that best completes the sentence.

16. A cubic foot of air _____ at sea level because the air molecules
    are compressed by the weight of overlying air.

    (A)   the heavier it is
    (B)   is heaviest
    (C)   that is heavier than
    (D)   the heaviest

LinguaForum

Time   Help   Confirm   Next

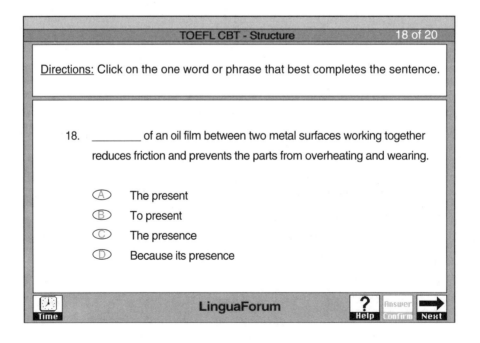

Directions: Click on the one underlined word or phrase that must be changed for the sentence to be correct.

17. Many <u>of the</u> stock ranches in Australia <u>owe</u> their <u>existence</u> to
          A   B   C

the country's <u>vastly</u> supply of water from artesian wells.
                      D

LinguaForum

Time Help Confirm Next

Directions: Click on the one word or phrase that best completes the sentence.

18. _____ of an oil film between two metal surfaces working together reduces friction and prevents the parts from overheating and wearing.

(A)   The present
(B)   To present
(C)   The presence
(D)   Because its presence

LinguaForum

Time Help Confirm Next

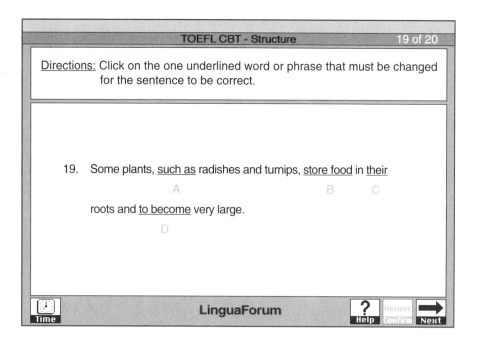

Directions: Click on the one underlined word or phrase that must be changed for the sentence to be correct.

19. Some plants, <u>such as</u> radishes and turnips, <u>store food</u> in <u>their</u>
       A   B C

roots and <u>to become</u> very large.
    D

LinguaForum

Time   **? Help**   Answer Confirm   **Next**

PRACTICE
TEST 9

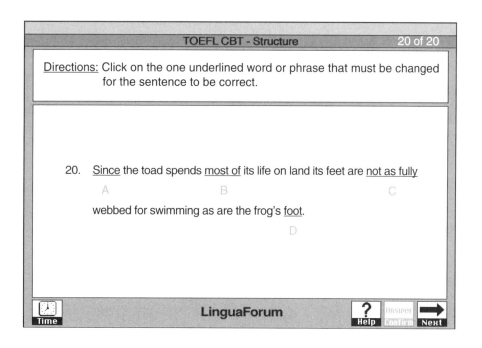

Directions: Click on the one underlined word or phrase that must be changed for the sentence to be correct.

20. <u>Since</u> the toad spends <u>most of</u> its life on land its feet are <u>not as fully</u>
   A   B   C

webbed for swimming as are the frog's <u>foot</u>.
             D

LinguaForum

Time   **? Help**   Answer Confirm   **Next**

SECTION 3
READING
Suggested Time: 70 Minutes

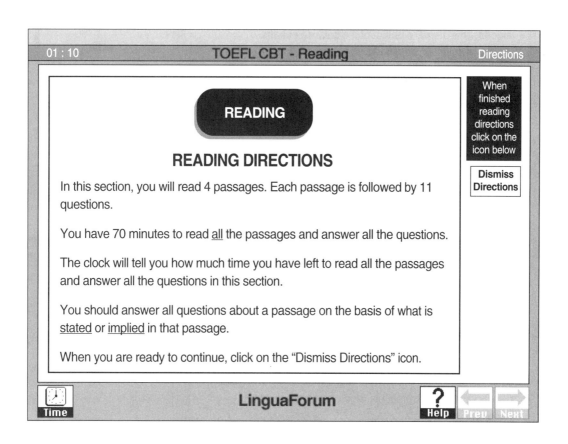

| 01 : 10 | TOEFL CBT - Reading | Directions |

READING

When finished reading directions click on the icon below

Dismiss Directions

READING DIRECTIONS

In this section, you will read 4 passages. Each passage is followed by 11 questions.

You have 70 minutes to read <u>all</u> the passages and answer all the questions.

The clock will tell you how much time you have left to read all the passages and answer all the questions in this section.

You should answer all questions about a passage on the basis of what is <u>stated</u> or <u>implied</u> in that passage.

When you are ready to continue, click on the "Dismiss Directions" icon.

Time | LinguaForum | ? Help | Prev | Next

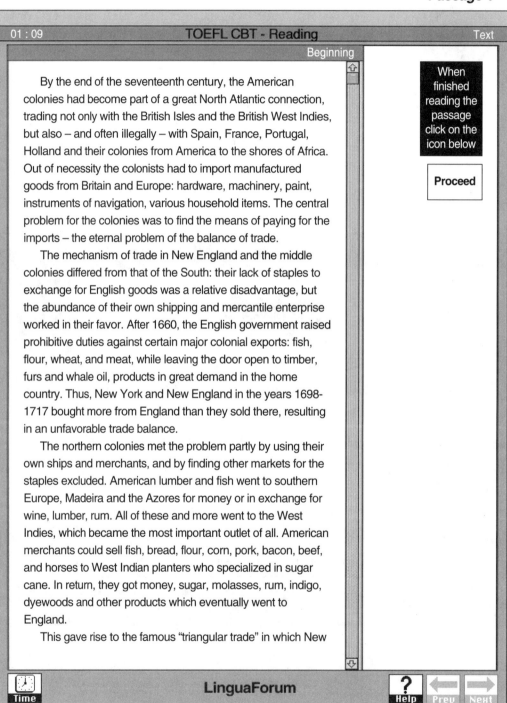

Passage 1

TOEFL CBT - Reading | Text

End

Englanders shipped rum to the west coast of Africa and bartered for slaves, took the slaves on the "Middle Passage" to the West Indies, and returned home with various commodities including molasses, from which they manufactured rum. In another version, they shipped provisions to the West Indies, carried sugar and molasses to England, and returned with manufactured goods from Europe.

When finished reading the passage click on the icon below

Proceed

Time | LinguaForum | Help | Prev | Next

PRACTICE
TEST 9

Passage 1

By the end of the seventeenth century, the American colonies had become part of a great North Atlantic connection, trading not only with the British Isles and the British West Indies, but also – and often illegally – with Spain, France, Portugal, Holland and their colonies from America to the shores of Africa. Out of necessity the colonists had to import manufactured goods from Britain and Europe: hardware, machinery, paint, instruments of navigation, various household items. The central problem for the colonies was to find the means of paying for the imports – the eternal problem of the balance of trade.

The mechanism of trade in New England and the middle colonies differed from that of the South: their lack of staples to exchange for English goods was a relative disadvantage, but the abundance of their own shipping and mercantile enterprise worked in their favor. After 1660, the English government raised prohibitive duties against certain major colonial exports: fish, flour, wheat, and meat, while leaving the door open to timber, furs and whale oil, products in great demand in the home country. Thus, New York and New England in the years 1698-1717 bought more from England than they sold there, resulting in an unfavorable trade balance.

The northern colonies met the problem partly by using their own ships and merchants, and by finding other markets for the staples excluded. American lumber and fish went to southern Europe, Madeira and the Azores for money or in exchange for wine, lumber, rum. All of these and more went to the West Indies, which became the most important outlet of all. American merchants could sell fish, bread, flour, corn, pork, bacon, beef, and horses to West Indian planters who specialized in sugar cane. In return, they got money, sugar, molasses, rum, indigo, dyewoods and other products which eventually went to England.

This gave rise to the famous "triangular trade" in which New

1. The main subject of the passage is

(A) the problem of trade imbalance in the American colonies

(B) the development of trade in the American colonies

(C) the triangular trade of the American colonies

(D) the rise of mercantilism in the American colonies

LinguaForum

?
Help

Prev

Next

Time

Reading

Passage 1

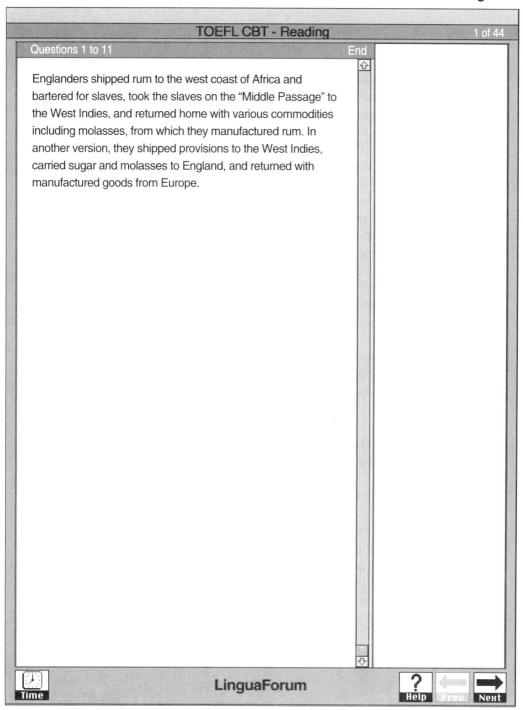

Questions 1 to 11

End

Englanders shipped rum to the west coast of Africa and bartered for slaves, took the slaves on the "Middle Passage" to the West Indies, and returned home with various commodities including molasses, from which they manufactured rum. In another version, they shipped provisions to the West Indies, carried sugar and molasses to England, and returned with manufactured goods from Europe.

PRACTICE
TEST 9

Time

LinguaForum

Help   Prev.   Next

Reading

Questions 1 to 11   Beginning

By the end of the seventeenth century, the American colonies had become part of a great North Atlantic connection, trading not only with the British Isles and the British West Indies, but also – and often illegally – with Spain, France, Portugal, Holland and their colonies from America to the shores of Africa. Out of necessity the colonists had to import manufactured goods from Britain and Europe: hardware, machinery, paint, instruments of navigation, various household items. The central problem for the colonies was to find the means of paying for the imports – the eternal problem of the balance of trade.

The mechanism of trade in New England and the middle colonies differed from that of the South: their lack of staples to exchange for English goods was a relative disadvantage, but the abundance of their own shipping and mercantile enterprise worked in their favor. After 1660, the English government raised prohibitive duties against certain major colonial exports: fish, flour, wheat, and meat, while leaving the door open to timber, furs and whale oil, products in great demand in the home country. Thus, New York and New England in the years 1698-1717 bought more from England than they sold there, resulting in an unfavorable trade balance.

The northern colonies met the problem partly by using their own ships and merchants, and by finding other markets for the staples excluded. American lumber and fish went to southern Europe, Madeira and the Azores for money or in exchange for wine, lumber, rum. All of these and more went to the West Indies, which became the most important outlet of all. American merchants could sell fish, bread, flour, corn, pork, bacon, beef, and horses to West Indian planters who specialized in sugar cane. In return, they got money, sugar, molasses, rum, indigo, dyewoods and other products which eventually went to England.

2. Look at the word their in the passage. Click on the word or phrase in the **bold** text that their refers to.

3. It can be inferred that the American colonies
Ⓐ were developing quickly as an industrial nation
Ⓑ depended heavily on Europe for survival
Ⓒ served as an important market for English goods from the mother country
Ⓓ relied on Europe for selling their products

4. The major problem of the colonies was
Ⓐ to develop goods to sell abroad
Ⓑ to export goods to England
Ⓒ to sell as much as possible
Ⓓ to find markets for their goods

Time   **LinguaForum**   ? Help   ← Prev   → Next

Reading

Passage 1

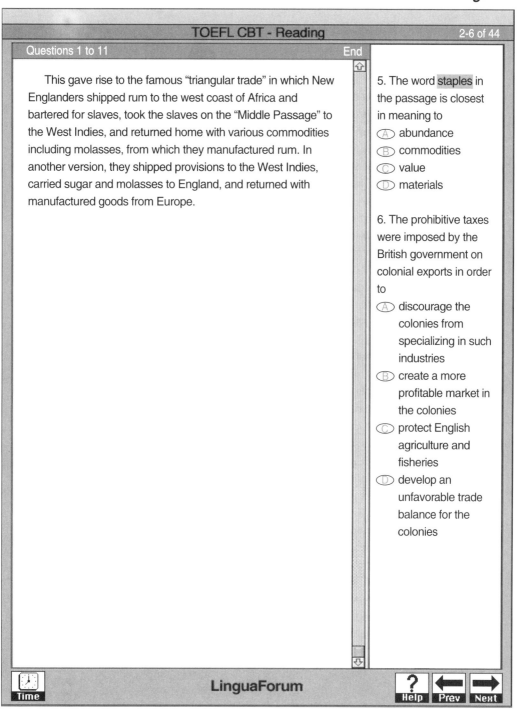

Questions 1 to 11   End

This gave rise to the famous "triangular trade" in which New Englanders shipped rum to the west coast of Africa and bartered for slaves, took the slaves on the "Middle Passage" to the West Indies, and returned home with various commodities including molasses, from which they manufactured rum. In another version, they shipped provisions to the West Indies, carried sugar and molasses to England, and returned with manufactured goods from Europe.

5. The word staples in the passage is closest in meaning to
Ⓐ abundance
Ⓑ commodities
Ⓒ value
Ⓓ materials

6. The prohibitive taxes were imposed by the British government on colonial exports in order to
Ⓐ discourage the colonies from specializing in such industries
Ⓑ create a more profitable market in the colonies
Ⓒ protect English agriculture and fisheries
Ⓓ develop an unfavorable trade balance for the colonies

PRACTICE
TEST 9

LinguaForum

? Help   ← Prev   → Next

Time

Passage 1

Questions 1 to 11   Beginning

By the end of the seventeenth century, the American colonies had become part of a great North Atlantic connection, trading not only with the British Isles and the British West Indies, but also – and often illegally – with Spain, France, Portugal, Holland and their colonies from America to the shores of Africa. Out of necessity the colonists had to import manufactured goods from Britain and Europe: hardware, machinery, paint, instruments of navigation, various household items. The central problem for the colonies was to find the means of paying for the imports – the eternal problem of the balance of trade.

➡ ■ The mechanism of trade in New England and the middle colonies differed from that of the South: their lack of staples to exchange for English goods was a relative disadvantage, but the abundance of their own shipping and mercantile enterprise worked in their favor. ■ After 1660, the English government raised prohibitive duties against certain major colonial exports: fish, flour, wheat, and meat, while leaving the door open to timber, furs and whale oil, products in great demand in the home country. ■ Thus, New York and New England in the years 1698-1717 bought more from England than they sold there, resulting in an unfavorable trade balance. ■

➡ The northern colonies met the problem partly by using their own ships and merchants, and by finding other markets for the staples excluded. ■ American lumber and fish went to southern Europe, Madeira and the Azores for money or in exchange for wine, lumber, rum. ■ All of these and more went to the West Indies, which became the most important outlet of all. American merchants could sell fish, bread, flour, corn, pork, bacon, beef, and horses to West Indian planters who specialized in sugar cane. ■ In return, they got money, sugar, molasses, rum, indigo, dyewoods and other products which eventually went to England. ■

This gave rise to the famous "triangular trade" in which New

7. The word outlet in the passage is closest in meaning to
(A) means
(B) opening
(C) exit
(D) passage

8. The colonies bought all of the following from the West Indies EXCEPT
(A) slaves
(B) sugar
(C) molasses
(D) indigo

9. The following sentence can be added to paragraph 2 or 3.

Other provisions went to Newfoundland.

Where would it best fit in the paragraph? Click on the square [■] to add the sentence to paragraph 2 or 3. Paragraphs 2 and 3 are marked with an arrow [➡].

Time   **LinguaForum**   Help Prev Next

Reading

Passage 1

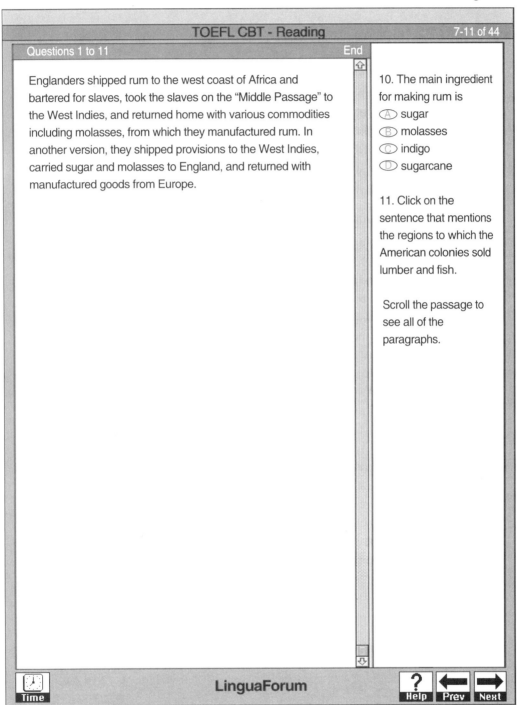

Questions 1 to 11   End

Englanders shipped rum to the west coast of Africa and bartered for slaves, took the slaves on the "Middle Passage" to the West Indies, and returned home with various commodities including molasses, from which they manufactured rum. In another version, they shipped provisions to the West Indies, carried sugar and molasses to England, and returned with manufactured goods from Europe.

10. The main ingredient for making rum is

   Ⓐ sugar

   Ⓑ molasses

   Ⓒ indigo

   Ⓓ sugarcane

11. Click on the sentence that mentions the regions to which the American colonies sold lumber and fish.

Scroll the passage to see all of the paragraphs.

PRACTICE TEST 9

Time   **LinguaForum**   ? Help   ← Prev   → Next

Pioneered by French anthropologist Claude Lévi-Strauss, structural anthropology analyzed cultural phenomena such as languages, myths, and kinship systems to discover what ordered patterns, or structures, they seemed to display.

Lévi-Strauss was struck by the contrast between the extraordinary variety of beliefs and customs throughout the world and the fact that the human brains that created this great variety are essentially the same everywhere. How could brains that are structured in the same way create different cultures? He reasoned that beneath the surface of individual cultures there must exist natural properties common to all. For an answer, Lévi-Strauss focused not on the customs and beliefs of specific cultures, but on the patterns or structures existing beneath the customs and beliefs of all cultures.

→ One such pattern is called opposition. Greek philosopher Heraclitus noted many opposites in the natural and social worlds: good vs. evil, life vs. death, etc. ■ He suggested that the entire world could be conceptualized in this dualistic way and others have agreed. ■ The reason people of all cultures tend to think in terms of opposites is that to think, we must classify, which means we must be able to distinguish between things. Thinking of two things as opposites is the simplest way to do this. ■ German philosopher Georg Hegel proposed that every idea implied its opposite, and by uniting an idea and its opposite, a process called synthesis, the two of them would create a single new idea, which in turn would give birth to its opposite, and so on. ■ This idea was later employed by the political philosopher Karl Marx, who interpreted human history as a continuous struggle between two opposite classes, the rulers and the ruled. ■

→ In the industrialized world, the red light of a traffic signal means "stop," green means "go." ■ To Lévi-Strauss, this is a mere external of culture, devoid of any deeper significance. ■ Much more meaningful is how these facts convey information to people: through the contrast between red and green and the switching from one color to another. ■ Red has a meaning only in relation to green. ■ It is the structure or pattern of opposites that provides the messages, not the specific colors considered independently of each other. This dual structure constitutes the meaning of "stop/go." ■

LinguaForum

12. The passage is primarily concerned with
    - Ⓐ dualistic philosophy
    - Ⓑ the history of dualistic thinking
    - Ⓒ the contribution made by Lévi-Strauss
    - Ⓓ the significance of structural anthropology

13. Look at the word they in the passage. Click on the word(s) or phrase in the **bold** text that they refers to.

14. Structural anthropology analyzes all of the following EXCEPT
    - Ⓐ myths
    - Ⓑ kinship systems
    - Ⓒ philosophy
    - Ⓓ languages

15. Structural anthropology studies mainly
    - Ⓐ the underlying universal pattern of different beliefs and customs
    - Ⓑ the ways in which human brains create different belief systems
    - Ⓒ the cultural beliefs and customs of specific cultures
    - Ⓓ the essential nature of the different cultures of the world

16. Which of the following could best replace the word struck in the passage?
    - Ⓐ Hit
    - Ⓑ Surprised
    - Ⓒ Sensitive
    - Ⓓ Impressed

17. Lévi-Strauss was looking for
    - Ⓐ a unique answer
    - Ⓑ a universal explanation
    - Ⓒ a radical discovery
    - Ⓓ a revolutionary insight

18. The word dualistic in the passage is closest in meaning to
    - Ⓐ duplicitous
    - Ⓑ paired
    - Ⓒ opposite
    - Ⓓ dichotomous

19. Classification is based upon
    - Ⓐ insight
    - Ⓑ perception
    - Ⓒ discrimination
    - Ⓓ understanding

20. Synthesis is
    - Ⓐ a form of thinking
    - Ⓑ a form of classification
    - Ⓒ a unification
    - Ⓓ a compromise

21. The following sentence can be added to paragraph 3 or 4.

    Much of Chinese philosophy is based on the idea of two opposing life forces: yin and yang.

    Where would it best fit in the paragraph? Click on the square [■] to add the sentence to paragraph 3 or 4.
    Paragraphs 3 and 4 are marked with an arrow [➡].

22. According to Lévi-Strauss, meaning arises from
    - Ⓐ the individual units that constitute the message
    - Ⓑ the dual relationship between the units of the message
    - Ⓒ the synthesis of the units that form the overall message
    - Ⓓ the struggling relationship among the units of the message

Passage 3

→ The tides are caused by the gravitational pull of the moon and sun and by the rotation of the earth, moon, and sun. ■ Strictly speaking, the moon does not rotate around the earth. Instead the earth and moon both rotate around a common point, their combined center of mass. ■ This rotation produces centrifugal force, which is the force that pushes you outward when you ride on a merry-go-round. ■ The centrifugal force just balances the gravitational attraction between the earth and moon – otherwise the two would either fly away from each other or crash together.■

→ Centrifugal force and the moon's gravity are not in perfect balance everywhere on the earth's surface, however. ■ On the side of the earth nearest the moon, the moon's gravity is stronger and pulls the water toward the moon. ■ On the side away from the moon, centrifugal force predominates, pushing the water away from the moon. ■ If the earth were completely covered with water, the water would form two bulges on opposite sides of the planet. ■

In addition to the rotation of the moon and the earth as mentioned above, the earth is spinning like a top on its own axis. As it does so, any given point on the planet's surface will first be under a bulge and then away from the bulge. High tide occurs when the point is under a bulge. Because the earth takes 24 hours to complete a rotation, the point will have two high tides and two low tides every day. Actually, the moon advances a little in its own orbit in the course of a day. It takes the point on earth an extra 50 minutes to catch up and come directly in line with the moon again. A full tidal cycle thus takes 24 hours and 50 minutes.

The sun produces tidal bulges in the same way as the moon. Though it is much larger than the moon, it is 400 times further away, and its effect on the tides is much less. When the sun and moon are in line with each other, which happens at the full and new moons, their effects add together. At these times, the tidal range, or difference in water level between successive high and low tides, is large. Such tides are called spring tides. This name is a misnomer because spring tides occur throughout the year.

Reading

23. What is the best title for this passage?
    - Ⓐ The Evolution of Tides
    - Ⓑ Why There are Tides
    - Ⓒ The Sun, Moon and Tides
    - Ⓓ The Rise and Fall of the Tides

24. All of the following cause tides EXCEPT
    - Ⓐ the gravitational pull of the sun
    - Ⓑ the rotation of the moon
    - Ⓒ the gravitational pull of the earth
    - Ⓓ the rotation of the sun

25. All of the following describe centrifugal force EXCEPT
    - Ⓐ outward push
    - Ⓑ balancing force between the moon and the earth
    - Ⓒ merry-go-round
    - Ⓓ inward pull

26. The centrifugal force is produced by
    - Ⓐ the gravitational pull of the earth
    - Ⓑ the rotation of the earth and the moon
    - Ⓒ the rotation of the moon and the sun
    - Ⓓ the gravitational pull of the sun

27. The following sentence can be added to paragraph 1 or 2.

    The water would be relatively deep under the bulges and shallow away from the bulges.

    Where would it best fit in the paragraph? Click on the square [■] to add the sentence to paragraph 1 or 2.
    Paragraphs 1 and 2 are marked with an arrow [➡].

28. The water is pulled towards the moon when
    - Ⓐ the moon's gravity is strongest
    - Ⓑ the earth is nearest the moon
    - Ⓒ the centrifugal force is least predominant
    - Ⓓ the centrifugal force is farthest from the earth

29. The word bulges in the passage is closest in meaning to
    - Ⓐ globes
    - Ⓑ curves
    - Ⓒ protrusions
    - Ⓓ rising

30. The passage supports all of the following statements EXCEPT
    - Ⓐ there is a total of four tides occurring every day
    - Ⓑ the earth takes 24 hours to spin on its own axis
    - Ⓒ a full tidal cycle takes more than 25 hours
    - Ⓓ the rotation of the moon is slightly faster than that of the earth

31. Look at the word its in the passage. Click on the word or phrase in the **bold** text that its refers to.

32. The passage implies that
    - Ⓐ the moon has the least influence in the creation of tides
    - Ⓑ the sun has the least influence in the creation of tides
    - Ⓒ distance is the key influence in the creation of tides
    - Ⓓ the range between the tides causes the height of the tides

33. The word misnomer in the passage is closest in meaning to
    - Ⓐ confusion
    - Ⓑ denomination
    - Ⓒ pseudonym
    - Ⓓ wrong name

PRACTICE TEST 9

Reading

Passage 4

   Before the invention of photography, art was confined to serving practical purposes. Painted images helped people to record, recognize and remember others. It was not until the appearance of the camera that art was relieved from the burden of record-keeping.

   Though photography was marveled at for its omniscience and its objectivity, it soon developed ways of distorting "reality" in order to shock the viewer into seeing new things that he had never imagined before. The result was a remarkable expansion in our ability to see.

→ Great changes in art have always had this effect, of course. ■ The introduction of perspective by Renaissance painters of the fifteenth century, as we have already pointed out, helped to make a man-centered world, with God's enveloping and all-seeing vision removed from it. ■ The development of better paints permitted easel paintings to supplant frescoes. ■ Thus art moved from church walls into even quite modest homes. ■ Other technical advances in the nineteenth century permitted painters to paint from nature in the open air. ■ But the modifications in our perception of the world brought about by photography may be more radical than any of those. ■

→ Though it is said that "the camera does not lie," there is no question that the camera *can* lie. A million publicity photos prove this to be so. ■ Nevertheless, the invention of photography has made it more difficult to maintain a sentimental view of the world. ■ A good photographer always manages to cut through even our most cherished illusions, that the poor are happy despite their poverty, or that suffering is always noble. ■

Time   **LinguaForum**   **?**   ←   →
                                                     Help Prev   Next

Reading

34. With what topic is the passage mainly concerned?
    - Ⓐ Great changes in art
    - Ⓑ The role of perspective in the evolution of art
    - Ⓒ Photography and the revolution of perspective
    - Ⓓ Photography and the distorted reality

35. The word relieved in the passage is closest in meaning to
    - Ⓐ released
    - Ⓑ assisted
    - Ⓒ eased
    - Ⓓ comforted

36. Photography is admired for
    - Ⓐ its transparency
    - Ⓑ its straightforwardness
    - Ⓒ its ability to open people's minds
    - Ⓓ its revolutionary technology

37. Look at the word its in the passage. Click on the word or phrase in the **bold** text that its refers to.

38. Great art is characterized primarily by its
    - Ⓐ revolutionary technique
    - Ⓑ radical influence
    - Ⓒ ability to expand vision
    - Ⓓ ability to show true reality

39. It can be inferred from the passage that frescoes are painted
    - Ⓐ on paper
    - Ⓑ in churches
    - Ⓒ on canvases
    - Ⓓ at private homes

40. The passage suggests that before the Renaissance, art
    - Ⓐ was primarily of religious nature
    - Ⓑ was financed by the church
    - Ⓒ was commissioned by nobility
    - Ⓓ was not addressed to the general public

41. Which of the following could best replace the word supplant in the passage?
    - Ⓐ Overcome
    - Ⓑ Defeat
    - Ⓒ Replace
    - Ⓓ Dismiss

42. Perspective before the Renaissance may be described as being
    - Ⓐ individual
    - Ⓑ divine
    - Ⓒ limited
    - Ⓓ focused

43. The following sentence can be added to paragraph 3 or 4.

    This, too, was a source of the revolutionary changes that produced impressionism.

    Where would it best fit in the paragraph? Click on the square [■] to add the sentence to paragraph 3 or 4.
    Paragraphs 3 and 4 are marked with an arrow [➜].

44. According to the passage, a good photographer
    - Ⓐ teaches us how to paint
    - Ⓑ shows the true image
    - Ⓒ shocks the viewer
    - Ⓓ creates illusions

PRACTICE TEST 9

Test
9

SECTION 4
WRITING
Suggested Time: 30 Minutes

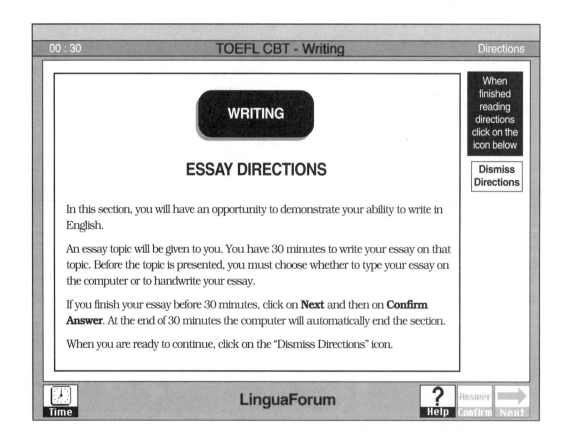

Writing

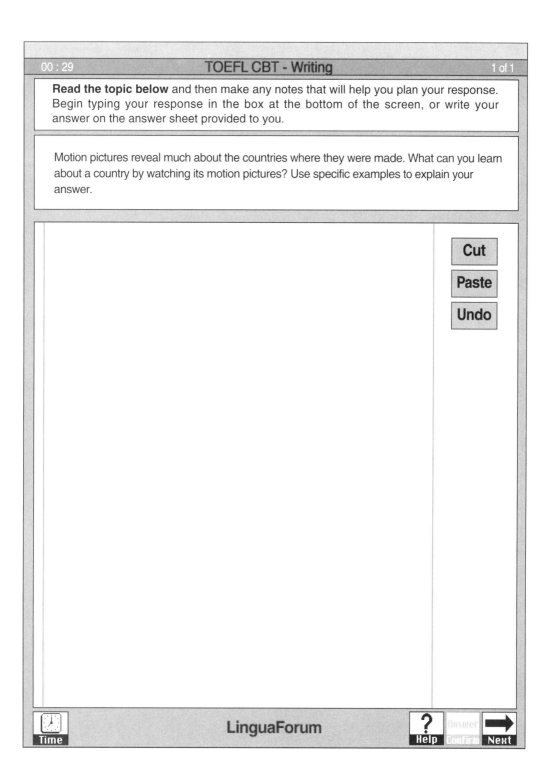

Practice Test 10

Listening: 40 Minutes (including listening time)
Structure: 20 Minutes
Reading: 90 Minutes
Writing: 30 Minutes

Suggested Total Time: 180 Minutes

ANSWER SHEET

Lingua TOEFL® CBT Test Book II
PRACTICE TEST 10

Name	
Sex	☐ male ☐ female
E-mail address	
Telephone No.	

No. of Correct Answers/Converted Score		
Listening		
Structure		
Reading		
Writing		
TOTAL		

Cut here.

Section 1: Listening

1. Ⓐ Ⓑ Ⓒ Ⓓ
2. Ⓐ Ⓑ Ⓒ Ⓓ
3. Ⓐ Ⓑ Ⓒ Ⓓ
4. Ⓐ Ⓑ Ⓒ Ⓓ
5. Ⓐ Ⓑ Ⓒ Ⓓ
6. Ⓐ Ⓑ Ⓒ Ⓓ
7. Ⓐ Ⓑ Ⓒ Ⓓ
8. Ⓐ Ⓑ Ⓒ Ⓓ
9. Ⓐ Ⓑ Ⓒ Ⓓ
10. Ⓐ Ⓑ Ⓒ Ⓓ
11. Ⓐ Ⓑ Ⓒ Ⓓ
12. Ⓐ Ⓑ Ⓒ Ⓓ
13. Chuck Yeager –
    Charles Lindbergh –
    The Wright brothers –
14. Ⓐ Ⓑ Ⓒ Ⓓ
15. Ⓐ Ⓑ Ⓒ Ⓓ
16. Ⓐ Ⓑ Ⓒ Ⓓ
17. René Descartes –
    Johannes Müller –
    Wilhelm Wundt –
18. Ⓐ Ⓑ Ⓒ Ⓓ
19. Ⓐ Ⓑ Ⓒ Ⓓ
20. Ⓐ Ⓑ Ⓒ Ⓓ
21. Ⓐ Ⓑ Ⓒ Ⓓ
22. Atomic weight –
    Atomic number –
    Density of water –
23.
24. Ⓐ Ⓑ Ⓒ Ⓓ
25. Ⓐ Ⓑ Ⓒ Ⓓ
26. Ⓐ Ⓑ Ⓒ Ⓓ
27. Ironclads –
    Pocahontas –
    Cornwallis –
28. Ⓐ Ⓑ Ⓒ Ⓓ
29. Ⓐ Ⓑ Ⓒ Ⓓ
30. Ⓐ Ⓑ Ⓒ Ⓓ

Section 2: Structure

1. Ⓐ Ⓑ Ⓒ Ⓓ
2. Ⓐ Ⓑ Ⓒ Ⓓ
3. Ⓐ Ⓑ Ⓒ Ⓓ
4. Ⓐ Ⓑ Ⓒ Ⓓ
5. Ⓐ Ⓑ Ⓒ Ⓓ
6. Ⓐ Ⓑ Ⓒ Ⓓ
7. Ⓐ Ⓑ Ⓒ Ⓓ
8. Ⓐ Ⓑ Ⓒ Ⓓ
9. Ⓐ Ⓑ Ⓒ Ⓓ
10. Ⓐ Ⓑ Ⓒ Ⓓ
11. Ⓐ Ⓑ Ⓒ Ⓓ
12. Ⓐ Ⓑ Ⓒ Ⓓ
13. Ⓐ Ⓑ Ⓒ Ⓓ
14. Ⓐ Ⓑ Ⓒ Ⓓ
15. Ⓐ Ⓑ Ⓒ Ⓓ
16. Ⓐ Ⓑ Ⓒ Ⓓ
17. Ⓐ Ⓑ Ⓒ Ⓓ
18. Ⓐ Ⓑ Ⓒ Ⓓ
19. Ⓐ Ⓑ Ⓒ Ⓓ
20. Ⓐ Ⓑ Ⓒ Ⓓ
21. Ⓐ Ⓑ Ⓒ Ⓓ
22. Ⓐ Ⓑ Ⓒ Ⓓ
23. Ⓐ Ⓑ Ⓒ Ⓓ
24. Ⓐ Ⓑ Ⓒ Ⓓ
25. Ⓐ Ⓑ Ⓒ Ⓓ

Section 3: Reading

1. Ⓐ Ⓑ Ⓒ Ⓓ
2. Ⓐ Ⓑ Ⓒ Ⓓ
3. Ⓐ Ⓑ Ⓒ Ⓓ
4. Ⓐ Ⓑ Ⓒ Ⓓ
5. Ⓐ Ⓑ Ⓒ Ⓓ
6. Ⓐ Ⓑ Ⓒ Ⓓ
7. Ⓐ Ⓑ Ⓒ Ⓓ
8. Ⓐ Ⓑ Ⓒ Ⓓ
9. Ⓐ Ⓑ Ⓒ Ⓓ
10. Ⓐ Ⓑ Ⓒ Ⓓ
11. Ⓐ Ⓑ Ⓒ Ⓓ
12. Ⓐ Ⓑ Ⓒ Ⓓ
13. Ⓐ Ⓑ Ⓒ Ⓓ
14. Ⓐ Ⓑ Ⓒ Ⓓ
15. Ⓐ Ⓑ Ⓒ Ⓓ
16. Ⓐ Ⓑ Ⓒ Ⓓ
17. Ⓐ Ⓑ Ⓒ Ⓓ
18. Ⓐ Ⓑ Ⓒ Ⓓ
19. Ⓐ Ⓑ Ⓒ Ⓓ
20. Ⓐ Ⓑ Ⓒ Ⓓ
21. Ⓐ Ⓑ Ⓒ Ⓓ
22. Ⓐ Ⓑ Ⓒ Ⓓ
23. Ⓐ Ⓑ Ⓒ Ⓓ
24. Ⓐ Ⓑ Ⓒ Ⓓ
25. Ⓐ Ⓑ Ⓒ Ⓓ
26.
27. Ⓐ Ⓑ Ⓒ Ⓓ
28.
29. Ⓐ Ⓑ Ⓒ Ⓓ
30. Ⓐ Ⓑ Ⓒ Ⓓ
31. Ⓐ Ⓑ Ⓒ Ⓓ
32. Ⓐ Ⓑ Ⓒ Ⓓ
33. Ⓐ Ⓑ Ⓒ Ⓓ
34. Ⓐ Ⓑ Ⓒ Ⓓ
35. Ⓐ Ⓑ Ⓒ Ⓓ
36.
37. Ⓐ Ⓑ Ⓒ Ⓓ
38. Ⓐ Ⓑ Ⓒ Ⓓ
39. Ⓐ Ⓑ Ⓒ Ⓓ
40.
41. Ⓐ Ⓑ Ⓒ Ⓓ
42. Ⓐ Ⓑ Ⓒ Ⓓ
43.
44.
45. Ⓐ Ⓑ Ⓒ Ⓓ
46.
47. Ⓐ Ⓑ Ⓒ Ⓓ
48. Ⓐ Ⓑ Ⓒ Ⓓ
49.
50.
51. Ⓐ Ⓑ Ⓒ Ⓓ
52.
53. Ⓐ Ⓑ Ⓒ Ⓓ
54. Ⓐ Ⓑ Ⓒ Ⓓ
55. Ⓐ Ⓑ Ⓒ Ⓓ

■ **Have you taken the official TOEFL Test?**

☐ Yes → if any
☐ No

PBT Score	
Listening	
Structure	
Reading	
Writing	
TOTAL	

CBT Score	
Listening	
Structure	
Reading	
Writing	
TOTAL	

■ **Educational background**

☐ middle/high school ☐ undergraduate ☐ graduate

SIGNED: _____
(SIGN YOUR NAME AS IF SIGNING A BUSINESS LETTER.)

DATE: ___ / ___ / ___
MO. DAY YEAR

LinguaForum
Copyright © 2002 by Lingua Forum, Inc. All rights reserved.

ANSWER SHEET

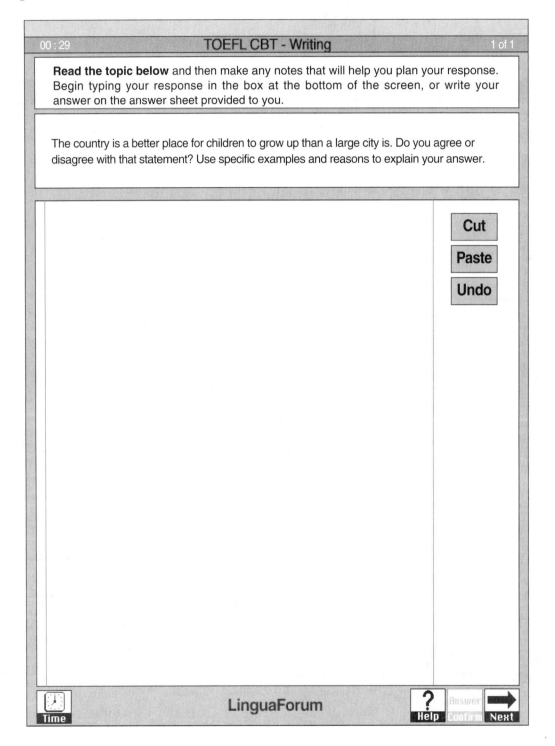

Read the topic below and then make any notes that will help you plan your response. Begin typing your response in the box at the bottom of the screen, or write your answer on the answer sheet provided to you.

The country is a better place for children to grow up than a large city is. Do you agree or disagree with that statement? Use specific examples and reasons to explain your answer.

Cut

Paste

Undo

Time

LinguaForum

? Help   Answer Confirm   Next

LinguaForum
Copyright © 2002 by Lingua Forum, Inc. All rights reserved.

Test
10

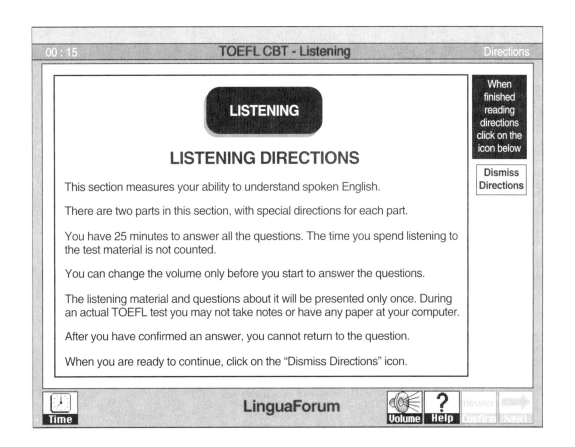

00 : 15	TOEFL CBT - Listening	Directions

LISTENING

LISTENING DIRECTIONS

This section measures your ability to understand spoken English.

There are two parts in this section, with special directions for each part.

You have 25 minutes to answer all the questions. The time you spend listening to the test material is not counted.

You can change the volume only before you start to answer the questions.

The listening material and questions about it will be presented only once. During an actual TOEFL test you may not take notes or have any paper at your computer.

After you have confirmed an answer, you cannot return to the question.

When you are ready to continue, click on the "Dismiss Directions" icon.

When finished reading directions click on the icon below

Dismiss Directions

Time   **LinguaForum**   Volume Help Answer Confirm Next

Test
10

SECTION 1
LISTENING

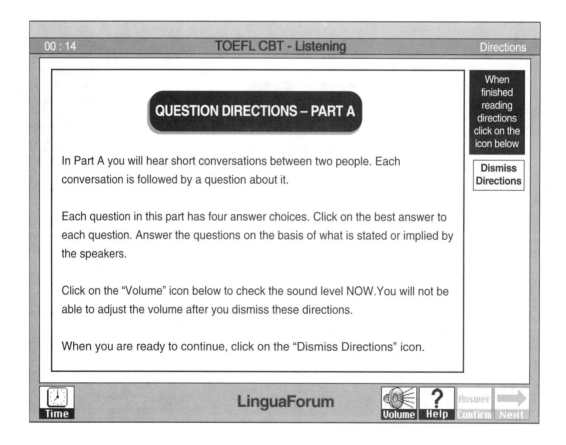

00 : 14 **TOEFL CBT - Listening** Directions

When finished reading directions click on the icon below

Dismiss Directions

QUESTION DIRECTIONS – PART A

In Part A you will hear short conversations between two people. Each conversation is followed by a question about it.

Each question in this part has four answer choices. Click on the best answer to each question. Answer the questions on the basis of what is stated or implied by the speakers.

Click on the "Volume" icon below to check the sound level NOW. You will not be able to adjust the volume after you dismiss these directions.

When you are ready to continue, click on the "Dismiss Directions" icon.

Time **LinguaForum** **Volume** **Help** **Confirm** **Next**

Listening

PRACTICE TEST 10

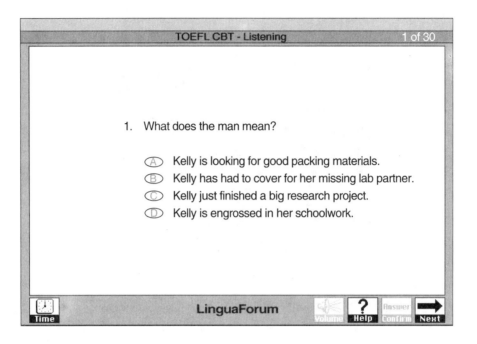

1. What does the man mean?

   Ⓐ Kelly is looking for good packing materials.
   Ⓑ Kelly has had to cover for her missing lab partner.
   Ⓒ Kelly just finished a big research project.
   Ⓓ Kelly is engrossed in her schoolwork.

LinguaForum

Time   Volume Help Confirm Next

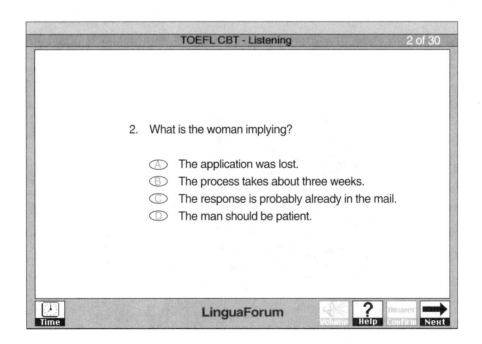

2. What is the woman implying?

   Ⓐ The application was lost.
   Ⓑ The process takes about three weeks.
   Ⓒ The response is probably already in the mail.
   Ⓓ The man should be patient.

LinguaForum

Time   Volume Help Confirm Next

271

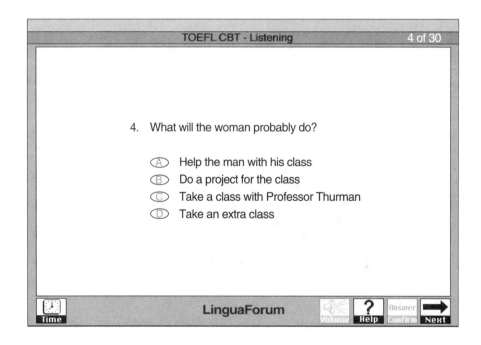

Question 5

**PRACTICE
TEST 10**

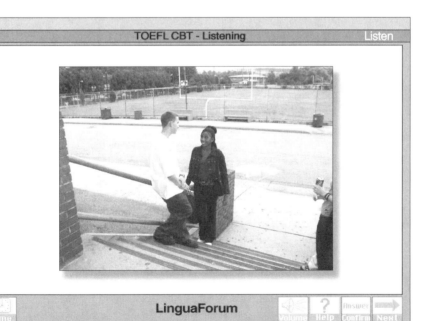

Question 6

273

Listening

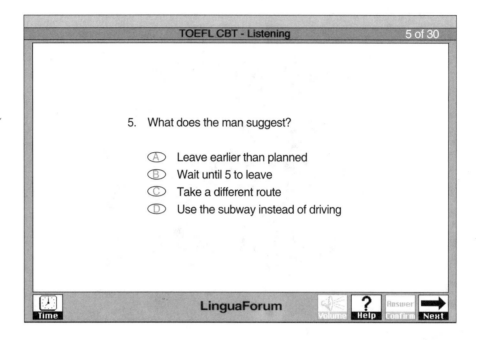

5. What does the man suggest?

Ⓐ Leave earlier than planned
Ⓑ Wait until 5 to leave
Ⓒ Take a different route
Ⓓ Use the subway instead of driving

LinguaForum

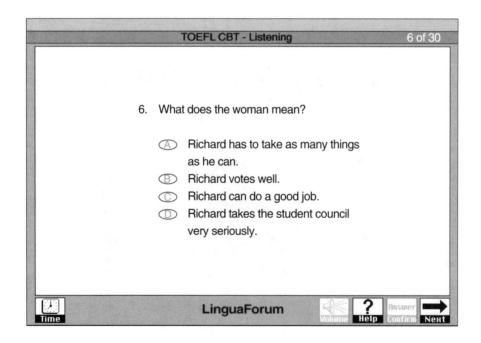

6. What does the woman mean?

Ⓐ Richard has to take as many things as he can.
Ⓑ Richard votes well.
Ⓒ Richard can do a good job.
Ⓓ Richard takes the student council very seriously.

LinguaForum

Question 7

Question 8

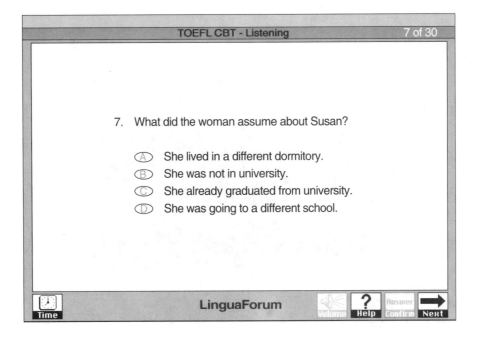

TOEFL CBT - Listening   7 of 30

7.   What did the woman assume about Susan?

   (A)   She lived in a different dormitory.
   (B)   She was not in university.
   (C)   She already graduated from university.
   (D)   She was going to a different school.

Time   LinguaForum   Volume   Help   Answer Confirm   Next

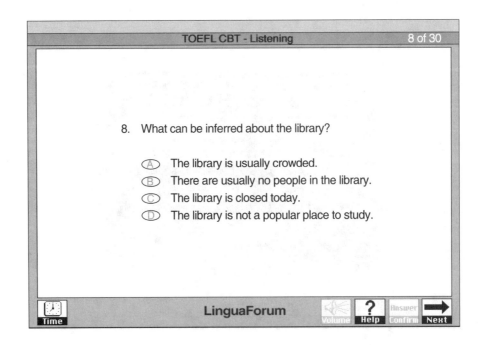

TOEFL CBT - Listening   8 of 30

8.   What can be inferred about the library?

   (A)   The library is usually crowded.
   (B)   There are usually no people in the library.
   (C)   The library is closed today.
   (D)   The library is not a popular place to study.

Time   LinguaForum   Volume   Help   Answer Confirm   Next

9. How much are the green sheets?

    (A) $37.60
    (B) $17.65
    (C) $16.45
    (D) $15.50

LinguaForum

Time   Volume Help Answer Confirm Next

10. What did Keith do?

    (A) Submitted a report
    (B) Recommended Michael's research
    (C) Followed Michael
    (D) Promised to write a report

LinguaForum

Time   Volume Help Answer Confirm Next

PRACTICE
TEST 10

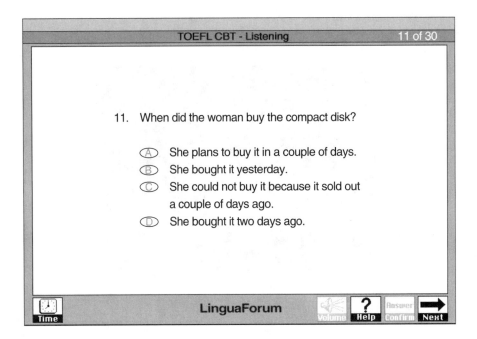

11. When did the woman buy the compact disk?

    Ⓐ She plans to buy it in a couple of days.
    Ⓑ She bought it yesterday.
    Ⓒ She could not buy it because it sold out
       a couple of days ago.
    Ⓓ She bought it two days ago.

LinguaForum

Time   Volume Help Confirm Next

Test
10

SECTION 1
LISTENING

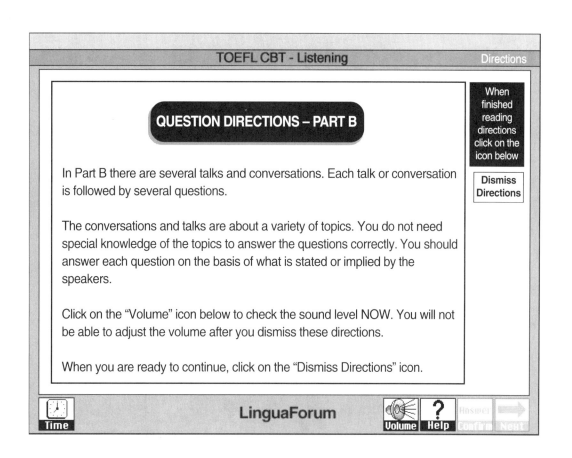

TOEFL CBT - Listening	Directions

QUESTION DIRECTIONS – PART B

In Part B there are several talks and conversations. Each talk or conversation is followed by several questions.

The conversations and talks are about a variety of topics. You do not need special knowledge of the topics to answer the questions correctly. You should answer each question on the basis of what is stated or implied by the speakers.

Click on the "Volume" icon below to check the sound level NOW. You will not be able to adjust the volume after you dismiss these directions.

When you are ready to continue, click on the "Dismiss Directions" icon.

When finished reading directions click on the icon below

Dismiss Directions

Time   **LinguaForum**   **Volume** **Help** Confirm Next

PRACTICE
TEST 10

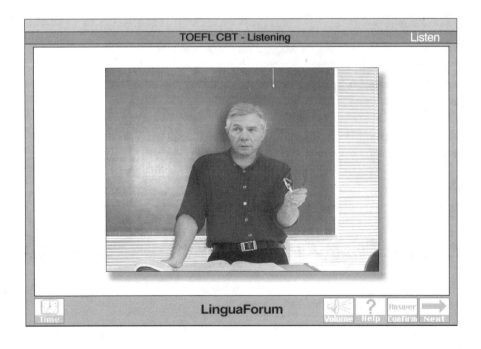

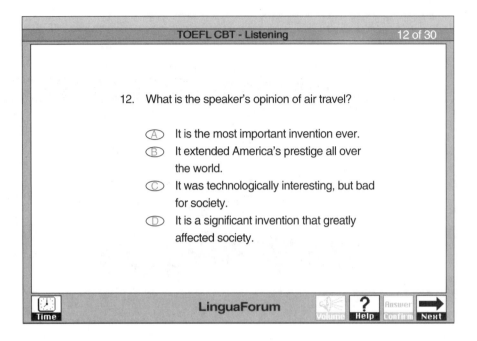

12.   What is the speaker's opinion of air travel?

Ⓐ   It is the most important invention ever.
Ⓑ   It extended America's prestige all over
      the world.
Ⓒ   It was technologically interesting, but bad
      for society.
Ⓓ   It is a significant invention that greatly
      affected society.

LinguaForum

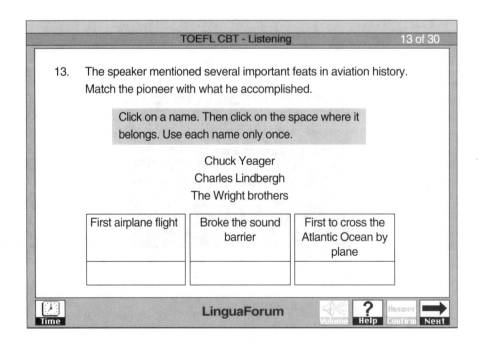

13.   The speaker mentioned several important feats in aviation history.
       Match the pioneer with what he accomplished.

       Click on a name. Then click on the space where it
       belongs. Use each name only once.

                    Chuck Yeager
                    Charles Lindbergh
                    The Wright brothers

First airplane flight	Broke the sound barrier	First to cross the Atlantic Ocean by plane

LinguaForum

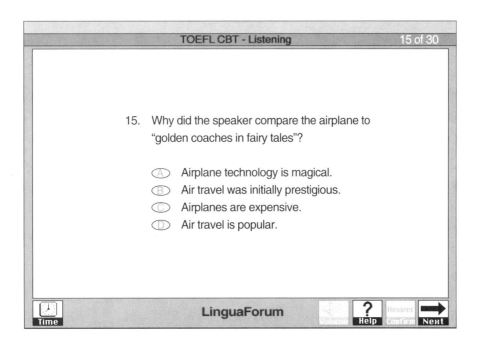

14.   How did the rise of air travel affect American society?

Click on 2 answers.

- ☐ A   It affected language.
- ☐ B   It became a sign of prestige.
- ☐ C   It became a sign of intelligence.
- ☐ D   It affected fairy tales.

LinguaForum   Volume   **?** Help   Answer Confirm   ➡ **Next**

Time

15.   Why did the speaker compare the airplane to "golden coaches in fairy tales"?

- Ⓐ   Airplane technology is magical.
- Ⓑ   Air travel was initially prestigious.
- Ⓒ   Airplanes are expensive.
- Ⓓ   Air travel is popular.

LinguaForum   Volume   **?** Help   Answer Confirm   ➡ **Next**

Time

PRACTICE
TEST 10

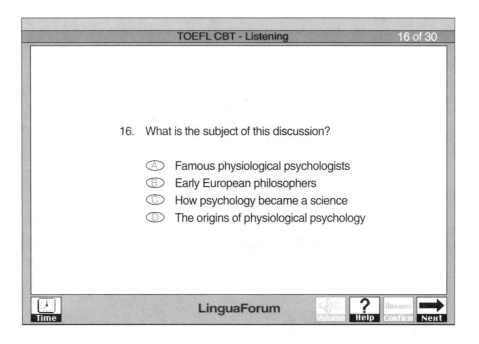

16. What is the subject of this discussion?

- (A) Famous physiological psychologists
- (B) Early European philosophers
- (C) How psychology became a science
- (D) The origins of physiological psychology

LinguaForum

Time | Volume | Help | Answer Confirm | Next

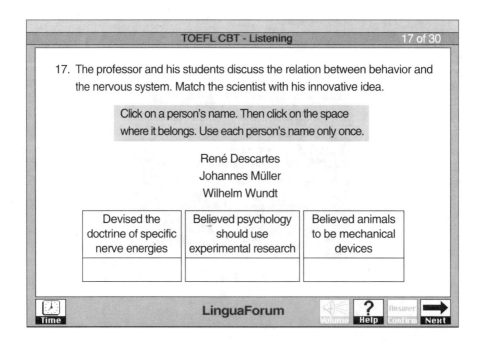

17. The professor and his students discuss the relation between behavior and the nervous system. Match the scientist with his innovative idea.

Click on a person's name. Then click on the space where it belongs. Use each person's name only once.

René Descartes
Johannes Müller
Wilhelm Wundt

Devised the doctrine of specific nerve energies	Believed psychology should use experimental research	Believed animals to be mechanical devices

LinguaForum

Time | Volume | Help | Answer Confirm | Next

18. What do psychologists today think about mind/body duality?

Click on 2 answers.

- [A] It is a useful tool, even if factually incorrect.
- [B] The world only consists of matter and energy.
- [C] It is a field of study much more complicated than in Descartes' time.
- [D] Scientists are no longer concerned with souls or non-material things.

Time

LinguaForum

Volume   **? Help**   Answer Confirm   **Next**

**PRACTICE
TEST 10**

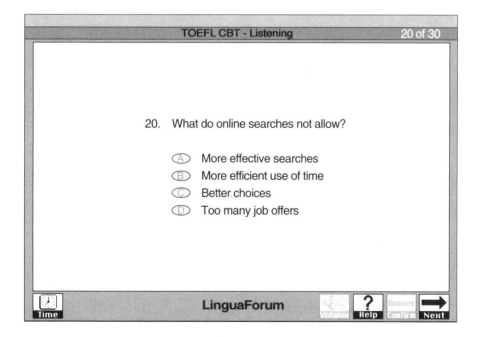

19. What is this dialogue about?

    Ⓐ Using search engines

    Ⓑ Online job searches

    Ⓒ Resumes

    Ⓓ Keywords

LinguaForum   Volume **?** Help Answer Confirm **➡** Next

Time

20. What do online searches not allow?

    Ⓐ More effective searches

    Ⓑ More efficient use of time

    Ⓒ Better choices

    Ⓓ Too many job offers

LinguaForum   Volume **?** Help Answer Confirm **➡** Next

Time

**PRACTICE
TEST 10**

Questions 21-25

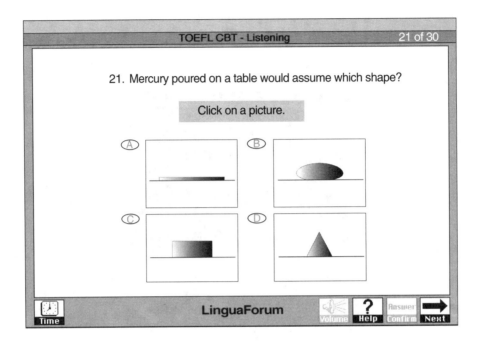

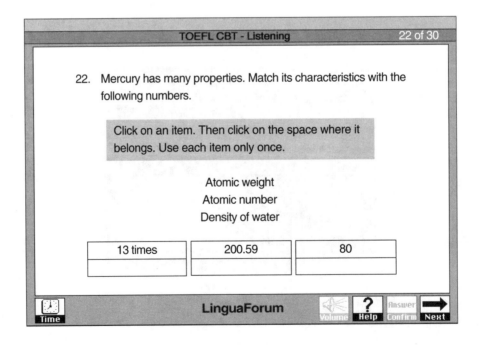

Listening

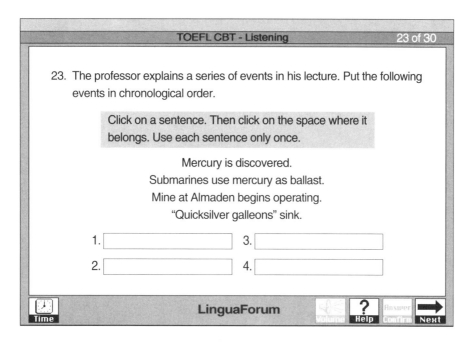

23. The professor explains a series of events in his lecture. Put the following events in chronological order.

Click on a sentence. Then click on the space where it belongs. Use each sentence only once.

Mercury is discovered.
Submarines use mercury as ballast.
Mine at Almaden begins operating.
"Quicksilver galleons" sink.

1. [　　　　　　]   3. [　　　　　　]
2. [　　　　　　]   4. [　　　　　　]

LinguaForum   Volume   Help   Confirm   Next   Time

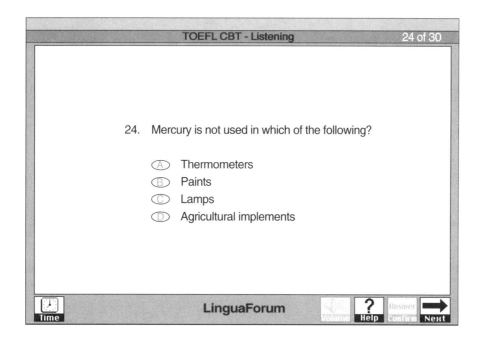

24. Mercury is not used in which of the following?

(A) Thermometers
(B) Paints
(C) Lamps
(D) Agricultural implements

LinguaForum   Volume   Help   Confirm   Next   Time

PRACTICE TEST 10

TOEFL CBT - Listening   25 of 30

25.   Mercury IS NOT

Click on 2 answers.

A   A metal
B   A solid at room temperature
C   Lighter than water
D   Used in insecticides

Time   LinguaForum   Volume   Help   Answer Confirm   Next

PRACTICE TEST 10

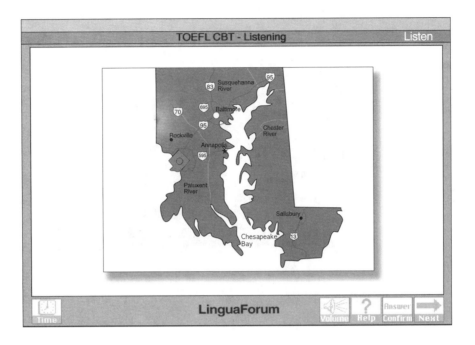

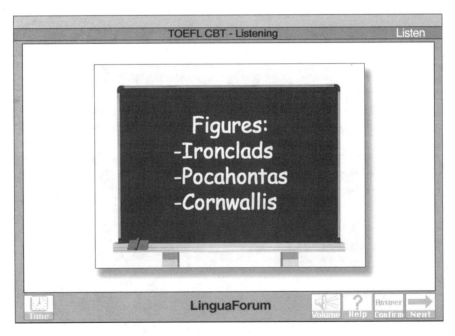

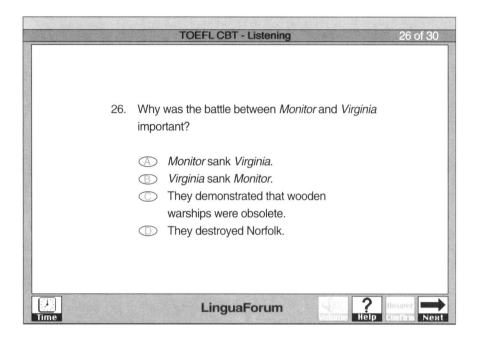

26. Why was the battle between *Monitor* and *Virginia* important?

  Ⓐ   *Monitor* sank *Virginia*.
  Ⓑ   *Virginia* sank *Monitor*.
  Ⓒ   They demonstrated that wooden warships were obsolete.
  Ⓓ   They destroyed Norfolk.

LinguaForum   Volume   Help   Confirm   Next

Time

PRACTICE
TEST 10

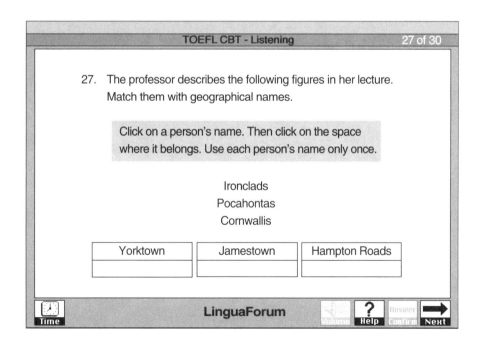

27. The professor describes the following figures in her lecture. Match them with geographical names.

Click on a person's name. Then click on the space where it belongs. Use each person's name only once.

Ironclads
Pocahontas
Cornwallis

Yorktown	Jamestown	Hampton Roads

LinguaForum   Volume   Help   Confirm   Next

Time

Listening

28. Which large cities are located in the Chesapeake Bay region?

Click on 2 answers.

A Seattle
B Denver
C Norfolk
D Baltimore

Time

LinguaForum

Volume Help Confirm Next

Listening

301

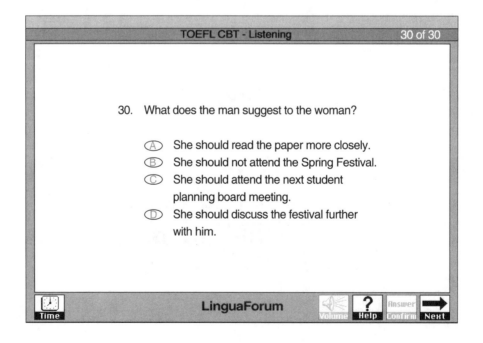

29. What can be inferred about the man?

- (A) He is not very interested in news about the university.
- (B) He thinks sports news is the most important kind of news.
- (C) He prefers to read about the university in a professional newspaper.
- (D) He wishes he knew more about the events of the university.

LinguaForum

30. What does the man suggest to the woman?

- (A) She should read the paper more closely.
- (B) She should not attend the Spring Festival.
- (C) She should attend the next student planning board meeting.
- (D) She should discuss the festival further with him.

LinguaForum

Test
10

SECTION 2
STRUCTURE
Suggested Time: 19 Minutes

PRACTICE
TEST 10

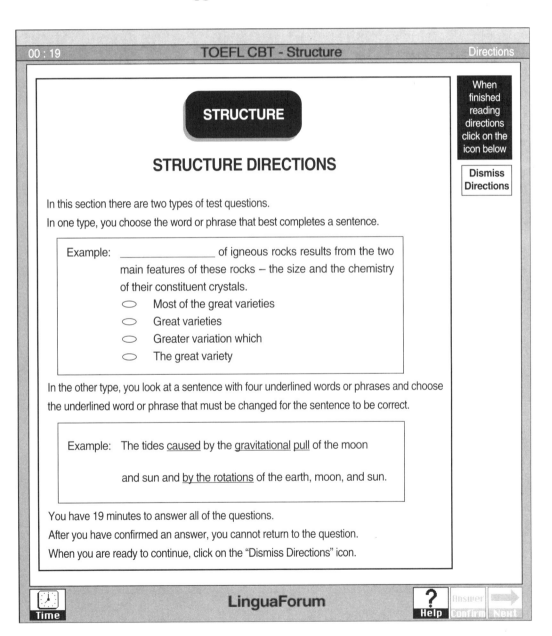

00 : 19   TOEFL CBT - Structure   Directions

STRUCTURE

When finished reading directions click on the icon below

Dismiss Directions

STRUCTURE DIRECTIONS

In this section there are two types of test questions.

In one type, you choose the word or phrase that best completes a sentence.

Example: _____ of igneous rocks results from the two main features of these rocks – the size and the chemistry of their constituent crystals.
- ○ Most of the great varieties
- ○ Great varieties
- ○ Greater variation which
- ○ The great variety

In the other type, you look at a sentence with four underlined words or phrases and choose the underlined word or phrase that must be changed for the sentence to be correct.

Example: The tides <u>caused</u> by the <u>gravitational</u> <u>pull</u> of the moon

and sun and <u>by the rotations</u> of the earth, moon, and sun.

You have 19 minutes to answer all of the questions.

After you have confirmed an answer, you cannot return to the question.

When you are ready to continue, click on the "Dismiss Directions" icon.

LinguaForum

?
Help   Answer Confirm Next

Time

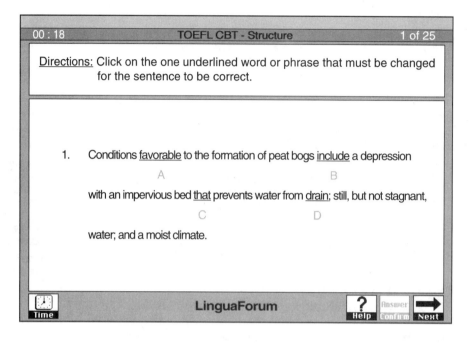

Directions: Click on the one underlined word or phrase that must be changed for the sentence to be correct.

1.   Conditions <u>favorable</u> to the formation of peat bogs <u>include</u> a depression
              A   B

with an impervious bed <u>that</u> prevents water from <u>drain</u>; still, but not stagnant,
                          C   D

water; and a moist climate.

LinguaForum

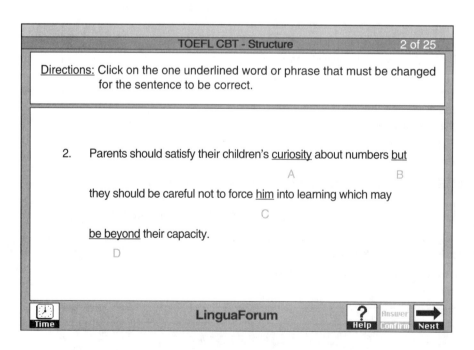

Directions: Click on the one underlined word or phrase that must be changed for the sentence to be correct.

2.   Parents should satisfy their children's <u>curiosity</u> about numbers <u>but</u>
                                              A   B

they should be careful not to force <u>him</u> into learning which may
                                     C

<u>be beyond</u> their capacity.
   D

LinguaForum

Structure

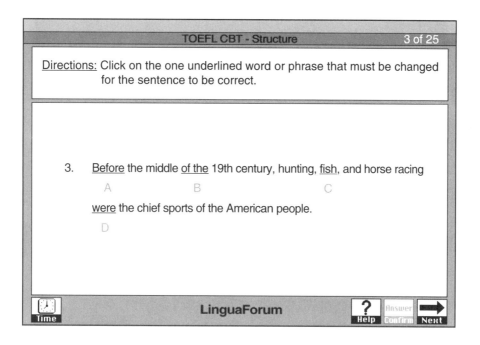

TOEFL CBT - Structure   3 of 25

Directions: Click on the one underlined word or phrase that must be changed
for the sentence to be correct.

3.   Before the middle of the 19th century, hunting, fish, and horse racing
          A   B   C

      were the chief sports of the American people.
          D

                          LinguaForum   ? Help Answer Confirm Next
Time

PRACTICE
TEST 10

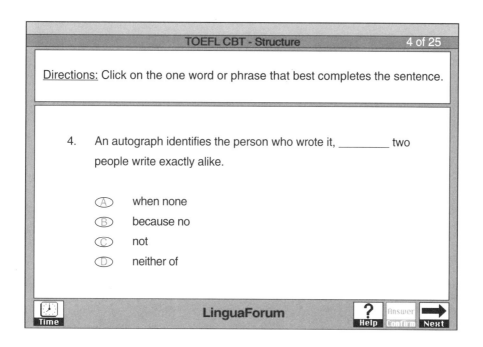

TOEFL CBT - Structure   4 of 25

Directions: Click on the one word or phrase that best completes the sentence.

4.   An autograph identifies the person who wrote it, _____ two
      people write exactly alike.

          Ⓐ   when none
          Ⓑ   because no
          Ⓒ   not
          Ⓓ   neither of

                          LinguaForum   ? Help Answer Confirm Next
Time

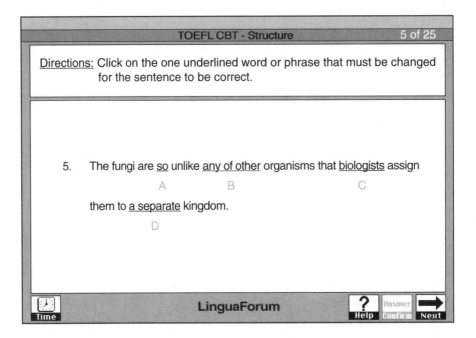

TOEFL CBT - Structure | 5 of 25

Directions: Click on the one underlined word or phrase that must be changed for the sentence to be correct.

5.   The fungi are <u>so</u> unlike <u>any of other</u> organisms that <u>biologists</u> assign
                              A   B   C

them to <u>a separate</u> kingdom.
                    D

Time   LinguaForum   ? Help Answer Confirm Next

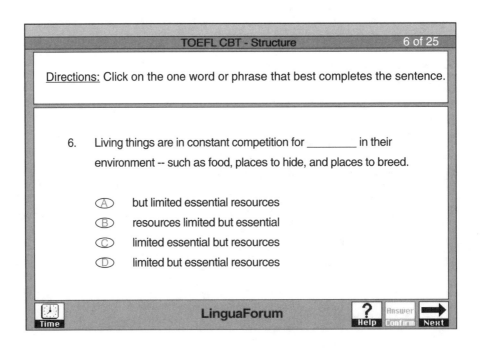

TOEFL CBT - Structure | 6 of 25

Directions: Click on the one word or phrase that best completes the sentence.

6.   Living things are in constant competition for _____ in their
        environment -- such as food, places to hide, and places to breed.

        Ⓐ   but limited essential resources
        Ⓑ   resources limited but essential
        Ⓒ   limited essential but resources
        Ⓓ   limited but essential resources

Time   LinguaForum   ? Help Answer Confirm Next

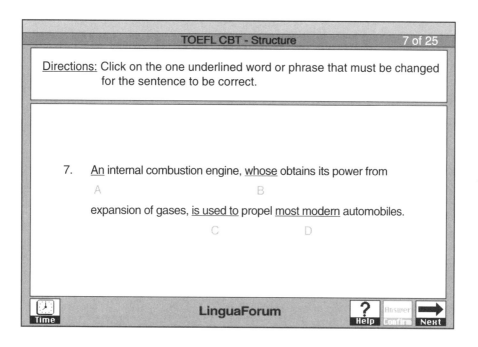

Directions: Click on the one underlined word or phrase that must be changed for the sentence to be correct.

7. <u>An</u> internal combustion engine, <u>whose</u> obtains its power from
       A   B

    expansion of gases, <u>is used to</u> propel <u>most modern</u> automobiles.
                         C   D

LinguaForum

Time   Help Confirm Next

PRACTICE
TEST 10

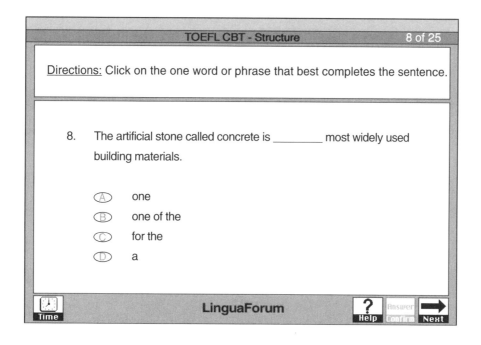

Directions: Click on the one word or phrase that best completes the sentence.

8. The artificial stone called concrete is _____ most widely used
    building materials.

    Ⓐ   one
    Ⓑ   one of the
    Ⓒ   for the
    Ⓓ   a

LinguaForum

Time   Help Confirm Next

Structure

<u>Directions:</u> Click on the one underlined word or phrase that must be changed for the sentence to be correct.

9.   Geography <u>is concerned</u> not only with the <u>distribution over</u> the face of
                      A   B

     the earth of physical things <u>or also</u> with the arrangement of people
                                   C

     and <u>their activities</u>.
           D

LinguaForum

? Help   Answer Confirm   ➡ Next

Time

<u>Directions:</u> Click on the one underlined word or phrase that must be changed for the sentence to be correct.

10.   Recorded history could not exist <u>until</u> men had invented methods of
                                 A

     writing and <u>had developed</u> an <u>accuracy</u> calendar <u>to measure</u> the
                    B   C   D

     passage of time.

LinguaForum

? Help   Answer Confirm   ➡ Next

Time

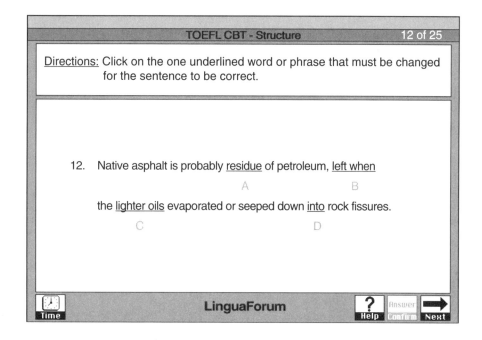

Directions: Click on the one word or phrase that best completes the sentence.

11. Seger cones are narrow pyramids about two inches high made

of various substances, _____ has a definite melting point.

- Ⓐ   which
- Ⓑ   each
- Ⓒ   each of which
- Ⓓ   they each

Time

LinguaForum

? **Answer**
Help **Confirm** **Next**

Directions: Click on the one underlined word or phrase that must be changed
for the sentence to be correct.

12. Native asphalt is probably <u>residue</u> of petroleum, <u>left when</u>

                   A   B

the <u>lighter oils</u> evaporated or seeped down <u>into</u> rock fissures.

           C   D

Time

LinguaForum

? **Answer**
Help **Confirm** **Next**

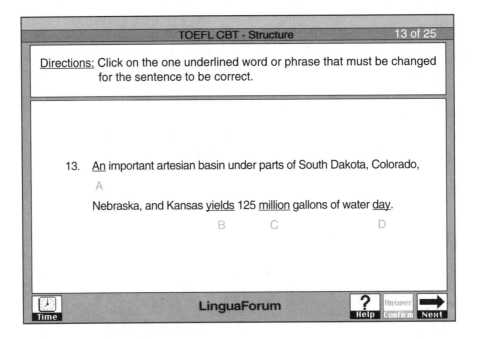

Directions: Click on the one underlined word or phrase that must be changed for the sentence to be correct.

13. <u>An</u> important artesian basin under parts of South Dakota, Colorado,
　　　A

Nebraska, and Kansas <u>yields</u> 125 <u>million</u> gallons of water <u>day</u>.
　　　　　　　　　　　B　　　　　C　　　　　　　　　D

LinguaForum

Time　Help　Confirm　Next

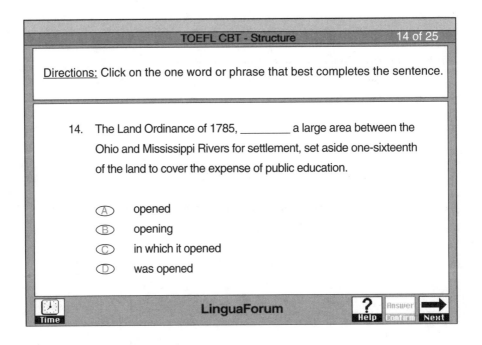

Directions: Click on the one word or phrase that best completes the sentence.

14. The Land Ordinance of 1785, _____ a large area between the Ohio and Mississippi Rivers for settlement, set aside one-sixteenth of the land to cover the expense of public education.

　(A)　opened
　(B)　opening
　(C)　in which it opened
　(D)　was opened

LinguaForum

Time　Help　Confirm　Next

Structure

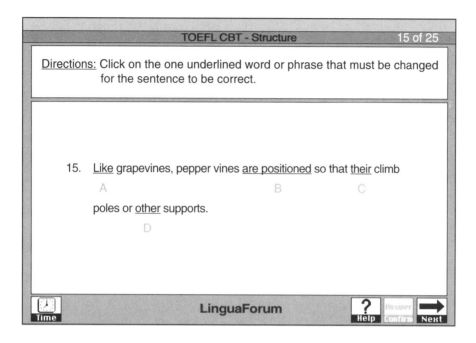

Directions: Click on the one underlined word or phrase that must be changed for the sentence to be correct.

15. Like grapevines, pepper vines are positioned so that their climb
     A   B   C

     poles or other supports.
              D

LinguaForum

? Help   Answer Confirm   Next

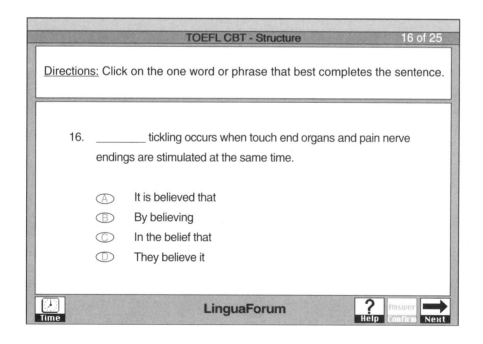

Directions: Click on the one word or phrase that best completes the sentence.

16. _____ tickling occurs when touch end organs and pain nerve
     endings are stimulated at the same time.

     Ⓐ   It is believed that
     Ⓑ   By believing
     Ⓒ   In the belief that
     Ⓓ   They believe it

LinguaForum

? Help   Answer Confirm   Next

PRACTICE
TEST 10

Structure

<u>Directions:</u> Click on the one underlined word or phrase that must be changed for the sentence to be correct.

17. <u>Dry</u> and desert land may <u>been turned</u> into gardens and pastures
      A   B

<u>by tapping</u> underground springs at a <u>depth</u> of sometimes nearly
      C   D

a mile.

LinguaForum

Time   ? **Help**   **Answer Confirm**   **Next**

<u>Directions:</u> Click on the one word or phrase that best completes the sentence.

18. _____ that carry engines with propellers to drive them through the air and rudders to steer them are called dirigibles or airships.

- (A) Balloons are
- (B) With balloons
- (C) Balloons
- (D) What balloons

LinguaForum

Time   ? **Help**   **Answer Confirm**   **Next**

Structure

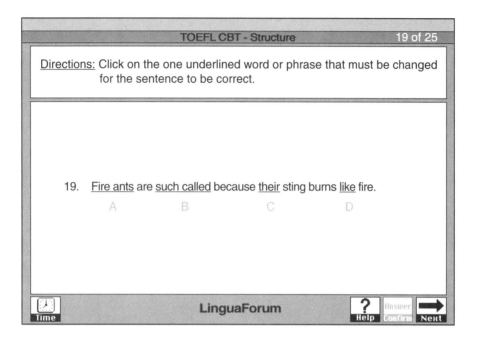

Directions: Click on the one underlined word or phrase that must be changed for the sentence to be correct.

19. Fire ants are such called because their sting burns like fire.
     A   B   C   D

LinguaForum

Time   Help Confirm Next

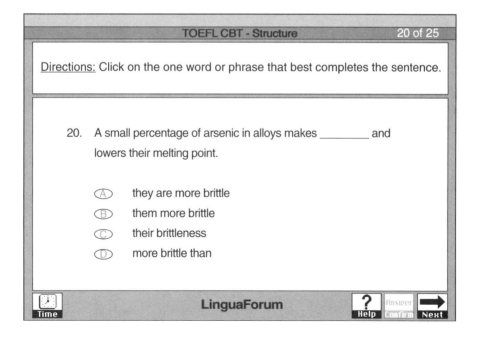

Directions: Click on the one word or phrase that best completes the sentence.

20. A small percentage of arsenic in alloys makes _____ and lowers their melting point.

     Ⓐ   they are more brittle
     Ⓑ   them more brittle
     Ⓒ   their brittleness
     Ⓓ   more brittle than

LinguaForum

Time   Help Confirm Next

Structure

<u>Directions:</u> Click on the one underlined word or phrase that must be changed
for the sentence to be correct.

21.   The heads of hunting <u>arrow</u> <u>were</u> oval <u>so</u> they could be
                                A   B   C

<u>withdrawn easily</u>.
        D

Time   **LinguaForum**   ?   Answer   ➡
                                                      Help Confirm Next

<u>Directions:</u> Click on the one word or phrase that best completes the sentence.

22.   Political maps _____ man-made, or cultural, features, such as the
      boundaries and location of nations, states, provinces, counties, and cities.

      Ⓐ   which emphasize
      Ⓑ   emphasize
      Ⓒ   emphasis on
      Ⓓ   to emphasize

Time   **LinguaForum**   ?   Answer   ➡
                                                      Help Confirm Next

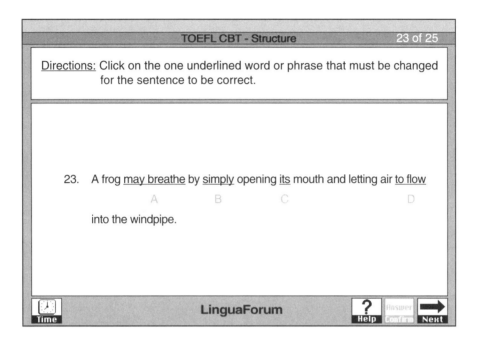

Directions: Click on the one underlined word or phrase that must be changed
for the sentence to be correct.

23.   A frog <u>may breathe</u> by <u>simply</u> opening <u>its</u> mouth and letting air <u>to flow</u>
              A   B   C   D

into the windpipe.

LinguaForum

Directions: Click on the one word or phrase that best completes the sentence.

24.   _____ their extreme hardness, diamonds have a number of
important industrial applications.

    (A)   Since
    (B)   Likewise
    (C)   Because of
    (D)   While

LinguaForum

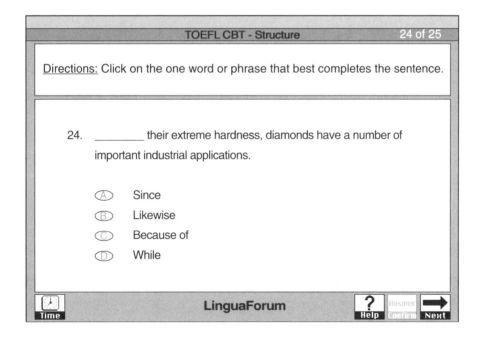

PRACTICE
TEST 10

Structure

Directions: Click on the one underlined word or phrase that must be changed for the sentence to be correct.

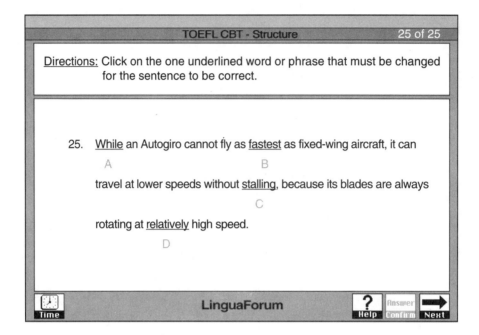

25. While an Autogiro cannot fly as fastest as fixed-wing aircraft, it can
    A   B

travel at lower speeds without stalling, because its blades are always
                                  C

rotating at relatively high speed.
            D

LinguaForum

Time   Help   Answer Confirm   Next

Test 10

SECTION 3
READING
Suggested Time: 90 Minutes

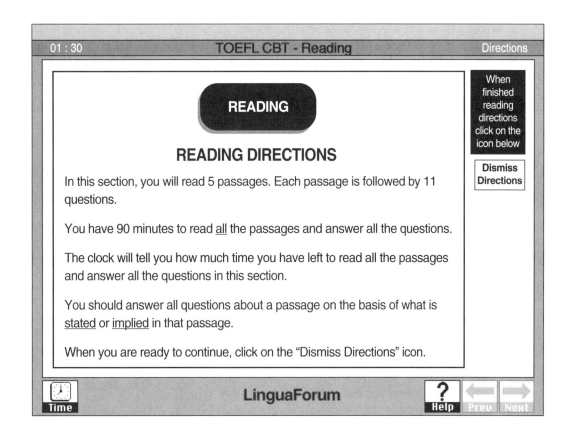

READING

READING DIRECTIONS

In this section, you will read 5 passages. Each passage is followed by 11 questions.

You have 90 minutes to read <u>all</u> the passages and answer all the questions.

The clock will tell you how much time you have left to read all the passages and answer all the questions in this section.

You should answer all questions about a passage on the basis of what is <u>stated</u> or <u>implied</u> in that passage.

When you are ready to continue, click on the "Dismiss Directions" icon.

When finished reading directions click on the icon below

Dismiss Directions

Time   **LinguaForum**   **Help** **Prev** **Next**

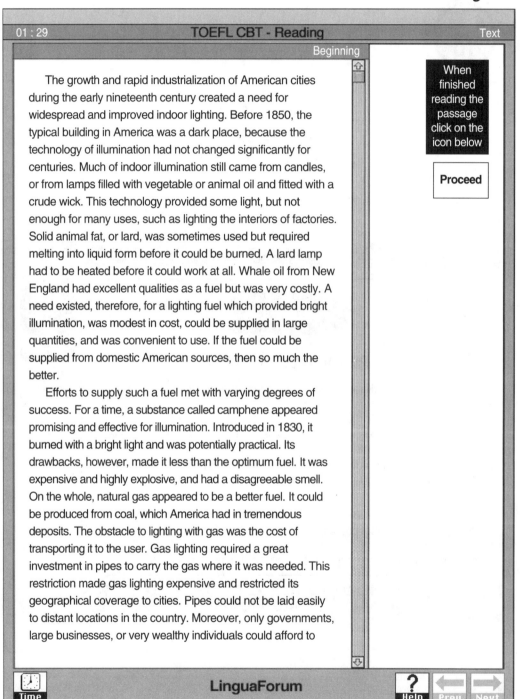

Passage 1

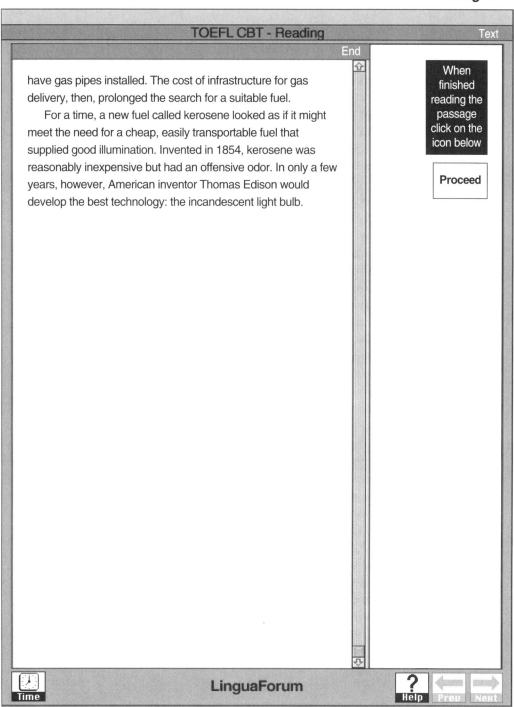

have gas pipes installed. The cost of infrastructure for gas delivery, then, prolonged the search for a suitable fuel.

For a time, a new fuel called kerosene looked as if it might meet the need for a cheap, easily transportable fuel that supplied good illumination. Invented in 1854, kerosene was reasonably inexpensive but had an offensive odor. In only a few years, however, American inventor Thomas Edison would develop the best technology: the incandescent light bulb.

When finished reading the passage click on the icon below

Proceed

LinguaForum

?
Help **Prev** **Next**

Time

PRACTICE
TEST 10

Reading

Passage 1

The growth and rapid industrialization of American cities during the early nineteenth century created a need for widespread and improved indoor lighting. Before 1850, the typical building in America was a dark place, because the technology of illumination had not changed significantly for centuries. Much of indoor illumination still came from candles, or from lamps filled with vegetable or animal oil and fitted with a crude wick. This technology provided some light, but not enough for many uses, such as lighting the interiors of factories. Solid animal fat, or lard, was sometimes used but required melting into liquid form before it could be burned. A lard lamp had to be heated before it could work at all. Whale oil from New England had excellent qualities as a fuel but was very costly. A need existed, therefore, for a lighting fuel which provided bright illumination, was modest in cost, could be supplied in large quantities, and was convenient to use. If the fuel could be supplied from domestic American sources, then so much the better.

Efforts to supply such a fuel met with varying degrees of success. For a time, a substance called camphene appeared promising and effective for illumination. Introduced in 1830, it burned with a bright light and was potentially practical. Its drawbacks, however, made it less than the optimum fuel. It was expensive and highly explosive, and had a disagreeable smell. On the whole, natural gas appeared to be a better fuel. It could be produced from coal, which America had in tremendous deposits. The obstacle to lighting with gas was the cost of transporting it to the user. Gas lighting required a great investment in pipes to carry the gas where it was needed. This restriction made gas lighting expensive and restricted its geographical coverage to cities. Pipes could not be laid easily to distant locations in the country. Moreover, only governments, large businesses, or very wealthy individuals could afford to

1. The passage is primarily concerned with
- (A) oil-burning lamps
- (B) the search for better illumination
- (C) why Edison succeeded
- (D) production of natural gas

LinguaForum

Reading

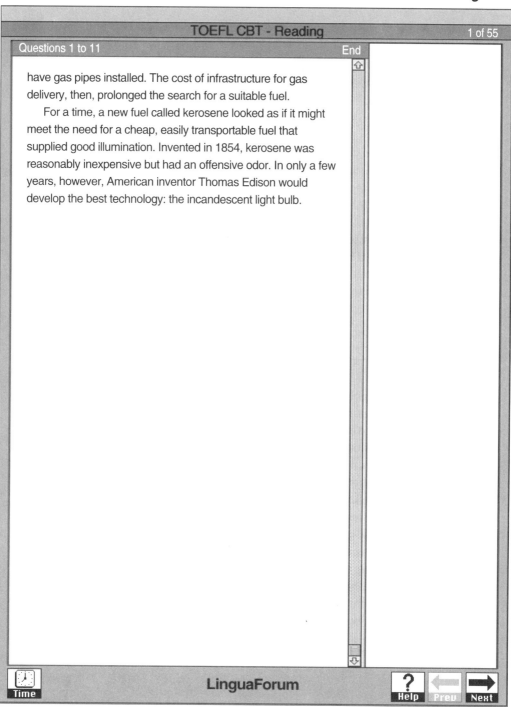

TOEFL CBT - Reading — 1 of 55

Questions 1 to 11 — End

have gas pipes installed. The cost of infrastructure for gas delivery, then, prolonged the search for a suitable fuel.

For a time, a new fuel called kerosene looked as if it might meet the need for a cheap, easily transportable fuel that supplied good illumination. Invented in 1854, kerosene was reasonably inexpensive but had an offensive odor. In only a few years, however, American inventor Thomas Edison would develop the best technology: the incandescent light bulb.

Time — LinguaForum — Help | Preu | Next

Reading

→ The growth and rapid industrialization of American cities during the early nineteenth century created a need for widespread and improved indoor lighting. Before 1850, the typical building in America was a dark place, because the technology of illumination had not changed significantly for centuries. ■ Much of indoor illumination still came from candles, or from lamps filled with vegetable or animal oil and fitted with a crude wick. This technology provided some light, but not enough for many uses, such as lighting the interiors of factories. ■ Solid animal fat, or lard, was sometimes used but required melting into liquid form before it could be burned. ■ A lard lamp had to be heated before it could work at all. Whale oil from New England had excellent qualities as a fuel but was very costly. ■ A need existed, therefore, for a lighting fuel which provided bright illumination, was modest in cost, could be supplied in large quantities, and was convenient to use. If the fuel could be supplied from domestic American sources, then so much the better. ■

→ **Efforts to supply such a fuel met with varying degrees of success. For a time, a substance called camphene appeared promising and effective for illumination. Introduced in 1830, it burned with a bright light and was potentially practical. Its drawbacks, however, made it less than the optimum fuel. ■ It was expensive and highly explosive, and had a disagreeable smell. On the whole, natural gas appeared to be a better fuel. ■ It could be produced from coal, which America had in tremendous deposits. The obstacle to lighting with gas was the cost of transporting it to the user. ■ Gas lighting required a great investment in pipes to carry the gas where it was needed. This restriction made gas lighting expensive and restricted its geographical coverage to cities. ■ Pipes could not be laid easily to distant locations in the country. Moreover, only**

2. Which properties did a good fuel require?

(A) It had to be low in cost.

(B) It could not burn with a bright flame.

(C) It required a strong odor.

(D) It had to be manufactured abroad.

3. Look at the word lighting in the passage. Click on the word or phrase in the bold text that is closest in meaning to lighting.

4. The following sentence can be added to paragraph 1 or 2.

The technology of illumination was still primitive.

Where would it best fit in the paragraph? Click on the square [■] to add the sentence to paragraph 1 or 2.
Paragraphs 1 and 2 are marked with an arrow [→].

Time   **LinguaForum**   ? ← →
                                                              Help Prev Next

Reading

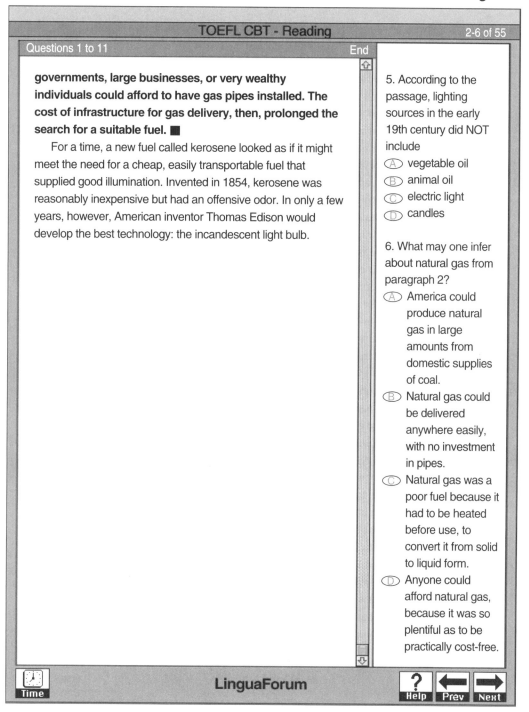

Questions 1 to 11   End

governments, large businesses, or very wealthy individuals could afford to have gas pipes installed. The cost of infrastructure for gas delivery, then, prolonged the search for a suitable fuel. ■

    For a time, a new fuel called kerosene looked as if it might meet the need for a cheap, easily transportable fuel that supplied good illumination. Invented in 1854, kerosene was reasonably inexpensive but had an offensive odor. In only a few years, however, American inventor Thomas Edison would develop the best technology: the incandescent light bulb.

5. According to the passage, lighting sources in the early 19th century did NOT include
- (A) vegetable oil
- (B) animal oil
- (C) electric light
- (D) candles

6. What may one infer about natural gas from paragraph 2?
- (A) America could produce natural gas in large amounts from domestic supplies of coal.
- (B) Natural gas could be delivered anywhere easily, with no investment in pipes.
- (C) Natural gas was a poor fuel because it had to be heated before use, to convert it from solid to liquid form.
- (D) Anyone could afford natural gas, because it was so plentiful as to be practically cost-free.

LinguaForum

Time   ? Help   ← Prev   → Next

Reading

Passage 1

Questions 1 to 11   Beginning

The growth and rapid industrialization of American cities during the early nineteenth century created a need for widespread and improved indoor lighting. Before 1850, the typical building in America was a dark place, because the technology of illumination had not changed significantly for centuries. Much of indoor illumination still came from candles, or from lamps filled with vegetable or animal oil and fitted with a crude wick. This technology provided some light, but not enough for many uses, such as lighting the interiors of factories. Solid animal fat, or lard, was sometimes used but required melting into liquid form before it could be burned. A lard lamp had to be heated before it could work at all. Whale oil from New England had excellent qualities as a fuel but was very costly. A need existed, therefore, for a lighting fuel which provided bright illumination, was modest in cost, could be supplied in large quantities, and was convenient to use. If the fuel could be supplied from domestic American sources, then so much the better.

Efforts to supply such a fuel met with varying degrees of success. For a time, a substance called camphene appeared promising and effective for illumination. Introduced in 1830, it burned with a bright light and was potentially practical. Its drawbacks, however, made it less than the optimum fuel. It was expensive and highly explosive, and had a disagreeable smell. On the whole, natural gas appeared to be a better fuel. It could be produced from coal, which America had in tremendous deposits. The obstacle to lighting with gas was the cost of transporting it to the user. Gas lighting required a great investment in pipes to carry the gas where it was needed. This restriction made gas lighting expensive and restricted its geographical coverage to cities. Pipes could not be laid easily to distant locations in the country. Moreover, only

7. Which of the following could best replace the word potentially in the passage?
Ⓐ Effectively
Ⓑ Promisingly
Ⓒ Clearly
Ⓓ Surely

8. Look at the word it in the passage. Click on the word or phrase in the **bold** text that it refers to.

9. Which of the following could best replace the word practical in the passage?
Ⓐ Actual
Ⓑ Promising
Ⓒ Speculative
Ⓓ Useful

Reading

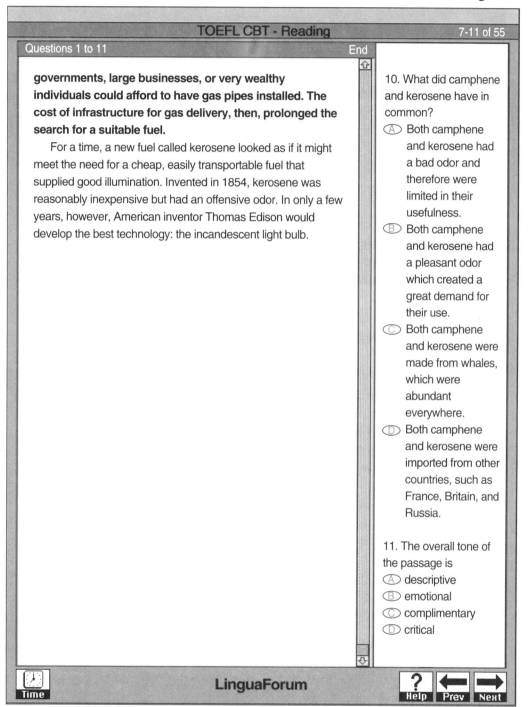

Questions 1 to 11 | End

governments, large businesses, or very wealthy individuals could afford to have gas pipes installed. The cost of infrastructure for gas delivery, then, prolonged the search for a suitable fuel.

For a time, a new fuel called kerosene looked as if it might meet the need for a cheap, easily transportable fuel that supplied good illumination. Invented in 1854, kerosene was reasonably inexpensive but had an offensive odor. In only a few years, however, American inventor Thomas Edison would develop the best technology: the incandescent light bulb.

10. What did camphene and kerosene have in common?

Ⓐ Both camphene and kerosene had a bad odor and therefore were limited in their usefulness.

Ⓑ Both camphene and kerosene had a pleasant odor which created a great demand for their use.

Ⓒ Both camphene and kerosene were made from whales, which were abundant everywhere.

Ⓓ Both camphene and kerosene were imported from other countries, such as France, Britain, and Russia.

11. The overall tone of the passage is

Ⓐ descriptive

Ⓑ emotional

Ⓒ complimentary

Ⓓ critical

Time

LinguaForum

? Help **← Prev** **→ Next**

PRACTICE TEST 10

Passage 2

The largest group of marine mammals is the cetaceans, the whales, dolphins and porpoises. No group of marine animals has captured our imaginations like the dolphins and whales. They have inspired countless legends and works of art and literature. The rescue of whales stranded on a beach or the birth of a killer whale in a oceanarium brings out strong emotions in all of us.

➡ Of all marine mammals, the cetaceans have made the most complete transition to aquatic life. ■ Whereas most other marine mammals return to land at least part of the time, cetaceans spend their entire lives in the water. ■ **Their bodies are streamlined and look remarkably fish-like. This is a dramatic example of convergent evolution, where different species develop similar structures because they have similar lifestyles. ■ Although they superficially resemble fishes, cetaceans breathe air and will drown if trapped below the surface. They are "warm blooded," have hair, though scanty, and produce milk for their young. ■**

➡ Cetaceans have a pair of front flippers, but the rear pair of limbs has disappeared. ■ Actually, the rear limbs are present in the embryo but fail to develop. In adults they remain only as small, useless bones. Like fishes, many cetaceans have a dorsal fin. ■ The muscular tail ends in a pair of fin-like, horizontal flukes. ■ Blubber provides insulation and buoyancy; body hair is practically absent. ■ Rather than being on the front of the head, the nostrils are on top, forming a single or double opening called the blowhole. ■

There are around 90 species of cetaceans. They are all marine except for five species of freshwater dolphins. Cetaceans are divided into two groups: the toothless, filter-feeding whales and the toothed, carnivorous whales, a group that includes the dolphins and porpoises.

The toothless whales are better known as the baleen whales. Instead of teeth they have rows of flexible, fibrous plates named baleen that hang from the upper jaw. Baleen is made of the same material as our hair and nails.

LinguaForum

Time   Help Prev Next

Reading

12. Which of the following would be the best title for the passage?
    - Ⓐ The Lovable Creatures of the Sea
    - Ⓑ The Story of the Cetaceans
    - Ⓒ Man's Best Friends: the Cetaceans
    - Ⓓ Endangered Species: the Cetaceans

13. Dolphins and whales
    - Ⓐ were once feared and thus avoided
    - Ⓑ appeal emotionally to people of all ages
    - Ⓒ are fast becoming extinct
    - Ⓓ are often found in aquariums

14. The cetaceans are known for their
    - Ⓐ strength
    - Ⓑ intelligence
    - Ⓒ size
    - Ⓓ friendliness

15. The passage supports which of the following statements?
    - Ⓐ Cetaceans live both on land and under the sea.
    - Ⓑ Cetaceans are not fishes.
    - Ⓒ Cetaceans are hairy creatures.
    - Ⓓ Cetaceans evolved into fishes.

16. Look at the word they in the passage. Click on the word or phrase in the **bold** text that they refers to.

17. Fishes and cetaceans are examples of convergent evolution because
    - Ⓐ they both share similar lifestyles
    - Ⓑ they both exhibit similar breathing patterns
    - Ⓒ they both share similar structures
    - Ⓓ they both live under the sea

18. Which of the following could best replace the word rear in the passage?
    - Ⓐ Lateral
    - Ⓑ Top
    - Ⓒ Side
    - Ⓓ Back

19. The following sentence can be added to paragraph 2 or 3.

    Cetacean nostrils differ from those of other mammals.

    Where would it best fit in the paragraph? Click on the square [■] to add the sentence to paragraph 2 or 3.
    Paragraphs 2 and 3 are marked with an arrow [➡].

20. The blowhole serves
    - Ⓐ to swim faster
    - Ⓑ to expel waste
    - Ⓒ for respiration
    - Ⓓ for signaling to fellow creatures

21. The word insulation in the passage is closest in meaning to
    - Ⓐ comfort
    - Ⓑ protection
    - Ⓒ nourishment
    - Ⓓ energy

22. All of the following describe baleen EXCEPT that
    - Ⓐ certain toothless whales are named after the fibrous plates
    - Ⓑ baleen whales are filter-feeding whales
    - Ⓒ dolphins and porpoises have rows of flexible, fibrous plates
    - Ⓓ baleen is made of the same material as human hair

PRACTICE TEST 10

Reading

Passage 3

➡ In the 19th century, railroads initiated a revolution in transportation in the United States. That revolution continued in the 20th century with the development of the mass-produced, affordable private automobile and a nationwide system of highways designed for cars. ■ Although American manufacturer Henry Ford is often given credit for inventing the automobile, early autos had been running in Europe for years when he transformed the automobile from a mechanical curiosity into an indispensable product: a standardized vehicle, produced by the millions, which even consumers with modest incomes could afford. ■ That product, in turn, transformed America by carrying the transportation revolution a tremendous step farther. ■ Railway trains in the 1800s had provided a means to move large numbers of people from one place to another. ■ Now automobiles supplied a way to give individuals unprecedented mobility, and to travel almost anywhere suitably firm, level ground existed. ■

➡ The impact of this new mode of transportation was all but incalculable, in both its economic and the social aspects. At first, the automobile was a symbol of status. An automobile advertised an individual's importance and sophistication, in much the same way that an advanced home computer system would serve as a status symbol in the late 1900s. The automobile also had a major influence on professions and trades. ■ A doctor making house calls by automobile became a familiar sight. A farmer with a truck could carry perishable produce to the city before it spoiled. Autos provided a quick, easy, and reliable way to travel all the way across a large city, or between the city and the country. The auto did not get sick or suffer exhaustion, as a horse might. ■ Standardized parts made repairs fast and easy. ■ In short, the private automobile was the missing piece which America had needed, so to speak, to give Americans true mobility. ■ Once that piece was in place, the United States became the most mobile society in history. The effect of automobiles, and the freedom of movement they provided, was felt everywhere; in other words, the "car culture" had arrived. ■

As Ford's machines put highway travel within the reach of almost everyone, America required a whole new infrastructure to support it. The country already had paved streets in its cities. Next, America needed a nationwide network of highways suitable for automobiles: paved arteries, or at least roads covered with gravel, on which cars could travel even in rainy weather without becoming trapped in mud. This network was quick to arrive. By the 1930s, it was possible to travel across much of the U.S. by car on paved highways. Yet the success of automobiles created a problem of congestion. The expression "traffic jam" entered the American language as automobile traffic increased. By the 1950s, the U.S. government could see that the nation faced a crisis in highway travel. A new system was needed; and the federal government took the lead in providing it. As an Interstate Highway System took shape on paper, the letter "I" was about to take on a new significance.

Time   **LinguaForum**   **?** **←** **→**
                                                                  Help **Prev** **Next**

Reading

23. Which of the following would be the best title for this passage?
    Ⓐ The Automobile and the Transportation Revolution in America
    Ⓑ American Farmers and the Automobile Culture
    Ⓒ Henry Ford as a Typical U.S. Manufacturer
    Ⓓ The Advantages of Standardized Auto Parts

24. Look at the word tremendous in the passage. Click on the word or phrase in the **bold** text which is OPPOSITE in meaning to tremendous.

25. It can be inferred from the passage that Henry Ford
    Ⓐ had helped create the railway network of the 1800s
    Ⓑ did not himself invent the automobile
    Ⓒ personally assembled all the automobiles produced in his factory
    Ⓓ hated horses and wanted to make them extinct

26. The following sentence can be added to paragraph 1 or 2.

    Where such conditions existed, motorists would no longer be tied to train schedules and railway routes; thanks to the automobile, one could simply get in the car and go nearly anywhere the terrain permitted.

    Where would it best fit in the paragraph? Click on the square [■] to add the sentence to paragraph 1 or 2.
    Paragraphs 1 and 2 are marked with an arrow [➡].

27. According to the passage, the automobile did NOT
    Ⓐ provide a symbol of status
    Ⓑ carry doctors on house calls
    Ⓒ help farmers transport perishable produce
    Ⓓ make Henry Ford president of the United States

28. Look at the word influence in the passage. Click on the word or phrase in the **bold** text which is closest in meaning to influence.

29. The phrase "car culture" in the passage describes
    Ⓐ the factory where Henry Ford's automobiles were assembled
    Ⓑ railway boxcars on which automobiles were transported to dealers
    Ⓒ the influence of automobiles and the freedom of movement they provided
    Ⓓ the educational level of the average motorist

30. Paragraph 2 supports paragraph 1 by explaining in detail
    Ⓐ the impact of automobiles on American society
    Ⓑ how automobiles were manufactured
    Ⓒ what early automobiles looked like
    Ⓓ how Henry Ford became a leading manufacturer

31. The word it in the passage most likely refers to
    Ⓐ America
    Ⓑ travel
    Ⓒ infrastructure
    Ⓓ culture

32. The phrase "traffic jam" in the passage is mentioned to provide an example of
    Ⓐ how automobiles affected the American language
    Ⓑ an expression invented by Henry Ford
    Ⓒ how newspapers described the emerging car culture
    Ⓓ how automobiles replaced railways as a leading means of travel

33. The paragraph after this passage most likely describes
    Ⓐ the emergence of private aircraft in the 20th century
    Ⓑ how automobiles transformed city planning in Los Angeles
    Ⓒ the construction of the huge Interstate Highway System
    Ⓓ how policemen dispersed traffic jams

Reading

Passage 4

➡ By photosynthesis, living systems incorporate carbon dioxide from the atmosphere into organic compounds. ■ In respiration, these compounds are broken down again into carbon dioxide and water. ■ These processes, viewed on a worldwide scale, result in the carbon cycle. The principal photosynthesizers in this cycle are plants and the phytoplankton, the marine algae. ■ They synthesize carbohydrates from carbon dioxide and water and release oxygen into the atmosphere. ■

➡ Some of the carbohydrates are used by the photosynthesizers themselves. ■ Plants release carbon dioxide from their roots and leaves, and marine algae release it into the water where it maintains an equilibrium with the carbon dioxide in the air. ■ Some of the carbohydrates are used by animals that feed on the living plants, on algae, and on one another, discharging carbon dioxide. ■ An enormous amount of carbon is contained in the dead bodies of plants and other organisms plus discarded leaves and shells, feces, and other waste materials that settle into the soil or sink to the ocean floors where they are consumed by small invertebrates, bacteria and fungi. ■ Carbon dioxide is also released by these processes into the reservoir of the air and oceans. ■

The natural processes of photosynthesis and respiration generally balance one another out. Over the long span of geologic time, the carbon dioxide concentration of the atmosphere has varied, but for the last 10,000 years it has remained relatively constant. By volume, it is a very small proportion of the atmosphere, only about 0.03 percent. It is important, however, because carbon dioxide, unlike most other components of the atmosphere, absorbs heat from the sun's rays. Since 1850, carbon dioxide concentrations in the atmosphere have been increasing, due to the use of fossil fuels, plowing of the soil, and destruction of forest land. A recent study predicts that the increase in carbon dioxide will increase the average temperature. The consequences cannot be known with certainty. In some parts of the world, there may be increased precipitation, while in other parts of the world, there may be lowered precipitation.

LinguaForum

Reading

34. With what topic is the passage mainly concerned?
    - Ⓐ The life cycle
    - Ⓑ Photosynthesis and life on Earth
    - Ⓒ Secrets of the atmosphere
    - Ⓓ The carbon cycle

35. Photosynthesis produces
    - Ⓐ carbohydrates
    - Ⓑ oxygen
    - Ⓒ carbon dioxide
    - Ⓓ water

36. Look at the word it in the passage. Click on the word or phrase in the **bold** text to which it refers.

37. Which of the following statements is true?
    - Ⓐ The carbon cycle consists of absorbing carbon dioxide from the atmosphere.
    - Ⓑ Other organisms besides plants and marine algae synthesize carbohydrates.
    - Ⓒ The organic compounds produced during photosynthesis consist of carbon dioxide and water.
    - Ⓓ In respiration, photosynthesizers release carbohydrates into the air.

38. The word discarded in the passage is closest in meaning to
    - Ⓐ rejected
    - Ⓑ useless
    - Ⓒ refined
    - Ⓓ discharged

39. Carbon is found in all of the following EXCEPT
    - Ⓐ ocean floors
    - Ⓑ ozone
    - Ⓒ waste
    - Ⓓ dead plants

40. Look at the word consumed in the passage. Click on the word or phrase in the **bold** text that is OPPOSITE in meaning to consumed.

41. The increase of heat is due to the
    - Ⓐ imbalance of carbon dioxide in the atmosphere and in the water
    - Ⓑ destruction of forest lands and the increase of pollution
    - Ⓒ decrease of oxygen release by plants into the atmosphere
    - Ⓓ high concentration of carbon dioxide in dead plants, waste, and shells

42. The tone of the author in paragraph 3 is
    - Ⓐ optimistic
    - Ⓑ pessimistic
    - Ⓒ cautious
    - Ⓓ conclusive

43. Click on the sentence that mentions the time that concentration of carbon dioxide has remained constant.

    Scroll the entire passage to see all of the paragraphs.

44. The following sentence can be added to paragraph 1 or 2.

    About 100 billion metric tons of carbon per year are bound into carbon compounds by photosynthesis.

    Where would it best fit in the paragraph? Click on the square [■] to add the sentence to paragraph 1 or 2.
    Paragraphs 1 and 2 are marked with an arrow [➡].

Paintings like the one by Christian Schussele entitled *Washington Irving and His Literary Friends at Sunnyside*, which depicts an astonishing number of elegantly clad notables in Irving's snug study, capture the fact that in the nineteenth century the American literary world was very small indeed, so narrow that most of the writers in this period knew each other, often intimately, or else knew much about each other. They lived, if not in each other's pockets, at least in each other's houses, or boardinghouses: Lemuel Shaw, from 1830 to 1860 chief justice of the Massachusetts Supreme Court and Herman Melville's father-in-law after 1847 for a time stayed in a Boston boardinghouse run by Ralph Waldo Emerson's widowed mother.

➡ Such intimacy was inevitable in a country which had only a few literary and publishing centers, all of them along the Atlantic seaboard. ■ Despite the acquisition of the Louisiana Territory from France in 1803 and the vast Southwest from Mexico in 1848, most of the writers lived all their lives in the original thirteen states, except for trips abroad, and their practical experience was of a compact country. ■

➡ Improvements in transportation occurred gradually and eventually shrank the country while territorial gains were enlarging it. ■ By the 1830s and 40s, railroads and steamboats were available, and such a literary figure as Whitman found himself using the steamboat, railroad and coach as he traveled slowly to New Orleans. ■ Despite frequent train wrecks, steamboat explosions and Atlantic shipwrecks, by the 1850s travel had ceased to be the hazardous adventure it once had been. ■ But the few American writers who saw much of the country were still provincials in their practical attitude toward their literary careers, for their publishers and purchasers were concentrated mainly in or near New York, Philadelphia and Boston. ■

LinguaForum

Reading

45. The main subject of the passage is
   - Ⓐ the US transportation system in the nineteenth century
   - Ⓑ the US literary world of the nineteenth century
   - Ⓒ the US literary dominance in the nineteenth century
   - Ⓓ major US literary figures of the nineteenth century

46. Look at the word small in the passage. Click on the word or phrase in the **bold** text that is closest to small.

47. The first paragraph suggests that
   - Ⓐ the literary circle was too small
   - Ⓑ the literary circle was too elitist
   - Ⓒ besides the literary circles, the elites of the period were well acquainted
   - Ⓓ the literary circle was far too intimate

48. The passage mentions the work of Schussele in order to
   - Ⓐ prove that the painter was famous
   - Ⓑ show that the camera did not exist
   - Ⓒ illustrate that literary figures were well acquainted
   - Ⓓ prove that portraits were popular at the time

49. Look at the word They in the passage. Click on the word or phrase in the **bold** text that They refers to.

50. The following sentence can be added to paragraph 2 or 3.

   Completed in 1825, the Erie Canal made possible transportation by steamboat.

   Where would it best fit in the paragraph? Click on the square [■] to add the sentence to paragraph 2 or 3.
   Paragraphs 2 and 3 are marked with an arrow [➡].

51. The second paragraph suggests that
   - Ⓐ the US made every effort to expand its territory
   - Ⓑ the US was hostile to its European neighbors
   - Ⓒ the US was largely occupied by Europeans during the eighteenth century
   - Ⓓ the US had no ambition to expand itself

52. Look at the word gradually in the passage. Click on the word or phrase in the **bold** text that best replaces gradually.

53. The center of US culture and politics during the nineteenth century was
   - Ⓐ Boston
   - Ⓑ New York
   - Ⓒ the east coast
   - Ⓓ Philadelphia

54. The passage mentions all of the following modes of transportation EXCEPT
   - Ⓐ trains
   - Ⓑ steamboats
   - Ⓒ coaches
   - Ⓓ sleighs

55. American writers of the nineteenth century remained on the East coast because
   - Ⓐ they disliked traveling
   - Ⓑ publishers and readers were all concentrated in Boston, New York and Philadelphia
   - Ⓒ traveling was too tiring and dangerous
   - Ⓓ outside the east coast, the literacy rate was low

PRACTICE
TEST 10

SECTION 4
WRITING
Suggested Time: 30 Minutes

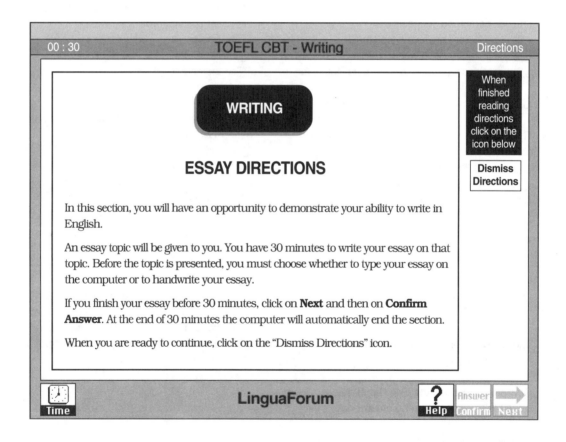

Writing

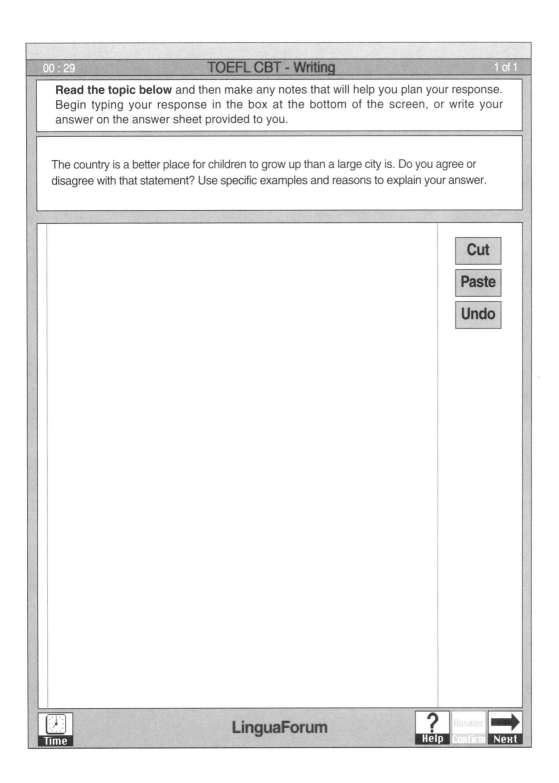

PRACTICE
TEST 10

Practice Test 11

Listening: 60 Minutes (including listening time)
Structure: 15 Minutes
Reading: 70 Minutes
Writing: 30 Minutes

Suggested Total Time: 175 Minutes

ANSWER SHEET

Lingua TOEFL® CBT Test Book II
PRACTICE TEST 11

Name	
Sex	☐ male ☐ female
E-mail address	
Telephone No.	

No. of Correct Answers/Converted Score		
Listening		
Structure		
Reading		
Writing		
TOTAL		

Section 1: Listening

1. Ⓐ Ⓑ Ⓒ Ⓓ
2. Ⓐ Ⓑ Ⓒ Ⓓ
3. Ⓐ Ⓑ Ⓒ Ⓓ
4. Ⓐ Ⓑ Ⓒ Ⓓ
5. Ⓐ Ⓑ Ⓒ Ⓓ
6. Ⓐ Ⓑ Ⓒ Ⓓ
7. Ⓐ Ⓑ Ⓒ Ⓓ
8. Ⓐ Ⓑ Ⓒ Ⓓ
9. Ⓐ Ⓑ Ⓒ Ⓓ
10. Ⓐ Ⓑ Ⓒ Ⓓ
11. Ⓐ Ⓑ Ⓒ Ⓓ
12. Ⓐ Ⓑ Ⓒ Ⓓ
13. Ⓐ Ⓑ Ⓒ Ⓓ
14. Ⓐ Ⓑ Ⓒ Ⓓ
15. Ⓐ Ⓑ Ⓒ Ⓓ
16. Ⓐ Ⓑ Ⓒ Ⓓ
17. Ⓐ Ⓑ Ⓒ Ⓓ
18. Ⓐ Ⓑ Ⓒ Ⓓ
19. Ⓐ Ⓑ Ⓒ Ⓓ
20.

She discovered ...

21. Ⓐ Ⓑ Ⓒ Ⓓ
22. Ⓐ Ⓑ Ⓒ Ⓓ
23. Ⓐ Ⓑ Ⓒ Ⓓ
24. Ⓐ Ⓑ Ⓒ Ⓓ
25. Ⓐ Ⓑ Ⓒ Ⓓ
26. Ⓐ Ⓑ Ⓒ Ⓓ
27. Ⓐ Ⓑ Ⓒ Ⓓ
28. Ⓐ Ⓑ Ⓒ Ⓓ
29. Ⓐ Ⓑ Ⓒ Ⓓ
30. Ⓐ Ⓑ Ⓒ Ⓓ
31.
32. Ⓐ Ⓑ Ⓒ Ⓓ
33. Ⓐ Ⓑ Ⓒ Ⓓ
34.

35. Frederick Olmsted –
    Andrew Downing –
    William Bryant –
36. Ⓐ Ⓑ Ⓒ Ⓓ
37. Ⓐ Ⓑ Ⓒ Ⓓ
38. Ⓐ Ⓑ Ⓒ Ⓓ
39. Ⓐ Ⓑ Ⓒ Ⓓ
40. Ⓐ Ⓑ Ⓒ Ⓓ
41.

42. Ⓐ Ⓑ Ⓒ Ⓓ
43. Ⓐ Ⓑ Ⓒ Ⓓ
44. Ⓐ Ⓑ Ⓒ Ⓓ
45. Ⓐ Ⓑ Ⓒ Ⓓ
46.

47. Ⓐ Ⓑ Ⓒ Ⓓ
48. Ⓐ Ⓑ Ⓒ Ⓓ
49. Ⓐ Ⓑ Ⓒ Ⓓ
50. Ⓐ Ⓑ Ⓒ Ⓓ

Section 2: Structure

1. Ⓐ Ⓑ Ⓒ Ⓓ
2. Ⓐ Ⓑ Ⓒ Ⓓ
3. Ⓐ Ⓑ Ⓒ Ⓓ
4. Ⓐ Ⓑ Ⓒ Ⓓ
5. Ⓐ Ⓑ Ⓒ Ⓓ
6. Ⓐ Ⓑ Ⓒ Ⓓ
7. Ⓐ Ⓑ Ⓒ Ⓓ
8. Ⓐ Ⓑ Ⓒ Ⓓ
9. Ⓐ Ⓑ Ⓒ Ⓓ
10. Ⓐ Ⓑ Ⓒ Ⓓ
11. Ⓐ Ⓑ Ⓒ Ⓓ
12. Ⓐ Ⓑ Ⓒ Ⓓ
13. Ⓐ Ⓑ Ⓒ Ⓓ
14. Ⓐ Ⓑ Ⓒ Ⓓ
15. Ⓐ Ⓑ Ⓒ Ⓓ
16. Ⓐ Ⓑ Ⓒ Ⓓ
17. Ⓐ Ⓑ Ⓒ Ⓓ
18. Ⓐ Ⓑ Ⓒ Ⓓ
19. Ⓐ Ⓑ Ⓒ Ⓓ
20. Ⓐ Ⓑ Ⓒ Ⓓ

Section 3: Reading

1. Ⓐ Ⓑ Ⓒ Ⓓ
2.
3.
4. Ⓐ Ⓑ Ⓒ Ⓓ
5. Ⓐ Ⓑ Ⓒ Ⓓ
6. Ⓐ Ⓑ Ⓒ Ⓓ
7.
8. Ⓐ Ⓑ Ⓒ Ⓓ
9.
10. Ⓐ Ⓑ Ⓒ Ⓓ
11. Ⓐ Ⓑ Ⓒ Ⓓ
12. Ⓐ Ⓑ Ⓒ Ⓓ
13. Ⓐ Ⓑ Ⓒ Ⓓ
14.
15. Ⓐ Ⓑ Ⓒ Ⓓ
16.
17. Ⓐ Ⓑ Ⓒ Ⓓ
18.
19. Ⓐ Ⓑ Ⓒ Ⓓ
20. Ⓐ Ⓑ Ⓒ Ⓓ
21.
22. Ⓐ Ⓑ Ⓒ Ⓓ
23. Ⓐ Ⓑ Ⓒ Ⓓ
24.
25. Ⓐ Ⓑ Ⓒ Ⓓ
26. Ⓐ Ⓑ Ⓒ Ⓓ
27.
28. Ⓐ Ⓑ Ⓒ Ⓓ
29.
30.

31. Ⓐ Ⓑ Ⓒ Ⓓ
32.
33. Ⓐ Ⓑ Ⓒ Ⓓ
34. Ⓐ Ⓑ Ⓒ Ⓓ
35. Ⓐ Ⓑ Ⓒ Ⓓ
36. Ⓐ Ⓑ Ⓒ Ⓓ
37. Ⓐ Ⓑ Ⓒ Ⓓ
38.
39. Ⓐ Ⓑ Ⓒ Ⓓ
40.
41. Ⓐ Ⓑ Ⓒ Ⓓ
42.
43. Ⓐ Ⓑ Ⓒ Ⓓ
44.

■ Have you taken the official TOEFL Test?

☐ Yes ——→ if any
☐ No

PBT Score	
Listening	
Structure	
Reading	
Writing	
TOTAL	

CBT Score	
Listening	
Structure	
Reading	
Writing	
TOTAL	

■ Educational background

☐ middle/high school   ☐ undergraduate   ☐ graduate

SIGNED: _____
(SIGN YOUR NAME AS IF SIGNING A BUSINESS LETTER.)

DATE: ____ / ____ / ____
　　　MO.　DAY　YEAR

Cut here.

LInguaForum

Copyright © 2002 by Lingua Forum, Inc. All rights reserved.

ANSWER SHEET

Lingua TOEFL® CBT Test Book II
PRACTICE TEST 11

Read the topic below and then make any notes that will help you plan your response. Begin typing your response in the box at the bottom of the screen, or write your answer on the answer sheet provided to you.

Imagine that the government intends to build a new university. Would your town be a good place to build the university? Why, or why not? Compare the advantages with the disadvantages of having a new university in your town. Use specific examples and reasons to explain your answer.

Cut

Paste

Undo

Time

LinguaForum

? Help   Answer Confirm   ➡ Next

LinguaForum

Copyright © 2002 by Lingua Forum, Inc. All rights reserved.

Test
11

SECTION 1
LISTENING
Suggested Time: 25 Minutes

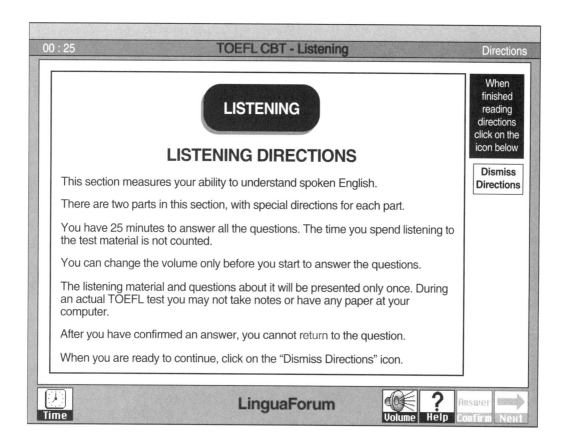

When finished reading directions click on the icon below

Dismiss Directions

LISTENING

LISTENING DIRECTIONS

This section measures your ability to understand spoken English.

There are two parts in this section, with special directions for each part.

You have 25 minutes to answer all the questions. The time you spend listening to the test material is not counted.

You can change the volume only before you start to answer the questions.

The listening material and questions about it will be presented only once. During an actual TOEFL test you may not take notes or have any paper at your computer.

After you have confirmed an answer, you cannot return to the question.

When you are ready to continue, click on the "Dismiss Directions" icon.

Time

LinguaForum

Volume   **Help**   **Answer Confirm**   **Next**

Test
11

SECTION 1
LISTENING

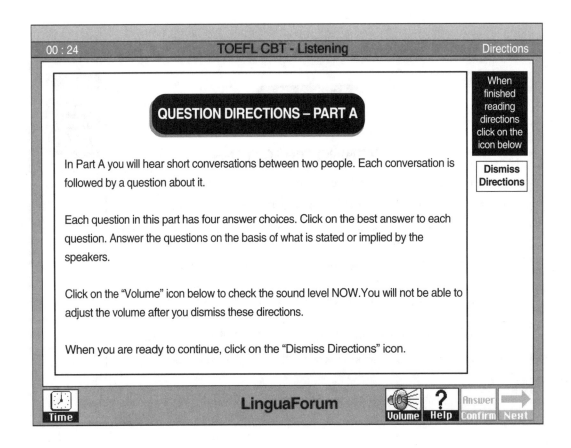

PRACTICE
TEST 11

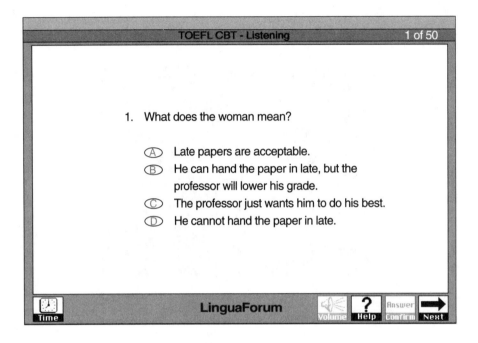

1. What does the woman mean?

    Ⓐ Late papers are acceptable.
    Ⓑ He can hand the paper in late, but the professor will lower his grade.
    Ⓒ The professor just wants him to do his best.
    Ⓓ He cannot hand the paper in late.

LinguaForum

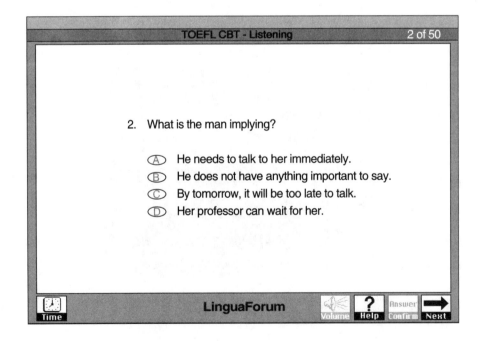

2. What is the man implying?

    Ⓐ He needs to talk to her immediately.
    Ⓑ He does not have anything important to say.
    Ⓒ By tomorrow, it will be too late to talk.
    Ⓓ Her professor can wait for her.

LinguaForum

PRACTICE
TEST 11

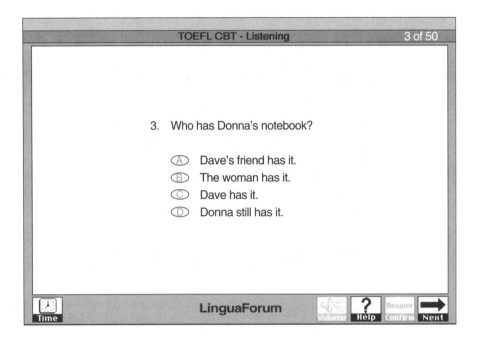

3. Who has Donna's notebook?

    Ⓐ   Dave's friend has it.
    Ⓑ   The woman has it.
    Ⓒ   Dave has it.
    Ⓓ   Donna still has it.

LinguaForum

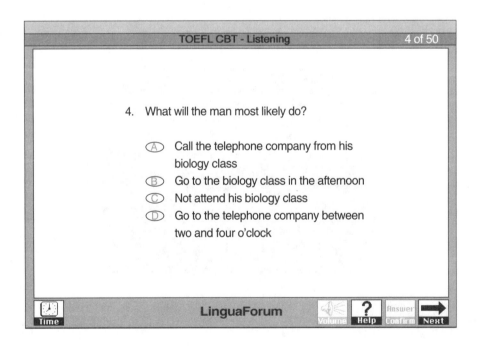

4. What will the man most likely do?

    Ⓐ   Call the telephone company from his
         biology class
    Ⓑ   Go to the biology class in the afternoon
    Ⓒ   Not attend his biology class
    Ⓓ   Go to the telephone company between
         two and four o'clock

LinguaForum

Question 5

Question 6

PRACTICE
TEST 11

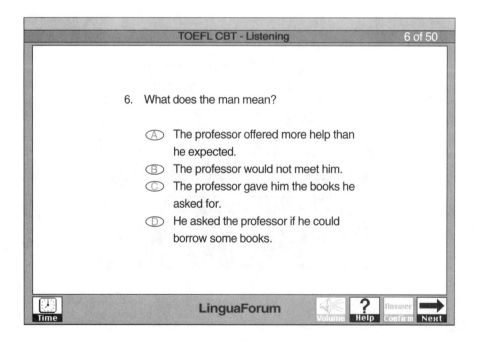

5. What does the woman suggest to the man?

    Ⓐ He should miss the seminar.
    Ⓑ He should eat dinner at home.
    Ⓒ He should not go to the concert.
    Ⓓ He should have dinner with her.

LinguaForum

6. What does the man mean?

    Ⓐ The professor offered more help than he expected.
    Ⓑ The professor would not meet him.
    Ⓒ The professor gave him the books he asked for.
    Ⓓ He asked the professor if he could borrow some books.

LinguaForum

TOEFL CBT - Listening
Listen

LinguaForum

Question 7

TOEFL CBT - Listening
Listen

LinguaForum

Question 8

PRACTICE
TEST 11

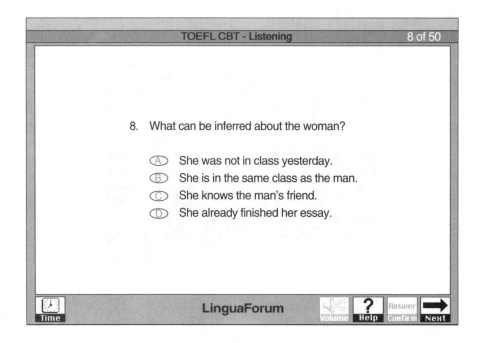

7. What did the woman assume about the man?

    Ⓐ   His French is not very good.
    Ⓑ   He did not like France.
    Ⓒ   He did not want to come back to school.
    Ⓓ   He did not go traveling.

LinguaForum

8. What can be inferred about the woman?

    Ⓐ   She was not in class yesterday.
    Ⓑ   She is in the same class as the man.
    Ⓒ   She knows the man's friend.
    Ⓓ   She already finished her essay.

LinguaForum

351

9. How far must the man walk to the library?

   (A)   He must walk to the corner.
   (B)   He must walk about 5 miles.
   (C)   He must walk 5 or 6 blocks.
   (D)   He must walk 3 blocks.

LinguaForum

Time   Volume   Help   Answer Confirm   Next

10. Why was Tori fired?

   (A)   She missed work because she was sick.
   (B)   She ruined an experiment.
   (C)   She was often late.
   (D)   She got angry with the professor.

LinguaForum

Time   Volume   Help   Answer Confirm   Next

Listening

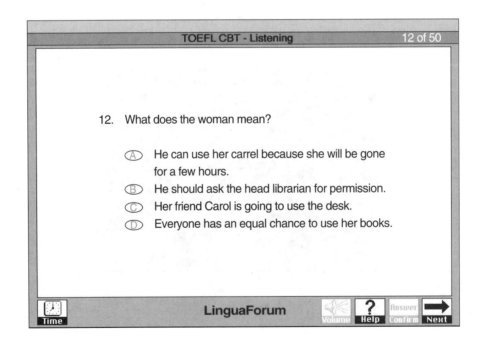

11. When does the man's flight leave Dallas?

- Ⓐ It leaves at 11:00.
- Ⓑ It leaves at 2:00.
- Ⓒ It leaves at 3:00.
- Ⓓ It leaves at 5:00.

LinguaForum

12. What does the woman mean?

- Ⓐ He can use her carrel because she will be gone for a few hours.
- Ⓑ He should ask the head librarian for permission.
- Ⓒ Her friend Carol is going to use the desk.
- Ⓓ Everyone has an equal chance to use her books.

LinguaForum

PRACTICE TEST 11

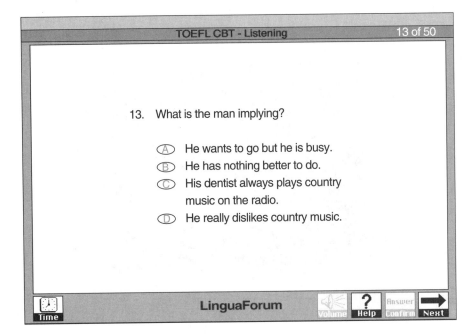

13. What is the man implying?

   Ⓐ   He wants to go but he is busy.
   Ⓑ   He has nothing better to do.
   Ⓒ   His dentist always plays country
         music on the radio.
   Ⓓ   He really dislikes country music.

LinguaForum

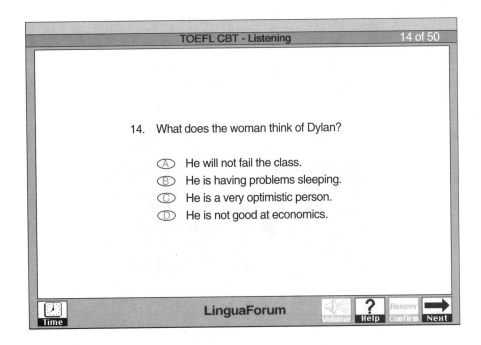

14. What does the woman think of Dylan?

   Ⓐ   He will not fail the class.
   Ⓑ   He is having problems sleeping.
   Ⓒ   He is a very optimistic person.
   Ⓓ   He is not good at economics.

LinguaForum

PRACTICE
TEST 11

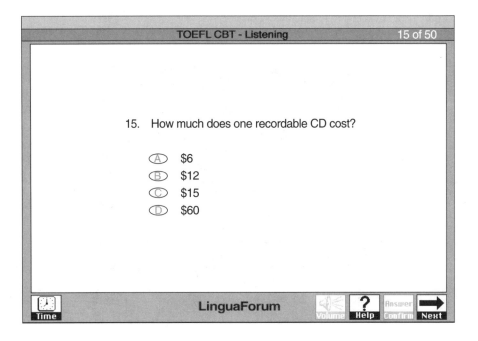

15. How much does one recordable CD cost?

(A) $6
(B) $12
(C) $15
(D) $60

LinguaForum

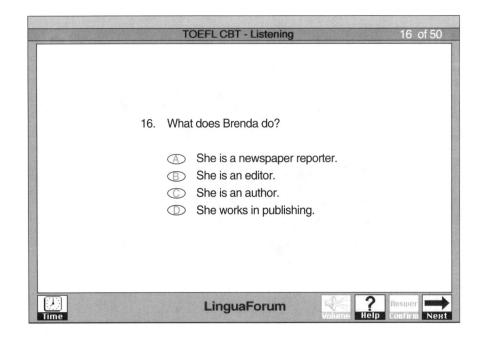

16. What does Brenda do?

(A) She is a newspaper reporter.
(B) She is an editor.
(C) She is an author.
(D) She works in publishing.

LinguaForum

Listening

PRACTICE
TEST 11

TOEFL CBT - Listening   17 of 50

17.   What is the man saying about the woman?

        Ⓐ   She needs to get better recommendations.
        Ⓑ   She will be accepted into graduate school.
        Ⓒ   She should have worried about her grades earlier.
        Ⓓ   She gives good advice.

Time   LinguaForum   Volume Help Confirm Next

Test
11

SECTION 1
LISTENING

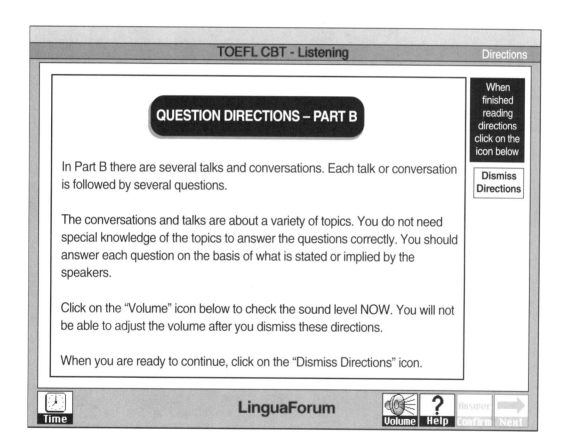

TOEFL CBT - Listening — Directions

When finished reading directions click on the icon below

Dismiss Directions

QUESTION DIRECTIONS – PART B

In Part B there are several talks and conversations. Each talk or conversation is followed by several questions.

The conversations and talks are about a variety of topics. You do not need special knowledge of the topics to answer the questions correctly. You should answer each question on the basis of what is stated or implied by the speakers.

Click on the "Volume" icon below to check the sound level NOW. You will not be able to adjust the volume after you dismiss these directions.

When you are ready to continue, click on the "Dismiss Directions" icon.

Time — LinguaForum — Volume | Help | Answer Confirm | Next

PRACTICE
TEST 11

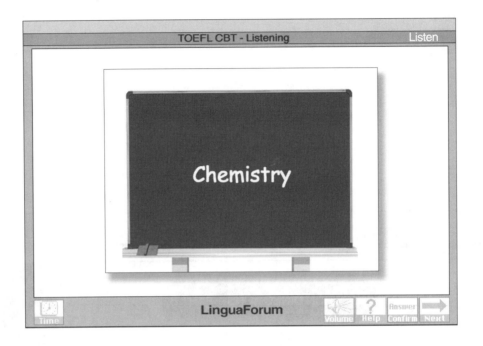

Listening

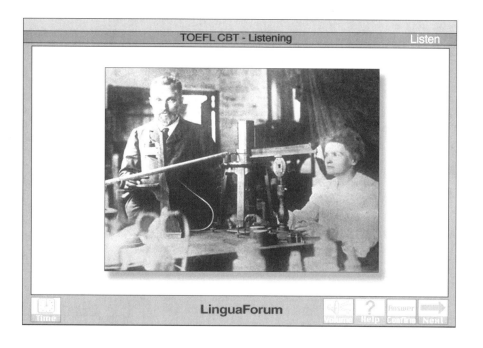

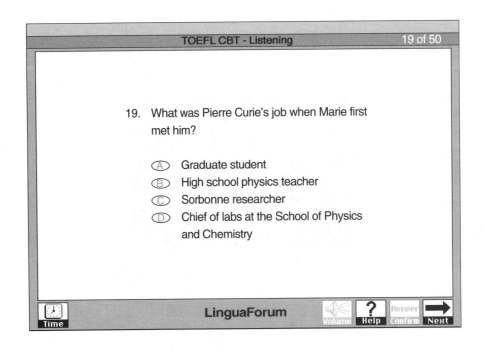

Listening

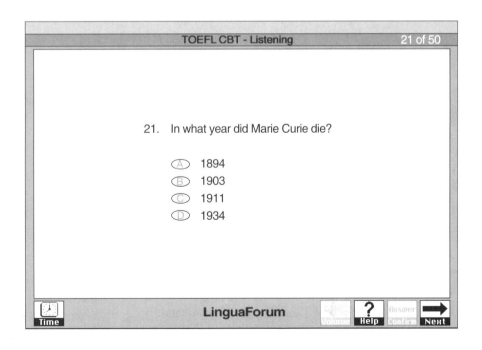

PRACTICE
TEST 11

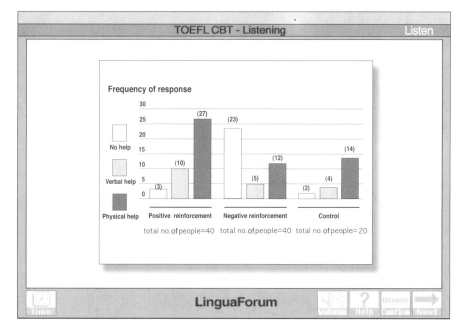

PRACTICE TEST 11

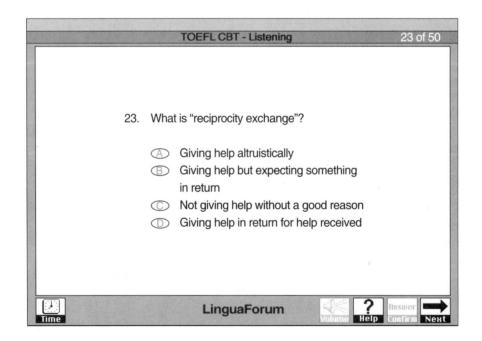

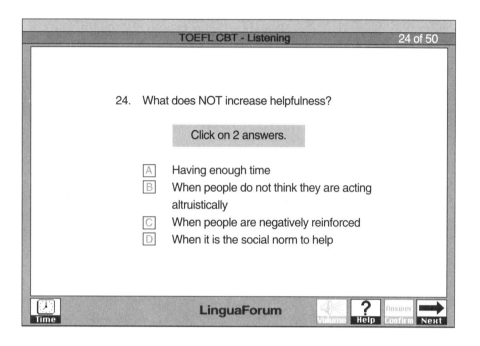

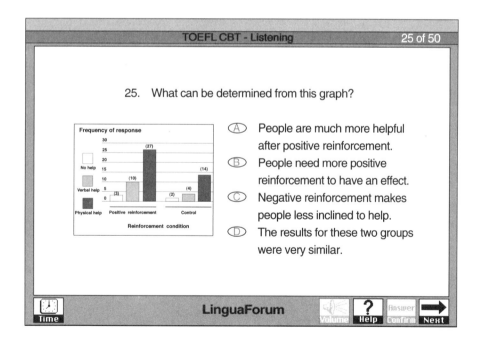

Listening

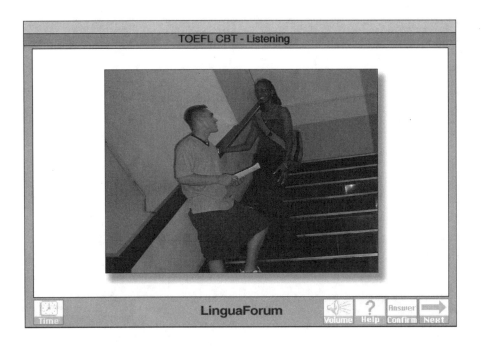

370

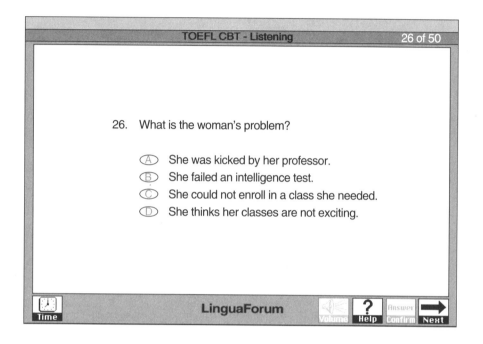

TOEFL CBT - Listening   26 of 50

26. What is the woman's problem?

   (A) She was kicked by her professor.
   (B) She failed an intelligence test.
   (C) She could not enroll in a class she needed.
   (D) She thinks her classes are not exciting.

LinguaForum

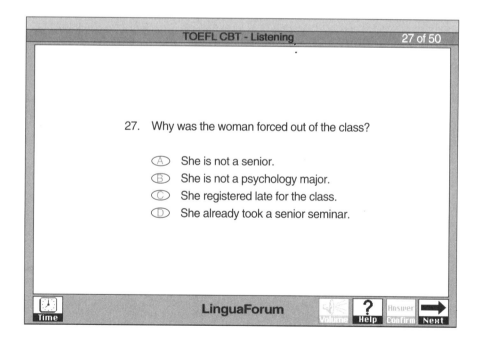

TOEFL CBT - Listening   27 of 50

27. Why was the woman forced out of the class?

   (A) She is not a senior.
   (B) She is not a psychology major.
   (C) She registered late for the class.
   (D) She already took a senior seminar.

LinguaForum

PRACTICE TEST 11

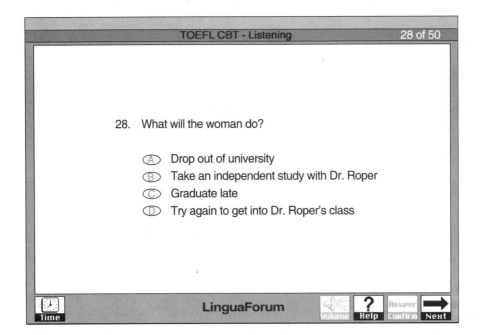

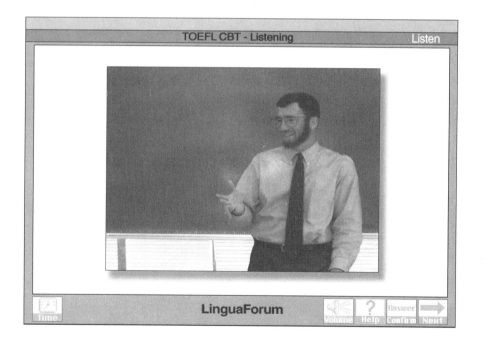

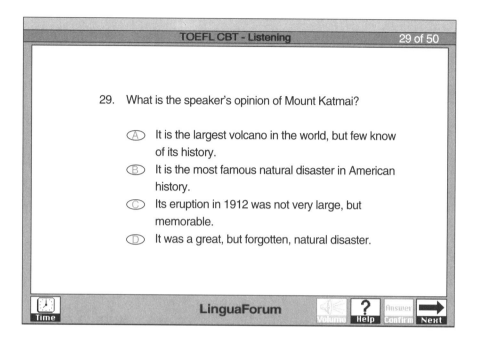

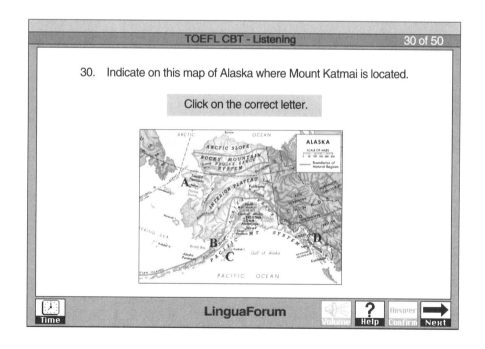

PRACTICE
TEST 11

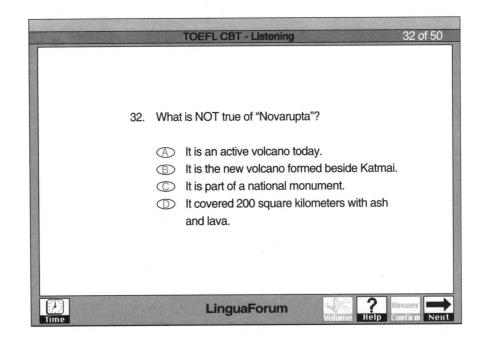

Listening

377

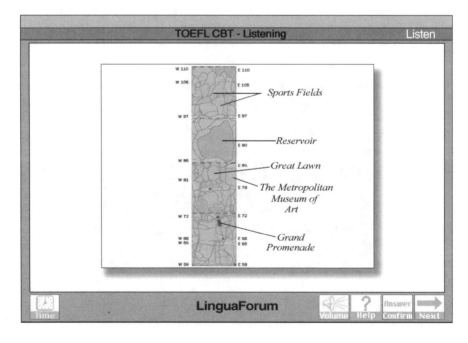

33.   What is the main topic of this lecture?

     Ⓐ   The landscapes of Frederick Olmsted
     Ⓑ   City parks in America
     Ⓒ   The growth of New York City
     Ⓓ   The most famous city park in America

LinguaForum

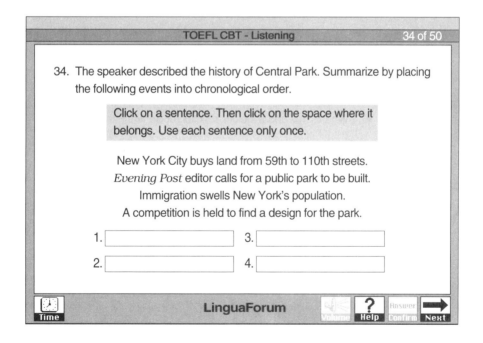

34.   The speaker described the history of Central Park. Summarize by placing the following events into chronological order.

> Click on a sentence. Then click on the space where it belongs. Use each sentence only once.

New York City buys land from 59th to 110th streets.
Evening Post editor calls for a public park to be built.
Immigration swells New York's population.
A competition is held to find a design for the park.

1. [＿＿＿＿＿＿＿]   3. [＿＿＿＿＿＿＿]

2. [＿＿＿＿＿＿＿]   4. [＿＿＿＿＿＿＿]

LinguaForum

PRACTICE
TEST 11

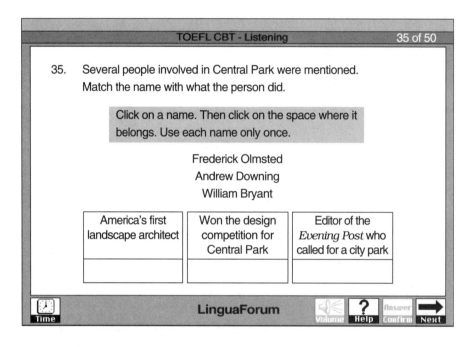

35.   Several people involved in Central Park were mentioned.
      Match the name with what the person did.

      Click on a name. Then click on the space where it
      belongs. Use each name only once.

                        Frederick Olmsted
                        Andrew Downing
                        William Bryant

America's first landscape architect	Won the design competition for Central Park	Editor of the *Evening Post* who called for a city park

LinguaForum

Time   Volume Help Confirm Next

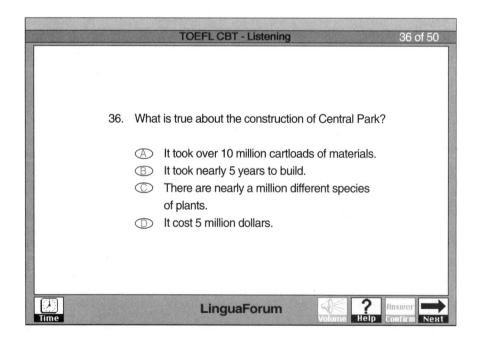

36.   What is true about the construction of Central Park?

      Ⓐ   It took over 10 million cartloads of materials.
      Ⓑ   It took nearly 5 years to build.
      Ⓒ   There are nearly a million different species
           of plants.
      Ⓓ   It cost 5 million dollars.

LinguaForum

Time   Volume Help Confirm Next

Listening

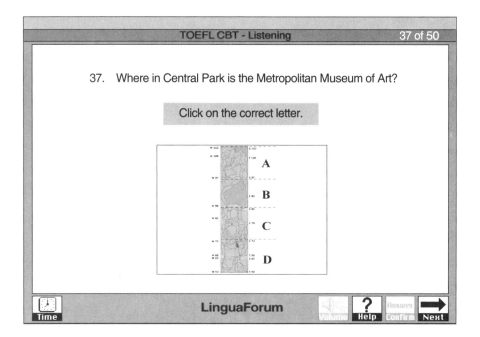

PRACTICE
TEST 11

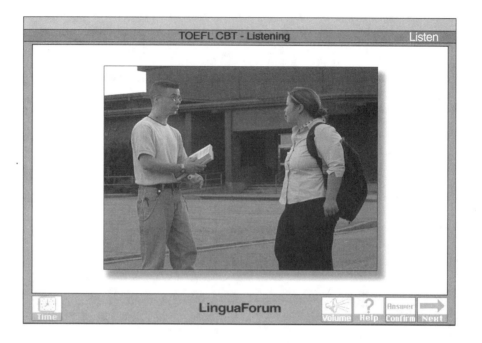

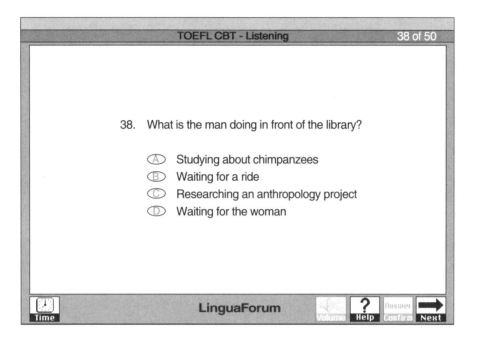

38. What is the man doing in front of the library?

   Ⓐ Studying about chimpanzees
   Ⓑ Waiting for a ride
   Ⓒ Researching an anthropology project
   Ⓓ Waiting for the woman

LinguaForum

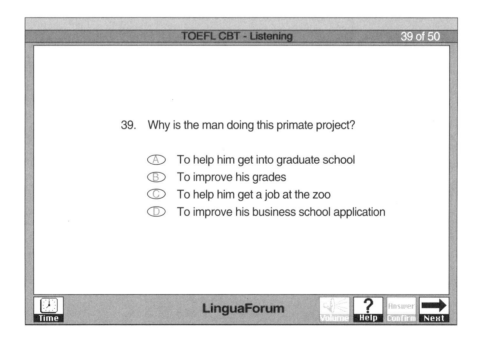

39. Why is the man doing this primate project?

   Ⓐ To help him get into graduate school
   Ⓑ To improve his grades
   Ⓒ To help him get a job at the zoo
   Ⓓ To improve his business school application

LinguaForum

**PRACTICE
TEST 11**

Listening

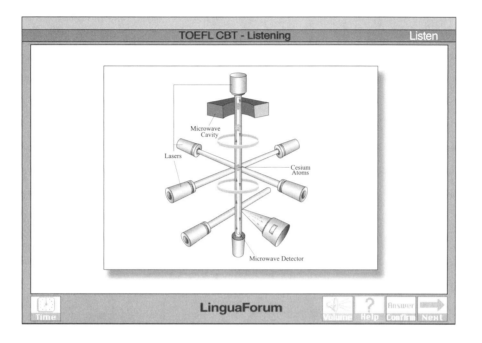

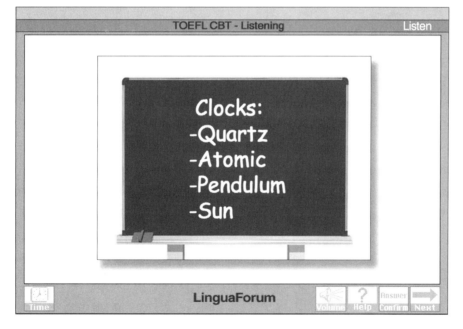

385

TOEFL CBT - Listening

40. What is the main topic of this discussion?

    Ⓐ How time was invented
    Ⓑ How clocks work
    Ⓒ How time began
    Ⓓ How time is measured

LinguaForum

Time   Volume   Help   Confirm   Next

TOEFL CBT - Listening

41. The professor mentioned several kinds of time-keeping devices. Put them into order, from least to most accurate.

    Click on a kind of clock. Then click on the space
    where it belongs. Use each type of clock only once.

        Quartz clock
        Atomic clock
        Pendulum clock
        Sun clock

1. [   ]   3. [   ]

2. [   ]   4. [   ]

LinguaForum

Time   Volume   Help   Confirm   Next

Listening

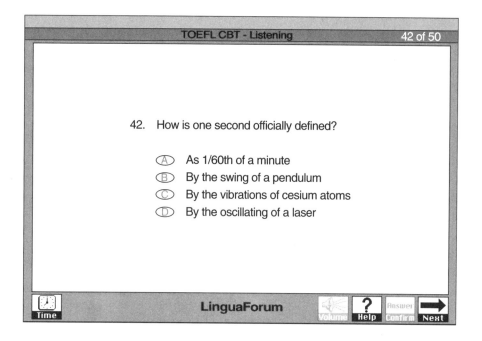

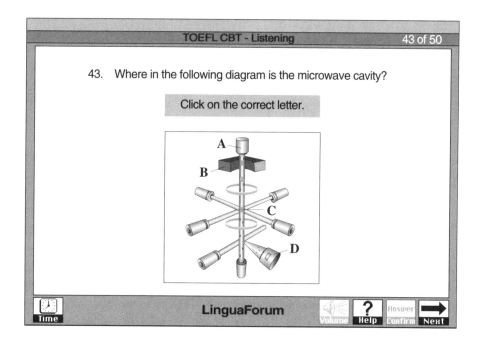

Listening

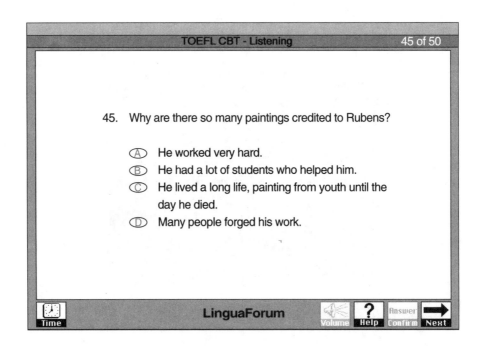

44. What is significant about Rubens' copy of "The Battle of Anghiari"?

    Ⓐ   It is a copy of a Leonardo da Vinci painting.
    Ⓑ   It was the last copy Rubens made.
    Ⓒ   It was Rubens' greatest painting.
    Ⓓ   It is the only surviving copy of that great work.

LinguaForum

45. Why are there so many paintings credited to Rubens?

    Ⓐ   He worked very hard.
    Ⓑ   He had a lot of students who helped him.
    Ⓒ   He lived a long life, painting from youth until the day he died.
    Ⓓ   Many people forged his work.

LinguaForum

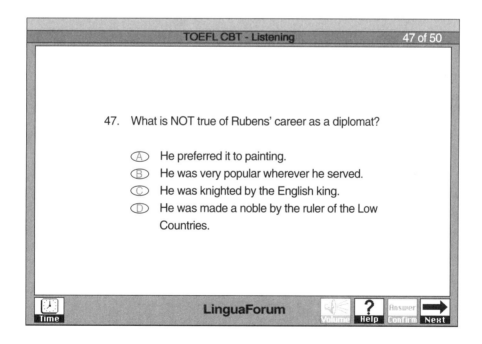

46. The professor explains the following events in Rubens' life. Put them into chronological order.

> Click on a sentence. Then click on the space where it belongs. Use each sentence only once.

He moved to Italy to study painting.
He became a court painter for a Spanish duke.
He became a nobleman.
He married Isabella Brandt.

1. [   ]　3. [   ]

2. [   ]　4. [   ]

Time　　LinguaForum　　Volume　Help　Confirm　Next

---

47. What is NOT true of Rubens' career as a diplomat?

(A) He preferred it to painting.
(B) He was very popular wherever he served.
(C) He was knighted by the English king.
(D) He was made a noble by the ruler of the Low Countries.

Time　　LinguaForum　　Volume　Help　Confirm　Next

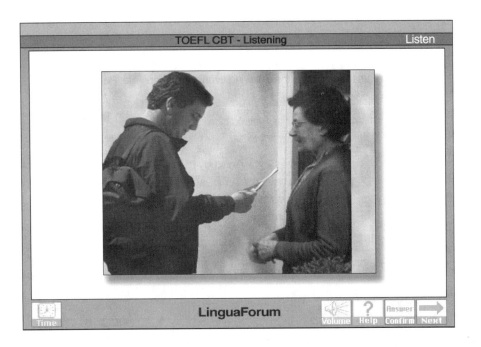

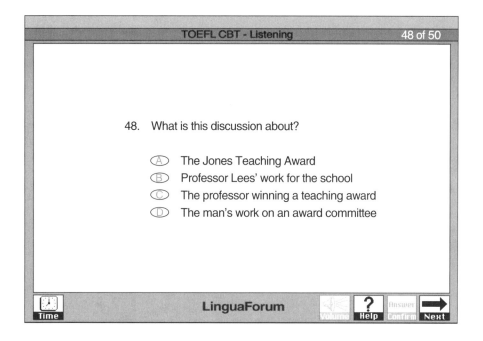

TOEFL CBT - Listening • 48 of 50

48. What is this discussion about?

Ⓐ The Jones Teaching Award
Ⓑ Professor Lees' work for the school
Ⓒ The professor winning a teaching award
Ⓓ The man's work on an award committee

LinguaForum

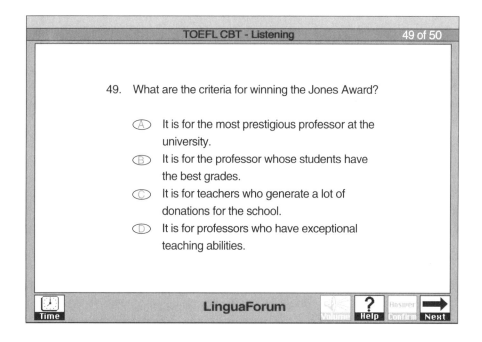

TOEFL CBT - Listening • 49 of 50

49. What are the criteria for winning the Jones Award?

Ⓐ It is for the most prestigious professor at the university.
Ⓑ It is for the professor whose students have the best grades.
Ⓒ It is for teachers who generate a lot of donations for the school.
Ⓓ It is for professors who have exceptional teaching abilities.

LinguaForum

PRACTICE TEST 11

TOEFL CBT - Listening   50 of 50

50.   What does the Awards Committee NOT ask
      the professor to do?

      Ⓐ   Write a speech
      Ⓑ   Attend the awards banquet
      Ⓒ   Provide a biography
      Ⓓ   Provide a teaching sample

Time   LinguaForum   Volume Help Confirm Next

Test
11

SECTION 2
STRUCTURE
Suggested Time: 15 Minutes

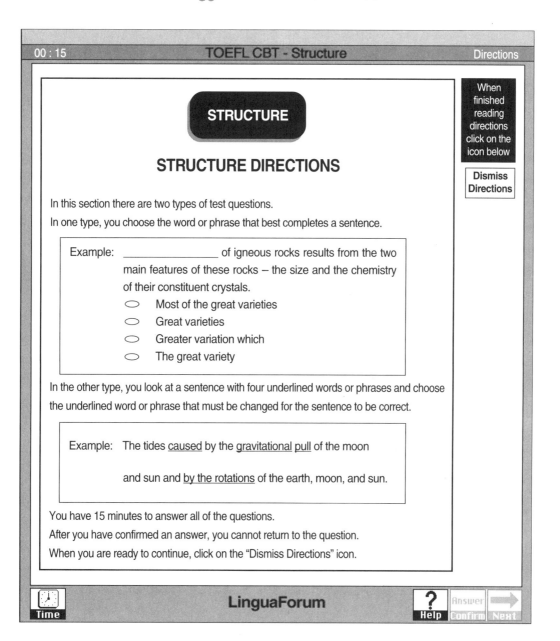

00 : 15   TOEFL CBT - Structure   Directions

When
finished
reading
directions
click on the
icon below

**Dismiss
Directions**

STRUCTURE

STRUCTURE DIRECTIONS

In this section there are two types of test questions.

In one type, you choose the word or phrase that best completes a sentence.

> Example: _____ of igneous rocks results from the two
> main features of these rocks – the size and the chemistry
> of their constituent crystals.
>   ⬭   Most of the great varieties
>   ⬭   Great varieties
>   ⬭   Greater variation which
>   ⬭   The great variety

In the other type, you look at a sentence with four underlined words or phrases and choose
the underlined word or phrase that must be changed for the sentence to be correct.

> Example: The tides <u>caused</u> by the <u>gravitational</u> <u>pull</u> of the moon
>
>   and sun and <u>by the rotations</u> of the earth, moon, and sun.

You have 15 minutes to answer all of the questions.

After you have confirmed an answer, you cannot return to the question.

When you are ready to continue, click on the "Dismiss Directions" icon.

Time   **LinguaForum**   ? Answer ⮕
                                        Help Confirm Next

PRACTICE
TEST 11

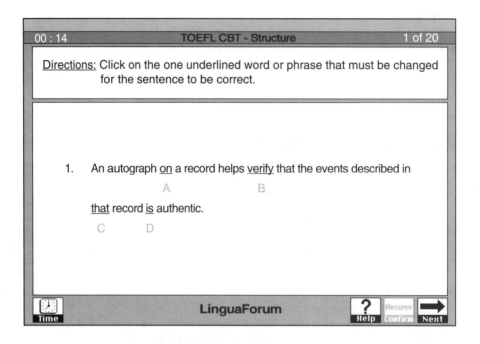

00 : 14 TOEFL CBT - Structure 1 of 20

Directions: Click on the one underlined word or phrase that must be changed
for the sentence to be correct.

1. An autograph <u>on</u> a record helps <u>verify</u> that the events described in
                A   B

   <u>that</u> record <u>is</u> authentic.
   C   D

LinguaForum

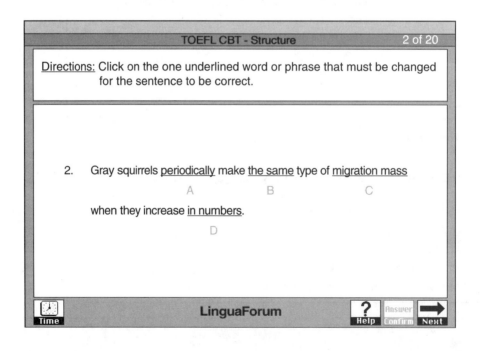

TOEFL CBT - Structure 2 of 20

Directions: Click on the one underlined word or phrase that must be changed
for the sentence to be correct.

2. Gray squirrels <u>periodically</u> make <u>the same</u> type of <u>migration mass</u>
                  A   B   C

   when they increase <u>in numbers</u>.
                       D

LinguaForum

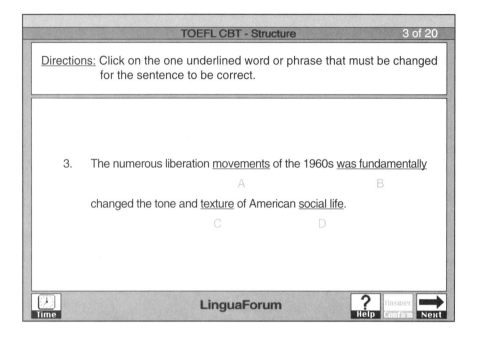

TOEFL CBT - Structure
3 of 20

Directions: Click on the one underlined word or phrase that must be changed for the sentence to be correct.

3. The numerous liberation <u>movements</u> of the 1960s <u>was fundamentally</u>
A   B

changed the tone and <u>texture</u> of American <u>social life</u>.
C   D

Time   **LinguaForum**   ? Help Answer Confirm → Next

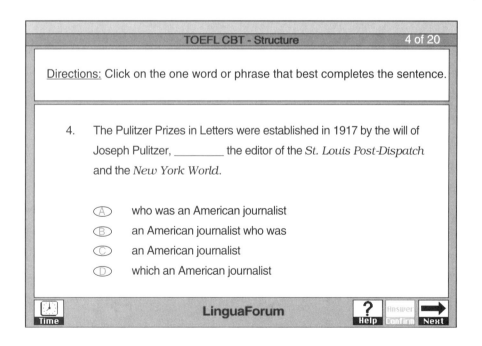

TOEFL CBT - Structure
4 of 20

Directions: Click on the one word or phrase that best completes the sentence.

4. The Pulitzer Prizes in Letters were established in 1917 by the will of Joseph Pulitzer, _____ the editor of the *St. Louis Post-Dispatch* and the *New York World*.

    Ⓐ   who was an American journalist
    Ⓑ   an American journalist who was
    Ⓒ   an American journalist
    Ⓓ   which an American journalist

Time   **LinguaForum**   ? Help Answer Confirm → Next

Structure

<u>Directions:</u> Click on the one underlined word or phrase that must be changed for the sentence to be correct.

5.   <u>Despite</u> the Great Depression, the United States <u>automobile industry</u>
     A   B

continued to <u>do</u> <u>scientific</u> and engineering progress.
               C   D

LinguaForum

Time | Help | Answer Confirm | Next

<u>Directions:</u> Click on the one word or phrase that best completes the sentence.

6.   In ancient Greece natural springs _____, and shrines to the gods were built around them.

    (A)   considered to be sacred
    (B)   which were considered as sacred
    (C)   were considered sacred
    (D)   consider it sacred

LinguaForum

Time | Help | Answer Confirm | Next

Structure

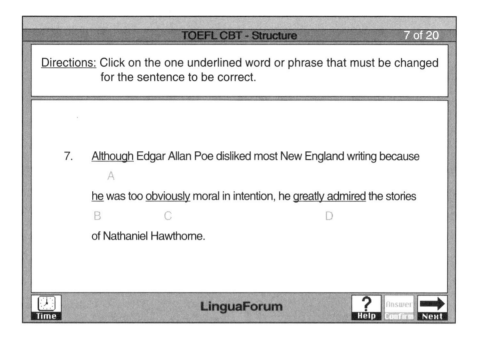

Directions: Click on the one underlined word or phrase that must be changed
for the sentence to be correct.

7.   <u>Although</u> Edgar Allan Poe disliked most New England writing because
      A

<u>he</u> was too <u>obviously</u> moral in intention, he <u>greatly admired</u> the stories
    B   C   D

of Nathaniel Hawthorne.

LinguaForum   ? Help   Answer Confirm   Next

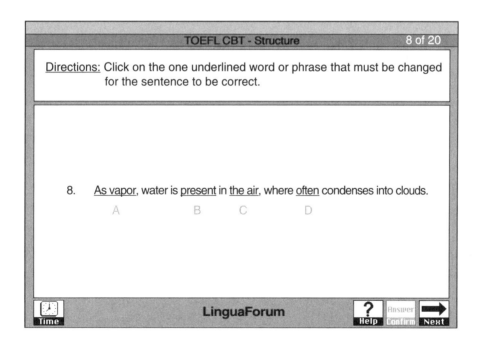

Directions: Click on the one underlined word or phrase that must be changed
for the sentence to be correct.

8.   <u>As vapor,</u> water is <u>present</u> in <u>the air,</u> where <u>often</u> condenses into clouds.
      A   B   C   D

LinguaForum   ? Help   Answer Confirm   Next

PRACTICE
TEST 11

Structure

<u>Directions:</u> Click on the one underlined word or phrase that must be changed for the sentence to be correct.

9.   Like the hairs of mammals and the scales of reptiles, feathers are

     _____ of the skin.

     Ⓐ   horny outgrowths

     Ⓑ   outgrown horny

     Ⓒ   outgrowths are horny

     Ⓓ   to outgrow horny

LinguaForum

?
Help   Answer Confirm   Next

Time

<u>Directions:</u> Click on the one underlined word or phrase that must be changed for the sentence to be correct.

10.   Like <u>all living</u> things, microorganisms can live and grow <u>only in an</u>

             A   B

   environment that is <u>favor</u> to <u>them</u>.

                    C   D

LinguaForum

?
Help   Answer Confirm   Next

Time

Structure

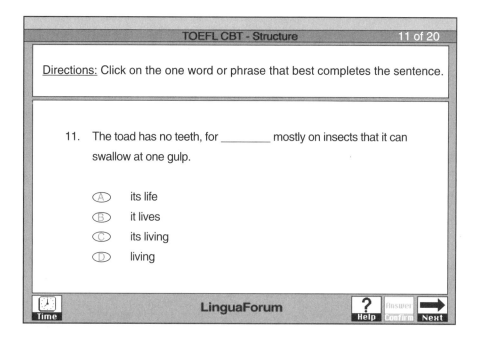

<u>Directions:</u> Click on the one word or phrase that best completes the sentence.

11. The toad has no teeth, for _____ mostly on insects that it can swallow at one gulp.

    Ⓐ   its life
    Ⓑ   it lives
    Ⓒ   its living
    Ⓓ   living

LinguaForum

Time   ? Help Answer Confirm Next

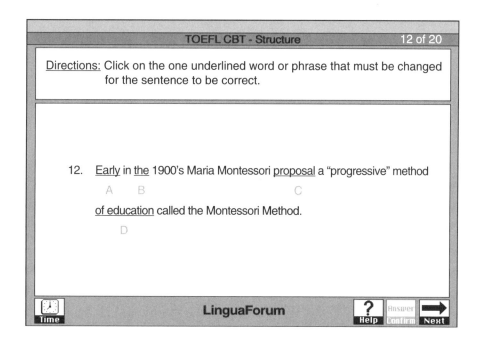

<u>Directions:</u> Click on the one underlined word or phrase that must be changed for the sentence to be correct.

12. <u>Early</u> in <u>the</u> 1900's Maria Montessori <u>proposal</u> a "progressive" method
    A   B   C

   <u>of education</u> called the Montessori Method.
      D

LinguaForum

Time   ? Help Answer Confirm Next

PRACTICE
TEST 11

Structure

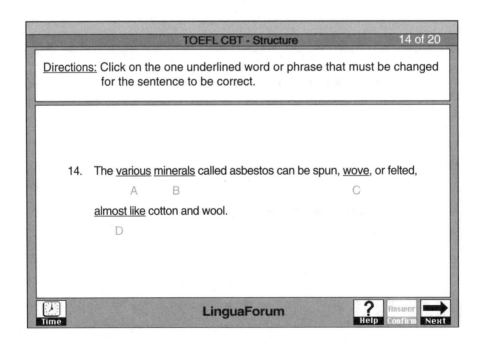

Directions: Click on the one word or phrase that best completes the sentence.

13. When the air becomes cooler, it cannot hold _____ as before.

     (A)   much more water

     (B)   not so much water

     (C)   more water than

     (D)   as much water

LinguaForum

? Help   Answer Confirm   Next

Time

Directions: Click on the one underlined word or phrase that must be changed for the sentence to be correct.

14. The <u>various</u> <u>minerals</u> called asbestos can be spun, <u>wove</u>, or felted,

         A   B   C

<u>almost like</u> cotton and wool.

      D

LinguaForum

? Help   Answer Confirm   Next

Time

Structure

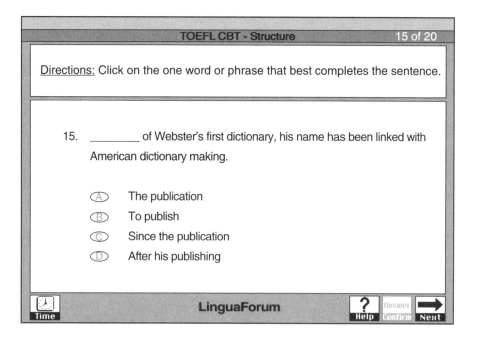

Directions: Click on the one word or phrase that best completes the sentence.

15. _____ of Webster's first dictionary, his name has been linked with American dictionary making.

    Ⓐ   The publication

    Ⓑ   To publish

    Ⓒ   Since the publication

    Ⓓ   After his publishing

LinguaForum   ? Help   Answer Confirm   Next   Time

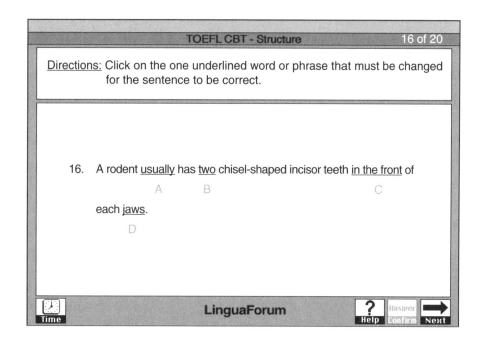

Directions: Click on the one underlined word or phrase that must be changed for the sentence to be correct.

16. A rodent <u>usually</u> has <u>two</u> chisel-shaped incisor teeth <u>in the front</u> of
              A   B   C

each <u>jaws</u>.
    D

LinguaForum   ? Help   Answer Confirm   Next   Time

PRACTICE TEST 11

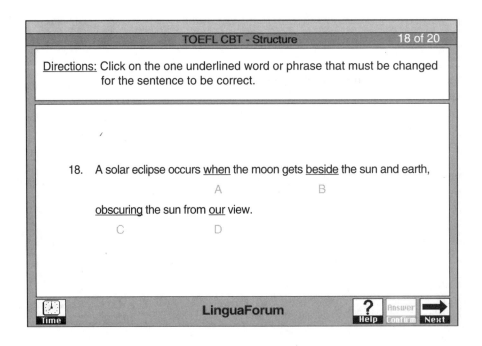

Directions: Click on the one word or phrase that best completes the sentence.

17. Root hairs do not develop at all in most plants _____ grow in water, such as the duckweed and the spatterdock, or yellow pond lily.

     (A) that
     (B) but
     (C) where they
     (D) they

LinguaForum

Time | Help | Answer Confirm | Next

Directions: Click on the one underlined word or phrase that must be changed for the sentence to be correct.

18. A solar eclipse occurs <u>when</u> the moon gets <u>beside</u> the sun and earth,
                                A   B

     <u>obscuring</u> the sun from <u>our</u> view.
        C   D

LinguaForum

Time | Help | Answer Confirm | Next

Structure

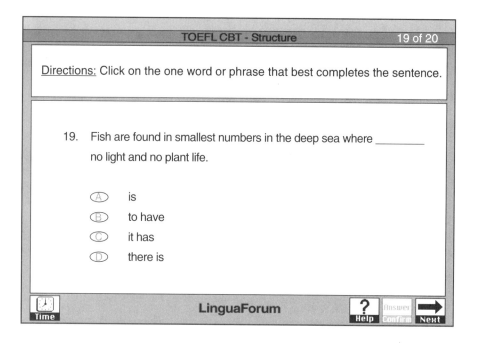

TOEFL CBT - Structure   19 of 20

Directions: Click on the one word or phrase that best completes the sentence.

19. Fish are found in smallest numbers in the deep sea where _____
no light and no plant life.

- (A) is
- (B) to have
- (C) it has
- (D) there is

LinguaForum

Time   Help Confirm Next

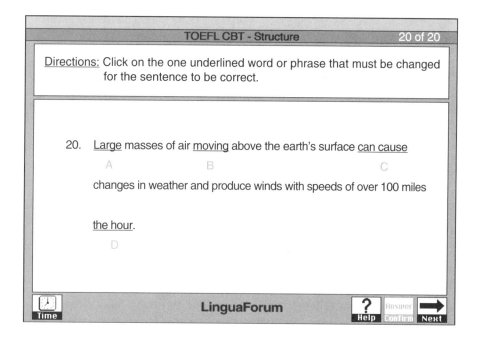

TOEFL CBT - Structure   20 of 20

Directions: Click on the one underlined word or phrase that must be changed
for the sentence to be correct.

20. Large masses of air moving above the earth's surface can cause
   A   B   C

changes in weather and produce winds with speeds of over 100 miles

the hour.
   D

LinguaForum

Time   Help Confirm Next

PRACTICE
TEST 11

Test
11

SECTION 3
READING
Suggested Time: 70 Minutes

READING

When finished reading directions click on the icon below

Dismiss Directions

READING DIRECTIONS

In this section, you will read 4 passages. Each passage is followed by 11 questions.

You have 70 minutes to read <u>all</u> the passages and answer all the questions.

The clock will tell you how much time you have left to read all the passages and answer all the questions in this section.

You should answer all questions about a passage on the basis of what is <u>stated</u> or <u>implied</u> in that passage.

When you are ready to continue, click on the "Dismiss Directions" icon.

Time

LinguaForum

?
Help   **Prev**   **Next**

PRACTICE
TEST 11

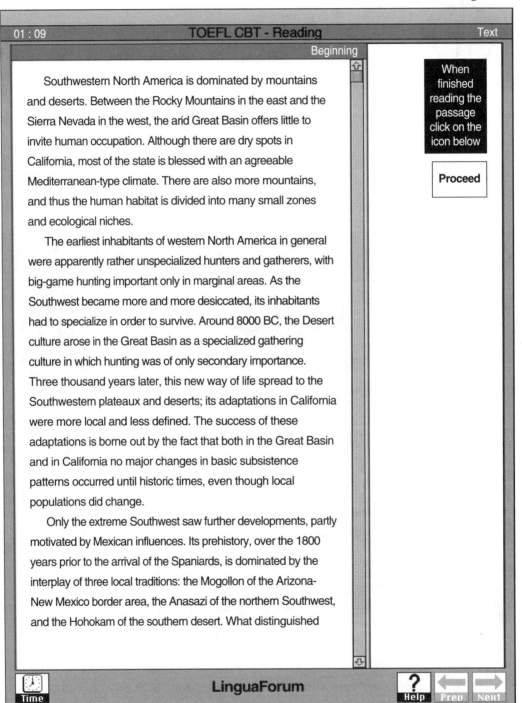

01 : 09   TOEFL CBT - Reading   Text

Beginning

When finished reading the passage click on the icon below

Proceed

Southwestern North America is dominated by mountains and deserts. Between the Rocky Mountains in the east and the Sierra Nevada in the west, the arid Great Basin offers little to invite human occupation. Although there are dry spots in California, most of the state is blessed with an agreeable Mediterranean-type climate. There are also more mountains, and thus the human habitat is divided into many small zones and ecological niches.

The earliest inhabitants of western North America in general were apparently rather unspecialized hunters and gatherers, with big-game hunting important only in marginal areas. As the Southwest became more and more desiccated, its inhabitants had to specialize in order to survive. Around 8000 BC, the Desert culture arose in the Great Basin as a specialized gathering culture in which hunting was of only secondary importance. Three thousand years later, this new way of life spread to the Southwestern plateaux and deserts; its adaptations in California were more local and less defined. The success of these adaptations is borne out by the fact that both in the Great Basin and in California no major changes in basic subsistence patterns occurred until historic times, even though local populations did change.

Only the extreme Southwest saw further developments, partly motivated by Mexican influences. Its prehistory, over the 1800 years prior to the arrival of the Spaniards, is dominated by the interplay of three local traditions: the Mogollon of the Arizona-New Mexico border area, the Anasazi of the northern Southwest, and the Hohokam of the southern desert. What distinguished

LinguaForum

?
Help   Prev   Next

Reading

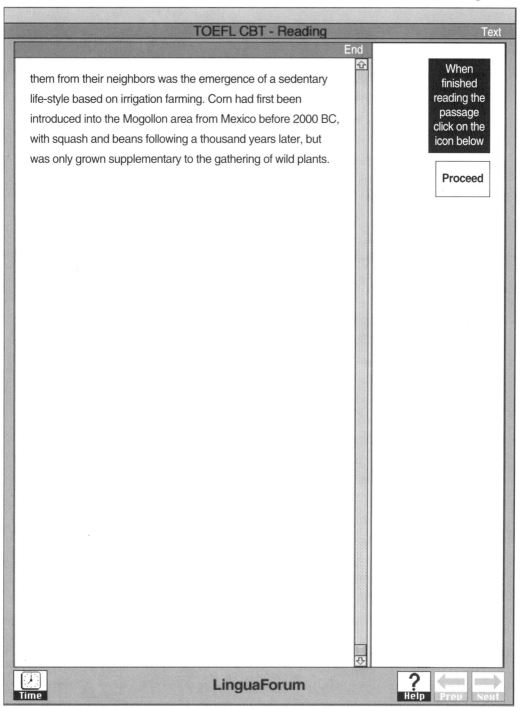

them from their neighbors was the emergence of a sedentary life-style based on irrigation farming. Corn had first been introduced into the Mogollon area from Mexico before 2000 BC, with squash and beans following a thousand years later, but was only grown supplementary to the gathering of wild plants.

When finished reading the passage click on the icon below

Proceed

TOEFL CBT - Reading

Text

End

LinguaForum

Time

Help   Prev   Next

PRACTICE TEST 11

Reading

Southwestern North America is dominated by mountains and deserts. Between the Rocky Mountains in the east and the Sierra Nevada in the west, the arid Great Basin offers little to invite human occupation. Although there are dry spots in California, most of the state is blessed with an agreeable Mediterranean-type climate. There are also more mountains, and thus the human habitat is divided into many small zones and ecological niches.

The earliest inhabitants of western North America in general were apparently rather unspecialized hunters and gatherers, with big-game hunting important only in marginal areas. As the Southwest became more and more desiccated, its inhabitants had to specialize in order to survive. Around 8000 BC, the Desert culture arose in the Great Basin as a specialized gathering culture in which hunting was of only secondary importance. Three thousand years later, this new way of life spread to the Southwestern plateaux and deserts; its adaptations in California were more local and less defined. The success of these adaptations is borne out by the fact that both in the Great Basin and in California no major changes in basic subsistence patterns occurred until historic times, even though local populations did change.

Only the extreme Southwest saw further developments, partly motivated by Mexican influences. Its prehistory, over the 1800 years prior to the arrival of the Spaniards, is dominated by the interplay of three local traditions: the Mogollon of the Arizona-New Mexico border area, the Anasazi of the northern Southwest, and the Hohokam of the southern desert. What distinguished

1. The main subject of the passage is

(A) the geography of Southwest United States

(B) the geography of the early inhabitants of the Southwest United States

(C) the historical and geographical background of the Southwest American Indians

(D) the Southwestern influence on the development of native American Indians

LinguaForum

?   ←   →
Help   Prev   Next

Reading

Passage 1

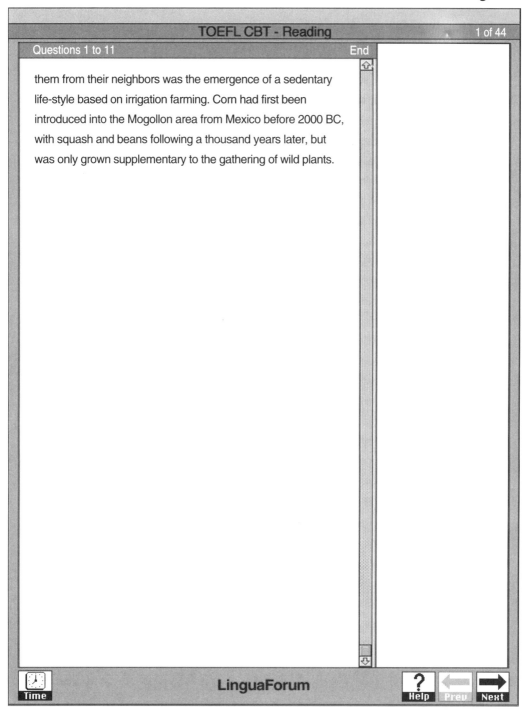

Questions 1 to 11   End

them from their neighbors was the emergence of a sedentary life-style based on irrigation farming. Corn had first been introduced into the Mogollon area from Mexico before 2000 BC, with squash and beans following a thousand years later, but was only grown supplementary to the gathering of wild plants.

LinguaForum

Time   Help   Prev   Next

PRACTICE TEST 11

Reading

Questions 1 to 11 | Beginning

→ **Southwestern North America is dominated by mountains and deserts.** ■ **Between the Rocky Mountains in the east and the Sierra Nevada in the west, the** arid **Great Basin offers little to invite human occupation.** ■ **Although there are dry spots in California, most of the state is blessed with an agreeable Mediterranean-type climate.** ■ There are also more mountains, and thus the human habitat is divided into many small zones and ecological niches. ■

→ The earliest inhabitants of western North America in general were apparently rather unspecialized hunters and gatherers, with big-game hunting important only in marginal areas. ■ As the Southwest became more and more desiccated, its inhabitants had to specialize in order to survive. Around 8000 BC, the Desert culture arose in the Great Basin as a specialized gathering culture in which hunting was of only secondary importance. ■ Three thousand years later, this new way of life spread to the Southwestern plateaux and deserts; its adaptations in California were more local and less defined. ■ The success of these adaptations is borne out by the fact that both in the Great Basin and in California no major changes in basic subsistence patterns occurred until historic times, even though local populations did change. ■

Only the extreme Southwest saw further developments, partly motivated by Mexican influences. Its prehistory, over the 1800 years prior to the arrival of the Spaniards, is dominated by the interplay of three local traditions: the Mogollon of the Arizona-New Mexico border area, the Anasazi of the northern Southwest, and the Hohokam of the southern desert. What distinguished them from their neighbors was the emergence of a sedentary

2. Look at the word arid in the passage. Click on the word or phrase in the **bold** text that is closest in meaning to arid.

3. The following sentence can be added to paragraph 1 or 2.

To the south, the Rockies level out into a plateau area which is drained by the Colorado River into the Gulf of California, and by the Rio Grande into the Gulf of Mexico, and ultimately drops off into the Gila Desert of southern Arizona.

Where would it best fit in the paragraph? Click on the square [■] to add the sentence to paragraph 1 or 2. Paragraphs 1 and 2 are marked with an arrow [→].

LinguaForum

Specialist Solutions for TOEFL® CBT

Reading

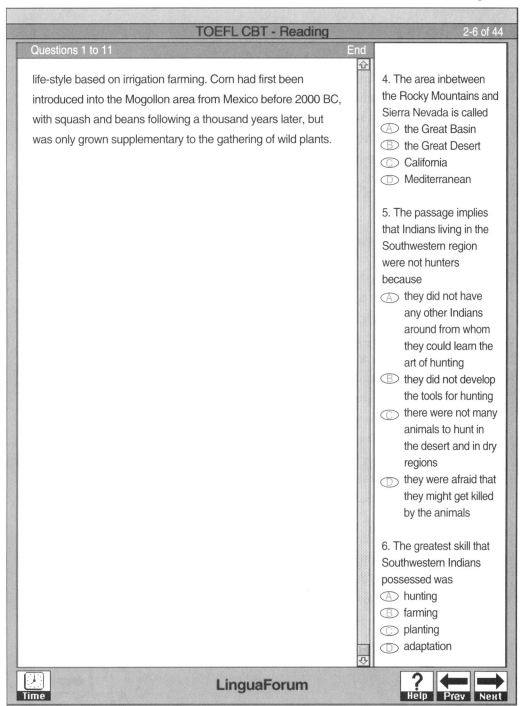

Questions 1 to 11   End

life-style based on irrigation farming. Corn had first been introduced into the Mogollon area from Mexico before 2000 BC, with squash and beans following a thousand years later, but was only grown supplementary to the gathering of wild plants.

4. The area inbetween the Rocky Mountains and Sierra Nevada is called
Ⓐ the Great Basin
Ⓑ the Great Desert
Ⓒ California
Ⓓ Mediterranean

5. The passage implies that Indians living in the Southwestern region were not hunters because
Ⓐ they did not have any other Indians around from whom they could learn the art of hunting
Ⓑ they did not develop the tools for hunting
Ⓒ there were not many animals to hunt in the desert and in dry regions
Ⓓ they were afraid that they might get killed by the animals

6. The greatest skill that Southwestern Indians possessed was
Ⓐ hunting
Ⓑ farming
Ⓒ planting
Ⓓ adaptation

LinguaForum

? Help ← Prev → Next

PRACTICE TEST 11

Reading

Passage 1

Questions 1 to 11 　　　　　　　　　　　　　　　Beginning

Southwestern North America is dominated by mountains and deserts. Between the Rocky Mountains in the east and the Sierra Nevada in the west, the arid Great Basin offers little to invite human occupation. Although there are dry spots in California, most of the state is blessed with an agreeable Mediterranean-type climate. There are also more mountains, and thus the human habitat is divided into many small zones and ecological niches.

The earliest inhabitants of western North America in general were apparently rather unspecialized hunters and gatherers, with big-game hunting important only in marginal areas. As the Southwest became more and more desiccated, its inhabitants had to specialize in order to survive. Around 8000 BC, the Desert culture arose in the Great Basin as a specialized gathering culture in which hunting was of only secondary importance. Three thousand years later, this new way of life spread to the Southwestern plateaus and deserts; its adaptations in California were more local and less defined. The success of these adaptations is borne out by the fact that both in the Great Basin and in California no major changes in basic subsistence patterns occurred until historic times, even though local populations did change.

Only the extreme Southwest saw further developments, partly motivated by Mexican influences. Its prehistory, over the 1800 years prior to the arrival of the Spaniards, is dominated by the interplay of three local traditions: the Mogollon of the Arizona-New Mexico border area, the

7. Look at the word marginal in the passage. Click on the word or phrase in the **bold** text that is closest in meaning to marginal.

8. The adaptations that developed as a result of the Desert Culture prevailed because
(A) no major geographical changes occurred that altered the subsistence patterns
(B) they were handed down from one generation to the next
(C) their influences were widespread throughout the southwestern United States
(D) there were no other major influences that affected the entire region

9. Look at the word Its in the passage. Click on the word or phrase in the **bold** text that Its refers to.

414

Reading

Specialist Solutions for TOEFL® CBT

Passage 1

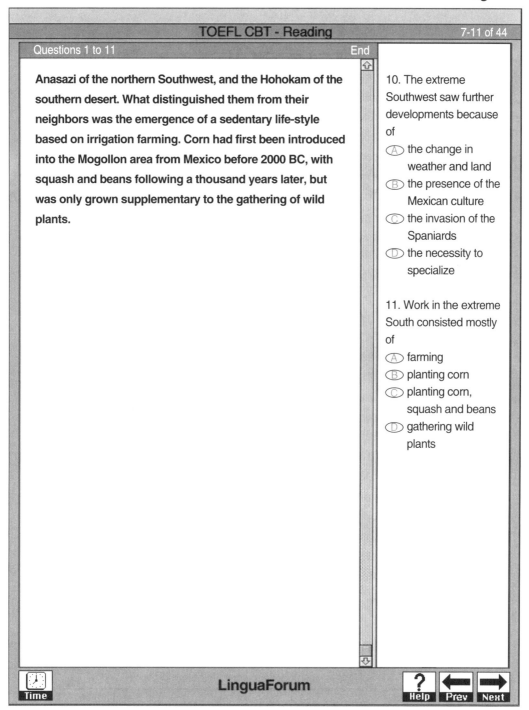

Questions 1 to 11   End

Anasazi of the northern Southwest, and the Hohokam of the southern desert. What distinguished them from their neighbors was the emergence of a sedentary life-style based on irrigation farming. Corn had first been introduced into the Mogollon area from Mexico before 2000 BC, with squash and beans following a thousand years later, but was only grown supplementary to the gathering of wild plants.

10. The extreme Southwest saw further developments because of
Ⓐ the change in weather and land
Ⓑ the presence of the Mexican culture
Ⓒ the invasion of the Spaniards
Ⓓ the necessity to specialize

11. Work in the extreme South consisted mostly of
Ⓐ farming
Ⓑ planting corn
Ⓒ planting corn, squash and beans
Ⓓ gathering wild plants

Time   LinguaForum   ? Help   ← Prev   → Next

PRACTICE TEST 11

Reading

An individual's DNA is as distinctive as a fingerprint and, in certain types of violent crime, more likely to be obtainable. The method for "DNA fingerprinting" which was devised by Alec Jeffreys of the University of Leicester in England, is basically simple. The eukaryotic genome contains many regions of simple-sequence DNA, identical short nucleotide sequences lined up in tandem and recurring thousands of times. Jeffreys noted that the number of repeated units in such regions differs distinctively from individual to individual. The regions can be excised from the total DNA by the use of appropriate restriction enzymes, placed on an electrophoretic gel, separated by length, denatured, and identified by a radioactive probe. When the process is completed, the end result, visible on x-ray film, looks like the bar code on a supermarket package.

→ Such a DNA bar code helped to convict Randall Jones, now on Death Row in Florida. Jones's car got stuck in the mud. ■ In search of a tow, he found a young couple asleep in a pickup truck parked by a fishing ramp. ■ He shot each of them in the head with a rifle, dragged their bodies into the woods, used the truck to pull out his car, and then went back and raped the woman. ■ In such cases, standard blood or semen analysis can identify a suspect with a certainty of about 90 to 95 percent, leaving some room for argument. ■ However, Jones's DNA pattern, which matched the sperm found in the victim's body, could occur in only one person out of 9.34 billion – about double the present population of the world.

→ Often only very small samples of biological evidence are found at a crime scene. ■ A gene amplification method known as PCR, or polymerase chain reaction, has been developed that can take a minute fragment of DNA and synthesize millions of copies. ■ Gene amplification has made it possible to obtain DNA fingerprints from trace amounts of blood and semen and even from the root of a single hair. ■ It has been used to speed up prenatal diagnosis of genetic disease and to detect latent virus infections. It also made possible the analysis of mitochondrial DNA from a wooly mammoth that died some 40,000 years ago. ■

LinguaForum

12. The main purpose of the passage is
   Ⓐ to introduce the case of Randall Jones
   Ⓑ to introduce the method of DNA fingerprinting
   Ⓒ to introduce the role of DNA in investigating crime
   Ⓓ to introduce the role of fingerprints in police investigation

13. Compared to fingerprints, DNA is
   Ⓐ distinctive
   Ⓑ more useful
   Ⓒ more obtainable
   Ⓓ more visible

14. Look at the word recurring in the passage. Click on the word or phrase in the **bold** text that is closest in meaning to recurring.

15. DNA fingerprinting is described as all of the following EXCEPT that
   Ⓐ it resembles a price tag
   Ⓑ it may be identified conclusively
   Ⓒ it is visible on x-ray film
   Ⓓ it looks like a bar code

16. Look at the word excised in the passage. Click on the word or phrase in the **bold** text that best replaces excised.

17. It can be inferred from the passage that Jones's murder was
   Ⓐ premeditated
   Ⓑ accidental
   Ⓒ passionate
   Ⓓ spontaneous

18. Look at the word he in the passage. Click on the word or phrase in the **bold** text that he refers to.

19. In the case of Jones, DNA proved to be
   Ⓐ more easily obtainable than blood or semen
   Ⓑ more accurate than blood or semen
   Ⓒ more useful than blood or semen
   Ⓓ more abundant than blood or semen

20. The second paragraph suggests that the DNA method
   Ⓐ may convict those who haven't committed crimes
   Ⓑ would also completely exonerate a defendant who was innocent
   Ⓒ is the preferred method of investigation by the police
   Ⓓ is more economical than blood or semen testing

21. The following sentence can be added to paragraph 2 or 3.

   This method involves adding a short primer at each end of a selected DNA sequence, separating the two strands of the double helix by heating, and exposing them to a bacterial DNA polymerase that recognizes the primers.

   Where would it best fit in the paragraph? Click on the square [■] to add the sentence to paragraph 2 or 3.
   Paragraphs 2 and 3 are marked with an arrow [➜].

22. The passage mentions other uses of DNA EXCEPT
   Ⓐ diagnosis of genetic disease
   Ⓑ diagnosis of cancerous cells
   Ⓒ latent virus infection
   Ⓓ investigation of crime

PRACTICE TEST 11

417

Reading

Passage 3

The electronic computer is so much a part of our everyday lives that the present generation has difficulty imagining the world without it. Computers regulate temperature in buildings and operate traffic signals at intersections. Computers sit on our desktops at work and at home. We carry computers in our briefcases and even in our pockets. Computers help doctors diagnose illness, schedule patients for surgery at hospitals, and help to operate the surgical equipment in the operating room. Computers process food, fuel, and bank transactions. Almost all developments in science and engineering today are made possible by computers. Name almost any form of human activity, and there is a high probability that electronic computers have something to do with it. **Computers are involved at the beginning, middle, and end of nearly everything we do. The invention of the computer is perhaps the most important single event of the 20th century.**

➡ **It may come as a surprise, then, to learn that the electronic computer is only about 60 years old. Many persons now alive were born and raised before it was even invented. ■ The emergence of the electronic computer was the culmination of a long series of events which began around the start of World War II. ■ The Germans were using a mechanical encryption machine called Enigma to generate codes for military use. ■ In principle, Enigma was so complex in its operation that its encoding was thought to be unbreakable. In fact, sophisticated machines were able to crack the German codes. One of the first code-breaking machines was built in Poland before the German invasion. Thereafter, progress was swift. The British quickly built much larger and more sophisticated machines, partly electronic and partly mechanical, to decipher German coded messages. ■**

➡ Such "electromechanical" devices were developed both in Britain and the United States during the war. ■ They were neither completely mechanical, as earlier computing machines had been, nor fully electronic, as later generations of computers would be. ■ It took about a decade to complete the transition from the mechanical era to the electronic era in computing. ■ Although there is some debate about who invented the first electronic (as opposed to electromechanical) computer, it is widely believed that the first completely electronic computer in the U.S. was the Electronic Numerical Integrator and Computer, or ENIAC, built at the University of Pennsylvania to help the Army calculate firing tables for artillery. ■ Filled with thousands of vacuum tubes, ENIAC was a huge machine which filled an entire room. ENIAC was completed too late to affect the war effort greatly, but provided the model for many later machines.

418

23. This passage is concerned primarily with
    - (A) the development of ENIAC and its influence on the U.S. war effort
    - (B) electromechanical British code-breaking machines in World War II
    - (C) the German invasion of Poland
    - (D) events culminating in the development of early electronic computers

24. Look at the word end in the passage. Click on the word or phrase in the **bold** text which is closest in meaning to end.

25. It is possible to infer from paragraph 1 that computers
    - (A) have a vast number and variety of applications because computers have become very small, efficient, and inexpensive
    - (B) have remained basically undeveloped since the end of World War II
    - (C) were principally responsible for Poland's invasion of Germany
    - (D) were principally responsible for Germany's invasion of Poland

26. According to the passage, electronic computers do NOT
    - (A) control temperature in buildings
    - (B) help operate surgical equipment in hospitals
    - (C) process bank transactions
    - (D) undergo surgery themselves

27. Look at the word invention in the passage. Click on the word or phrase in the **bold** text which is closest in meaning to invention.

28. According to the passage, paragraph 2 supports paragraph 1 by
    - (A) explaining the recent origin of the electronic computer and early developments leading to its invention
    - (B) describing how Polish machines were smuggled to Britain to keep them from being captured by the Germans
    - (C) describing how Poland stole a German Enigma machine from a railway station
    - (D) explaining how Enigma machines were distributed to German submarines for use at sea

29. The following sentence can be added to paragraph 2 or 3.

    These machines were so successful that the British were able to read German communications before Hitler himself could see them.

    Where would it best fit in the paragraph? Click on the square [■] to add the sentence to paragraph 2 or 3.
    Paragraphs 2 and 3 are marked with an arrow [➡].

30. Look at the word it in the passage. Click on the word in the **bold** text to which it refers.

31. According to the passage, it took about a decade to complete
    - (A) the German invasion of Poland
    - (B) the construction of ENIAC
    - (C) the invention of the vacuum tube
    - (D) the transition from the mechanical era to the electronic era in computing

32. Look at the word crack in the passage. Click on the word or phrase in the **bold** text which is closest in meaning to crack.

33. The overall tone of this passage may be described as
    - (A) indifferent
    - (B) sarcastic
    - (C) critical
    - (D) descriptive

PRACTICE TEST 11

Reading

The word "opium" comes from the Greek *opion*, meaning "poppy juice." Since the time of the Greeks, poppy juice and its derivatives such as morphine have been used for the control of pain. They are the most potent painkillers known, and their physiological effects are greatly enhanced by the fact that they produce euphoria. They are also highly addictive, and although the pharmaceutical industry, urged on by the possibility of great profits, has made repeated attempts to develop an opium derivative that is non-addictive, its efforts have been uniformly unsuccessful.

→ All substances with opiate action are related chemically and have similarities in their three-dimensional structures. ■ Thus, it was long suspected that opiates act upon the brain by binding to specific membrane receptors. Investigators were able to show that the central nervous system does, indeed, have receptors for opiates. ■ Such receptors have been found not just in humans but in all other vertebrates tested. Why would vertebrate brains have opiate receptors? Only one answer seemed logical: Because vertebrate brains themselves must produce opiates. ■ This rather startling conclusion triggered a search for naturally occurring substances with opiate activity. Many such internal opiates have now been isolated, and they have been given the name of endorphins, for endogenous morphine-like substances. ■

→ **Two types of endorphins are recognized. One group, known as the enkephalins, is** widespread **in the central nervous system and is also abundant in the adrenal medulla.** ■ **The other endorphins are produced mainly by the pituitary gland and perhaps by other tissues as well.** ■ **The endorphins are of great interest to medical researchers because of the insight** they **may afford into the relief of two extremely serious medical problems, opiate addiction and pain.** ■ **They are believed to function as natural analgesics or pain relievers. Individuals in stressful situations have often reported being unaware of what later proved to be an** utterly **painful injury, and so being able to continue to function in a life- or victory-threatening situation.** ■

Time   **LinguaForum**   **Help** **Prev** **Next**

34. The passage discusses primarily
    - (A) the origin and history of opium
    - (B) the different kinds of painkillers
    - (C) the importance of endorphins
    - (D) the role of internal opiates: the endorphins

35. Opium is used as
    - (A) poppy juice
    - (B) a painkiller
    - (C) a drug derivative
    - (D) a prevention against drug addiction

36. The pharmaceutical industry has tried to make non-addictive opium because
    - (A) it fears that patients will become addicts
    - (B) it fears that other drugs will not function
    - (C) it wants to create a substantial profit for itself
    - (D) it wants to help people feel better

37. Opiates act upon by the brain by
    - (A) triggering the membrane receptors
    - (B) detaching the membrane receptors
    - (C) stimulating the membrane receptors
    - (D) binding to the membrane receptors

38. The following sentence can be added to paragraph 2 or 3.

    These receptors are located primarily in the spinal cord, brainstem, and brain regions in which drives and emotions are thought to be translated into complex actions.

    Where would it best fit in the paragraph? Click on the square [■] to add the sentence to paragraph 2 or 3.
    Paragraphs 2 and 3 are marked with an arrow [➜].

39. All of the following describe endorphins EXCEPT
    - (A) morphine-like
    - (B) natural
    - (C) addictive
    - (D) internal

40. Look at the word widespread in the passage. Click on the word or phrase in the **bold** text that is closest in meaning to widespread.

41. Endorphins are found in the following places EXCEPT
    - (A) endocrine glands
    - (B) pituitary gland
    - (C) adrenal medulla
    - (D) central nervous system

42. Look at the word they in the passage. Click on the word or phrase in the **bold** text that they refers to.

43. All of the following are examples of persons in stressful or life- or victory-threatening situations EXCEPT
    - (A) soldiers on a battlefield
    - (B) marathon runners
    - (C) television repairmen
    - (D) tennis players

44. Look at the word utterly in the passage. Click on the word or phrase in the **bold** text that utterly refers to.

PRACTICE TEST 11

Test
11

SECTION 4
WRITING
Suggested Time: 30 Minutes

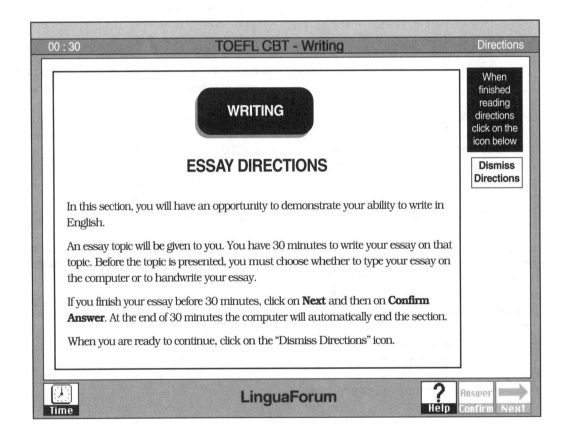

| 00 : 30 | TOEFL CBT - Writing | Directions |

WRITING

When finished reading directions click on the icon below

Dismiss Directions

ESSAY DIRECTIONS

In this section, you will have an opportunity to demonstrate your ability to write in English.

An essay topic will be given to you. You have 30 minutes to write your essay on that topic. Before the topic is presented, you must choose whether to type your essay on the computer or to handwrite your essay.

If you finish your essay before 30 minutes, click on **Next** and then on **Confirm Answer**. At the end of 30 minutes the computer will automatically end the section.

When you are ready to continue, click on the "Dismiss Directions" icon.

Time

LinguaForum

? Help | **Answer Confirm** | **Next**

Writing

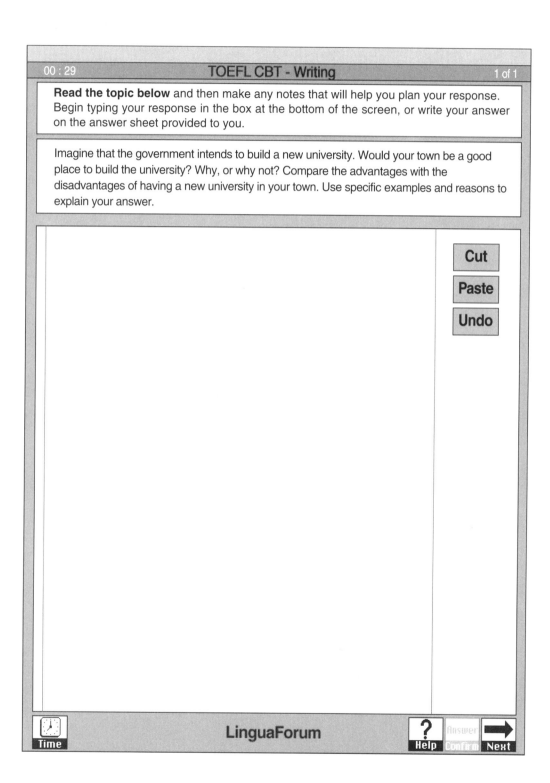

Practice Test 12

Listening: 40 Minutes (including listening time)
Structure: 20 Minutes
Reading: 90 Minutes
Writing: 30 Minutes

Suggested Total Time: 180 Minutes

ANSWER SHEET

Lingua TOEFL® CBT Test Book II
PRACTICE TEST 12

Name	
Sex	☐ male ☐ female
E-mail address	
Telephone No.	

No. of Correct Answers/Converted Score

Listening		
Structure		
Reading		
Writing		
TOTAL		

Section 1: Listening

1. Ⓐ Ⓑ Ⓒ Ⓓ
2. Ⓐ Ⓑ Ⓒ Ⓓ
3. Ⓐ Ⓑ Ⓒ Ⓓ
4. Ⓐ Ⓑ Ⓒ Ⓓ
5. Ⓐ Ⓑ Ⓒ Ⓓ
6. Ⓐ Ⓑ Ⓒ Ⓓ
7. Ⓐ Ⓑ Ⓒ Ⓓ
8. Ⓐ Ⓑ Ⓒ Ⓓ
9. Ⓐ Ⓑ Ⓒ Ⓓ
10. Ⓐ Ⓑ Ⓒ Ⓓ
11. Ⓐ Ⓑ Ⓒ Ⓓ
12. Ⓐ Ⓑ Ⓒ Ⓓ
13. Adam Smith –

   Alfred Marshall –

   John Maynard Keynes –
14. Ⓐ Ⓑ Ⓒ Ⓓ
15. Ⓐ Ⓑ Ⓒ Ⓓ
16. Ⓐ Ⓑ Ⓒ Ⓓ
17. Light bulb –

   Repeater –

   Ticker –
18.

19. Ⓐ Ⓑ Ⓒ Ⓓ
20. Ⓐ Ⓑ Ⓒ Ⓓ
21. Ⓐ Ⓑ Ⓒ Ⓓ
22. Ⓐ Ⓑ Ⓒ Ⓓ
23. Ⓐ Ⓑ Ⓒ Ⓓ
24. Ⓐ Ⓑ Ⓒ Ⓓ
25. Ⓐ Ⓑ Ⓒ Ⓓ
26.

27.

28. Ⓐ Ⓑ Ⓒ Ⓓ
29. Ⓐ Ⓑ Ⓒ Ⓓ
30. Ⓐ Ⓑ Ⓒ Ⓓ

Section 2: Structure

1. Ⓐ Ⓑ Ⓒ Ⓓ
2. Ⓐ Ⓑ Ⓒ Ⓓ
3. Ⓐ Ⓑ Ⓒ Ⓓ
4. Ⓐ Ⓑ Ⓒ Ⓓ
5. Ⓐ Ⓑ Ⓒ Ⓓ
6. Ⓐ Ⓑ Ⓒ Ⓓ
7. Ⓐ Ⓑ Ⓒ Ⓓ
8. Ⓐ Ⓑ Ⓒ Ⓓ
9. Ⓐ Ⓑ Ⓒ Ⓓ
10. Ⓐ Ⓑ Ⓒ Ⓓ
11. Ⓐ Ⓑ Ⓒ Ⓓ
12. Ⓐ Ⓑ Ⓒ Ⓓ
13. Ⓐ Ⓑ Ⓒ Ⓓ
14. Ⓐ Ⓑ Ⓒ Ⓓ
15. Ⓐ Ⓑ Ⓒ Ⓓ
16. Ⓐ Ⓑ Ⓒ Ⓓ
17. Ⓐ Ⓑ Ⓒ Ⓓ
18. Ⓐ Ⓑ Ⓒ Ⓓ
19. Ⓐ Ⓑ Ⓒ Ⓓ
20. Ⓐ Ⓑ Ⓒ Ⓓ
21. Ⓐ Ⓑ Ⓒ Ⓓ
22. Ⓐ Ⓑ Ⓒ Ⓓ
23. Ⓐ Ⓑ Ⓒ Ⓓ
24. Ⓐ Ⓑ Ⓒ Ⓓ
25. Ⓐ Ⓑ Ⓒ Ⓓ

Section 3: Reading

1. Ⓐ Ⓑ Ⓒ Ⓓ
2. Ⓐ Ⓑ Ⓒ Ⓓ
3. Ⓐ Ⓑ Ⓒ Ⓓ
4. Ⓐ Ⓑ Ⓒ Ⓓ
5. Ⓐ Ⓑ Ⓒ Ⓓ
6. Ⓐ Ⓑ Ⓒ Ⓓ
7. Ⓐ Ⓑ Ⓒ Ⓓ
8. Ⓐ Ⓑ Ⓒ Ⓓ
9. Ⓐ Ⓑ Ⓒ Ⓓ
10. Ⓐ Ⓑ Ⓒ Ⓓ
11. Ⓐ Ⓑ Ⓒ Ⓓ
12. Ⓐ Ⓑ Ⓒ Ⓓ
13. Ⓐ Ⓑ Ⓒ Ⓓ
14. Ⓐ Ⓑ Ⓒ Ⓓ
15. Ⓐ Ⓑ Ⓒ Ⓓ
16. Ⓐ Ⓑ Ⓒ Ⓓ
17. Ⓐ Ⓑ Ⓒ Ⓓ
18. Ⓐ Ⓑ Ⓒ Ⓓ
19. Ⓐ Ⓑ Ⓒ Ⓓ
20. Ⓐ Ⓑ Ⓒ Ⓓ
21. Ⓐ Ⓑ Ⓒ Ⓓ
22. Ⓐ Ⓑ Ⓒ Ⓓ
23. Ⓐ Ⓑ Ⓒ Ⓓ
24. Ⓐ Ⓑ Ⓒ Ⓓ
25. Ⓐ Ⓑ Ⓒ Ⓓ
26. Ⓐ Ⓑ Ⓒ Ⓓ
27. Ⓐ Ⓑ Ⓒ Ⓓ
28.
29. Ⓐ Ⓑ Ⓒ Ⓓ
30. Ⓐ Ⓑ Ⓒ Ⓓ

31.
32.
33. Ⓐ Ⓑ Ⓒ Ⓓ
34. Ⓐ Ⓑ Ⓒ Ⓓ
35. Ⓐ Ⓑ Ⓒ Ⓓ
36. Ⓐ Ⓑ Ⓒ Ⓓ
37. Ⓐ Ⓑ Ⓒ Ⓓ
38. Ⓐ Ⓑ Ⓒ Ⓓ
39. Ⓐ Ⓑ Ⓒ Ⓓ
40. Ⓐ Ⓑ Ⓒ Ⓓ
41. Ⓐ Ⓑ Ⓒ Ⓓ
42.
43.
44. Ⓐ Ⓑ Ⓒ Ⓓ
45. Ⓐ Ⓑ Ⓒ Ⓓ
46. Ⓐ Ⓑ Ⓒ Ⓓ
47.
48.
49. Ⓐ Ⓑ Ⓒ Ⓓ
50. Ⓐ Ⓑ Ⓒ Ⓓ
51. Ⓐ Ⓑ Ⓒ Ⓓ
52. Ⓐ Ⓑ Ⓒ Ⓓ
53. Ⓐ Ⓑ Ⓒ Ⓓ
54. Ⓐ Ⓑ Ⓒ Ⓓ
55. Ⓐ Ⓑ Ⓒ Ⓓ

Cut here.

■ **Have you taken the official TOEFL Test?**

☐ Yes   → if any

☐ No

PBT Score	
Listening	
Structure	
Reading	
Writing	
TOTAL	

CBT Score	
Listening	
Structure	
Reading	
Writing	
TOTAL	

■ **Educational background**

☐ middle/high school   ☐ undergraduate   ☐ graduate

SIGNED: _____

(SIGN YOUR NAME AS IF SIGNING A BUSINESS LETTER.)

DATE: ____ / ____ / ____

MO.   DAY   YEAR

LinguaForum

Copyright © 2002 by Lingua Forum, Inc. All rights reserved.

ANSWER SHEET

Lingua TOEFL® CBT Test Book II
PRACTICE TEST 12

Read the topic below and then make any notes that will help you plan your response. Begin typing your response in the box at the bottom of the screen, or write your answer on the answer sheet provided to you.

One can make decisions quickly, or after thinking long and carefully. Some people say it is always wrong to make a decision quickly. Do you agree or disagree with that view? Use specific examples and reasons to support your answer.

Cut

Paste

Undo

Time

LinguaForum

? Help

Answer Confirm

→ Next

LinguaForum
Copyright © 2002 by Lingua Forum, Inc. All rights reserved.

Test
12

SECTION 1
LISTENING
Suggested Time: 15 Minutes

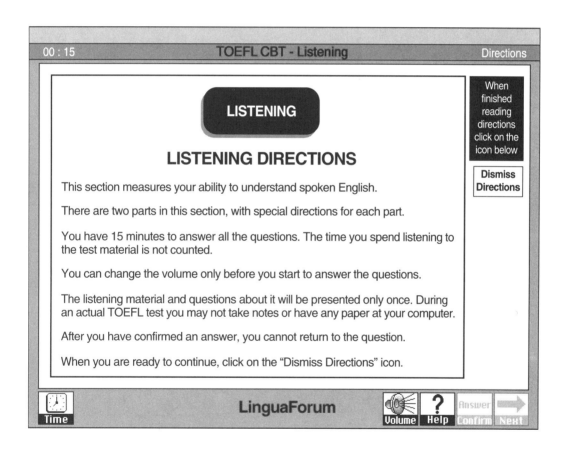

Test
12

SECTION 1
LISTENING

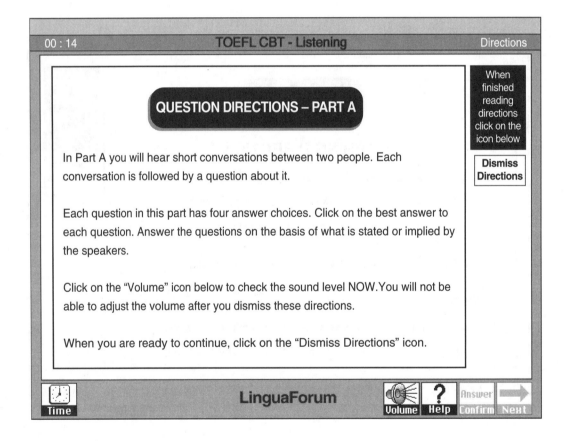

| 00 : 14 | TOEFL CBT - Listening | Directions |

QUESTION DIRECTIONS – PART A

When finished reading directions click on the icon below

Dismiss Directions

In Part A you will hear short conversations between two people. Each conversation is followed by a question about it.

Each question in this part has four answer choices. Click on the best answer to each question. Answer the questions on the basis of what is stated or implied by the speakers.

Click on the "Volume" icon below to check the sound level NOW. You will not be able to adjust the volume after you dismiss these directions.

When you are ready to continue, click on the "Dismiss Directions" icon.

LinguaForum

Time | Volume | Help | Answer Confirm | Next

PRACTICE
TEST 12

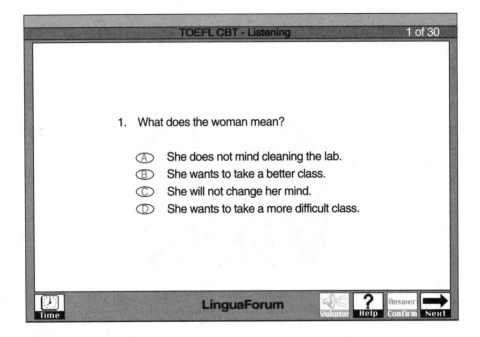

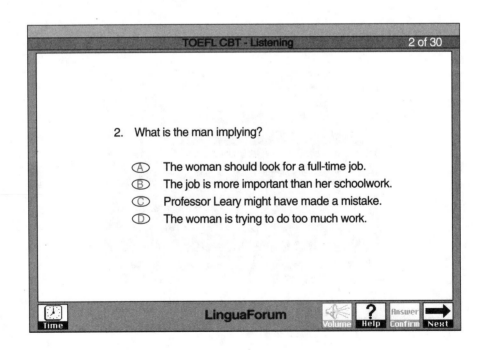

Listening

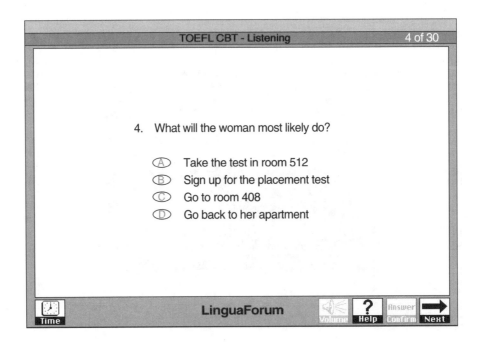

3. Who cut the woman's hair?

- Ⓐ Adam
- Ⓑ The woman's friend
- Ⓒ Adam's brother
- Ⓓ The man

Time   LinguaForum   Volume Help Confirm Next

4. What will the woman most likely do?

- Ⓐ Take the test in room 512
- Ⓑ Sign up for the placement test
- Ⓒ Go to room 408
- Ⓓ Go back to her apartment

Time   LinguaForum   Volume Help Confirm Next

PRACTICE
TEST 12

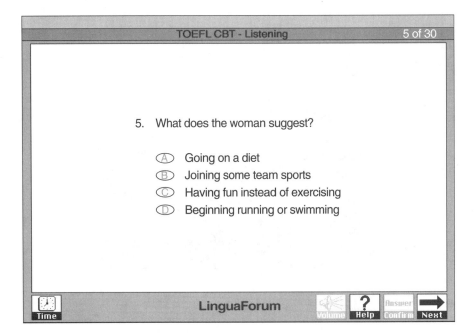

5. What does the woman suggest?

    Ⓐ Going on a diet
    Ⓑ Joining some team sports
    Ⓒ Having fun instead of exercising
    Ⓓ Beginning running or swimming

LinguaForum

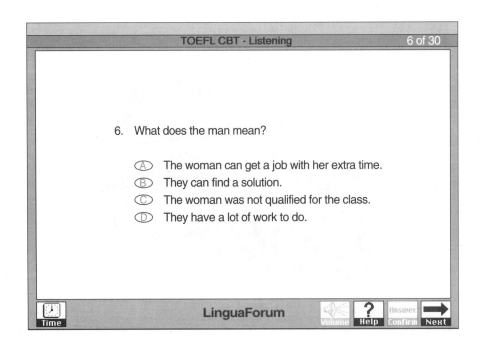

6. What does the man mean?

    Ⓐ The woman can get a job with her extra time.
    Ⓑ They can find a solution.
    Ⓒ The woman was not qualified for the class.
    Ⓓ They have a lot of work to do.

LinguaForum

Listening

437

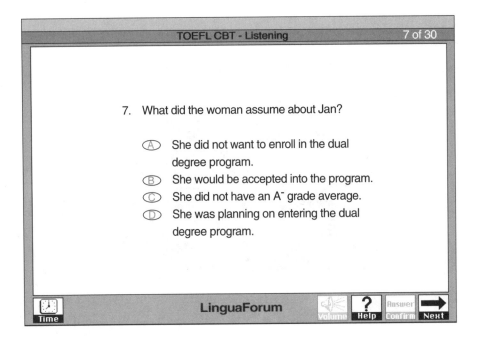

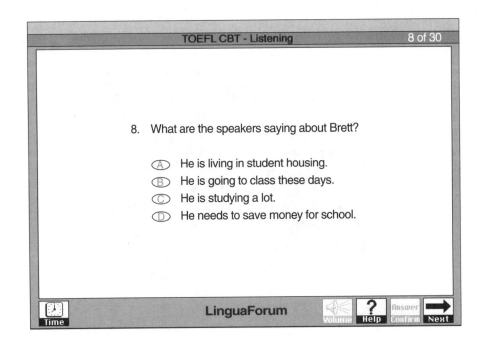

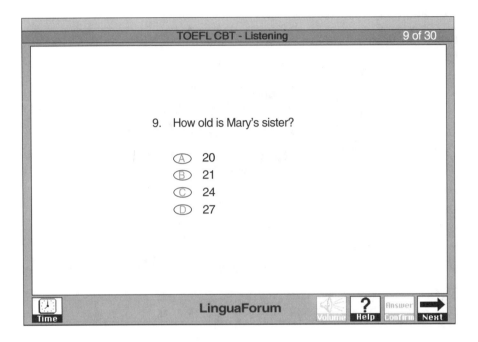

9. How old is Mary's sister?

    (A)   20
    (B)   21
    (C)   24
    (D)   27

LinguaForum

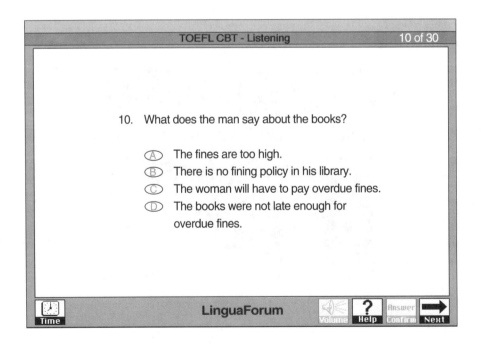

10. What does the man say about the books?

    (A)   The fines are too high.
    (B)   There is no fining policy in his library.
    (C)   The woman will have to pay overdue fines.
    (D)   The books were not late enough for
          overdue fines.

LinguaForum

Listening

PRACTICE TEST 12

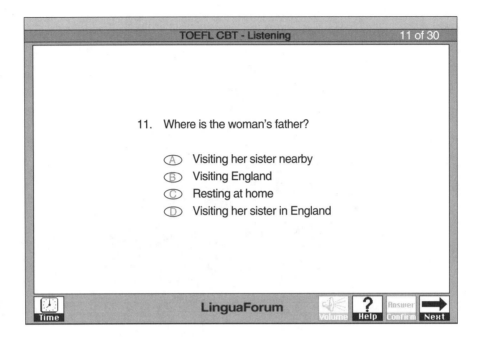

Test
12

SECTION 1
LISTENING

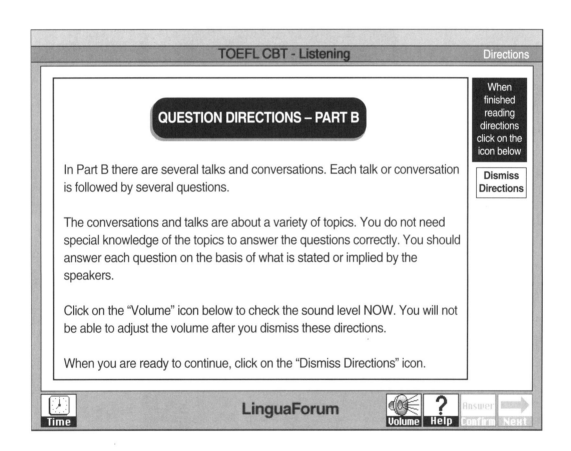

TOEFL CBT - Listening — Directions

QUESTION DIRECTIONS – PART B

In Part B there are several talks and conversations. Each talk or conversation is followed by several questions.

The conversations and talks are about a variety of topics. You do not need special knowledge of the topics to answer the questions correctly. You should answer each question on the basis of what is stated or implied by the speakers.

Click on the "Volume" icon below to check the sound level NOW. You will not be able to adjust the volume after you dismiss these directions.

When you are ready to continue, click on the "Dismiss Directions" icon.

When finished reading directions click on the icon below

Dismiss Directions

Time   LinguaForum   Volume Help Confirm Next

PRACTICE
TEST 12

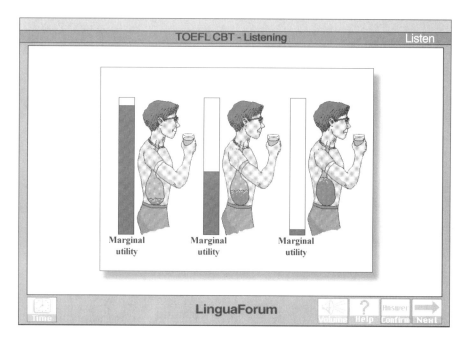

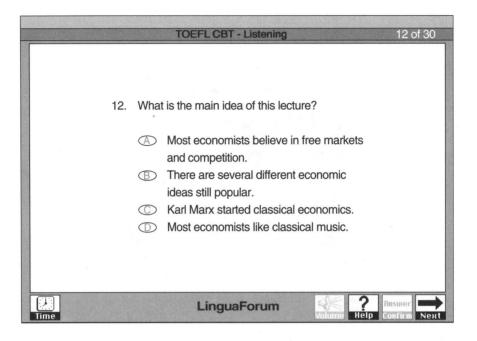

12.   What is the main idea of this lecture?

   Ⓐ   Most economists believe in free markets
          and competition.
   Ⓑ   There are several different economic
          ideas still popular.
   Ⓒ   Karl Marx started classical economics.
   Ⓓ   Most economists like classical music.

LinguaForum

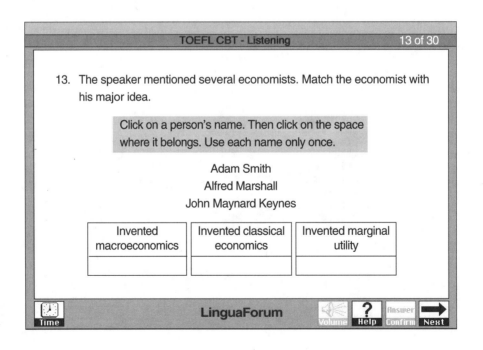

13.   The speaker mentioned several economists. Match the economist with
       his major idea.

       Click on a person's name. Then click on the space
       where it belongs. Use each name only once.

                        Adam Smith
                      Alfred Marshall
                   John Maynard Keynes

Invented macroeconomics	Invented classical economics	Invented marginal utility

LinguaForum

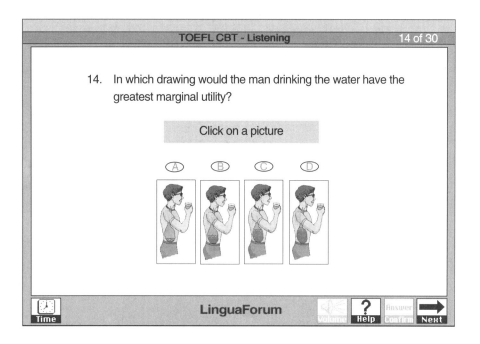

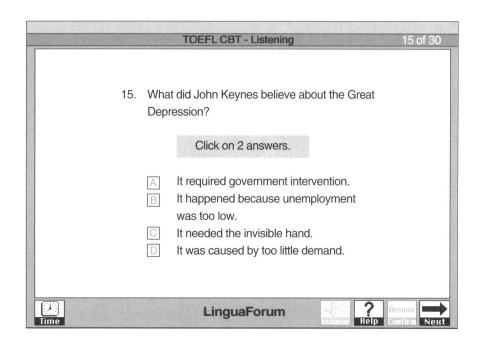

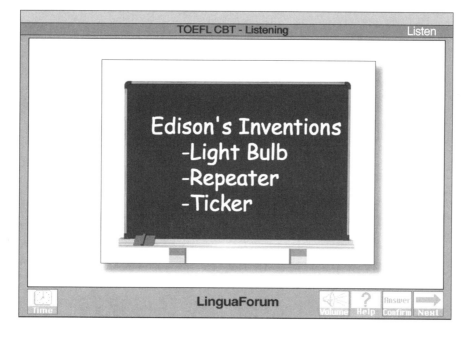

Questions 16-19

449

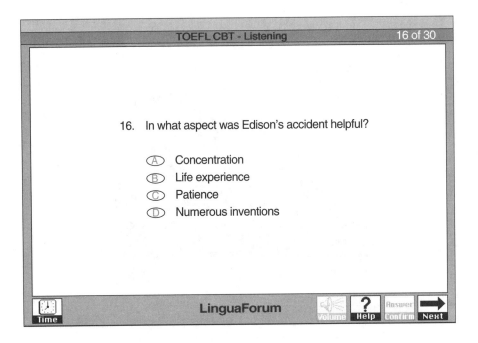

16. In what aspect was Edison's accident helpful?

    Ⓐ Concentration
    Ⓑ Life experience
    Ⓒ Patience
    Ⓓ Numerous inventions

LinguaForum

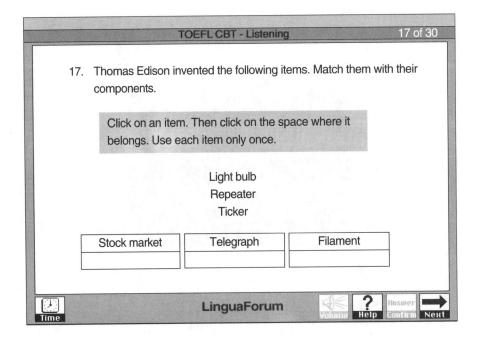

17. Thomas Edison invented the following items. Match them with their components.

Click on an item. Then click on the space where it belongs. Use each item only once.

Light bulb
Repeater
Ticker

Stock market	Telegraph	Filament

LinguaForum

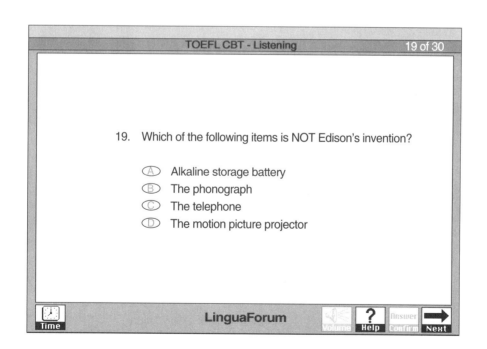

Questions 20-21

452

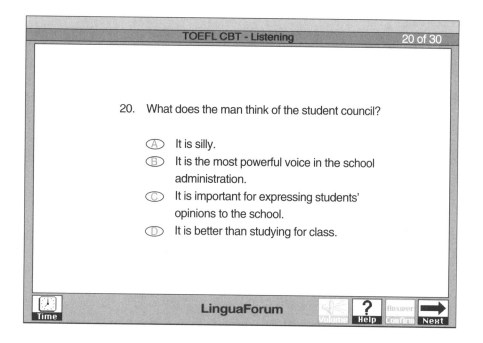

20. What does the man think of the student council?

    Ⓐ   It is silly.
    Ⓑ   It is the most powerful voice in the school administration.
    Ⓒ   It is important for expressing students' opinions to the school.
    Ⓓ   It is better than studying for class.

LinguaForum

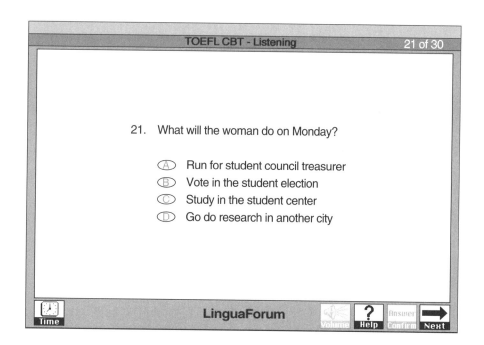

21. What will the woman do on Monday?

    Ⓐ   Run for student council treasurer
    Ⓑ   Vote in the student election
    Ⓒ   Study in the student center
    Ⓓ   Go do research in another city

LinguaForum

PRACTICE TEST 12

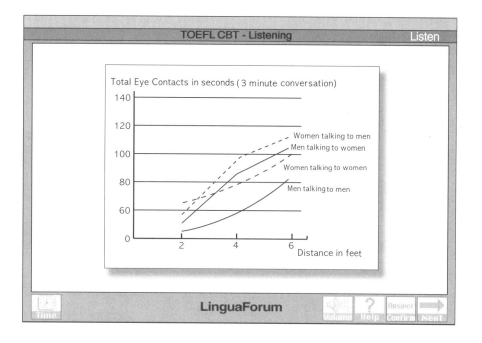

PRACTICE
TEST 12

Questions 22-24

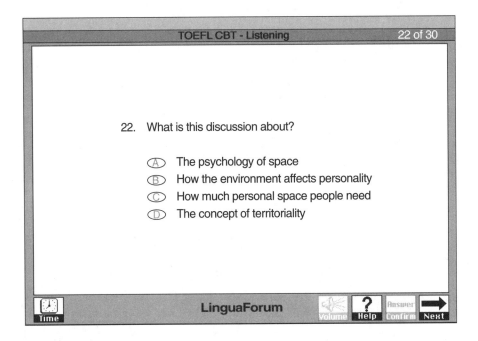

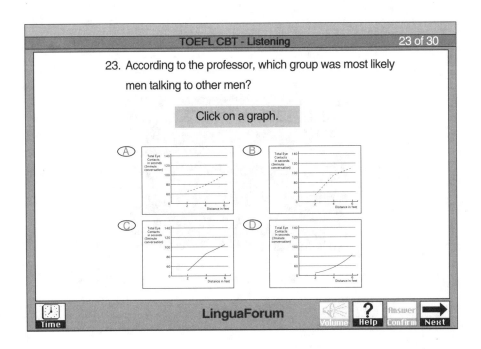

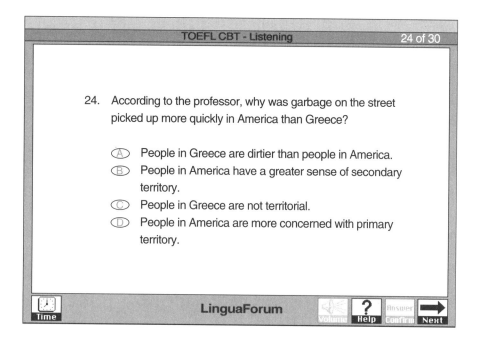

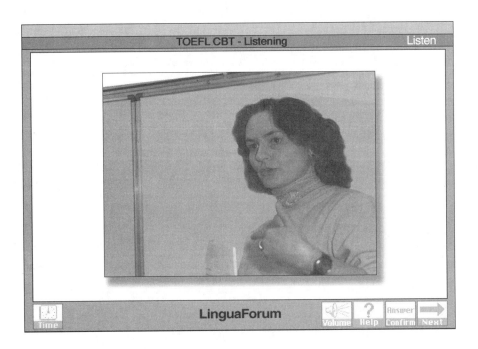

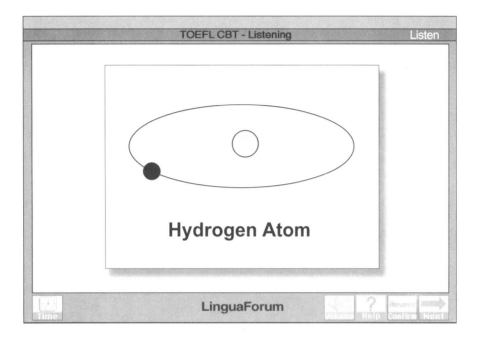

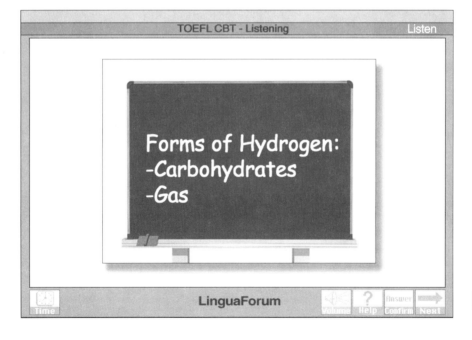

Questions 25-28

**PRACTICE
TEST 12**

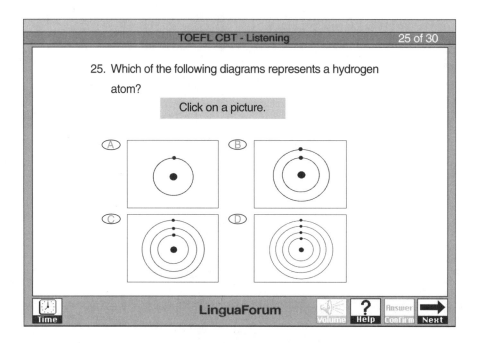

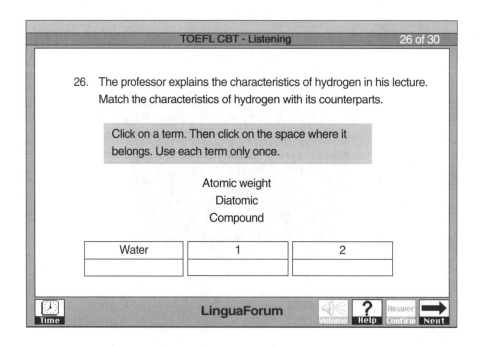

27. Although there is very little free hydrogen in our atmosphere, it combines easily with oxygen in the atmosphere to produce water. Put the following events in chronological order.

Click on a sentence. Then click on the space where it belongs. Use each sentence only once.

Hydrogen gas burns, forming water.
Hydrogen gas is collected.
Hydrogen atoms separate from oxygen atoms.
Water undergoes electrolysis.

1. _____　　3. _____

2. _____　　4. _____

Time　　　　　**LinguaForum**　　　Volume　Help　Confirm　Next

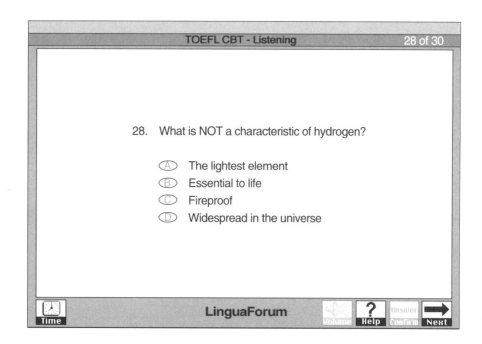

28.　What is NOT a characteristic of hydrogen?

(A)　The lightest element
(B)　Essential to life
(C)　Fireproof
(D)　Widespread in the universe

Time　　　　　**LinguaForum**　　　Volume　Help　Confirm　Next

PRACTICE
TEST 12

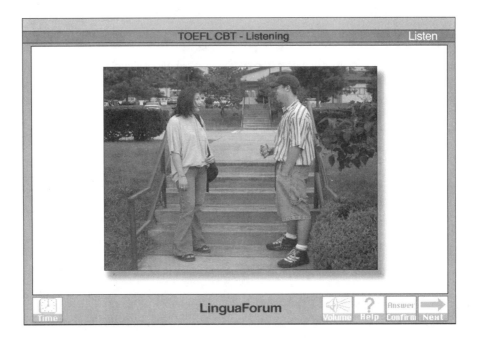

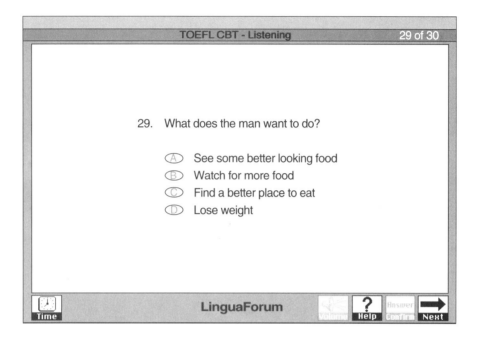

29. What does the man want to do?

- Ⓐ See some better looking food
- Ⓑ Watch for more food
- Ⓒ Find a better place to eat
- Ⓓ Lose weight

LinguaForum

Time Volume Help Answer Confirm Next

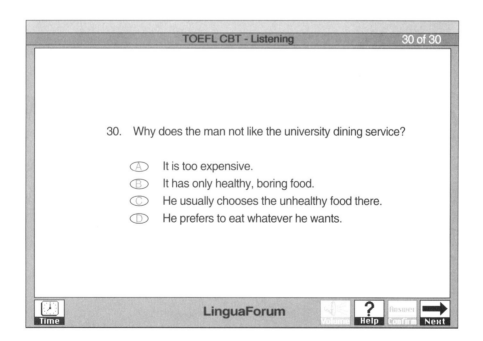

30. Why does the man not like the university dining service?

- Ⓐ It is too expensive.
- Ⓑ It has only healthy, boring food.
- Ⓒ He usually chooses the unhealthy food there.
- Ⓓ He prefers to eat whatever he wants.

LinguaForum

Time Volume Help Answer Confirm Next

PRACTICE
TEST 12

Test
12

SECTION 2
STRUCTURE

Suggested Time: 19 Minutes

| 00 : 19 | TOEFL CBT - Structure | Directions |

STRUCTURE

STRUCTURE DIRECTIONS

When finished reading directions click on the icon below

Dismiss Directions

In this section there are two types of test questions.

In one type, you choose the word or phrase that best completes a sentence.

> Example: _____ of igneous rocks results from the two
> main features of these rocks – the size and the chemistry
> of their constituent crystals.
> ○ Most of the great varieties
> ○ Great varieties
> ○ Greater variation which
> ○ The great variety

In the other type, you look at a sentence with four underlined words or phrases and choose the underlined word or phrase that must be changed for the sentence to be correct.

> Example: The tides <u>caused</u> by the <u>gravitational</u> <u>pull</u> of the moon
>
> and sun and <u>by the rotations</u> of the earth, moon, and sun.

You have 19 minutes to answer all of the questions.

After you have confirmed an answer, you cannot return to the question.

When you are ready to continue, click on the "Dismiss Directions" icon.

Time

LinguaForum

?
Help | Answer | **Confirm** | **Next**

PRACTICE
TEST 12

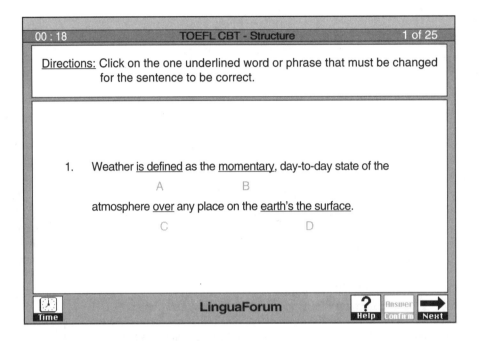

Directions: Click on the one underlined word or phrase that must be changed for the sentence to be correct.

1. Weather <u>is defined</u> as the <u>momentary</u>, day-to-day state of the
                A   B

atmosphere <u>over</u> any place on the <u>earth's the surface</u>.
          C   D

LinguaForum

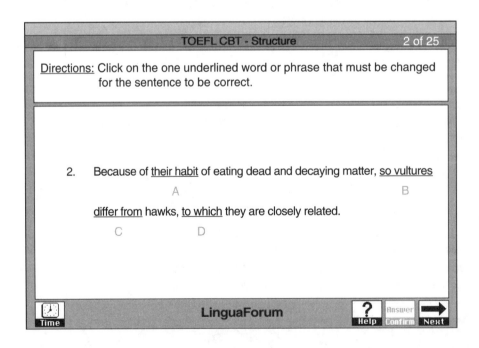

Directions: Click on the one underlined word or phrase that must be changed for the sentence to be correct.

2. Because of <u>their habit</u> of eating dead and decaying matter, <u>so vultures</u>
               A   B

<u>differ from</u> hawks, <u>to which</u> they are closely related.
  C   D

LinguaForum

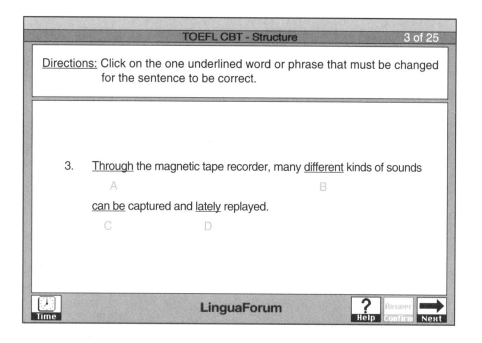

Directions: Click on the one underlined word or phrase that must be changed for the sentence to be correct.

3.   <u>Through</u> the magnetic tape recorder, many <u>different</u> kinds of sounds
       A   B

<u>can be</u> captured and <u>lately</u> replayed.
   C   D

LinguaForum

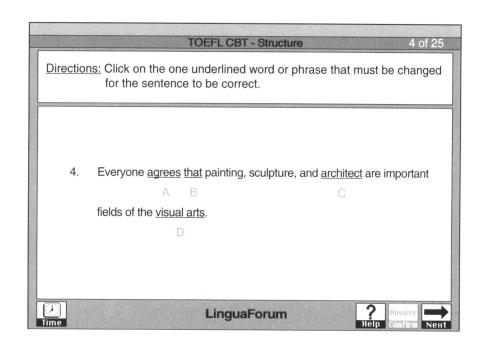

Directions: Click on the one underlined word or phrase that must be changed for the sentence to be correct.

4.   Everyone <u>agrees</u> <u>that</u> painting, sculpture, and <u>architect</u> are important
           A   B   C

fields of the <u>visual arts</u>.
         D

LinguaForum

PRACTICE
TEST 12

467

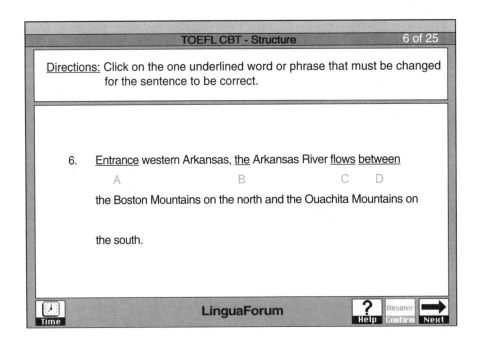

Directions: Click on the one word or phrase that best completes the sentence.

5.   Warming hastens evaporation, since the warmer the liquid,

_____ will have enough speed to escape.

(A)   which more molecules

(B)   many molecules

(C)   the more molecules

(D)   than the molecules

Time   LinguaForum   Help Confirm Next

Directions: Click on the one underlined word or phrase that must be changed for the sentence to be correct.

6.   Entrance western Arkansas, the Arkansas River flows between
      A   B   C   D

the Boston Mountains on the north and the Ouachita Mountains on

the south.

Time   LinguaForum   Help Confirm Next

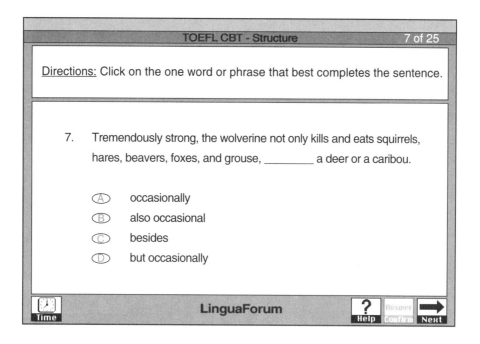

TOEFL CBT - Structure   7 of 25

<u>Directions:</u> Click on the one word or phrase that best completes the sentence.

7.   Tremendously strong, the wolverine not only kills and eats squirrels, hares, beavers, foxes, and grouse, _____ a deer or a caribou.

     Ⓐ   occasionally
     Ⓑ   also occasional
     Ⓒ   besides
     Ⓓ   but occasionally

LinguaForum

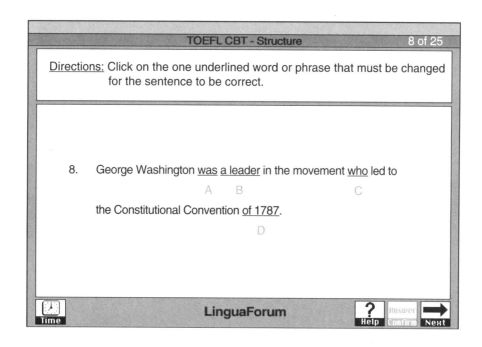

TOEFL CBT - Structure   8 of 25

<u>Directions:</u> Click on the one underlined word or phrase that must be changed for the sentence to be correct.

8.   George Washington <u>was</u> <u>a leader</u> in the movement <u>who</u> led to
                  A   B   C

   the Constitutional Convention <u>of 1787</u>.
                       D

LinguaForum

PRACTICE
TEST 12

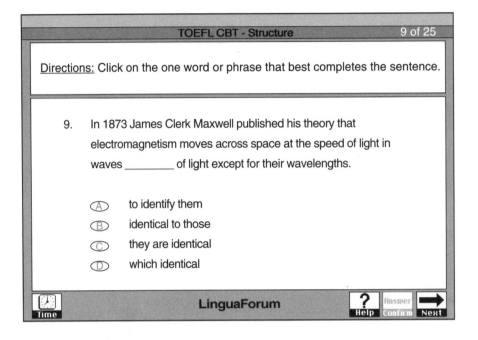

Directions: Click on the one word or phrase that best completes the sentence.

9. In 1873 James Clerk Maxwell published his theory that
    electromagnetism moves across space at the speed of light in
    waves _____ of light except for their wavelengths.

    (A)   to identify them
    (B)   identical to those
    (C)   they are identical
    (D)   which identical

LinguaForum

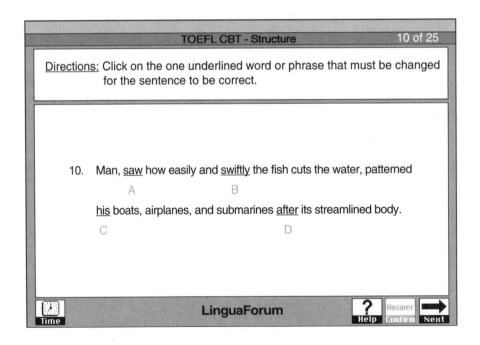

Directions: Click on the one underlined word or phrase that must be changed
           for the sentence to be correct.

10. Man, saw how easily and swiftly the fish cuts the water, patterned
              A   B

     his boats, airplanes, and submarines after its streamlined body.
     C   D

LinguaForum

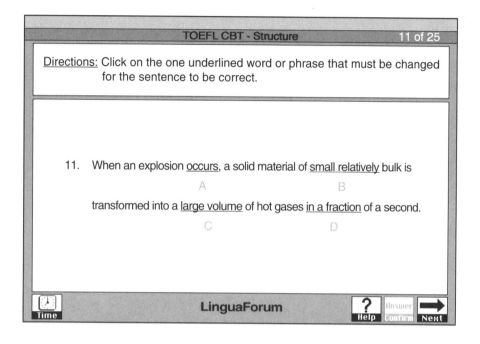

TOEFL CBT - Structure — 11 of 25

Directions: Click on the one underlined word or phrase that must be changed for the sentence to be correct.

11. When an explosion <u>occurs</u>, a solid material of <u>small relatively</u> bulk is
                       A   B

    transformed into a <u>large volume</u> of hot gases <u>in a fraction</u> of a second.
                    C   D

LinguaForum   ? Help   Answer Confirm   → Next

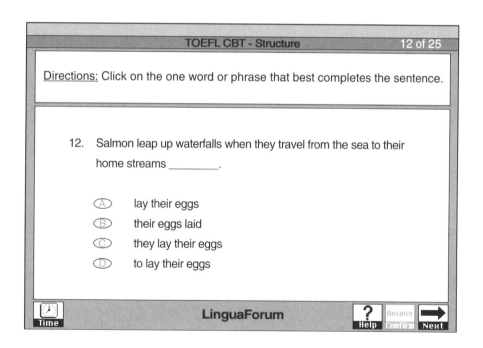

TOEFL CBT - Structure — 12 of 25

Directions: Click on the one word or phrase that best completes the sentence.

12. Salmon leap up waterfalls when they travel from the sea to their home streams _____.

    (A) lay their eggs
    (B) their eggs laid
    (C) they lay their eggs
    (D) to lay their eggs

LinguaForum   ? Help   Answer Confirm   → Next

PRACTICE TEST 12

Structure

Directions: Click on the one underlined word or phrase that must be changed for the sentence to be correct.

13.   From June 21st <u>until</u> December 21st, <u>the length</u> of daylight in the
                           A   B

northern hemisphere <u>progressive</u> decreases to a <u>minimum</u>.
                                      C   D

Time   **LinguaForum**   **?** Answer ➡
                                                           Help Confirm Next

Directions: Click on the one word or phrase that best completes the sentence.

14.   Whether water is in a liquid state, a solid state, or a gaseous state,
       _____ chemical makeup remains the same.

       Ⓐ   its
       Ⓑ   whose
       Ⓒ   but the
       Ⓓ   it is

Time   **LinguaForum**   **?** Answer ➡
                                                           Help Confirm Next

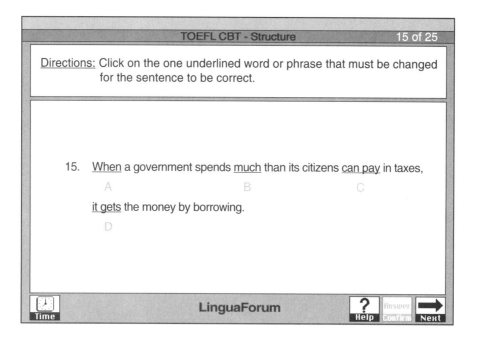

TOEFL CBT - Structure   15 of 25

Directions: Click on the one underlined word or phrase that must be changed for the sentence to be correct.

15. When a government spends much than its citizens can pay in taxes,
     A   B   C

     it gets the money by borrowing.
     D

LinguaForum

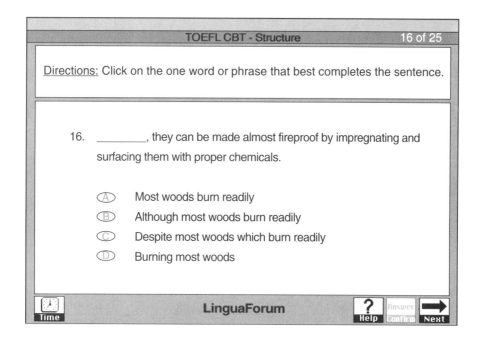

TOEFL CBT - Structure   16 of 25

Directions: Click on the one word or phrase that best completes the sentence.

16. _____, they can be made almost fireproof by impregnating and surfacing them with proper chemicals.

     (A) Most woods burn readily
     (B) Although most woods burn readily
     (C) Despite most woods which burn readily
     (D) Burning most woods

LinguaForum

PRACTICE
TEST 12

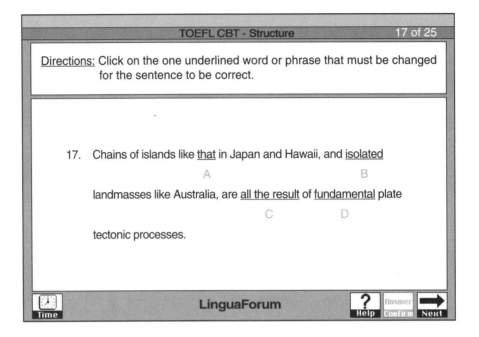

Directions: Click on the one underlined word or phrase that must be changed for the sentence to be correct.

17. Chains of islands like <u>that</u> in Japan and Hawaii, and <u>isolated</u>
                              A   B

landmasses like Australia, are <u>all the result</u> of <u>fundamental</u> plate
                                        C   D

tectonic processes.

LinguaForum

Time   Help Answer Confirm Next

Directions: Click on the one word or phrase that best completes the sentence.

18. Atmospheric pressure is measured at weather stations by an aneroid
barometer, _____ flexible metal vacuum box that expands or
contracts with changes in pressure.

Ⓐ   is a
Ⓑ   which is
Ⓒ   a
Ⓓ   and it is

LinguaForum

Time   Help Answer Confirm Next

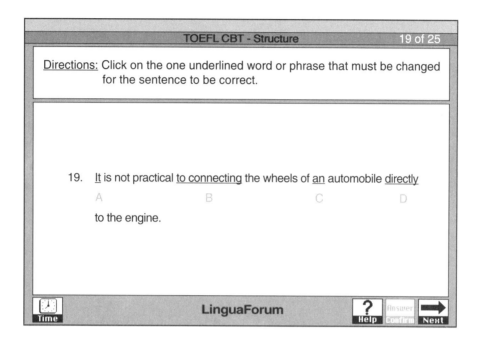

Directions: Click on the one underlined word or phrase that must be changed for the sentence to be correct.

19.   <u>It</u> is not practical <u>to connecting</u> the wheels of <u>an</u> automobile <u>directly</u>
        A   B   C   D

     to the engine.

LinguaForum

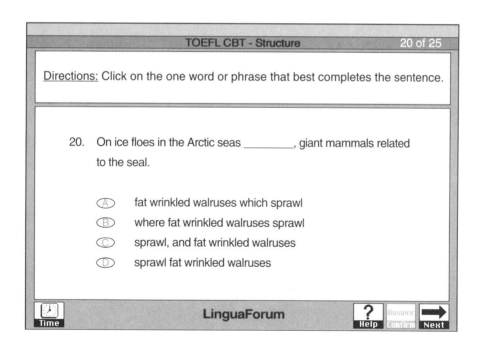

Directions: Click on the one word or phrase that best completes the sentence.

20.   On ice floes in the Arctic seas _____, giant mammals related to the seal.

     (A)   fat wrinkled walruses which sprawl
     (B)   where fat wrinkled walruses sprawl
     (C)   sprawl, and fat wrinkled walruses
     (D)   sprawl fat wrinkled walruses

LinguaForum

PRACTICE
TEST 12

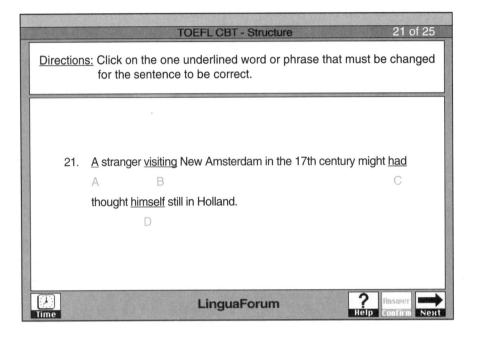

Directions: Click on the one underlined word or phrase that must be changed for the sentence to be correct.

21. <u>A</u> stranger <u>visiting</u> New Amsterdam in the 17th century might <u>had</u>
   A   B   C

thought <u>himself</u> still in Holland.
       D

LinguaForum

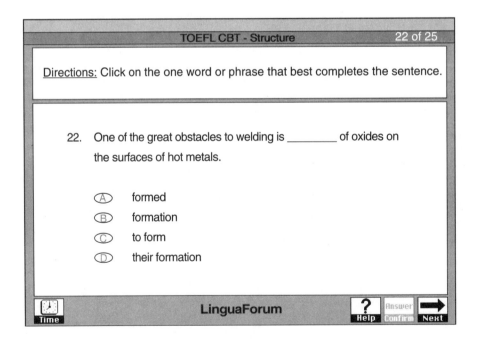

Directions: Click on the one word or phrase that best completes the sentence.

22. One of the great obstacles to welding is _____ of oxides on the surfaces of hot metals.

   Ⓐ   formed
   Ⓑ   formation
   Ⓒ   to form
   Ⓓ   their formation

LinguaForum

Structure

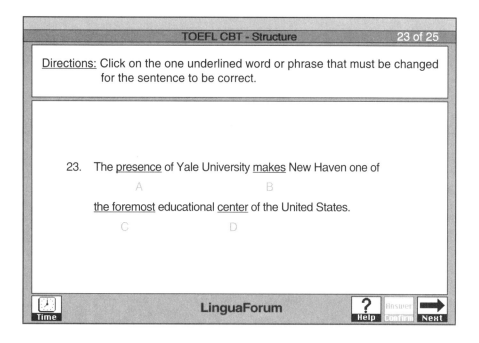

Directions: Click on the one underlined word or phrase that must be changed for the sentence to be correct.

23.   The <u>presence</u> of Yale University <u>makes</u> New Haven one of
                 A   B

the foremost <u>educational</u> <u>center</u> of the United States.
           C   D

LinguaForum

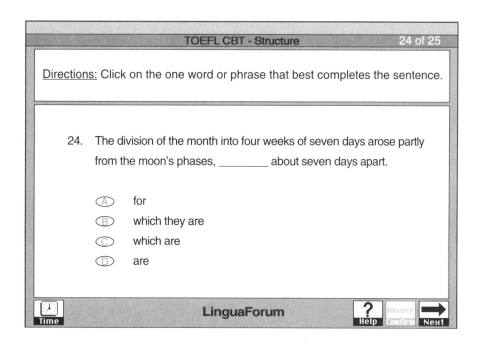

Directions: Click on the one word or phrase that best completes the sentence.

24.   The division of the month into four weeks of seven days arose partly
      from the moon's phases, _____ about seven days apart.

      Ⓐ   for
      Ⓑ   which they are
      Ⓒ   which are
      Ⓓ   are

LinguaForum

PRACTICE TEST 12

477

Structure

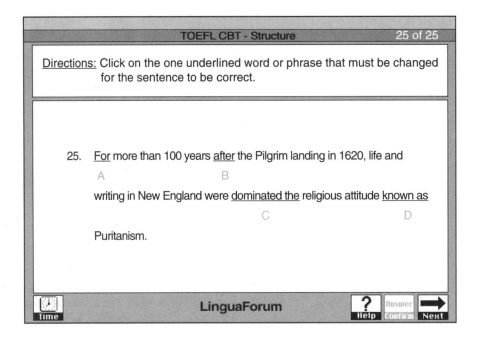

<u>Directions:</u> Click on the one underlined word or phrase that must be changed for the sentence to be correct.

25. <u>For</u> more than 100 years <u>after</u> the Pilgrim landing in 1620, life and

    A   B

writing in New England were <u>dominated the</u> religious attitude <u>known as</u>

                                    C   D

Puritanism.

LinguaForum

Time   **?** Help   Answer Confirm   Next

Test
12

SECTION 3
READING
Suggested Time: 90 Minutes

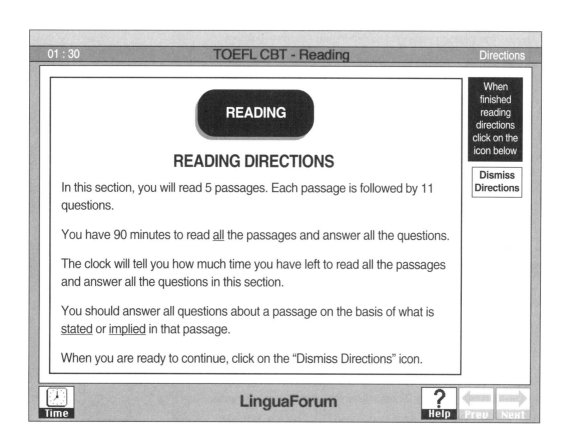

| 01 : 30 | TOEFL CBT - Reading | Directions |

When finished reading directions click on the icon below

Dismiss Directions

READING

READING DIRECTIONS

In this section, you will read 5 passages. Each passage is followed by 11 questions.

You have 90 minutes to read <u>all</u> the passages and answer all the questions.

The clock will tell you how much time you have left to read all the passages and answer all the questions in this section.

You should answer all questions about a passage on the basis of what is <u>stated</u> or <u>implied</u> in that passage.

When you are ready to continue, click on the "Dismiss Directions" icon.

Time   **LinguaForum**   **? Help**   Prev   Next

PRACTICE TEST 12

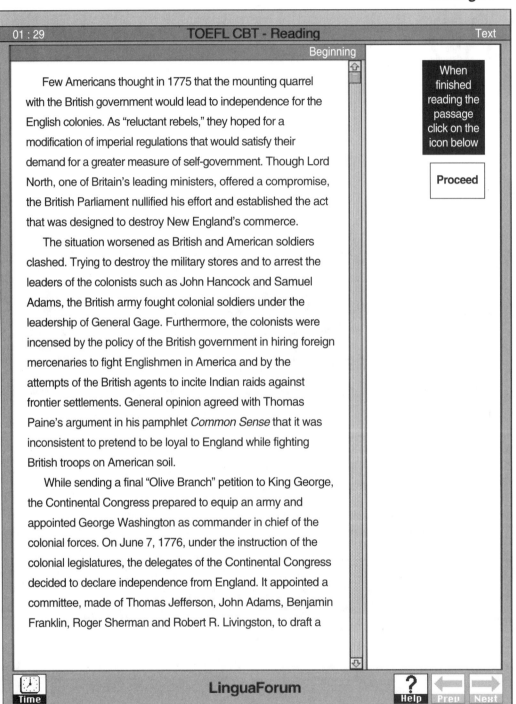

01 : 29   TOEFL CBT - Reading   Text

Beginning

When finished reading the passage click on the icon below

Proceed

    Few Americans thought in 1775 that the mounting quarrel with the British government would lead to independence for the English colonies. As "reluctant rebels," they hoped for a modification of imperial regulations that would satisfy their demand for a greater measure of self-government. Though Lord North, one of Britain's leading ministers, offered a compromise, the British Parliament nullified his effort and established the act that was designed to destroy New England's commerce.

    The situation worsened as British and American soldiers clashed. Trying to destroy the military stores and to arrest the leaders of the colonists such as John Hancock and Samuel Adams, the British army fought colonial soldiers under the leadership of General Gage. Furthermore, the colonists were incensed by the policy of the British government in hiring foreign mercenaries to fight Englishmen in America and by the attempts of the British agents to incite Indian raids against frontier settlements. General opinion agreed with Thomas Paine's argument in his pamphlet *Common Sense* that it was inconsistent to pretend to be loyal to England while fighting British troops on American soil.

    While sending a final "Olive Branch" petition to King George, the Continental Congress prepared to equip an army and appointed George Washington as commander in chief of the colonial forces. On June 7, 1776, under the instruction of the colonial legislatures, the delegates of the Continental Congress decided to declare independence from England. It appointed a committee, made of Thomas Jefferson, John Adams, Benjamin Franklin, Roger Sherman and Robert R. Livingston, to draft a

LinguaForum

Time   Help   Prev   Next

Passage 1

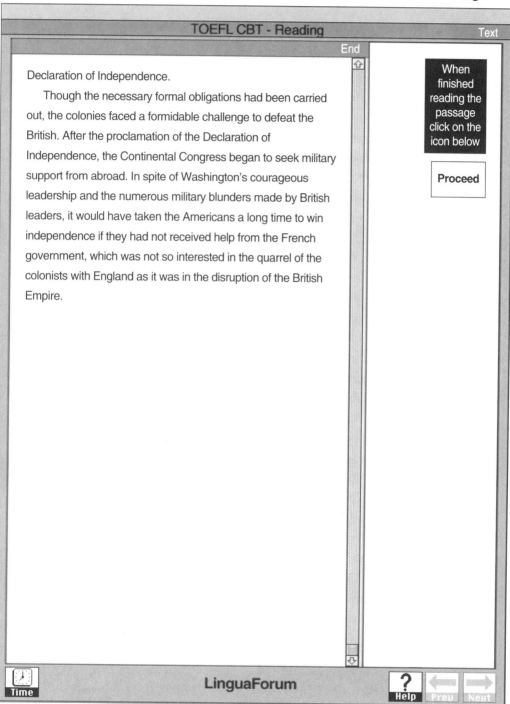

TOEFL CBT - Reading   Text

End

Declaration of Independence.

Though the necessary formal obligations had been carried out, the colonies faced a formidable challenge to defeat the British. After the proclamation of the Declaration of Independence, the Continental Congress began to seek military support from abroad. In spite of Washington's courageous leadership and the numerous military blunders made by British leaders, it would have taken the Americans a long time to win independence if they had not received help from the French government, which was not so interested in the quarrel of the colonists with England as it was in the disruption of the British Empire.

When finished reading the passage click on the icon below

Proceed

Time   **LinguaForum**   ? Help   Prev   Next

Passage 1

Questions 1 to 11   Beginning

Few Americans thought in 1775 that the mounting quarrel with the British government would lead to independence for the English colonies. As "reluctant rebels," they hoped for a modification of imperial regulations that would satisfy their demand for a greater measure of self-government. Though Lord North, one of Britain's leading ministers, offered a compromise, the British Parliament nullified his effort and established the act that was designed to destroy New England's commerce.

The situation worsened as British and American soldiers clashed. Trying to destroy the military stores and to arrest the leaders of the colonists such as John Hancock and Samuel Adams, the British army fought colonial soldiers under the leadership of General Gage. Furthermore, the colonists were incensed by the policy of the British government in hiring foreign mercenaries to fight Englishmen in America and by the attempts of the British agents to incite Indian raids against frontier settlements. General opinion agreed with Thomas Paine's argument in his pamphlet *Common Sense* that it was inconsistent to pretend to be loyal to England while fighting British troops on American soil.

While sending a final "Olive Branch" petition to King George, the Continental Congress prepared to equip an army and appointed George Washington as commander in chief of the colonial forces. On June 7, 1776, under the instruction of the colonial legislatures, the delegates of the Continental Congress decided to declare independence from England. It appointed a committee, made of Thomas Jefferson, John Adams, Benjamin Franklin, Roger Sherman and Robert R. Livingston, to draft a Declaration of Independence.

1. Which of the following would be the best title for the passage?
   Ⓐ The Declaration of Independence
   Ⓑ The Decline of the British Empire
   Ⓒ The American War for Independence
   Ⓓ The Continental Congress and the British Empire

LinguaForum

Passage 1

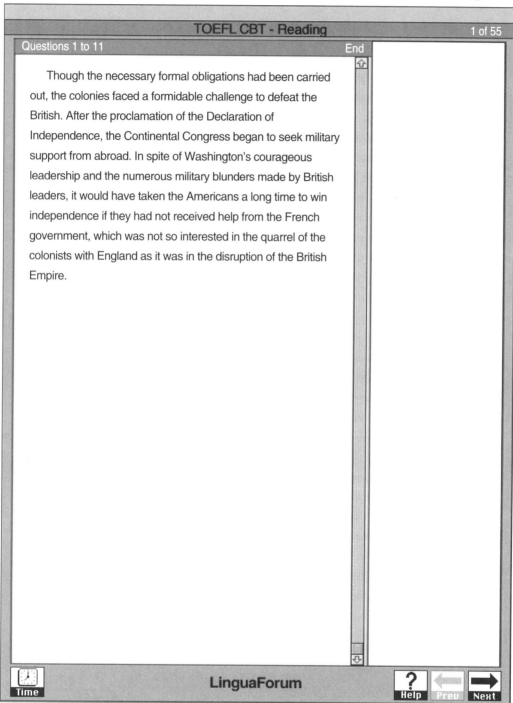

Though the necessary formal obligations had been carried out, the colonies faced a formidable challenge to defeat the British. After the proclamation of the Declaration of Independence, the Continental Congress began to seek military support from abroad. In spite of Washington's courageous leadership and the numerous military blunders made by British leaders, it would have taken the Americans a long time to win independence if they had not received help from the French government, which was not so interested in the quarrel of the colonists with England as it was in the disruption of the British Empire.

LinguaForum

Time

Help Prev Next

PRACTICE TEST 12

Few Americans thought in 1775 that the mounting quarrel with the British government would lead to American Independence. As "reluctant rebels," they hoped for a modification of imperial regulations that would satisfy their demand for a greater measure of self-government. Though Lord North, one of Britain's leading ministers, offered a compromise, the British Parliament nullified his effort and established the act that was designed to destroy New England's commerce.

The situation worsened as British and American soldiers clashed. Trying to destroy the military stores and to arrest the leaders of the colonists such as John Hancock and Samuel Adams, the British army fought colonial soldiers under the leadership of General Gage. Furthermore, the colonists were incensed by the policy of the British government in hiring foreign mercenaries to fight Englishmen in America and by the attempts of the British agents to incite Indian raids against frontier settlements. General opinion agreed with Thomas Paine's argument in his pamphlet *Common Sense* that it was inconsistent to pretend to be loyal to England while fighting British troops on American soil.

→ ■ While sending a final "Olive Branch" petition to King George, the Continental Congress prepared to equip an army and appointed George Washington as commander in chief of the colonial forces. ■ On June 7, 1776, under the instruction of the colonial legislatures, the delegates of the Continental Congress decided to declare independence from England. ■ It appointed a committee, made of Thomas Jefferson, John Adams, Benjamin Franklin, Roger Sherman and Robert R.

---

2. Look at the word their in the passage. Click on the word or phrase in the **bold** text that their refers to.

3. The first paragraph implies that
- (A) the colonists were eagerly seeking confrontation with England
- (B) the British government was willing to renounce its colonies in America
- (C) the fights with the British forces were becoming more hostile
- (D) the colonists were attempting to seek self-government and not complete independence from England

4. The phrase lead to in the passage could best be replaced by
- (A) follow to
- (B) result in
- (C) direct to
- (D) influence

LinguaForum   ? Help   ← Prev   → Next

Time

Reading

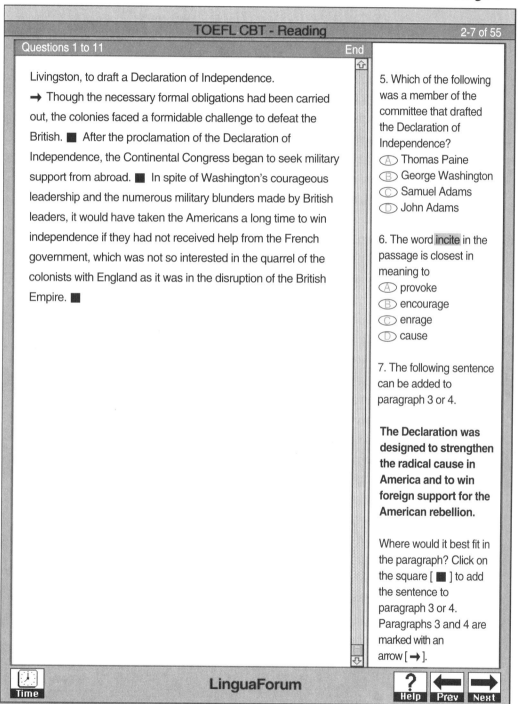

Questions 1 to 11   End

Livingston, to draft a Declaration of Independence.

→ Though the necessary formal obligations had been carried out, the colonies faced a formidable challenge to defeat the British. ■ After the proclamation of the Declaration of Independence, the Continental Congress began to seek military support from abroad. ■ In spite of Washington's courageous leadership and the numerous military blunders made by British leaders, it would have taken the Americans a long time to win independence if they had not received help from the French government, which was not so interested in the quarrel of the colonists with England as it was in the disruption of the British Empire. ■

5. Which of the following was a member of the committee that drafted the Declaration of Independence?
Ⓐ Thomas Paine
Ⓑ George Washington
Ⓒ Samuel Adams
Ⓓ John Adams

6. The word incite in the passage is closest in meaning to
Ⓐ provoke
Ⓑ encourage
Ⓒ enrage
Ⓓ cause

7. The following sentence can be added to paragraph 3 or 4.

The Declaration was designed to strengthen the radical cause in America and to win foreign support for the American rebellion.

Where would it best fit in the paragraph? Click on the square [■] to add the sentence to paragraph 3 or 4. Paragraphs 3 and 4 are marked with an arrow [→].

Time   LinguaForum   **? Help**   **← Prev**   **→ Next**

Passage 1

Few Americans thought in 1775 that the mounting quarrel with the British government would lead to independence for the English colonies. As "reluctant rebels," they hoped for a modification of imperial regulations that would satisfy their demand for a greater measure of self-government. Though Lord North, one of Britain's leading ministers, offered a compromise, the British Parliament nullified his effort and established the act that was designed to destroy New England's commerce.

The situation worsened as British and American soldiers clashed. Trying to destroy the military stores and to arrest the leaders of the colonists such as John Hancock and Samuel Adams, the British army fought colonial soldiers under the leadership of General Gage. Furthermore, the colonists were incensed by the policy of the British government in hiring foreign mercenaries to fight Englishmen in America and by the attempts of the British agents to incite Indian raids against frontier settlements. General opinion agreed with Thomas Paine's argument in his pamphlet *Common Sense* that it was inconsistent to pretend to be loyal to England while fighting British troops on American soil.

While sending a final "Olive Branch" petition to King George, the Continental Congress prepared to equip an army and appointed George Washington as commander in chief of the colonial forces. On June 7, 1776, under the instruction of the colonial legislatures, the delegates of the Continental Congress decided to declare independence from England. It appointed a committee, made of Thomas Jefferson, John Adams, Benjamin Franklin, Roger Sherman and Robert R. Livingston, to draft a Declaration of Independence.

8. It can be inferred that Paine's *Common Sense*
(A) attacked the Indians who were obstructing the settlements on the frontier
(B) declared war on the foreign countries that were helping England
(C) challenged the authority of the colonists
(D) proposed independence from England

9. The passage supports which of the following statements?
(A) The Continental Congress made every effort to seek a compromise with the British government.
(B) The Declaration of Independence was drafted by those still loyal to the British Crown.
(C) Though outwardly expressing peace, the colonists were working towards independence.
(D) The colonists sought to provoke the British by attacking their posts.

LinguaForum

?   Help   ← Prev   → Next

Time

Reading

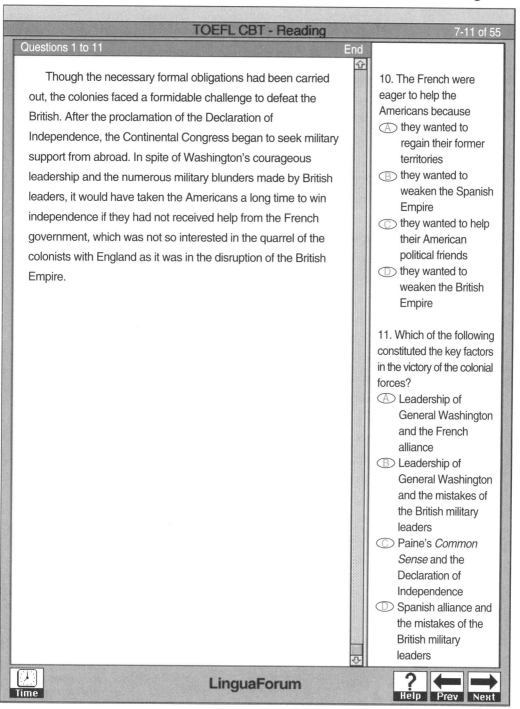

Questions 1 to 11   End

Though the necessary formal obligations had been carried out, the colonies faced a formidable challenge to defeat the British. After the proclamation of the Declaration of Independence, the Continental Congress began to seek military support from abroad. In spite of Washington's courageous leadership and the numerous military blunders made by British leaders, it would have taken the Americans a long time to win independence if they had not received help from the French government, which was not so interested in the quarrel of the colonists with England as it was in the disruption of the British Empire.

10. The French were eager to help the Americans because
  (A) they wanted to regain their former territories
  (B) they wanted to weaken the Spanish Empire
  (C) they wanted to help their American political friends
  (D) they wanted to weaken the British Empire

11. Which of the following constituted the key factors in the victory of the colonial forces?
  (A) Leadership of General Washington and the French alliance
  (B) Leadership of General Washington and the mistakes of the British military leaders
  (C) Paine's *Common Sense* and the Declaration of Independence
  (D) Spanish alliance and the mistakes of the British military leaders

Time   **LinguaForum**   ? Help   ← Prev   → Next

PRACTICE TEST 12

Passage 2

➡ Much of the North American landscape has been shaped by glaciation, the formation and movement of great sheets of ice, or glaciers, across the continent. North America is believed to have undergone several major periods of glaciation. ■ During the most recent glacial period, the northern part of the continent, including part of what is now the northern United States, is thought to have been buried under a layer of ice several kilometers thick. ■ The weight of this ice was so tremendous that it actually depressed, or bent downward, the crust of the Earth in some places, even as it scoured the surface of the continent. ■ The advancing glaciers left more dramatic evidence of their passage in the form of large basins, or depressed areas, which filled with water after the glaciers melted and disappeared. ■

➡ **Several of these enormous water-filled basins are known today as the Great Lakes. Important avenues of maritime commerce, they have played an important part in the history of the United States and Canada and have made seaports out of cities such as Chicago, Milwaukee, Marquette, and Duluth, which lie hundreds of kilometers from the Atlantic Ocean.** ■ The Great Lakes are connected to the Atlantic Ocean by the St. Lawrence River, which flows into the Gulf of St. Lawrence and from there to the Atlantic. ■

Before the most recent glaciation, the location of the present-day Great Lakes was an area of low elevation in an inland plain. The southward-moving sheet of ice, flowing into the lowest-lying portions of the plain, eroded the lowlands even more deeply. At its greatest extent, the ice sheet reached as far south as the modern Ohio River valley. Then, global climate became warmer, and the glacial ice began to melt and retreat, leaving behind the deep basins which now contain the Great Lakes. Other glacial landforms were created from the moraines, or deposits of ground and fragmented rock, left behind by the shrinking glaciers. Moraines in some places acted as great natural dams which trapped water from the melted ice. The glacial debris also accumulated in long, sinuous ridges which indicate where rivers of water from the melting glaciers once ran.

488

12. This passage is concerned mainly with
    - (A) the earliest glacial periods in North America
    - (B) the formation of the Great Lakes by glaciation and related processes
    - (C) how moraines are deposited by advancing and retreating glaciers
    - (D) maritime commerce on the Great Lakes in the 20th century

13. According to the passage, glaciers
    - (A) elevated the crust of North America by pressing down on the north pole
    - (B) protected North American vegetation under a cover of ice and snow
    - (C) formed what is now the state of Florida
    - (D) depressed the crust, scoured the land, and created basins

14. The word scoured in the passage is closest in meaning to
    - (A) blamed
    - (B) mounted
    - (C) eroded
    - (D) buried

15. The following sentence can be added to paragraph 1 or 2.

    Exactly why these periods occurred is uncertain, but glaciation is believed to be related to irregularities in the Earth's rotation.

    Where would it best fit in the paragraph? Click on the square [■] to add the sentence to paragraph 1 or 2.
    Paragraphs 1 and 2 are marked with an arrow [➡].

16. Which of the following could best replace the word advancing in the passage?
    - (A) Northward-moving
    - (B) Southward-moving
    - (C) Eastward-moving
    - (D) Westward-moving

17. The word depressed in the passage could best be replaced by
    - (A) bad
    - (B) barren
    - (C) lowest-lying
    - (D) disappeared

18. From paragraph 1, we may infer that the most recent period of glaciation in North America DID NOT
    - (A) affect the southern United States by scouring the crust
    - (B) deposit moraine in what is now the northern United States
    - (C) scour the crust of present-day Canada and the northern United States
    - (D) depress the crust under the tremendous weight of glacial ice

19. Look at the word they in the passage. Click on the words in the **bold** text which they refers to.

20. According to the passage, glaciation created
    - (A) the cities of Duluth, Milwaukee, Marquette, and Chicago
    - (B) the Atlantic Ocean and the Gulf of St. Lawrence
    - (C) the Mississippi River delta on the shore of the Gulf of Mexico
    - (D) basins which later became the Great Lakes

21. Cities on the Great Lakes, mentioned in the passage, include
    - (A) Norfolk, Suffolk, Richmond, and Harrisonburg
    - (B) Durham, Raleigh, Charlotte, and Kitty Hawk
    - (C) San Francisco, Oakland, Fremont, and Hayward
    - (D) Duluth, Milwaukee, Marquette, and Chicago

22. Paragraph 2 supports paragraph 1 by
    - (A) describing examples of glacially-created basins (the Great Lakes), their economic importance, and their coastal cities
    - (B) providing examples of glacially-created mountains
    - (C) explaining how Marquette, Milwaukee, and Duluth received their names
    - (D) describing how the explorer Marquette navigated the Ohio River

PRACTICE TEST 12

Consumption refers to all the ways in which goods, services, and nonmaterial things produced are used. Far from merely satisfying basic wants and needs, consumption in most societies has a wide range of purposes, one of the most important of which is to symbolize social prestige. In some societies, consumption as a mark of status is a potent device for establishing political influence, as in the case of the Kwakiutl.

➡ ■ **The link between production and consumption has proven instructive to economic anthropologists. In gatherer-and-hunter societies, this link is direct. ■ Since each family accumulates food and other necessities for itself, gatherers and hunters have no need for an institutionalized redistributive system in which goods are amassed by one person or organization and then distributed to the needy. A person able to acquire a surplus distributes it directly among the less fortunate, without much fanfare, much less a bid for power. ■ In any society, the more remote the connection between production and eventual consumption, the more likely it is that consumption has functions that go beyond the satisfaction of immediate need. ■**

➡ Consumption for prestige was a central value of traditional Native Americans of the Northwest Coast, who developed it to a high art. ■ A village chief would give a huge feast for another chief with whom he had some political dispute. All the villagers under the rule of both chiefs would be invited. ■ **This potlatch, as it was called, represented a way for the host to win the political support of both sets of villagers. A potlatch host's primary concern was to increase his own prestige relative to his rival's, and to this end he would throw the most massive, most elaborate potlatch possible, sometimes bankrupting himself in the process. ■ Although potlatch customs differed somewhat among the various Northwest Coast groups, most chiefs would stop at nothing to impress their guests. ■ In the destructive potlatch of the Kwakiutl, hosts went so far as to destroy their most valued possessions in front of their guests. They were sending their rivals the message that they were so wealthy they could afford to indulge in wanton waste.**

Reading

23. The main subject of the passage is
    - (A) the different forms of consumption
    - (B) the function of consumption in primitive societies
    - (C) the concept of consumption and an example
    - (D) the phenomenon of potlatch and its significance

24. Consumption is all of the following EXCEPT
    - (A) satisfaction of basic needs
    - (B) form of production
    - (C) form of storage
    - (D) mark of status

25. Look at the word distributed in the passage. Click on another word or phrase in the **bold** text that is OPPOSITE in meaning to distributed.

26. All of the following relate to consumption as satisfaction of basic needs EXCEPT
    - (A) does not need redistributive system
    - (B) is common in hunter-gatherer societies
    - (C) distributes necessities directly
    - (D) is a bid for power

27. The second paragraph suggests that the value of goods depends on
    - (A) production
    - (B) consumption
    - (C) distribution
    - (D) marketing

28. Look at the word necessities in the passage. Click on another word or phrase in the **bold** text that is closest in meaning to necessities.

29. Potlatch is described as primarily
    - (A) a form of high art in Native American Indian culture
    - (B) a form of power struggle in Native American Indian culture
    - (C) a symbolic gathering for Native American Indians
    - (D) a form of privilege reserved for the chosen members of a village

30. All of the following describe a potlatch EXCEPT
    - (A) an elaborate feast
    - (B) a bitter struggle
    - (C) a spectacular show
    - (D) a competitive gathering

31. Look at the word his in the passage. Click on the word or phrase in the **bold** text that his refers to.

32. The following sentence can be added to paragraph 2 or 3.

    He would shower his guests with food and gifts – artworks, blankets, fish oil, and household utensils such as carved wooden boxes and spoons.

    Where would it best fit in the paragraph?
    Click on the square [■] to add the sentence to paragraph 2 or 3.
    Paragraphs 2 and 3 are marked with an arrow [➡].

33. The power of the Indian chief depended mostly on
    - (A) the amount of gifts offered to the villagers
    - (B) the votes of the villagers
    - (C) the amount of sacrifice of his wealth
    - (D) the amount of gifts offered to the gods

Reading

Most species of marine algae are represented by the forms popularly known as seaweeds. This, however, is a rather unfortunate term. For one thing, the word weeds does not do justice to these conspicuous and often elegant inhabitants of rocky shores and other marine environments. Some biologists opt for the more formal name of *macrophytes*. On the other hand, the term seaweeds is useful in distinguishing them from the unicellular algae. The structures of seaweeds are far more complex than those of unicellular algae, and reproduction is also more elaborate. Seaweeds are all eukaryotic, as opposed to prokaryotic, which are the simplest type of cells that lack organelles. Most are multicellular, but some forms consisting of single cells or simple filaments are considered seaweeds. This is because the classification of seaweeds is based not only on structure but also on other features such as the types of pigments and food storage products.

➡ ■ Although more complex than unicellular algae, seaweeds still lack the complex structures and reproductive mechanisms characteristic of the higher, mostly terrestrial plants. ■ Most specialists include them in the kingdom Protista. There are some who disagree and assign them instead to the kingdom Plantae, together with the higher plants. ■

➡ **The range of variation observed among the multicellular algae is spectacular. Those we see on rocky shores at low tide are usually small and sturdy as an adaptation to withstand waves. ■ Kelps found offshore in cold waters are true giants that form dense underwater forests. ■ The multicellular condition of seaweeds allows many adaptations not available to unicellular forms. ■ They can grow tall and rise off the bottom. ■ This provides new opportunities as well as challenges: wave action and turbulence, competition for space and light, and the problem of predatory sea urchins and fish. ■**

Reading

34. With what topic is the passage mainly concerned?
  - Ⓐ Macrophytes
  - Ⓑ Unicellular algae
  - Ⓒ Marine inhabitants
  - Ⓓ Kingdoms of marine biology

35. The author considers the use of the term weeds in the first paragraph to be
  - Ⓐ helpful
  - Ⓑ critical
  - Ⓒ misleading
  - Ⓓ irrelevant

36. The first paragraph suggests that eukaryotic cells
  - Ⓐ are the most common in the marine environment
  - Ⓑ contain organelles
  - Ⓒ are the simplest types of cells
  - Ⓓ are related to the prokaryotic cells

37. All of the following describe seaweeds EXCEPT
  - Ⓐ multicellular algae
  - Ⓑ complex
  - Ⓒ macrophytes
  - Ⓓ prokaryotic

38. Which of the following could best replace the word consipicuous in the passage?
  - Ⓐ Attractive
  - Ⓑ Abundant
  - Ⓒ Highly visible
  - Ⓓ Important

39. All of the following are used to classify seaweeds EXCEPT
  - Ⓐ origin
  - Ⓑ structure
  - Ⓒ food storage products
  - Ⓓ types of pigments

40. The difference between the Protista and Plantae kingdoms is that
  - Ⓐ the latter includes terrestrial plants while the former includes less complex plants
  - Ⓑ the latter includes terrestrial plants while the former includes complex plants
  - Ⓒ the latter includes only unicellular plants while the former includes complex plants
  - Ⓓ the former includes only complex plants while the latter includes terrestrial plants

41. The word include in the passage is closest in meaning to
  - Ⓐ involve
  - Ⓑ assign
  - Ⓒ contain
  - Ⓓ complete

42. The following sentence can be added to paragraph 2 or 3.

  Some small, delicate ones live as epiphytes or parasites on other seaweeds.

  Where would it best fit in the paragraph? Click on the square [■] to add the sentence to paragraph 2 or 3.
  Paragraphs 2 and 3 are marked with an arrow [➡].

43. Look at the word They in the passage. Click on the word or phrase in the **bold** text that They refers to.

44. The passage suggests that the adaptations of multicellular algae are
  - Ⓐ useful
  - Ⓑ advantageous
  - Ⓒ disadvantageous
  - Ⓓ inappropriate

PRACTICE TEST 12

Reading

Passage 5

➡ Melville's life, works and reputation are the stuff of legend. ■ With very little formal education, he **turned** his early South Sea adventuring to literary use, charming readers in Britain and the United States with his first book, *Typee*, the story of his captivity by a Polynesian tribe. ■ Once established as a popular young author, he simultaneously began exploring philosophy and experimenting with literary style and form. ■ Some readers were outraged, and for the rest of Melville's brief career he was torn between his own urge toward aesthetic and philosophical adventuring and the public's demand for **racy** sea stories which did not disturb **its** opinion on politics, religion and metaphysics.

■ By his mid-thirties, broken in reputation and health, he ceased writing fiction, gradually passing into a stern and neglected middle age as a deputy customs inspector in Manhattan. ■

➡ During the forty years he lived after publishing *Moby Dick*, Melville withdrew into the privacy of his family while men like G. W. Curtis, R. H. Stoddard, E. C. Stedman, T. B. Aldrich, E. P. Whipple and R. W. Gilder reigned over a magazine-dominated literary domain whose intellectual and artistic values formed a counterpart to the prevailing shoddiness of political values in post-Civil War America. ■ Rediscovered by a few English readers just before his death, Melville was all but forgotten for another thirty years. ■

Finally the centennial of this birth brought about a revival of interest; by the 1920s, literary and cultural historians began to see Melville as the archetypal artist in a money-grubbing century hostile to all grandeur of intellect and spirit. That was a new distortion, but the "Melville Revival" of the 1920s succeeded in establishing him as one of the greatest American writers, although it took another decade or two for him to gain much space in college textbooks. The facts of his life are as poignant – and as archetypal – as the legends.

Time | LinguaForum | ? Help ← Prev → Next

Reading

45. This passage is likely to be found in the following publications EXCEPT
    - Ⓐ introduction to the anthology of American literature
    - Ⓑ a beginner's guide to fiction writing
    - Ⓒ literary biography of American Writers
    - Ⓓ newspaper article on the new edition of one of Melville's works

46. The word turned in the passage is closest in meaning to
    - Ⓐ move
    - Ⓑ direct
    - Ⓒ convert
    - Ⓓ model

47. Look at the word its in the passage. Click on the word or phrase in the **bold** text that its refers to.

48. The following sentence can be added to paragraph 1 or 2.

    As the earliest personal account of the South Seas to have the readability and suspense of adventure fiction, it made a great sensation, capturing the imagination of both the literary reviewers and the reading public.

    Where would it best fit in the paragraph? Click on the square [■] to add the sentence to paragraph 1 or 2.
    Paragraphs 1 and 2 are marked with an arrow [➡].

49. The passage implies that Melville based much of his work on
    - Ⓐ his childhood and family life
    - Ⓑ his early school years and college life
    - Ⓒ his adventurous life as a sailor traveling the South Seas
    - Ⓓ his travels around the world

50. The word racy in the passage could best be replaced by
    - Ⓐ sexy
    - Ⓑ racist
    - Ⓒ violent
    - Ⓓ stimulating

51. According to the passage, Melville stopped writing because
    - Ⓐ he was tired of being rejected by publishers
    - Ⓑ he became ill and lost much of his reputation
    - Ⓒ he lost inspiration to continue writing
    - Ⓓ he decided to sail

52. The passage mentions the following editors who reigned on the literary scene during Melville's latter years EXCEPT
    - Ⓐ G. W. Chester
    - Ⓑ R. H. Stoddard
    - Ⓒ E. P. Whipple
    - Ⓓ R. W. Gilder

53. Melville took which of the following jobs after writing *Moby Dick*?
    - Ⓐ Editor of a literary journal
    - Ⓑ Sea captain
    - Ⓒ Port inspector
    - Ⓓ Deputy customs inspector

54. The passage supports which of the following statements?
    - Ⓐ Throughout his writing career, Melville sought to please the public and wrote many sea stories.
    - Ⓑ After the publication of his first works until his death, Melville enjoyed great fame and admiration.
    - Ⓒ It was only after his death that Melville received much deserved fame and respect.
    - Ⓓ During his career, Melville eagerly sought both literary and financial success.

55. Paragraph 2 suggests the following EXCEPT that
    - Ⓐ after his death, literary historians were all proposing their versions of the "true" Melville
    - Ⓑ though he was hailed as a great writer after his death, it still took much time to be widely accepted
    - Ⓒ literary historians could only imagine Melville's life, for they had no biographical evidence
    - Ⓓ during his lifetime, Melville did not enjoy lasting literary and financial success

PRACTICE TEST 12

SECTION 4
WRITING
Suggested Time: 30 Minutes

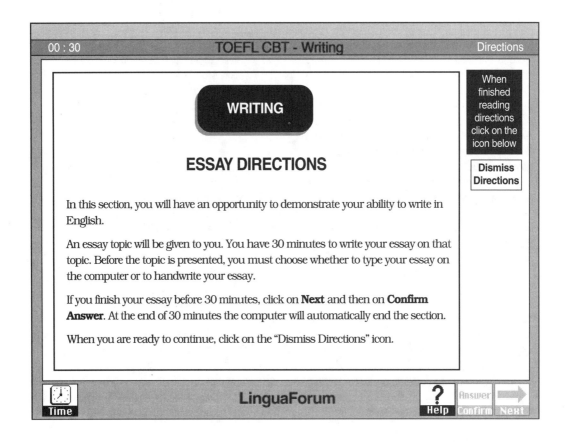

Writing

Read the topic below and then make any notes that will help you plan your response. Begin typing your response in the box at the bottom of the screen, or write your answer on the answer sheet provided to you.

One can make decisions quickly, or after thinking long and carefully. Some people say it is always wrong to make a decision quickly. Do you agree or disagree with that view? Use specific examples and reasons to support your answer.

Cut

Paste

Undo

Time

LinguaForum

Help   Confirm   Next

Answer

PRACTICE
TEST 12

LISTENING SCRIPT

Practice Test ❼

Listening Script Part A

1.   (woman)   Hey, congratulations.
    (man)   For what?
    (woman)   I heard that you got an assistantship.
    (man)   You must be thinking of my roommate. I'm not going to try to teach next year while I'm studying full-time.
    (narrator)   What does the man mean?

2.   (man)   I've been so busy with exams that I haven't had time to do my Christmas shopping for my roommate. But at least I know what I'm going to get him.
    (woman)   Oh, what's that?
    (man)   I've decided I'm going to get him a video game for his computer.
    (woman)   Are you sure he'd like that?
    (narrator)   What does the woman imply about the man's roommate?

3.   (woman)   Why did Peter pick Janice for the leading part in the play? Naomi is a much better actress.
    (man)   That's true, but she doesn't sing nearly as well.
    (narrator)   According to the woman, who is the best actor?

4.   (woman)   Where is the best place to buy cakes?
    (man)   Well, the Dutch Oven is the best place, but it's closed right now. Why don't you try Mama's Bake Shop on Clark Street?
    (narrator)   What will the woman most likely do next?

5.   (man)   I've got to quit smoking, but it's really hard. I've even joined a support group, but it didn't help much.
    (woman)   You can do it. I smoked for ten years, but I finally gave it up.
    (man)   But I have no willpower. I tried chewing gum. I tried everything, but I couldn't do it.
    (woman)   I know it's hard. I failed to quit many times. But then I got one of those nicotine patches. Why don't you try it?
    (narrator)   What does the woman suggest?

6.   (woman)   Mary never understands my jokes.
    (man)   Yes she does. It just takes a while for them to sink in.
    (narrator)   What does the man mean?

7.   (man)   Congratulations! I just saw your name on the graduation list.
    (woman)   Then someone else must have the same name. I'm not graduating until next spring.
    (narrator)   What had the man assumed?

8.   (woman)   Who's in charge of course requests?
    (man)   That would be me.
    (woman)   Could you please sign my course request form?
    (man)   I'm sorry, but you'll have to get your advisor's signature on it first.
    (narrator)   What can be inferred about the man?

9.   (man)   Where did you get such a great looking bookbag?
     (woman)   They were on sale at the student book center. Two for the price of one for $29.95, so Leanne and I both got one.
     (narrator)   How much did the two bags cost?

10. (woman)   I'm starving. Where did you put the leftover pizza?
     (man)   I threw it out. But I'm sure there's something else to eat in the house.
     (narrator)   What can we say about the man?

11. (man)   I thought you only had classes in the morning, between nine and twelve o'clock.
     (woman)   I did. But then my ten o'clock history class was cancelled, and the only other class available that fulfilled my requirement was at 2.
     (man)   I know you prefer classes in the morning, but two o'clock isn't so bad, is it?
     (woman)   Well, I suppose it's better than an evening class.
     (narrator)   What time was the woman's history class supposed to be?

12. (woman)   How's your political science class going?
     (man)   The class itself is great. It's just the recitation that's horrible.
     (woman)   Oh, that's right. You don't like the teaching assistant, do you?
     (man)   No. He makes fun of his students' mistakes.
     (narrator)   What does the man mean?

13. (man)   Were you able to find everything you needed?
     (woman)   There wasn't anyone working in the stacks to help me!
     (narrator)   What is the woman implying?

14. (woman)   I'm really excited about our trip this weekend. How far away is San Diego, anyway?
     (man)   Well, it's fifty miles to Long Beach, and Long Beach is about ninety miles from San Diego.
     (narrator)   What can be inferred from the conversation?

15. (man)   The tickets for the best seats in the concert hall cost $60.
     (woman)   That's more than I wanted to pay. How about the $15 seats in the top balcony?
     (man)   Those seats are too far away. We wouldn't be able to see a thing. But the middle balcony is $35 and the lower balcony is $45.
     (woman)   Well, the $45 seats are still too expensive, but I guess if we really want to enjoy the concert, those are the ones we should buy.
     (narrator)   How much are the tickets the woman decides to buy?

16. (woman)   I never see you out jogging any more. What happened to your exercise program?
     (man)   I walk now. It's less stress on the feet and knees. I've been playing some tennis, too, though.
     (narrator)   What are the speakers talking about?

17. (man)   Matt told me that he was really interested in journalism.
     (woman)   Yes, but when he declared his major he chose biology.
     (narrator)   What can be inferred about Matt?

Listening Script Part B

Questions 18-21

Listen to part of a lecture in a marine biology class. The professor is talking about fiddler crabs.

There are many species of fiddler crabs inhabiting the mud and sand flats of estuaries and sheltered coasts. They are found mostly in the tropics and subtropics, but some species are found as far north as southern California and Boston Harbor. Fiddlers are deposit feeders; that is, they feed at low tide, using their pincers to scoop mud up into their mouth. The detritus in the mud is extracted with the help of brush-like mouthparts. Water is pumped from the gill chambers into the mouth to make the lighter detritus float and thus help separate it from the mud. The detritus is swallowed, and the clean mud is spat out on the substrate in neat little balls. During high tide, they return to their burrows in the mud. This lifestyle requires a very good biological clock to synchronize its activities to the tides. In fact, if you were to put a fiddler crab into an isolated environment, with constant light and temperature, it would continue to be active at the times corresponding to low tide, and sit quietly at the times corresponding to high tide. Fiddlers also have an interesting sex life. While female fiddlers have two identical, small claws, males have one tremendously enlarged claw, either right or left, often colored or with markings in many species. Males use their big claw to advertise their sex and their availability, as well as to threaten other males who might be around. At low tide, the males hang around their burrows, waving their claws wildly, trying to attract the female crabs' attention.
In areas with several species of fiddler crabs, the waving takes on special patterns to distinguish one species from another. Some species wave their claws back and forth, while others wave up and down, or whatever. Some even beat the claw on the ground or vibrate a joint on their claw to make sounds.

18. Which best describes the habitat of fiddler crabs?

19. The professor describes the following steps of how the fiddler crab eats. Put them into the proper order.

20. What is the following a picture of?

21. What is NOT a method the male fiddler crab uses to attract the female's attention?

Questions 22-24

Listen to a professor and two students discussing information from a political science class.

(professor)   Every nation in the world must deal with one or more other nations. What can you tell me about the field of International Relations?

(woman)   Well, it's a relatively young field of study, encompassing international law, trade, and organizations, as well as world politics.

(professor)   That's right. For much of history, there were no international relations because often the world had just one dominating empire in an area, like the Roman Empire, and other powerful nations existed too far away to have any interaction. Or else there were no international relations because there were simply too many small powers, local and disordered. In European history, this was called feudalism. Only in the 18th and 19th centuries, with the formation of the modern nation-state in Europe, did modern international relations begin. Now, in terms of power relationships, what are the two things all nations want?

(man)   Security and national interest?

(professor)   Exactly. Security might be military, economic, or political. And often what promotes one nation's security harms another's.

(woman)   Like how Turkey is building new irrigation systems to make it more secure economically. But by doing so, less water will flow down to Syria – a country that is not friends with Turkey, but that needs water just as badly.

(professor)   That's a very good example. And what is the central idea of state interaction?

(woman)   Sovereignty – the idea that no nation has to account to anyone else for what goes on within its own borders.

(professor)   Good. So international relations is about how nations further their security and national interest as much as possible, while also insisting on their sovereignty. There are two major systems of thought relating all these issues. The first is "realism" – the idea that each nation should take care of itself, doing whatever is in its own interest. However, "national interest" can be a very difficult idea to pin down, and ultimately this theory does not explain how states act very well. In response, a much more complicated set of systems, called "behavioralism," has been developed. Behavioralism looks at many interrelated social conditions that affect nations, like class issues, psychology, game theory and human adaptation.

22. What is the main topic of this discussion?

23. Some different systems of international relations were mentioned. Match the system with the description of it.

24. What are the two schools of thought in International Relations?

Questions 25-26

Listen to part of a conversation between two people.

(woman)	I've decided to join the school golf team.
(man)	Golf team? I didn't even know we had a golf team.
(woman)	We sure do. In fact, our university is one of the best in the state.
(man)	So why would you want to join the golf team?
(woman)	I love golf. It's really a lot of fun, and most importantly, it's really competitive. I love that feeling of competing with someone, or even competing with myself. Anyhow, I played it all the time in high school, but I never thought I'd have a chance to play it in university. But I tried out anyway, and I did really well.
(man)	Is the golf team a big commitment?
(woman)	Not too bad. We go out to play at least three mornings a week, and every afternoon we meet behind the gym to practice our driving and putting.
(man)	Does the school have its own golf course?
(woman)	No, but that's one of the best parts of the golf team – we get to play on the best courses all over the area for free. Some of them are really expensive, too.
(man)	That is a good deal, I guess – if you like golf.
(woman)	You don't?
(man)	I like to exercise, but I prefer team sports and sports that are more athletic. Golf is like a nice walk, and I really like being outdoors, but I don't consider it a real sport.
(woman)	You should give it a try. You might be surprised.

25. What does the woman most like about golf?

26. Which exercise would the man most likely enjoy?

Questions 27-31

Listen to part of a lecture in an engineering class. The professor is talking about cables.

Before the age of satellite communication and the Internet, most long distance communication had to go through cables. Great copper cables for telegrams and telephones were laid across the deep bottom of the world's oceans, bringing the world together in a revolutionary way.

The first successful telegraph cable across the Atlantic was laid in 1866. When radiotelephoning began in 1927, it seemed that cable laying would soon become obsolete. Radiotelephone service, however, presented certain disadvantages. It could not be expanded because the number of high-frequency bands that radio uses is limited. Radio is also subject to atmospheric disturbances. It produces static, and its signals tend to fade. In addition, the conversations are not strictly private. These are important considerations to governments and business in times of peace and war.

In 1956 the first telephone cable was completed across the Atlantic. Actually, it consisted of two cables about 20 miles apart. Each one carried the voice in one direction. The two cables could carry just 36 conversations – double the capacity of the radiotelephone, but a fraction of what is possible today.

In order for that telephone cable to work, a kind of electronic amplifier was needed. Those "repeaters," built into the cable every 40 miles, boosted the signal. That first cable spans the Atlantic, 2,250 miles long between Newfoundland and Scotland.

Ocean cables must be well insulated to protect them from the many potential injuries they might incur. At the core of a telegraph cable is a central copper wire which carries the electric current, about a fifth of an inch in diameter. A layer of plastic insulation covers the central wire, which is in turn wrapped in a layer of steel wires for strength. Finally, tarred hemp cords on the outside keep the steel wires from corroding. The life span of an undersea cable is about 30 to 40 years.

The thickness of the cable depends on where it is laid. At the greatest depths, the cable is safer, so it is slightly less than an inch thick, and weighs about one ton per mile. In shallower water, it is more exposed to damage, therefore it is heavily reinforced, increasing the diameter to between 2 and 3 inches, and the weight to more than 10 tons a mile.

In spite of advances in technology, telegraph and telephone cables still play an important role in modern communications. The most common place the cable runs is from the east coast of America to England, but there are many other routes, across the Pacific Ocean, the South Atlantic, and almost anywhere else. Over 400,000 miles of telegraph cable cover the floors of the world's oceans – enough to go around the whole planet 16 times. And there is almost as much telephone cable, too, in spite of its late start in 1956. Now, with fiber optic cables being installed all around the world, there is no telling how many miles of cable might one day be in place.

27. What is the main topic of this lecture?

28. What is NOT a disadvantage of radio-transmitted telephone service?

29. The following is a cross-section of an undersea cable. Indicate what part of the cable is the tarred hemp cord.

30. How much does the greatest depth ocean cable weigh?

31. Indicate where on the map there is the greatest number of underwater cables.

Questions 32-35

Listen to a professor and two students discussing information from an American history class. The class is on American society.

(professor)   So Alexis de Tocqueville, in his seminal work, *Democracy in America*, recognized the democratic foundations of America, as well as the incredible changes that were taking place in that period in America.

(woman)   Professor, what were these changes that Tocqueville talked about?

(professor)   There were many. The whole of America was in great flux in the first half of the nineteenth century. Just look at the population. In 1790, there were less than 4 million people in the entire country, but by the early 1850s, there were about 24 million – six times as many people. That means the population of America was doubling every generation, about every 22 years.

(man)   I guess that's why there was so much westward expansion.

(professor)   Yes, all those new people needed space to live, so many of them turned west. But many others moved to the cities. America went from 5 cities with 250,000 people in 1820 to 26 in 1850. Boston, Philadelphia, and New York all had their populations triple in that same time period. There was major growth throughout the northeast and west, but little in the American South.

(woman)   What about New Orleans and Baltimore? They are in the South.

(professor)   Yes, there were major Southern cities, but they were at the periphery of the South. There was nothing remotely that size in Virginia, North Carolina or elsewhere in the heart of the South; cities there barely grew at all in this period.

(woman)   All the expansion must have really changed how Americans worked, too.

(professor)   That's certainly true. Agriculture went from employing three-quarters of all Americans in 1820, to two-thirds in 1850. And the share of the economy dedicated to manufacturing soared, from only 8 percent of the economy, to over a third. It was the start of the industrial revolution in America.

(woman)   Did this change life a lot?

(professor)   Oh, yes. Industrialization totally changed the makeup of cities. It changed the traditional master/apprentice relationship to a more impersonal employer/employee relationship. And as manufacturers grew larger, operations could no longer be done out of the owner's home. Major cities started to sort themselves into districts: areas where businesses congregated, places where the employers lived, and other neighborhoods for the working class.

32.   What is the topic of this discussion?

33.   Where did the expanding population go?

34.   What part of this chart represents agricultural workers in 1850?

35.   What is NOT an example of how industrialization changed the makeup of cities?

Questions 36-38

Listen to part of a conversation between two speakers.

(man)	Listen, Jen, a bunch of us have decided to form a study group for Psych class. You want in?
(woman)	That sounds like a good idea. That class has been giving me all kinds of problems since day one.
(man)	We're all in the same boat; that's why we're forming the study group.
(woman)	When are you planning on meeting?
(man)	That isn't settled yet. Someone suggested Tuesday nights, but that isn't very convenient for me. I prefer Wednesday nights; they're best for me.
(woman)	Oh. Neither of those days is very good for me. How about Sunday afternoons?
(man)	Actually, that's not bad, either. I have some free time on Sunday afternoons, and that way we could look at all the work from the previous week.
(woman)	I wonder if Sunday would be good for everyone else, though?
(man)	I'll make some phone calls this evening and see what everyone says. But I think that should work out okay. Assuming the time is okay, how should we organize these study sessions?
(woman)	Well, we could rotate group leaders – have someone different every week. That person would be responsible for organizing that Sunday's meeting – leading discussions, getting someone to review the lectures, maybe getting someone else to talk about the readings.
(man)	And maybe someone else could generate a list of sample questions for us to answer, like the kind we might get on the exam.
(woman)	That's a really good idea.

36. What is the main topic of this discussion?

37. What does the man think about meeting Sundays?

38. What would the group leader NOT be responsible for?

Questions 39-42

Listen to part of a lecture in a business class. The professor is talking about insurance.

Insurance is a legal contract that protects people from the financial costs that result from loss of life or health, from lawsuits or property damage. It provides a means for individuals and societies to cope with some of the risks faced in everyday life. By doing so, it serves an invaluable function in society, helping companies protect their property and make business operations safer.

Insurance is also a core element of civilization. Historians believe insurance first developed in ancient Babylonia, where Iraq is today, around 3,000 BC. In fact, one of the oldest known examples of writing deals with this. King Hammurabi's Code, written around 1,800 BC, gave the rules that governed the practices of early risk-sharing. For instance, the code dictated that traders had to repay merchants who financed trading voyages unless thieves stole the goods, in which case the debts would be cancelled.

Around 200 BC in ancient Greece and Rome, people started to form "benevolent societies" – organizations whose members paid dues that went towards paying for the burial of members who died. In the Middle Ages, those organizations developed into craft guilds, providing benefits to members and their families.

Modern insurance really began in England in the 16th century when the first known life insurance policy was offered. After the great fire of London in 1666, groups began to offer fire insurance, too. One of the most famous modern insurance companies, Lloyd's of London, actually started as a bar where sailors met and would make informal insurance arrangements with each other.

In America, Benjamin Franklin offered the first insurance, beginning in 1730. All the insurance companies until 1792 were private, for the members of a guild or some other group. But in 1792, the Insurance Company of North America started to offer the first public insurance policies.

After the Civil War, the size of the insurance industry expanded very rapidly – from $5 million in 1840 to $9 billion by the turn of the century. Today, nearly 5% of the entire American workforce is in some way associated with the insurance industry.

39. What is the speaker's opinion of insurance?

40. The speaker described the history of insurance. Summarize by placing the following events into the correct order.

41. What did ancient Greek and Roman "benevolent societies" do?

42. What was significant about the Insurance Company of North America?

Questions 43-47

Listen to part of a lecture in an anthropology class. The professor is talking about the history of writing.

Writing is such an intrinsic part of civilization, and yet it is a relatively recent invention. The oldest writings in the world are only about 5,000 years old, starting with the Sumerians, and then spreading to the Egyptians. Long before any kind of real writing began, people tried to communicate in a more permanent form than the spoken word. The earliest kind of written communication used ideas in the form of pictures and was called "ideography." Primitive ideography is very limited, however. Actual things could be drawn easily enough, but verbs were much harder, and more abstract ideas were nearly impossible.

There were three great steps needed to turn this simple ideography into the full alphabet. The first step was using signs to stand for actual word sounds, not just ideas: like the difference between a "plus" sign and spelling p-l-u-s, plus. The Sumerians did this first, soon followed by the Egyptians and their "hieroglyphics." In this new form of writing, individual signs stand for specific, individual words, not just ideas.

But writing continued to develop. Having a different sign for every single word would require knowing thousands of different signs, and abstract ideas and grammar are still difficult to express. A way of overcoming this problem is to turn to sound devices. For example, by using the character for a bee and the character for the leaf of a tree, one can combine them, "bee" plus "leaf," to form "belief." This kind of writing is called "word-syllabic." By using the sounds of known words and combining them, one can make the sounds for other words.

Word-syllabic writing is still very pictographic; that is, it uses signs that one could recognize, such as a face, mountain, or tree. However, over time, these writing systems often become highly abbreviated and greatly changed.

This represents the next radical change in writing. It first occurred in Syria and Palestine around 1000 BC. They developed a writing system from the Egyptian word-syllabic system; however, they eliminated all word-signs entirely, and those syllable signs with more than one consonant. This limited their syllabaries to about 30 signs, all beginning with a consonant, but ending in any vowel. With 30 signs, one could make all the sounds of the language, without any picture reference any longer.

Many societies used this syllabic system, but the Phoenicians were the most successful at it. The Phoenicians simplified their syllabary even further, down to 22 syllabic signs; and, more importantly, they began to spread this system. It spread rapidly around the Middle East, eastward to Persia and India, and westward to Greece, Italy, and the rest of Europe.

However, this was still not a true alphabet: the Phoenician writing system lacked vowels. This third step was done by the Greeks, who took five Phoenician letters they did not need and turned them into vowels.

43. How old is writing?

44. What is significant about the Phoenicians?

45. Why was the Phoenician language still not an alphabet?

46. The professor explains several steps in the evolution of writing. Put them into proper order.

47. The following picture is an example of what kind of writing?

Questions 48-50

Listen to part of a conversation between two speakers.

(man)	Excuse me; I'm having trouble finding a particular book.
(woman)	No problem. What are you looking for?
(man)	It's a famous art book, about modernism – that's an artistic period earlier this century.
(woman)	I see. And is it an art criticism book or a graphic book – I mean, an art book that features pictures?
(man)	I'm not sure. Why?
(woman)	Because the main library only would have art criticism. If you want to find a pictorial art book, you need to go to the Irving Art Library.
(man)	I didn't know there was a separate library for art books.
(woman)	Actually, there are nine different libraries on campus. Usually, the main library is the right place, but there are several libraries specializing in particular contents.
(man)	So how do I know what library to go to?
(woman)	From the call number on the book. After the main Library of Congress number we add a two-letter code. "M-A" is the main library, "S-C" is the science library, and "I-A" is the Irving Art Library.
(man)	Well, after the call number it says "M-A." So this is the right library after all.
(woman)	Okay. Most art books are on the 4th floor, in the west wing. Try looking for it there.
(man)	Thanks a lot.

48. What is the man looking for?

49. How does one know what library a book will be in?

50. Where is the man's book?

Practice Test ❽

Listening Script Part A

1. (man)   Did you hear that Steve's going for the mayor's scholarship?
   (woman)   Yeah, I did. It's a very competitive scholarship, though. Lots of people are applying for it.
   (man)   But at least Dave's working really hard. He's always studying.
   (woman)   Even though he's doing his best, he doesn't really have a chance of winning the mayor's scholarship.
   (narrator) What does the woman mean?

2. (woman)   I heard you and Cody went to that big concert last night.
   (man)   Yeah. The two of us had been waiting in line for over 2 days for those tickets.
   (woman)   So what did you and Cody think of it?
   (man)   After all that work to get the tickets, we left halfway through.
   (narrator) What is the man implying?

3. (man)   That's a great looking haircut. You must have gone to an expensive salon.
   (woman)   No, I just had my mother do it.
   (narrator) Who cut the woman's hair?

4. (woman)   Are you going to read those books here in the library?
   (man)   I think I'd rather check them out and read them at home.
   (narrator) What will the man probably do?

5. (man)   This class with Dr. Finch is really tough. He gave me a "D" on my last paper.
   (woman)   That's not good. You can't afford to get another grade like that.
   (man)   I know. But I'm not sure what our professor wants for this next paper, either.
   (woman)   Well, if I were you, I'd write a rough copy and ask Dr. Finch to look at it.
   (narrator) What does the woman suggest the man do?

6. (woman)   Did you hear about Mike?
   (man)   No. What happened to him?
   (woman)   His notebook computer was stolen. He took it with him to the library, and while he was getting a book, someone took it.
   (man)   I'm not surprised. I've told him time after time to keep his computer locked up.
   (narrator) What does the man mean?

7. (man)   I'm sorry, but have we met?
   (woman)   I don't think so. I don't live around here. I'm just visiting for a couple of days.
   (man)   Oh, are you Tanya Lords' sister?
   (woman)   No, I'm not. She's my cousin.
   (narrator) What did the man assume about the woman?

8. (woman)   I enjoy waiting for the nibble and the fight, but I don't like putting the worm on the hook.
   (man)   You don't have to use worms for bait.
   (woman)   You don't?
   (man)   No. You can use flies or even cheese. I've gotten good catches with all of them.
   (narrator) What are the people talking about?

511

9.   (man)   Have you decided to follow the coast or take the interstate to Maine?
     (woman)   I think I'll follow the coast, maybe even stop for a picnic along the way in New Hampshire.
     (man)   That's a good idea.
     (woman)   And coming back, I'll take the interstate through Boston and stop there to see a friend.
     (narrator)   Where will the woman have a picnic?

10. (woman)   I'm going over to the student union building to get some coffee. Do you want some?
     (man)   Actually, I would love some tea.
     (woman)   Do you want any cream in your tea?
     (man)   No, I take it plain.
     (narrator)   What does the woman want to know?

11. (man)   You know, Pam, you look a lot more healthy than you did a few months ago.
     (woman)   Thanks. I guess it's all that exercise I've been doing.
     (man)   Are you still running and working out every day?
     (woman)   No, more like every other day these days.
     (narrator)   What does the woman say about her exercising?

Listening Script Part B

Questions 12-15

Listen to part of a lecture in a film class. The professor is talking about science fiction and popular culture.

Science fiction is very popular these days – in books, in movies, and on TV. Unfortunately, popular science fiction often is a lot more "fiction" and not so much "science."

One of the most common problems is faster-than-light travel. We know that is impossible, as it violates Einstein's basic theory of space and time, but on *Star Trek* and other science fiction shows, spaceships jump from star to star and galaxy to galaxy like you or I might want to drive to another city. The closest star to Earth, Proxima Centauri, is over three light years away. That means traveling at the speed of light, the fastest speed anyone theoretically could travel, it would take three years to make it to our nearest neighbor. Other stars and galaxies are routinely thousands and millions of light years away, making intergalactic travel an impossibility.

Even if we grant that such space travel somehow was possible, there is no shortage of other errors in popular science fiction. In *Star Wars* and other films, space ships swoop across the screen, their engines emitting a great roar. However, since space is a void, sound waves cannot travel. There is no sound in space; it is utterly silent.

Gravity is another mystery in these films. Gravity depends mostly on mass. Spaceships are tiny compared to the mass of earth. In space there should be practically no gravity. And yet people in science fiction routinely walk around on their spaceships in space as comfortably as they would on earth. There have been a few, scarce films that bothered to portray the science of space flight somewhat realistically. In *2001: A Space Odyssey*, the ship must rotate to create artificial gravity. Outside the spaceship, there is total silence. And the voyage from Earth to Jupiter takes many months. But such films are the exception, not the rule. While this may be enjoyable, you should look elsewhere to learn about science.

12. What is the subject of this lecture?

13. What is wrong with space travel, as portrayed in most science fiction?

14. The professor describes the characteristics of a few movies in his lecture. Match the film title with what the professor said about the film.

15. What does the speaker NOT say about the movie *2001: A Space Odyssey*?

Questions 16-18

Listen to a professor and two students discussing information from an art class. The class is on Rembrandt.

(professor)	Let's continue our examination of famous painters from the Low Countries and talk about Rembrandt. Born Rembrandt van Rijn, Rembrandt was born in 1606 in Leyden, Holland. He was from a middle class family and made it to university where he decided he was not cut out to be a scholar, so he asked his father to allow him to become a painter. What was unusual about his artistic training?
(man)	Rembrandt never went to Italy to study, as was the custom then. Instead, he studied in Leyden for a few years, and then moved to Amsterdam when he was 18.
(professor)	That's right. Although he never went to Italy, he learned a lot about Renaissance painting from his teacher, Pieter Lastman. What is considered special about Rembrandt's painting style?
(woman)	Well, he's really well known for his chiaroscuro – his use of strongly contrasting lights and darks.
(professor)	Good, and what else?
(man)	He was also very good at revealing character. When he was 25, he painted *The Anatomy Lesson*, which made him really famous. Rembrandt painted a group of doctors crowded around, each with a very distinctive style. Because he was good at showing character, he became a very popular portrait painter.
(professor)	For many years, yes, that's true. But over time, Rembrandt fell out of fashion. People complained that his paint was too thick and dark.
(woman)	Like in his most famous painting, *The Night Watch*. That painting is really a daytime scene, but because his chiaroscuro was so strong, and because the painting has darkened with age, people think it is a nighttime painting.
(man)	Yes, its real name is *Parade of the Civic Guard*. Rembrandt painted it the year his wife died, in 1642. It is generally considered his most famous painting. But Rembrandt did not lose popularity until later in his life, many years after painting that picture.
(woman)	How about Rembrandt's etchings? Those are famous, too.
(professor)	True. In fact, many people consider Rembrandt to be the greatest etcher of all time. And he also was very good at drawing. But when he drew Amsterdam, he always drew its older buildings, often while they were being torn down; he never drew the new buildings.

16. What was different about Rembrandt's education?

17. Why are Rembrandt's paintings famous?

18. Rembrandt used several media for his works. Match the medium with Rembrandt's reputation for how he used it.

Questions 19-20

Listen to part of a conversation between two students.

(man)	So, are you all ready for graduation?
(woman)	Not yet. I still have a couple of papers to turn in. Nothing major, though.
(man)	You'd better hurry up. You only have a couple more days until the final deadline.
(woman)	I know. And with my family coming down to see me graduate, I'm really busy, too.
(man)	My family is already here; that's why I had to get all my work done ahead of time. Has the school announced yet who is going to speak at graduation?
(woman)	Not yet. I don't think they've decided yet. Last I heard, the decision was down to Ian Hacking and Robert Philips.
(man)	Robert Philips, the news anchor? I'd like to hear him speak. His news program is one of my favorites.
(woman)	Really? I'd prefer Ian Hacking.
(man)	I don't even know who he is.
(woman)	Dr. Hacking is a famous mathematician.
(man)	A mathematician? That sounds like he'd be really boring.
(woman)	Not at all. First of all, he's a really good speaker. I heard him once at a symposium, and he was really funny and engaging. Secondly, he's one of the smartest people in the world. I think most people just want to hear Robert Philips because he's a celebrity.
(man)	I think having a celebrity is important. Having a well-known celebrity at graduation is very prestigious for the university. And graduation is an important time; people want someone memorable. Not just the students, but for their parents and relatives coming down to see them graduate.
(woman)	I just think it's sad most people consider someone on TV more important than a great scholar.

19. Why is the man already ready for graduation?

20. What does the woman think of the graduation speaker debate?

Questions 21-24

Listen to part of a lecture in a nautical science class. The professor is talking about the clipper ships.

In the mid-19th century, the U.S. maritime industry produced a spectacular kind of ship never seen before or since: the clipper. The long-hulled clipper ship was designed to carry relatively small amounts of valuable cargo and small numbers of passengers at high speed between the Atlantic and Pacific coasts of the United States. Such ships were required as the western territories of the United States opened to development, because transcontinental railroad service was not yet available.

The clipper ship was unique. It was built for speed, and very little else. While clipper ships were not rapid by modern standards, they were rapid by the standards of sailing vessels at that time. They might take four months to go from New York to San Francisco, and one ship, named *the Oriental*, shocked the world when it made the journey from Hong Kong to London, England in only 97 days. They could travel over 600 kilometers a day; one famous clipper, *the Sovereign*, could even manage about 22 knots, or 40 kilometers per hour – a respectable speed even in the age of steamships, and unprecedented in the age of sail.

Clippers could not carry large amounts of cargo. They did carry tremendous amounts of sail, to take full advantage of every bit of wind. A clipper ship under full sail was an unforgettable sight. One distinctive feature of a clipper ship was its sharply raked bow, like a knife blade, which was known as the "clipper bow" and continued in use long after the age of sail had ended.

Impressive though they were, clipper ships ruled the seas only briefly. They had serious weaknesses. Wooden construction made them vulnerable to fire. One ship, *The Great Republic*, was completely destroyed in a fire before it was ever launched. Also, even as the speedy clipper ships raced along the seas, another means of transportation – the railroad – was about to make the clipper ship obsolete, only a few short years after the first clipper set sail.

21. What is the speaker's attitude towards the clipper?

22. What was NOT a special feature of the clipper?

23. The speaker mentioned several different clipper ships. Match the ship name and for what it was famous.

24. Why did the speaker say the clipper ships were successful for only a short time?

Questions 25-28

Listen to part of a lecture in a fairy tale class. The professor is talking about Hans Christian Andersen.

Everyone knows the fairy tales written by Hans Christian Andersen. And although people all around the world today read his stories, translated into nearly every language, his path to fame and success was not an easy one.

Hans Christian was not from a wealthy family. His father was a poor cobbler. He was not well educated, but read stories like the "Arabian Nights" to Hans Christian when he could. Hans Christian's dad died when he was only 11 years old.

When Hans Christian was a young boy, he was considered a fool – too dreamy and impractical. In his early schooling, he showed creativity and a fondness for acting and the arts, but was otherwise bored by school. After his father died, Hans Christian went to school increasingly less often. He had a good memory, and could memorize plays and books easily, but was more interested in telling stories than reading his lessons.

His mother tried to put him to work when he was thirteen, but Hans Christian had no interest in any of the jobs she got for him. So when he turned 14, he left for Copenhagen, the capital of Denmark, by himself. For the next three years, Hans Christian was bitterly poor. He took what work he could, and never gave up. But when he turned 17, he got a lucky break. A director of the Royal Theater named Jonas Collin read a play written by Hans Christian and thought he had talent, but lacked education. So Collin sent Hans Christian back to school. It was another traumatic experience. Hans Christian was several years older than his fellow students, and the teacher was abusive to the young boy. Eventually, Collin took Hans Christian out of school and placed him under a private tutor. Hans Christian was 23 before he passed the university entrance examinations, but almost immediately, he started to get published. His first books were poems, plays, and novels.

By 1833, Hans Christian was so successful, the king gave him money to travel in Europe. It wasn't until he was 30 years old that Hans Christian published his first book of fairy tales. He gave the book little thought and intended to return to his poems and novels, but the public reaction to those fairy tales was overwhelming.

Throughout his life, Hans Christian Andersen wrote 156 fairy tales. He lived to 70 years of age, was never married, but had a great number of friends. He was greatly honored by his countrymen, including by a great festival when he was 62. Hans Christian himself became like his story of the ugly duckling – after a difficult childhood, he grew to be the gorgeous swan and pride of Denmark.

25. What is the theme of this biography?

26. How did Hans Christian do in school?

27. The professor explains a series of events of Hans Christian Andersen's life. Put them into chronological order.

28. Why does the speaker say Hans Christian Andersen's life was like his story of the Ugly Duckling?

Questions 29-30

Listen to part of a conversation between two people.

(woman)	Did you hear the school is going to be offering a new major starting next year?
(man)	No, I didn't. What's that all about?
(woman)	It's called "American Civilization."
(man)	So how's that different than American History?
(woman)	It's broader than just history. This course encompasses anything and everything about America – history, literature, culture, politics, economy, urban studies – you name it.
(man)	Then American Civilization is more a combination of many other majors; it won't be offering new classes?
(woman)	I guess not.
(man)	Is the department going to have an office?
(woman)	Sure. It's going to be in the History building for now, on the third floor where the Regional Science office used to be.
(man)	So are you thinking about enrolling in this new major?
(woman)	I am. You know I've had a terrible time deciding on a major. My interests are too interdisciplinary for any one field. By studying American Civilization, I could bring together a wide range of interests into one package.
(man)	That sounds like it could be a good idea for you. But I think I'd prefer something more focused. I wouldn't want to concentrate on any single country.
(woman)	Fair enough. We can still take courses together about American Literature.

29. What is starting at the university?

30. What is most likely true about the man?

Practice Test ⑨

Listening Script Part A

1.   (man)   Hi Ruth. Have you been here studying all day?
       (woman)   Pretty much, though to be honest, I did sleep for a little while.
       (man)   I know, let's go study in the park for a while. The fresh air would be good for us.
       (woman)   Oh, I can't move. I just started a new exercise class at the gym this morning.
       (narrator)   What does the woman mean?

2.   (woman)   So everyone agrees to help with the cooking. Matthew is going to make dessert. And Luke is going to make an appetizer. I'll cook the main dish.
       (man)   That sounds like a great dinner.
       (woman)   But are you going to join us for dinner later?
       (man)   If only I'd finished my lab report, I'd have gladly joined you.
       (narrator)   What will the man most likely do?

3.   (man)   I saw Alex's computer was working again. It was really a mess. Did he fix it himself?
       (woman)   No, it was too damaged, so he had it fixed by his friend Bernie.
       (narrator)   Who fixed Alex's computer?

4.   (woman)   You said you were going to write up a copy of the lesson I missed. Do you have time to do it before you go?
       (man)   I'd like to, but I have to get to the copy center before it closes. Don't worry; I'll get it done.
       (narrator)   What is the man implying?

5.   (man)   This physiology class is really challenging. Right now we have to design rehabilitation programs for people who've been injured.
       (woman)   I remember that assignment. It was pretty tough, but Dr. Jones is a good teacher.
       (man)   Do you know what kind of exercise is appropriate for someone coming back from an ankle sprain?
       (woman)   No, but you could look under "exercise" in your physiology textbook.
       (narrator)   What does the woman suggest?

6.   (woman)   Unfortunately, you haven't had enough basic courses to take an advanced class in economics.
       (man)   Can't I persuade you to bend the rules this once?
       (narrator)   What does the man mean?

7.   (man)   Did you see Ken's science fair project? It's really impressive. I wouldn't be surprised if he won an award.
       (woman)   Oh, then the science fair wasn't cancelled after all?
       (narrator)   What is the woman assuming?

8.   (woman)   Excuse me, I seem to be a little lost.
       (man)   Sure. What're you looking for?
       (woman)   I'm looking for the reference desk. I thought it was on the first floor.
       (man)   It is. This is the basement. You need to go past the book return desk, and take a left to the stairs.
       (narrator)   What kind of place are the speakers probably talking about?

9.   (woman)   Is it true that they make a lot of pottery around the Columbia River?
      (man)   Oh, yes. That's because there's an abundance of the right kind of clay.
      (narrator)   What is true about the Columbia River area?

10. (man)   Professor Headley is the best English teacher I've ever had.
      (woman)   Really? I took one of her introductory courses and didn't think much of it.
      (narrator)   What do these people think of Professor Headley's courses?

11. (woman)   Hi, Dan. I heard you were looking for me.
      (man)   I was wondering if you wanted to see that new comedy movie.
      (woman)   Trish and I saw it last week. But I wouldn't mind seeing it again.
      (man)   Perfect. Then let's get together at your place around eight and go together.
      (narrator)   When will the man and woman meet?

12. (man)   Professor Ford gave me a great grade for my experiment mixing those gases.
      (woman)   I don't understand how you were able to make the experiment work. I tried over and over
                 again, but nothing worked.
      (man)   By mixing the gases at a lower temperature, I was able create a more stable experiment.
                 It was no big deal.
      (woman)   I disagree. It was certainly a major breakthrough.
      (narrator)   What does the woman mean?

13. (woman)   We should meet up in the library after dinner and do some studying.
      (man)   No thanks. I think I've done more than enough studying for one day.
      (narrator)   What is the man implying?

14. (man)   I really like the looks of Dr. Richards' seminar on the history of economic reasoning. Can
                 I get the application form for his class?
      (woman)   I'm sorry, but that class is open to economics majors only.
      (narrator)   What can be inferred about the man?

15. (woman)   Thanks for the information. It feels like you know just about everything about this school.
      (man)   I should. I've been here long enough.
      (woman)   So how long have you been going to school here?
      (man)   I'm just finishing off my second year of graduate school now, but I also did all four years
                 of undergraduate school here, and I lived in the area during my senior year of high
                 school, too.
      (narrator)   How long has the man attended the university?

16. (woman)   I'm tired of waiting around for John. He's always late. At least Diane always gets here on time.
      (man)   True enough, but her punctuality doesn't nearly make up for her inefficiency.
      (narrator)   What does the man think about Diane?

17. (man)   Where'd you get that great-looking certificate? It looks really impressive.
      (woman)   Oh, from Dr. Reynolds. He had a little party where he gave them out to all his honors students.
      (narrator)   What can be inferred about the woman?

Listening Script Part B

Questions 18-21

Listen to part of a lecture in an earth science class. The professor is talking about the Chandler wobble.

Earth science can be a mysterious field of study. Our planet is subject to so many far-ranging forces, it is often difficult to determine what affects what. But with better models, computers, and new data, those mysteries are slowly being explained.

One of the older scientific mysteries about the Earth is the so-called "Chandler wobble." It was first noticed by the American businessman-turned-astronomer Seth Carlo Chandler in 1891. He discerned one of several wobbling motions the Earth makes as it rotates on its axis, like how a top wobbles as it spins. Even after a century of observation, scientists could not decide on what was causing this particular wobble – about 40 feet every 433 days. Since the wobble is so small, scientists calculated that the wobble should diminish to nothing in just 68 years, unless some force were constantly replenishing it. What could that force be? Many explanations were guessed at over the years. Most geologists thought it was the movement of the earth's crust. Meteorologists thought it was atmospheric phenomena. And environmentalists thought the force was the changes in the ice fields on the polar caps.

But finally, it looks like that mystery has been discovered. It appears the principal cause of the Chandler Wobble is fluctuating pressure on the bottom of the oceans. Changes in temperature and salinity affect the pressure of the deep ocean depths, and those changes help create a wobble. In fact, scientists think the wobble is two-thirds caused by the ocean, and one-third by atmospheric fluctuations.

This is just one, seemingly minor, example. But it is a good example of the kind of new discovery that has become possible in recent years only because of better data and a better understanding of the oceans that has emerged. The new research going on these days is interdisciplinary, taking advantage of the discoveries made in a myriad of fields, not just one.

18. What is this lecture about?

19. What is the significant question about the Chandler wobble?

20. The professor explains the Chandler wobble, which is one of the older scientific mysteries about the Earth. Match the hypothesis about Chandler's wobble with the group who believed it.

21. What is the major force behind Chandler's wobble?

Questions 22-25

Listen to part of a lecture in a geography class. The professor is talking about cartography.

If the earth were flat, there would be no problem in representing its surface on a flat sheet of paper. But the earth is a sphere, and a spherical surface cannot be flattened.

The transfer of a spherical surface to a flat surface is known as a projection. When a sphere is represented upon a flat surface, there is always some distortion – distortion of distances, distortion of direction, distortion of the sizes or shapes of areas. Equal-area projections distort shape and direction badly but show the relative sizes of areas correctly. Conformal projections distort size but show shapes and directions correctly. The projection chosen depends on the purposes of a particular map. Since accuracy in one property must be sacrificed to gain accuracy in another, accuracy is sought for the properties where it is most essential.

Map projections are often classified according to the type of surface onto which the globe is projected or transferred – cylinder, cone, or plane. In the cylindrical projection, the surface of the globe is transferred to a cylinder. The globe touches the cylinder along only one line, usually the equator. Only at this point is the map totally accurate. When the cylinder is unrolled, the meridians and parallels are straight and cross each other at right angles. The meridians are always the same distance from each other, even though on a globe, they come together at the poles.

The most famous kind of cylindrical projection is the Mercator map. The Mercator map preserves shape and direction. It was primarily designed for use in navigation, and any straight line on it has the same compass direction throughout its length. The Mercator, however, is not an equal-area projection. The Mercator greatly exaggerates the sizes of areas in the polar regions.

Plane maps are made by transferring the image of the globe to a plane which touches the globe at one point. If the origin of the projection is on one side of the globe, as in this picture, a stereographic projection is formed. For the orthographic projection, the projection is moved infinitely far away, creating an image that most resembles a photo of the globe.

By moving the origin of the projection to the center of the globe, the result is a gnomonic projection. In the polar gnomonic projection, both the parallels and the meridians get farther and farther apart approaching the edges, and there is a great distortion of size and shape. However, the gnomonic projection has a quality useful in navigation – any straight line on it is a great circle, that is, the shortest distance between any two places on the earth. The earth is a sphere, so often the shortest distance between two points is not what a Mercator projection would suggest.

Sometimes, the maps are split into several lobes, each focusing on a central landmass or ocean. These are called interrupted projections, and they show equal areas and minimize distortions within each area. Goode's Homolosine Projection is the most famous of this type.

22. Why do all maps distort?

23. What is most useful about a Mercator map?

24. Which of these maps is a cylindrical projection?

25. The professor explains map projections in his lecture. Match these maps with their names.

Questions 26-27

Listen to part of a conversation between two speakers.

(man)	Hey, Jane. How're you doing?
(woman)	Not too good. I really made a mess of my statistics test yesterday.
(man)	That's too bad. What happened? I thought you said statistics wasn't very difficult.
(woman)	It's not. But I've been so busy working on a short story for my creative writing class, I forgot to prepare for the statistics test.
(man)	That's right, you're taking creative writing this semester. I was surprised you decided to take a class like that. You're normally a very mathematical person. I don't think of you as a writer.
(woman)	Neither did I. I never meant to take a writing class, but I had to take an English class to fulfill a graduation requirement. And I was so late in registering for classes last semester that this creative writing class was the only thing still available that fit my timetable. But now look at me! I'm enjoying writing so much that I'm neglecting my other classes.
(man)	That's great. Except what are you going to do about your statistics class?
(woman)	Oh, it's actually not a huge problem. I already talked to my professor about it, and she's agreed to let me do some extra work to make up for it.
(man)	That's really nice of her. You have Professor Childs, don't you?
(woman)	That's right.
(man)	Professor Childs is probably the nicest professor in the department. I wish I could have taken more classes with her.

26. What is the woman's problem?

27. What can be inferred about the man?

Questions 28-31

Listen to part of a lecture in a cultural studies class. The professor is talking about a sense of history.

One might say that the American people live entirely for the present and care nothing about the past. Americans lack what many other nations would call a "sense of history." The early 1900s seem almost as remote to most Americans as the reign of Julius Caesar. Even reasonably well-educated and thoughtful Americans tend to take a skeptical view of history and historians.

At the same time, however, Americans have a heartfelt – though muddled – perception of history, in the form of nostalgia, or a longing for "the good old days" when life was supposedly simpler and more enjoyable. Many businesses and products have arisen to make money from such nostalgia for an America that never really existed.

A remarkably large industry, for example, is devoted to marketing "old-time radio." Broadcasts from the 1930s and 1940s, such as Jack Benny's comedy program and various mystery dramas, have found a new life in recordings that bring back pleasant memories for millions of listeners.

Television also has capitalized on nostalgia through comedies such as *Happy Days*, about America in the 1950s. Popular in the late 1970s, *Happy Days* used nostalgia to make the audience laugh.

Another successful American TV series of the 1970s, *The Waltons*, was more sentimental and focused on the life of a rural family during the great depression of the 1930s.

Movies, too, regularly recycle old ideas in an attempt to profit from nostalgia. Films like *Charlie's Angels* and *Star Trek* were more popular than the original television shows ever were.

Nostalgia-related products in the United States appear to emerge in a cycle of approximately 20 to 25 years. That's about how long it takes for unpleasant memories of a decade to fade and be replaced by "confabulations," or invented "memories" and myths of that era. Only then can nostalgia arise, after the passage of years has diminished the awareness that the "good old days" did not seem especially good at the time. Because in truth, the "happy" 1950s were in fact painful and tumultuous for many Americans, and rural life during the 1930s was harsh and difficult.

28. What is the main idea of this talk?

29. The speaker mentioned many examples of nostalgia. Match the medium and the example of nostalgia.

30. What can be inferred about the *Happy Days* television program?

31. What does the speaker say about the cycle of nostalgia?

Questions 32-35

Listen to a professor and her students discussing information from a linguistics class. The class is on language.

(professor)   So then, the Phoenicians developed the world's first syllabic writing, using signs that represented individual consonant sounds instead of whole words. And by doing so, they reduced the number of characters needed to write their language from the thousands, like in Egyptian hieroglyphics, to just 22. But this was still not a real alphabet. What was missing?

(man)   Vowels. The Phoenician writing system didn't have any vowels.

(professor)   Exactly. But vowels did not just suddenly appear overnight. Immediately after the Phoenicians spread to Greece around 900 BC, the Greek writing resembled the Phoenician writing a lot, but over time it changed. The Phoenicians had many weak consonants. Some of them, the Greeks just dropped. But six different weak consonants were used to indicate specific vowel sounds. Eventually, since the Greeks had no use for those characters as consonants, they turned into the Greek vowel sounds – a, e, u, long e, i, and o.

(woman)   Later on, the Greeks also changed how language was written. Most older languages, including Phoenician, were written from right to left. The Greeks, though, eventually changed from right to left to from left to right, like we use today.

(professor)   Very good. All those changes then passed around to other cultures – to the Etruscans in Italy, to the Copts in Egypt (where it replaced hieroglyphics), and to the Slavic peoples in Eastern Europe. Latin writing derived from the Etruscans, then formed the basis for all the modern western languages.

(woman)   Professor, what about upper- and lower-case letters? Where did they come from?

(professor)   Good question. They are a relatively recent invention; the ancient Greeks, Romans, and others only had one form, no capitals or small letters. But in Medieval times, two forms of writing developed. Carefully drawn, squarish letters that resembled Latin characters were used for formal documents, and faster, more rounded "cursive" writing was used for less formal documents. These two styles eventually came to be used side-by-side in handwritten books. With the rise of the printing press in the Renaissance, these two types of letters were fully distinguished. And so today, capital letters mimic Latin letters, and small letters resemble the medieval cursive.

32. What is the topic of this seminar?

33. What were the most significant changes to writing made by the Greeks?

34. A professor and two students discuss a series of historical events. Place the following events in order.

35. How were upper- and lower-case letters invented?

Questions 36-38

Listen to part of a conversation between two speakers.

(woman)	I'm sorry, but could you help me? I'm having trouble registering for next semester.
(man)	What happens to be the problem?
(woman)	I'm not sure what classes I have to take, and what ones are only electives.
(man)	Let's take a look at your schedule.
(woman)	See, both Anthropology 100 and the major seminar are scheduled at 1 PM.
(man)	But if you want to be an Anthropology major, you have to take the seminar first.
(woman)	But I really wanted to take Anthropology 100.
(man)	I think you're going to have to wait until next semester. What else?
(woman)	Well, those two Cultural Anthropology classes, 150 and 151, look really interesting.
(man)	Sure, but they are sequence classes. You can't take 151 until you've finished 150.
(woman)	I see. And how about Anthropology 50?
(man)	The Social Anthropology survey? You can take that anytime.
(woman)	Hmmm ... that's only three classes. What else can I take?
(man)	You can always take non-major classes. You need a couple of non-Anthropology classes for your major-related electives – Statistics or Computers, for instance. Biology is related, too. It's always good to take a wide array of classes; you don't want your classes to get too monotonous.
(woman)	Thanks for all your help.
(man)	No problem. But remember, whatever you choose, get the form okayed by the department, signed by your advisor, and handed in to the Registrar's office by next Monday, or you'll miss registration.

36. What best describes this conversation?

37. Why can't the woman take both Anthropology 100 and the major seminar?

38. What course does the man NOT describe as major-related?

Questions 39-42

Listen to part of a lecture in an anthropology class. The professor is talking about the Stone Age.

The Stone Age refers to the rugged time early in the development of human culture, before the use of metals, when tools and weapons were made of stone. The dates of the Stone Age vary considerably for different parts of the world. It began in Africa as early as 2.5 million years ago, in Asia about 1.8 million years ago, and perhaps only 1 million years ago in Europe. In the Americas, the Stone Age began with the coming of the first peoples about 30,000 years ago. The Stone Age ended only around 3-4,000 BC in Europe and Asia, and later elsewhere.

The process of blade tool making developed about 40,000 years ago. Before that, much more simple stone tools were used. To make stone tools requires some ingenuity. The toolmaker used a wooden hammer and a piece of bone to strike downward on the edge of a platform of rock. This knocked off several long bladelike pieces from around the edge. Then the hammer or bone was used further on the blade flake to remove smaller flakes, shaping the blade into a finished tool.

Using this process, many different tools could be made. The large, heavy ground-edge blade was used as an axe. The flaked-edge blade was used as an adze, for woodworking. The smaller blade was used for slicing meat. And the arrowhead was used for hunting.

The Stone Age has been divided into three eras – the Paleolithic, the Mesolithic, and the Neolithic. The Paleolithic was the longest period, going from the beginning of the Stone Age to about 15,000 years ago. At first, only very simple stone and bone tools were used in that cold age, when food was scarce and life difficult.

After 15,000 years ago, the start of the Mesolithic period, warmer weather made food more available, and humans began to spread. Tools were adapted and refined.

The start of agricultural villages about 10,000 years ago marked the beginning of the Neolithic period. Stone tools became highly polished and varied. By about 6000 BC, pottery first appeared, and in some places, copper began to be used.

39. What is the speaker's attitude towards the Stone Age?

40. The professor described how the Stone Age came to different parts of the world at different times. Put the following world regions into the correct order according to when the Stone Age first came. Go from oldest to most recent.

41. What was the blade pictured here used for?

42. The speaker mentioned several periods within the Stone Age. Match the period to its characteristic.

Questions 43-47

Listen to part of a lecture in a biology class. The professor is talking about cloning.

Developments in genetic science are pioneering some of the most important advances in medicine these days.

Cloning is one of the most dramatic examples of genetic science. A clone is a group of genes, cells, or complete organisms in which all of the group's members have the same genetic constitution. Clones occur in nature, especially in the case of simple organisms, such as bacteria and viruses, which produce merely by asexual production; that is, by replicating by themselves with their own DNA. They also occur in humans and other animals when a single fertilized egg divides and separates to form two or more identical individuals, as with identical twins.

Artificial cloning of selected genes is one of the most significant breakthroughs ever made in biology and has powerful implications for both science and industry. Once the desired gene is obtained, the cloning can be left to organisms such as bacteria, which, under suitable conditions, reproduce almost indefinitely. In this way, enormous quantities of the particular gene may be produced. Gene cloning is most commonly done in the laboratory by means of the "polymerase chain reaction," or PCR. This can produce millions of copies of a single gene in a matter of hours.

Far more daunting an enterprise than gene cloning is the cloning of whole animals, which has only recently been done. In order to clone a complete animal, one needs a complete sample of its DNA; since every cell in an animal's body has a complete copy, this is not difficult. This DNA is then introduced into the ovum or egg of another animal of the same species after that egg's original DNA has been removed. The egg is then inserted into a surrogate animal's womb, and the pregnancy proceeds as normal.

Another important advance in genetic medicine is genetically modified food, or GM for short. This is increasingly common in the food industry. By changing a plant's genes, scientists can make foods that last longer before going bad, have better color, or resist disease.

A third key genetic advance is the creation of transgenic animals. A transgenic animal is not a clone, but an animal whose genes contain DNA taken from another source. It is now possible to create transgenic pigs in order to provide organs for human transplant. If, for example, a human gene is introduced at the one-cell stage of a pig embryo's development, the organ taken from the resulting pig will be less likely to be rejected by the human.

However, all these advances are controversial. For example, scientists recently discovered that pigs carry a virus that can infect human cells. This is normally not a problem, but organs taken from a transgenic pig could cause that virus to cross over to humans. Similarly, some scientists warn that cloning and other forms of genetic modification could create unforeseen consequences that could be dangerous to human life.

43. What is the main topic of this lecture?

44. What is NOT a genetic advance mentioned in the lecture?

45. What is an example of a clone?

46. The speaker discussed the animal cloning process. Summarize that process by putting the following steps into the correct order.

47. Why are these technological developments controversial?

Questions 48-50

Listen to part of a conversation between two speakers.

(woman)	Can I ask you something, Dave?
(man)	Sure. Ask away.
(woman)	Well, I was thinking about trying out for the drama club's next play this spring. Do you think I should go for it?
(man)	Definitely! Our university's drama club is really good. If you got a part, it would be a unique experience for you. You know I was in their play last year, and I think it was the most important thing I've done since I came to college.
(woman)	Important? Why's that?
(man)	Because performing on stage can really change you. It gave me a lot of confidence in myself and helped me be less shy. It lets you learn a lot about yourself. What play are they going to produce this year?
(woman)	"A Midsummer Night's Dream."
(man)	Shakespeare? That's really hard. Who do you want to be?
(woman)	I'm not 100% sure yet. I was thinking about Tatiana, the Faerie Queen.
(man)	A good choice. I bet you could be a good Faerie Queen. It's a good part, really interesting, but not the biggest female part in the play, so you should have a little less competition for the part.
(woman)	That was what I was thinking, too. I was just worried that it might be too hard.
(man)	It certainly does take a lot of time. You need to take an easier course load, or else you'll just get too swamped with work, and it will hurt your grades. But with some good planning and time management, you can do it.

48. What does the woman want to do?

49. What is NOT a reason the man thinks acting is good?

50. Why does the man recommend trying out for Tatiana?

Practice Test ⑩

Listening Script Part A

1. (woman)   I miss Kelly. She's a lot of fun.
    (man)   Yeah, Kelly is always nice to hang out with.
    (woman)   So where's she been lately? I haven't seen her for weeks.
    (man)   That's because she's wrapped up in her research.
    (narrator) What does the man mean?

2. (man)   Hi. I applied for a student loan, but I haven't heard anything yet.
    (woman)   Okay, let me check our files. Did you submit your request on time?
    (man)   I sure did. I sent my application in three weeks ago.
    (woman)   Well, that's why you haven't heard from us. It takes six weeks to process applications.
    (narrator) What is the woman implying?

3. (woman)   Brian, did you invite Ethan to Alex's party?
    (man)   I thought they weren't getting along so well these days, so I figured I shouldn't say anything.
    (narrator) Who is having a party?

4. (man)   I heard Professor Thurman will let you do a project for extra credit.
    (woman)   Really? That's great! I could use some.
    (narrator) What will the woman probably do?

5. (woman)   So I'm going to pick you guys up and drive us all to our professor's house?
    (man)   Yeah, it should be a lot of fun. When are we going to go?
    (woman)   We don't have to be there until 5, so I'll probably just leave around 4.
    (man)   The traffic is really bad, though. You'd better leave a few minutes before that.
    (narrator) What does the man suggest?

6. (man)   There are so many people running in the student council elections. I have no idea who I'm going to vote for. Like for council president, I can't decide if I like Charles or Linda more.
    (woman)   Actually, I was thinking of voting for Richard.
    (man)   Richard? You would seriously vote for Richard for student council president?
    (woman)   Well, I think he has what it takes.
    (narrator) What does the woman mean?

7. (man)   Say, do you remember Susan from high school?
    (woman)   Sure. It's been ages since I've seen her, though.
    (man)   I just saw Susan last week. She started attending this university just this semester.
    (woman)   So she _did_ finally enter university.
    (narrator) What did the woman assume about Susan?

8. (woman)   I don't think I've ever seen the library this empty before.
    (man)   It certainly is quiet today.
    (woman)   It is really strange to see so few people in the library, isn't it?
    (man)   It sure is. I wonder where everybody is?
    (narrator)   What can be inferred about the library?

9. (man)   I'm trying to decide which sheets to buy for my new bed. I found some nice blue ones for $37.50, but the green ones only cost $16.45.
    (woman)   If you're looking to save money, I know a store selling sheets for $15.50.
    (narrator)   How much are the green sheets?

10. (woman)   Your lab is producing a lot of great research these days.
    (man)   A lot of that is thanks to Michael. He got some great results from his experiments last year.
    (woman)   And did you follow up on his experiments?
    (man)   Keith has. And his report looks very promising, too.
    (narrator)   What did Keith do?

11. (man)   I heard the university orchestra just released a recording of Beethoven's 7th Symphony.
    (woman)   Yeah, it's getting a lot of good reviews, and I like it, too.
    (man)   Do you know if the CD is being sold at the campus music store yet?
    (woman)   I bought it the day before yesterday.
    (narrator)   When did the woman buy the compact disk?

Listening Script Part B

Questions 12-15

Listen to part of a lecture in a sociology of technology class. The professor is talking about air travel.

One of the most striking developments in 20th-century America, and by extension the world, was the emergence of commercial air travel.

The Wright Brothers' initial flight at Kitty Hawk, North Carolina, in 1903 lasted only a few seconds and covered a distance of only about 30 meters, but that was only the beginning. Charles Lindbergh flew across the Atlantic Ocean in 1927. Chuck Yeager broke the sound barrier. Within only a few years, the beginnings of a transcontinental and international airline network were in place. The Wrights' unsophisticated biplane developed into large passenger-carrying aircraft capable of flying thousands of kilometers without refueling. By 1970, air travel had become as commonplace as journeys by rail, and airlines had all but forced ocean liners, once the monarchs of the oceans, out of business.

Commercial air travel also marked a significant change in American social history. Travel by air became a symbol of prestige. As airliners became the rulers of the skies, their passengers came to be seen as a kind of "royalty" themselves, because they either had enough status to require the uniquely rapid transportation that aircraft provided, or had the money to afford the price of an airline ticket. A special breed of people traveled by swift aircraft, whereas those who enjoyed less favor had to be content with poky ground transportation. Aircraft were more than merely a means of getting from Point A to Point B in a short time. They also were modern equivalents of the golden coaches in fairy tales.

Because social standing was so important an element of airline travel, it is no surprise that air travel affected the American language as well. When commercial jet aircraft entered passenger service, they became the vehicles of choice for glamorous individuals, who flitted from coast to coast and continent to continent by jet – and became known as the "jet set." Anything improved, accelerated, or made more sophisticated was described as "jet-propelled," and the word "jet" came to have connotations of wealth, power, and influence.

12. What is the speaker's opinion of air travel?

13. The speaker mentioned several important feats in aviation history. Match the pioneer with what he accomplished.

14. How did the rise of air travel affect American society?

15. Why did the speaker compare the airplane to "golden coaches in fairy tales"?

Questions 16-18

Listen to a professor and her students discussing information from a psychology class. The class is on physiological psychology.

(man)	Professor? This is sort of off-topic, but a few of us have been wondering: where did physiological psychology come from?
(professor)	That's actually an interesting question, Brad. What is physiological psychology?
(woman)	It's a branch of psychology concerned with the relation between behavior and the sense organs and the nervous system.
(professor)	Right, Valerie. And one of the first people to think about that relation was René Descartes, the 17th century French philosopher. To Descartes, animals were just mechanical devices; their behavior was controlled by environmental stimuli. Even humans were mechanical devices, but with one exception – mind. Descartes believed in a body/mind duality; that is, the mind existed outside of the body, and was not subject to the mechanical laws the body was.
(woman)	Do people still believe in mind/body duality?
(professor)	Not in physiological psychology. Like most scientists these days, we believe that the world consists of matter and energy, and that nonmaterial entities such as souls are not a part of the universe.
(woman)	What about Johannes Müller? I thought he was also an important experimentalist.
(professor)	He was. And Müller was also the person who came up with the doctrine of specific nerve energies – that electrical impulses, carried along nerves, go to specific areas of the brain. Eye impulses to the eye part of the brain, or sound impulses to the sound part. His ideas set the stage for further research on the brain itself, an integral part of physiological psychology. But the first real advocate of physiological psychology was Wilhelm Wundt in the latter part of the 19th century. Physiological psychology grew out of general psychology in the 19th century. Indeed, the first textbook of psychology was written by researcher Wilhelm Wundt and titled *Principles of Physiological Psychology*. Wundt also was the first person who tried to make psychology more like a science, advocating experimental research instead of only thinking about ideas.

16. What is the subject of this discussion?

17. The professor and his students discuss the relation between behavior and the nervous system. Match the scientist with his innovative idea.

18. What do psychologists today think about mind/body duality?

Questions 19-20

Listen to part of a conversation between two speakers.

(man)	Graduation is a month away, and my job search is leading nowhere.
(woman)	How are you handling it?
(man)	I'm looking in all the newspapers but finding no good jobs.
(woman)	Searching newspapers is pointless. Try an online search instead.
(man)	How do I perform an online search?
(woman)	Go to the computer and call up a search engine. Then type in keywords to direct your search. Your keywords might be "Jobs" and the name of your specialty.
(man)	All right. I'll type in "Jobs" and "Journalism." What next?
(woman)	The search engine will give you a set of links for jobs in journalism. The links might lead to websites for newspapers, magazines, employment agencies, or whatever. See if they look promising. If they do, then submit your resume.
(man)	Can I do that online?
(woman)	Yes, of course. You can send out 50 resumes online in the time it would take to send five resumes by mail.
(man)	So an online job search will improve my chance of finding a job.
(woman)	Certainly. I've already received two job offers after searching and applying online. I'll have a job as soon as I graduate.

19. What is this dialogue about?

20. What do online searches not allow?

Questions 21-25

Listen to part of a lecture in a chemistry class. The professor is talking about the element mercury.

An element with unusual but highly useful properties, mercury is the only metal that is a liquid at ordinary room temperature. Its chemical symbol, Hg, is derived from two Greek words meaning "silver water." Its atomic number, or the number of positively charged particles in its core or nucleus, is 80. Its atomic weight, or total weight of particles in the atom, is 200.59. Although mercury, like water, is a fluid at room temperature, mercury is more than 13 times heavier than water and does not moisten surfaces which it touches. Its characteristics include a high boiling point, which makes mercury practical for use in thermometers and other scientific instruments. When poured onto a flat, level surface, mercury assumes the form of slightly flattened droplets, or spheroids, with shiny gray surfaces. If touched with one's finger, a droplet of mercury splits apart into two or more smaller spheroids, which then rejoin easily when brought together again. Mercury flows easily and rapidly, and for this reason is commonly known as "quicksilver," meaning "living silver." Spain and Italy produce much of the world's supply of mercury.

The United States also produces mercury, most of it from the state of California. Mercury has been known and used since ancient times. It occurs widely in the form of a red ore called cinnabar. When the ore is heated, mercury vapor is released and then condensed to form liquid mercury. The world's leading mercury mine, the Almaden mine in Spain, is believed to have been in operation since approximately 800 B.C. During Spain's colonial era, mercury was especially valuable because it played an important part in refining gold. Ships carrying mercury between Spain and Spain's colonies in the Americas were known as the "quicksilver galleons." Some of these ships were wrecked in a storm. Centuries later, divers exploring the wrecks found pools of liquid mercury on the bottom of the sea. The mercury had not dissolved in sea water for hundreds of years.

Mercury has had many applications. It has been used in medicines since the Middle Ages, and in modern dentistry as an ingredient of metal fillings for teeth. Because mercury expands when heated, it is used in devices for sensing and regulating temperature. Mercury is also important to batteries, and mercury vapor is used in certain kinds of lamps. Mercury is toxic and therefore has applications as a poison in insecticides and fungicides. Bright red paints may contain mercury. It has had important applications in shipping, where mercury-based paints have been used to prevent marine organisms from attaching themselves to ships' hulls. In some 20th-century submarines, mercury was used as ballast because it is heavy and can be pumped from one tank to another. The toxicity of mercury became an environmental issue in the 1970s, when it was discovered that metallic mercury released into rivers from factories was converted by bacteria into methyl mercury, a poison which accumulates in the bodies of fish and of humans who eat them. Methyl mercury can damage the brain.

21. Mercury poured on a table would assume which shape?

22. Mercury has many properties. Match its characteristics with the following numbers.

23. The professor explains a series of events in his lecture. Put the following events in chronological order.

24. Mercury is not used in which of the following?

25. Mercury IS NOT

Questions 26-28

Listen to part of a lecture in a geography class. The professor is talking about Chesapeake Bay.

One of the most historic and important bodies of water in the United States is Chesapeake Bay, an estuary in eastern Virginia and Maryland. More than 300 km long, Chesapeake Bay extends northward from the great harbor at Hampton Roads to the city of Baltimore and beyond. Several large rivers flow into the bay from the west, including the Potomac, Rappahannock, York and James Rivers.

The bay has long been a vital avenue of commerce and transportation. It also has been an important fishery. Although the bay's output of fish and shellfish declined during the late 20th century, Chesapeake oyster beds were once so productive and valuable that gun battles were fought on the water over their ownership as late as the 1950s. These battles are remembered as the "oyster wars."

Much of early American history took place on or near Chesapeake Bay. The legendary meeting between Pocahontas and Captain John Smith, for example, took place near the English colony at Jamestown.

Chesapeake Bay and its tributaries were the scene of important military action during the Revolutionary War and the War Between the States. The British General Cornwallis surrendered to George Washington at Yorktown on the York River in 1781, thus ending the Revolutionary War. Just over 80 years later, the ironclad warships *Monitor* and *Virginia* had an inconclusive but nonetheless historic duel in Hampton Roads. This battle demonstrated the superiority of ironclads over wooden warships.

A large military presence remains in Chesapeake Bay, especially at the huge U.S. Navy base in Norfolk. Civilian activities on the bay range from recreation to shipping.

26. Why was the battle between *Monitor* and *Virginia* important?

27. The professor describes the following figures in her lecture. Match them with geographical names.

28. Which large cities are located in the Chesapeake Bay region?

Questions 29-30

Listen to part of a conversation between two speakers.

(woman)	Did you see the headlines in the school paper this morning?
(man)	No, I never read the school newspaper.
(woman)	You don't? Why not?
(man)	Because I don't think it's very reliable. School newspapers in general are pretty amateurish, but ours is particularly bad.
(woman)	Sure, it's not some big, professional paper, but the students work really hard on it and they do the best they can. Besides, where else can you get news about what's going on at our school?
(man)	Well, I'm most interested in how our school sports teams do, and they're all written about in the local newspaper. Anyhow, what did you want to talk to me about?
(woman)	I just read in the paper this morning that the school was planning on canceling the Spring Festival this year.
(man)	I heard about that. That's what I mean by how you can't trust our school paper.
(woman)	What do you mean? Isn't it true?
(man)	No. I serve on the student planning board that works with the school to organize the Spring Festival every year. In last night's meeting, the school said they wanted us to find more private financing for the festival, but they didn't cancel anything.
(woman)	Oh, the newspaper article made it sound very different. Are you sure that's what happened?
(man)	You can come to our next meeting and see for yourself if you want. We'll be discussing the Spring Festival further.

29. What can be inferred about the man?

30. What does the man suggest to the woman?

Practice Test ⑪

Listening Script Part A

1. (man)   I need to get an extension from Dr. Sanders. I didn't get my paper finished that was due today.
   (woman)   What happened to it?
   (man)   I was up late, finishing off my paper, when there was a power failure in the dorm. My whole paper got erased before I had a chance to print it.
   (woman)   Dr. Sanders said late papers were not acceptable.
   (narrator)   What does the woman mean?

2. (woman)   Hi, Brandon. How are you?
   (man)   Pretty good, Kelly. I'm glad I met you; there's something I've been meaning to talk to you about.
   (woman)   Actually, I have to get something from my professor. Wait here, and I'll be back in five minutes.
   (man)   Don't bother. I'll talk to you about it tomorrow.
   (narrator)   What is the man implying?

3. (man)   What happened to Donna's notebook? She said I could use it.
   (woman)   I'm sorry, I forgot. I lent it to my friend, Dave.
   (narrator)   Who has Donna's notebook?

4. (woman)   I talked to the telephone company. They said they can send someone over tomorrow between 2 and 4, but there'll have to be someone at home to let him in.
   (man)   I guess I'll have to skip my biology class tomorrow afternoon. We can't go without a telephone any longer.
   (narrator)   What will the man most likely do?

5. (man)   My schedule has gotten all mixed up tonight. I'm worried I'm going to have to miss the concert.
   (woman)   But we've been planning on this for weeks.
   (man)   I know, but I have a seminar that goes until 6. The concert starts at 7:30. That doesn't give me enough time to drive home, eat dinner, and drive back to the concert hall.
   (woman)   I've got an idea. Why don't I pick you up straight from the seminar? We can have dinner downtown together, and that'll give us plenty of time to get to the concert.
   (narrator)   What does the woman suggest to the man?

6. (woman)   Did Professor Cooper agree to meet with you to help you with your project?
   (man)   Not only that, but he also gave me a bunch of books of his that related to my project. That was more than I could have asked for!
   (narrator)   What does the man mean?

7. (man)   I'm happy to be back at school, but I really did enjoy France. The weather was great, I met a lot of people, and I really improved my French.
   (woman)   Oh, so you _did_ go traveling after all.
   (narrator)   What did the woman assume about the man?

8. (woman)   I can't believe Professor Campbell assigned us an essay and a book report for next week.
   (man)   That is a lot of work. So when is the essay due?
   (woman)   You don't know? Weren't you in class yesterday?
   (man)   No, I had to take my friend to the airport.
   (narrator)   What can be inferred about the woman?

538

9.   (man)   Excuse me, I'm looking for the law library. Could you tell me where it is?

     (woman)   Sure. Go left here until you get to the corner, then take a right and walk two blocks. Take another right, and it's dead ahead about another three blocks.

     (narrator) How far must the man walk to the library?

10. (woman) I feel really sorry that Professor Spelling fired Tori from our lab. I'll miss her, even though I know she was late a lot and sometimes missed days because she was sick.

     (man)   It wasn't that. She made a mistake on one of the experiments that ruined about two weeks' worth of work. It was a dumb mistake, and Dr. Spelling got really angry at her.

     (narrator) Why was Tori fired?

11. (woman) There's a seat available on the direct flight to Fort Worth, leaving at 6 pm and arriving at 11. But it's full fare.

     (man)   Oh, I really wanted to save a couple of dollars. Are there any student fares?

     (woman) The best I can do is an 11 o'clock flight that arrives in Dallas at 2. But there's a three-hour stopover until your connecting flight to Fort Worth.

     (man)   That's kind of inconvenient, but I guess I'll take it.

     (narrator) When does the man's flight leave Dallas?

12. (man)   I can't believe how crowded the library is today. There isn't a seat available anywhere.

     (woman) That's why I always rent a carrel, so I know I have a place to sit and keep my books.

     (man)   Do you mind if I use your carrel for a while?

     (woman) Go right ahead. I'm not going to be back in the library until around 7 or so this evening.

     (narrator) What does the woman mean?

13. (woman) Jack, I have an extra ticket to the country music concert tonight. Would you like to come with me?

     (man)   I think I'd prefer to go to the dentist.

     (narrator) What is the man implying?

14. (man)   Did you hear Dylan say he was going to fail economics? I'm worried about him.

     (woman) I wouldn't lose any sleep over it. Last time Dylan told me he was going to fail a course, he got the best mark in the class.

     (narrator) What does the woman think of Dylan?

15. (woman) The student computer store is having a sale on accessories. That's great. I could totally use some new accessories for my computer. Did you see how much for a new mouse?

     (man)   They're around $15. That's about $10 off their usual price.

     (woman) And how much for recordable CDs?

     (man)   They're $6 apiece, or $60 for a dozen. That's a pretty good price, considering they're really high quality discs.

     (narrator) How much does one recordable CD cost?

16. (man)   Brenda's been so busy lately. I haven't met her or even talked to her in ages. Do you know what's she up to these days?

     (woman) She had some short stories published last year, so these days she's trying to get a novel about some young journalists accepted.

     (narrator) What does Brenda do?

17. (woman) I really want to go to graduate school, but my grades weren't so good.

     (man)   With your recommendations, you have nothing to worry about.

     (narrator) What is the man saying about the woman?

Listening Script Part B

Questions 18-21

Listen to part of a lecture in a chemistry class. The professor is talking about Marie Curie.

By discovering radium, Marie Curie – along with her husband, Pierre – did much to revolutionize theories about matter and the universe. She is an inspiring example of scientific achievement at a time when women were not commonly involved in scientific research.

Marie was born in Warsaw in 1867, when it was under Russian rule. Her father taught physics at a Warsaw high school. Marie finished high school at 15 years old. She had the best grades in her class. After graduating, she taught in the high school before enrolling in the school of science at the Sorbonne in Paris in 1891.

There, she met Pierre, who was already the chief of laboratory work in the School of Physics and Chemistry. In 1895, they were married.

At that time, the radioactivity of uranium had just been discovered, and physicists were excited about the find. Marie Curie experimented with various minerals until she became convinced that an undiscovered radioactive element existed. Pierre joined in her research, and in 1898 they announced the discovery of two new elements – polonium and radium. After four years of experimenting, Marie Curie successfully isolated the new elements in the small shed that was her only laboratory.

The Curies shared the Nobel Prize for physics in 1903, but Pierre died soon after. Marie Curie won the Nobel Prize for chemistry by herself in 1911. After her husband died, Marie was forced to raise her daughters on her own. She died at Haute-Savoie on July 4th, 1934.

18. For what achievement is Marie Curie most famous?

19. What was Pierre Curie's job when Marie first met him?

20. The professor mentioned a series of events from Marie Curie's life. Place them into chronological order.

21. In what year did Marie Curie die?

Questions 22-25

Listen to a professor and two students discussing information from a sociology class. The class is on help.

(professor)	Let's continue with our work on why people help each other. What are the two kinds of help?
(woman)	There's altruistic help and egoistic help. Egoism is helping behavior based on a person's own sense of self-gratification, while altruism has as its ultimate goal a benefit to another person. The focus is solely on the other, without conscious attention focused on one's own self-interest.
(man)	And true altruism comes from empathy – sharing the feelings of and having compassion for, the perceived welfare of another person.
(professor)	You're both right. When a person is in need, empathy would suggest the emotions of sympathy, compassion, and tenderness. And that sets the stage for altruistic help. So when do we help other people?
(man)	When we see other people help, we're more inclined to help; when we have the time; when we think about people being altruistic, people are more helpful; and when it is the social norm to help – like if someone helped us, we should return the help.
(professor)	Those are all correct. The last one, helping in exchange for receiving help, is called "reciprocity exchange."
(woman)	And when help is rewarded, it becomes more common.
(professor)	That's right. Moss and Page performed a simple study about this. A passerby was first approached by a stranger and asked directions to a particular part of town. Almost always the passerby willingly gave the stranger directions. The stranger, who was actually part of the team, responded by saying something positive, such as "Thank you"; or by saying something negative, such as grumbling, "I can't understand you. Never mind, I'll ask someone else"; or by saying something neutral such as "OK." This reinforced the passerby – positively, negatively, or not at all. Then the passerby saw a woman drop a small bag on the round and apparently fail to notice it. As you can see in this chart, people who had been positively reinforced in their earlier encounter with a stranger were much more likely to try to help the woman get her package than people who had been negatively reinforced.

22. What is the subject of this discussion?

23. What is "reciprocity exchange"?

24. What does NOT increase helpfulness?

25. What can be determined from this graph?

Questions 26-28

Listen to part of a conversation between two speakers.

(man)	Chris, what's wrong? You look really stressed.
(woman)	I just got kicked out of Dr. Roper's psychology seminar.
(man)	Not the seminar about intelligence testing! Oh, you were really excited about that class. What happened?
(woman)	The class was oversubscribed. There's supposed to be a limit of 12 people in the senior seminars, but I guess there was a computer error, because there were 15 people who thought they were in the class. Three people had to get cut.
(man)	But why you?
(woman)	The department has rules about who gets priority for classes. People who've already taken a senior seminar and non-majors have a lower priority – people who aren't graduating seniors, too. I know that technically I already took a seminar, but I've changed my major concentration since then, so I really needed this class.
(man)	So what are you going to do?
(woman)	Well, there's no way I can get into Dr. Roper's seminar – it's totally full. I could take the seminar next semester, but then I won't be able to graduate on time.
(man)	You could try to take an independent study with Dr. Roper.
(woman)	What's that?
(man)	Design your own class, something that covers most of the same material as the seminar. Then get Dr. Roper to agree to be your supervisor, and you could report directly to him.
(woman)	That's a really good idea. I'm going to try it.

26. What is the woman's problem?

27. Why was the woman forced out of the class?

28. What will the woman do?

Questions 29-32

Listen to part of a lecture in an American history class. The professor is talking about natural catastrophes.

One of the greatest natural catastrophes in the history of the United States, the eruption of Mount Katmai in Alaska in 1912 is all but forgotten today, but tremendous quantities of ash issued from the eruption, which generated an explosion that was heard more than 1,000 km away.

The volcano is located near Kodiak Island, where the Alaska Peninsula, the western "tail" of the state, joins the mainland. Before its eruption in 1912, Mount Katmai stood almost 2,500 m tall and was at the center of a cluster of volcanoes.

The eruption began with a series of earthquakes felt in Katmai village near the volcano starting on June 2, 1912. The earthquakes continued for the next three days. No one was able to observe what was happening on the mountain during this time, because clouds enshrouded the volcano. Then, just after noon on June 6, a thick cloud of ash emanated from the volcano, surrounded the peak, and cast the land into darkness for two and a half days. Ash fell on Juneau, some 1,000 km to the southeast. Some 1,400 km north of Katmai, another ashfall blanketed the Yukon Valley. Gases released by the volcano dissolved in water in the air and formed an acidic mist.

On that first day alone, Mount Katmai cast out approximately 8 cubic km of ash and rock. It expelled so much solid material in this eruption that the peak was left unsupported inside, and on June 7th, it collapsed. Where a huge volcano once had stood, there was now a great natural bowl, big enough for a whole city to fit inside. During the eruption, a new volcano formed from a vent in the side of Katmai. It was called Novarupta, and from it a vast, terrifically hot flow of ash spewed out over an area of more than 200 square kilometers. Fiery gases continued to escape for years afterward from this plain of hot ash, which was named the "Valley of 10,000 Smokes" and was proclaimed a national monument by President Woodrow Wilson. Katmai has been quiet for 80 years now, but will it remain quiet indefinitely?

29. What is the speaker's opinion of Mount Katmai?

30. Indicate on this map of Alaska where Mount Katmai is located.

31. The speaker described the events related to the eruption of Mount Katmai. Summarize his lecture by putting the following events into the correct chronological order.

32. What is NOT true of "Novarupta"?

Questions 33-37

Listen to part of a lecture in a city planning class. The professor is talking about a city park.

Cities all around the world have large, elaborate parks for their citizens to come and rest themselves from the frenetic pace of everyday life. And the most famous city park in America in undoubtedly New York City's Central Park.

At the beginning of the 19th century, New York City had grown to some 60,000 people, most of them located in lower Manhattan. But the waves of immigrants that flooded into New York beginning in the 1830s quickly swelled the population – to more than 300,000 in the 1840s, and to over half-a-million by 1850. Needless to say, the city was incredibly crowded and chaotic. Incessant noise and poor sanitation adversely affected everyone.

The first public figure to call for open green spaces within the city was the editor of the *Evening Post* newspaper, William Bryant. In 1844 he called for the creation of a large public park. He joined forces with America's first landscape architect, Andrew Downing, to pressure city officials to set aside land before the fast-growing city swallowed everything up. In a rare moment of public consensus, all the political figures in the city agreed on the necessity of a large, public park. Between 1853 and 1856 the city paid over $5 million to buy undeveloped land from 59th Street to 110th Street and between 5th and 6th Avenues.

The city then sponsored a public competition to design the new Central Park. Out of 33 entries, they chose the plan submitted by Frederick Law Olmsted. Olmstead wanted to make a park that was, in his words, "of great importance as the first real park made in this century – a democratic development of the highest significance."

The project was a mammoth undertaking. The land was full of rock, mud, and swamp. The sand was too poor to support the trees Olmsted envisioned, so 500,000 cubic feet of topsoil was brought in from New Jersey. Nearly 5 million trees, shrubs and other plants were planted, representing more than 1,400 different species. In all, more than 10 million cartloads of materials were hauled through the park, a process that took nearly 20 years. Thirty-six bridges and archways were built, along with 4 man-made bodies of water. Finally, sunken roads had to be installed beneath the park to allow for traffic to cross from one side to the other.

But the end product was spectacular. Within the park, curving pathways gave visitors a succession of views as they walked through the park. The north end of the park featured many sporting grounds where people could play sports like baseball or soccer. In the middle, a giant water reservoir created a gorgeous-looking lake. South of the lake were the Metropolitan Museum of Art and many large lawns. The southern end of the park was dominated by the grand promenade, the only constructed, formal piece of architecture in the park.

33. What is the main topic of this lecture?

34. The speaker described the history of Central Park. Summarize by placing the following events into chronological order.

35. Several people involved in Central Park were mentioned. Match the name with what the person did.

36. What is true about the construction of Central Park?

37. Where in Central Park is the Metropolitan Museum of Art?

Questions 38-39

Listen to part of a conversation between two people.

(woman)	Hi, Michael. What're you doing here in front of the library?
(man)	I'm waiting for my ride. Scott and I are going to drive out to the zoo for our anthropology project.
(woman)	Really? What are you doing at the zoo?
(man)	We've been studying a chimpanzee colony there, looking at their social interactions.
(woman)	That sounds like a fun project.
(man)	It's a lot of fun. But it's also a lot of work. We have to travel all the way out to the zoo and back four times every week – that's over an hour of driving each time. Then we have to do all the actual research, which can take two or three hours.
(woman)	You're right; that is a lot of work. How can you get your work done for all your other classes?
(man)	Well, to be honest, this project is probably hurting my other grades. But by doing this primate study, I'm pretty much guaranteed of getting into graduate school. That's what's important to me.
(woman)	I didn't know you were interested in doing that. I thought you wanted to go to business school.
(man)	No, I changed my mind about that a while ago.

38. What is the man doing in front of the library?

39. Why is the man doing this primate project?

Questions 40-43

Listen to a professor and his students discussing information from a physics class. The class is about time.

(man)   Professor? We've been talking a lot about time over the last couple of weeks. But how do we measure time precisely?

(professor)   Well, for most of history, we did not have accurate means of keeping track of time. Early peoples used the sun, moon, and the stars to gain a basic idea of how time flowed, but all of those are uncertain and irregular. What was a major improvement on this situation?

(woman)   When Galileo made the pendulum clock in the 16th century.

(professor)   That's right. By adding the pendulum, Galileo added the idea of regularity to time measurement. Since a pendulum swings in a regular manner, a major source of error was eliminated. However, since a pendulum typically swings twice per second, it was not a very reliable timepiece either. The quartz clock is better; it vibrates over 32,000 times a second, so that is reasonably good. But what is most reliable way of measuring time?

(man)   The atomic clock?

(professor)   Very good. In fact, these days, atomic clocks are more accurate than the Earth, so they have to be readjusted periodically for the Earth.

(woman)   How does an atomic clock operate?

(professor)   Atomic clocks are based on the oscillations, or vibrations, of cesium atoms. In fact, a second is now defined as precisely 9,192,631,770 oscillations of cesium radiation. The most accurate is called the atomic fountain, pictured here. The atomic fountain uses three pairs of lasers to trap and cool a ball of several million cesium atoms. The lasers launch the ball upward through a field of microwave radiation. As the atoms fall through the microwave cavity, many of them are excited and change energy state. A detector unit measures how many of the atoms are excited. The microwave frequency is fine-tuned in order to excite as many of the cesium atoms as possible. When the microwave frequency is just right, so that nearly all the cesium atoms get excited when they pass through, then the microwave frequency is nearly the same as the cesium atoms' frequency. This is complicated, but incredibly accurate. In fact, the atomic fountain is precise to within one second every ten billion years.

40. What is the main topic of this discussion?

41. The professor mentioned several kinds of time-keeping devices. Put them into order, from least to most accurate.

42. How is one second officially defined?

43. Where in the following diagram is the microwave cavity?

Questions 44-47

Listen to part of a lecture in an art class. The professor is talking about Peter Paul Rubens.

Peter Paul Rubens was born in 1577 in the Low Countries, what we today call Belgium, in the city of Antwerp. He was young when his mother died, and his mother sent him to be a young page in the court of an old princess when he was thirteen. Rubens found this life very boring, however, and as he began to show signs of a talent in art, he asked his mother to send him away to study art. From 1591 to 1600, Rubens studied art with a variety of artists around the Low Countries.

Rubens did well and learned quickly; however, in those days, Italy was the center of the art world. So at 23 years old, Rubens moved to Venice to study the great art of the Renaissance. In fact, Rubens' copy of Leonardo da Vinci's "The Battle of Anghiari" is the only record we have of that great work.

While in Venice, Rubens met the Spanish Duke of Mantua and became his court painter. He moved to Spain for 8 years, where he became a most famous and respected painter.

After his mother died, Rubens returned to Antwerp, where he became a court painter for the Spanish rulers of the Low Countries. He continued to become ever more successful. In 1609 he married Isabella Brandt, and over the next few years, he painted her often.

Rubens was so famous that many young artists wanted to work with him. In 1611 alone he turned down over one hundred prospective students. But he also accepted many others. There are so many paintings with Rubens' name on them that he could not have possibly painted them all. For most of them, he made the preliminary sketch, then let his students make the full-size painting. Rubens would then make the finishing touches and sign it.

At the time, there were many conflicts between the countries of Europe, and Rubens became a diplomat. He served in Paris, Spain, and England on various diplomatic missions, where he was well liked and successful. The English king knighted him, and the rulers of the Low Countries made Rubens a nobleman of the royal household.

After many years of serving abroad, Rubens asked to return home. He gave up the courtly life to concentrate on his paintings, before dying in 1640.

44. What is significant about Rubens' copy of "The Battle of Anghiari"?

45. Why are there so many paintings credited to Rubens?

46. The professor explains the following events in Rubens' life. Put them into chronological order.

47. What is NOT true of Rubens' career as a diplomat?

Questions 48-50

Listen to part of a conversation between two speakers.

(man)	Professor Lees?
(woman)	Yes? What can I do for you?
(man)	I'm on the Jones' Teaching Award committee. Do you know us?
(woman)	Yes, I do. Every year, you select a teacher to be honored for his or her teaching ability.
(man)	That's right. It's an old and prestigious award, given to professors who really give something special to their students and to the school, who go above and beyond what's expected of them. And this year, we would like to honor you with the Jones' Teaching Award.
(woman)	Wow, I'm very flattered.
(man)	You deserve it, professor. Actually, I nominated you myself. When I had problems last semester, you scheduled so many additional office hours to help me out. I never would have passed Calculus if not for you.
(woman)	I don't know about that. You're a very good student.
(man)	But I know you've done that for many students. And everyone is doubly impressed that you can make subjects like introductory algebra interesting.
(woman)	So what happens next?
(man)	We're going to have an awards ceremony and banquet for you at the end of the semester. We need to find a time that's good for you. We were hoping you'd talk a little about your teaching philosophy and methods. And in order to introduce you properly, we'll need a good biography of you.
(woman)	I can give you a copy of my CV right now; that should do for a biography. My schedule is rather busy these days. When do you need to know a ceremony date?
(man)	If you could let us know by the end of the week, that would be great.

48. What is this discussion about?

49. What are the criteria for winning the Jones Award?

50. What does the Awards Committee NOT ask the professor to do?

Practice Test ⑫

Listening Script Part A

1. (man)   I'm not sure if you should be taking a research lab with Dr. Smith. She's really tough.
   (woman)   But she's also the best. If I want to do original research, I have to work with her.
   (man)   But Dr. Smith is really hard to work with. You'll be swamped with extra work all semester.
   (woman)   It'll take more than that to put me off.
   (narrator)   What does the woman mean?

2. (woman)   Hi, Vic. I'm glad I ran into you. I have some great news.
   (man)   Really? What is it?
   (woman)   Professor Leary just hired me to work in his lab. The hours are a little heavy, but it should be really interesting.
   (man)   Do you think you can work on your honors thesis and hold a job at the same time?
   (narrator)   What is the man implying?

3. (man)   That's a fantastic new haircut. Where'd you get it done?
   (woman)   Oh, I didn't go to a hair salon or anything. I just had my friend's brother, Adam, do it for me. He's really good.
   (narrator)   Who cut the woman's hair?

4. (woman)   This is room 512? I signed up on the phone to write a placement test. I thought it was here.
   (man)   No, this is the department office. You can sign up here for the placement test, but the test itself is in room 408. If you've already signed up, you can go straight down.
   (narrator)   What will the woman most likely do?

5. (man)   I've really put on a lot of weight over the past couple of years. I should go on a diet.
   (woman)   Dieting isn't very good for you. Exercise is a much healthier way of losing weight.
   (man)   I tried jogging and swimming and a bunch of different ways of exercising, but they were all so boring, I kept quitting.
   (woman)   You know, I had the same problem for the longest time. Then I joined some of the intramural sports teams. They're a lot more fun of a way to exercise.
   (narrator)   What does the woman suggest?

6. (woman)   I really need some advice. My schedule is totally ruined for next semester.
   (man)   It's okay. It can't be that bad.
   (woman)   It is that bad. I really needed to take this research seminar, but the professor just cancelled the class.
   (man)   Well, sit down and let's talk. I'm sure we can work it out.
   (narrator)   What does the man mean?

7. (man)   I'm so happy for Jan. This is really great news, isn't it?
   (woman)   What is? I didn't hear anything about Jan.
   (man)   You didn't? Well, I'm really happy for her. She actually made it into the dual degree program.
   (woman)   She did? I thought you needed at least an A⁻ average to get into that program.
   (narrator)   What did the woman assume about Jan?

8.   (woman)   Did you notice that Brett was working down at the housing office *again*? I think he's been there every day this week.

    (man)   He certainly has been there a lot lately.

    (woman)   I just don't understand why he hurt his grades like that. Why would Brett put in so many hours working for the housing office?

    (man)   He has to if he wants to afford next semester's tuition.

    (narrator)   What are the speakers saying about Brett?

9.   (man)   Mary, your sister, is in the same year as us, but she seems a lot younger than you. How old is she anyway?

    (woman)   Well, she's a little more than three years younger than me, and I'm going to turn 24 next week.

    (narrator)   How old is Mary's sister?

10.   (woman)   I'm here to return some books. Sorry, I know you're only supposed to have them a couple of weeks, but I had them a couple of days longer.

    (man)   That's okay. Let me scan them in for you.

    (woman)   Does your school have overdue fines for the books? At my school, you have to pay 10 cents for every day the books are overdue.

    (man)   We do, too, but you have a three-day grace period. You're okay.

    (narrator)   What does the man say about the books?

11.   (man)   Hi, Suzanne. Has your Dad gotten back from his business trip to England yet?

    (woman)   He got back early this morning. But he's over at my sister's place at the moment.

    (narrator)   Where is the woman's father?

Listening Script Part B

Questions 12-15

Listen to part of a lecture from an economics class. The professor is talking about economic principles.

For much of history, people did not understand how money, production, and consumption all affected each other – in other words, they did not understand economics. Over the years, many competing theories arose about how economics worked. The rise of nations created mercantilism. Karl Marx and others advocated communism. Only now do most economists agree on what's called "classical economics." Although there are many different schools of classical economics, most agree on certain broad principles such as private property, free markets and competition.

Classical economics began in 1776 with the publication of *The Wealth of Nations* by the Scottish philosopher Adam Smith. This book is most famous for introducing the idea of "the invisible hand." By the invisible hand, Smith meant that the economy did not need to be controlled by the government. Instead, he believed each person individually pursuing his private interests actually satisfied the public good. He believed that government involvement in the economy would only lead to inefficiency and problems.

British economist Alfred Marshall, in his 1890 book *Principles of Economics*, introduced the idea of marginal utility. In economics, "utility" refers to the satisfaction or enjoyment a person gets from doing something. Marginal utility refers to the enjoyment you get from each additional item you consume. Consider someone drinking a glass of water. If he is very thirsty, then his first drink of water will have a very high marginal utility – he really likes it. But as he gets less thirsty, each drink will be less enjoyable. When he is no longer thirsty at all, he will stop drinking because it is no longer enjoyable. In economics, this idea is very powerful.

Finally, John Maynard Keynes was a very influential economist. He was a student of Marshall and a believer in classical economics until the Great Depression came in the 1930s. The invisible hand did not work, and despite governments remaining distant, the economy continued to get worse. In his book, *The General Theory of Employment, Interest, and Money*, published in 1935, Keynes introduced powerful new economic ideas. He believed that the Great Depression and the massive unemployment of the times were caused by a lack of demand. In other words, because so few people had jobs, they could not buy anything. And because nothing was bought, companies could not make money. As a result, he believed that it was the government's job to help the economy in extraordinary times. When the economy was very weak, the government should spend more money to increase demand and keep businesses strong.

In writing these ideas, Keynes single-handedly invented the field of macroeconomics, the study of economics at the national level. Before Keynes, classical economics was only interested in microeconomics, that is, the actions of people and companies.

12. What is the main idea of this lecture?

13. The speaker mentioned several economists. Match the economist with his major idea.

14. In which drawing would the man drinking the water have the greatest marginal utility?

15. What did John Keynes believe about the Great Depression?

Questions 16-19

Listen to part of a lecture being given in a history class. The professor is talking about Thomas Edison.

The most famous inventor in the history of the United States, Thomas Edison was born in 1847 in Ohio. His formal education lasted only three months. Largely self-educated, he became a brilliant and highly productive inventor. By the time of his death in 1931, Edison had more than 1,000 patents on his inventions, which included the incandescent light bulb. While still a boy, he published a successful newspaper from an office in the baggage car of a train. He also had an accident which left him deaf for the rest of his life. Afterward, Edison said his deafness was an advantage, because it allowed him to work without distraction. One of Edison's early inventions was a "telegraph repeater," which relayed telegraph messages automatically from one line to another. He later received a large payment after inventing a "ticker," or reporting device for stock market quotations. Edison used that money to start a business of his own, but had to leave the business because of poor health. When his health improved, Edison became a full-time inventor with a laboratory in Menlo Park, New Jersey. In addition to the light bulb, he invented the phonograph, the alkaline storage battery, and the motion picture projector. Edison also made major improvements to early telephones. Edison was known for his patience and his power of concentration. While working on the first incandescent electric light, for example, he collected some 40,000 pages of notes. He experimented with many different materials before he found a filament that glowed for 40 hours continuously. In the final years of his life, Edison worked on inventions for the navy. As a result of his research, a method was developed for making synthetic rubber. Edison was married twice and had six children. One of his sons became governor of New Jersey. Edison died a wealthy and famous man. His laboratory in West Orange, New Jersey, is preserved as a national historic site.

16. In what aspect was Edison's accident helpful?

17. Thomas Edison invented the following items. Match them with their components.

18. The professor explains a series of events in Edison's life. Put them into chronological order.

19. Which of the following items is NOT Edison's invention?

Questions 20-21

Listen to part of a conversation between two people.

(man)	Are you excited about the student council elections next Monday?
(woman)	Student council elections? I hadn't heard anything about them.
(man)	How could you miss out on the campaign? Every tree and fencepost on campus has a campaign poster attached to it.
(woman)	I guess I've been busy studying for my classes. I don't have a lot of time to waste on silly student activities.
(man)	Silly? But the student council is important for all of us at the university. It's the student voice in how the school is run.
(woman)	Not for me. I can't think of anything the student council has done to make my life any easier.
(man)	Well, what about the student center? You like to study there, don't you?
(woman)	Sure.
(man)	But the school was thinking of turning that building into administrative offices. It was opposition by the student council that made them change their mind. And it was the student council that made the school improve the dining facilities in the student center, too.
(woman)	I sure do like studying there more now that they have a good coffee shop.
(man)	That's why it's important for you to vote in the student elections. I'm going to be running for council treasurer. I hope I can get your support.
(woman)	I guess you're right. Unfortunately, on Monday I'll be in New York, doing research for my art history class.

20. What does the man think of the student council?

21. What will the woman do on Monday?

Questions 22-24

Listen to a professor and two students discussing information from a psychology class. The class is on space.

(professor)   For all people and animals, the space around them is an important part of their daily lives. Territory and personal space are two aspects of our environment. What do I mean by 'personal space'?

(woman)   Personal space is the bubble of space that people attempt to keep around them when they interact.

(professor)   That's right, Julie. People have a sense of ownership of the space around their bodies. The amount of that space may differ by culture, but it exists to varying degrees everywhere. Gender and age also affect it. In one experiment, psychologists put someone in a room with a second person and told them to talk. An observer behind a one-way mirror recorded the amount of eye contact maintained by the subject. As the distance between the subject and the second person decreased, so did the amount of eye contact. Why?

(man)   Because the subject was made uncomfortable. When he lost his personal space, the subject felt too much intimacy for being close to a stranger, and tried to create a sense of psychological distance by avoiding eye contact.

(professor)   Very good, Paul. Notice how the amount of eye contact differs by gender. Women talking to women were most comfortable at the closest space. And women talking to men were most comfortable at a greater distance. Men talking to men were the most uncomfortable at any distance. Now, territoriality is similar and also an important part of how people relate to their space. How is it different than personal space?

(man)   Personal space refers to the space around a person; it moves with him or her. But territoriality is the persistent attachment to an area or object.

(professor)   Right again. Humans have a sense of proprietorship over their territory, in that they can dispose of it as they wish, and they will defend it even to the point of aggression.

(man)   People also have different levels of territory. Home is a kind of primary territory, a place you protect more carefully. A regular place you go to would be a secondary territory; this is a bridge between primary and public territory. Public territory is open to anyone, and no one has a particular claim on it.

(professor)   That's right. And what people consider primary, secondary, and public can differ from culture to culture. For example, in Greece, tourists are often surprised to find a lot of litter and trash on the streets. This does not mean Greek people are untidy. Rather, Greeks draw a sharper line than Americans between private and public territory.
In an experiment, researchers put litter in people's yards, in front of their homes, and down the streets in America and Greece. In both countries, the trash on their yards was quickly picked up, but the litter around the homes was picked up much more quickly in America than in Greece. That's because Americans often view the sidewalk and curb in front of the home as a secondary territory, and are more inclined to keep it clean. Most Greek homes, however, have a fence or hedge clearly separating private property from public.

22. What is this discussion about?

23. According to the professor, which group was most likely men talking to other men?

24. According to the professor, why was garbage on the street picked up more quickly in America than Greece?

Questions 25-28

Listen to part of a lecture in a chemistry class. The professor is talking about the element hydrogen.

The most common element in the universe, hydrogen is also the lightest and the simplest. The hydrogen atom consists of a single proton, or positively charged particle, and a single electron, or negatively charged particle. In the periodic table of the elements, hydrogen has the lowest atomic number, 1, and the lowest atomic weight, also 1. Because hydrogen is the most widespread element in the universe, hydrogen is found almost everywhere. Stars like our sun consist mostly of hydrogen. Giant planets like Jupiter and Saturn have large amounts of hydrogen in their atmospheres. Most of our Earth's surface is made up of a hydrogen compound, namely water, whose molecule includes one atom of oxygen and two atoms of hydrogen. Because water is essential to life as we know it, hydrogen is therefore essential to life as well. Hydrogen is also essential to life because hydrogen forms weak bonds with other atoms, and these bonds can be made and unmade easily. These weak bonds are vital to living things, because they allow biochemical reactions to occur with a minimum of energy. Hydrogen, in the form of the water molecule, is part of "carbohydrates," the sugars and starches which animals, including humans, use for food.

Although a hydrogen compound covers much of the Earth's surface, there is very little free hydrogen in our atmosphere. Free hydrogen combines easily with oxygen in the atmosphere to produce water. Hydrogen can be isolated from water by a process called "electrolysis," which uses an electrical current to break apart water molecules into hydrogen and oxygen. On Earth, gaseous hydrogen usually takes the form of a "diatomic" molecule, meaning that two atoms of hydrogen are joined together. Gaseous hydrogen burns in oxygen with an extremely hot flame. Hydrogen makes a very clean fuel, because the only product of combustion is harmless water. Hydrogen's low atomic weight made it, during the 19th and early 20th centuries, the choice to provide lift for flying machines called "dirigibles." A dirigible was a passenger-carrying airship filed with huge bags of hydrogen gas. Because hydrogen is lighter than air, a dirigible was capable of rising without using any energy to create lift, unlike airplanes, which are heavier than air and must use great amounts of energy to generate lift. Hydrogen's tendency to catch fire and burn, however, made it dangerous to use in airships. If its hydrogen caught fire, then a dirigible would explode, burn and crash. A spectacular crash of this kind occurred when the German dirigible *Hindenburg* burned at Lakehurst, New Jersey, following a crossing of the Atlantic Ocean.

25. Which of the following diagrams represents a hydrogen atom?

26. The professor explains the characteristics of hydrogen in his lecture. Match the characteristics of hydrogen with its counterparts.

27. Although there is very little free hydrogen in our atmosphere, it combines easily with oxygen in the atmosphere to produce water. Put the following events in chronological order.

28. What is NOT a characteristic of hydrogen?

Questions 29-30

Listen to part of a conversation between two speakers.

(man)	I really need to start watching what I eat.
(woman)	Really? You look okay.
(man)	Thanks, but I gained five pounds last month. It's because I eat too much junk food.
(woman)	That's not good for you. You should sign up for the university dining program. They offer a lot of good, healthy food, and the price is pretty reasonable.
(man)	Yeah, but they also have a lot of unhealthy food. When I have a choice, I usually make a bad one.
(woman)	Well, no one can make you eat better, except yourself.
(man)	I was thinking of skipping lunch, instead.
(woman)	That's not healthy at all. In fact, skipping meals can make you gain weight. Your body worries that it might be starving, so it converts more energy to fat for storage.
(man)	I didn't know that. What should I do?
(woman)	Exercise is the best thing. Exercising not only burns calories while you exercise, but you also burn more calories all during the day – even while sleeping. And eating healthy is important. If you eat sensibly, your body works more efficiently. You should be able to eat a lot and still lose weight.
(man)	Exercising? That sounds like a lot of work.
(woman)	Then why not play a sport? You like basketball. Why don't you sign up for one of those intramural leagues? It's better than just watching sports on television. I play three times each week.
(man)	Wow. I bet you're really in shape.

29. What does the man want to do?

30. Why does the man not like the university dining service?

ANSWER KEY

Listening ➡

	ANSWER		ANSWER
1	B	30	A
2	C	31	C
3	A	32	C
4	B	33	A, D
5	A	34	D
6	B	35	B
7	D	36	A
8	A	37	C
9	C	38	B
10	C	39	C
11	B	40	King Hammurabi's Code
12	D		The first life insurance
13	C		The first fire insurance
14	A		The first insurance in America
15	C	41	B
16	B	42	A
17	A	43	B
18	C	44	D
19	It scoops mud up into its mouth.	45	A
	Water is pumped in to separate detritus ...	46	Ideogram
	The detritus is swallowed.		Word-syllabic
	The clean mud is spat out.		Syllabic
20	A		Alphabet
21	D	47	B
22	D	48	C
23	Feudalism – Many small, disorganized ...	49	B
	Empire – One single state dominant	50	D
	International relations – The interaction of ...		
24	A, D		
25	D		
26	C		
27	B		
28	C, D		
29	A		

Structure ➡

	ANSWER		ANSWER
1	B (the theory)	11	C (its)
2	D (that is characteristic)	12	B
3	C (exact)	13	B (uses)
4	C	14	D
5	C (no)	15	B (there is)
6	B	16	D
7	B (remaining)	17	D (uses)
8	A	18	C
9	A (make)	19	D (confused)
10	D	20	A (In)

Reading ➡

	ANSWER		ANSWER
1	B	23	C
2	D	24	(the famous) box camera
3	C	25	B
4	A	26	C
5	(Colonial) merchants	27	A
6	C	28	C
7	B	29	D (own eyes? ■ Before the)
8	C	30	B
9	C	31	C
10	D	32	B
11	F (the harbor. ■ The Quebec)	33	C
12	C	34	B
13	C	35	D
14	A	36	(The) arts or skills
15	B	37	C
16	(blind) fish	38	B
17	B	39	D (academic community. ■ The convenient)
18	H (each other. ■ There is)	40	A
19	B	41	B
20	A	42	B
21	D	43	B
22	C	44	C

Writing ➡

Imagine that a university intends to start a new research institution in your country, for research in either business or farming. Which of these purposes would you favor, and why? Provide specific reasons for your choice.

Business already has numerous research centers. A list of them would fill several pages. Moreover, business is its own research institution, always studying sales figures and other data to determine what sells best and who will buy what. Therefore, I favor an agricultural research center.

All societies and nations, no matter how advanced in business, are basically agricultural. Everyone needs to eat. No country can succeed unless it does a good job of feeding its people. The former Soviet Union had great trouble with agriculture. Now the Soviet Union is history. There is a lesson here. In the last analysis, everything depends on food.

Also, agriculture faces tremendous challenges in the years just ahead. Crops are becoming weak. That is, they have been bred so selectively for high yield that they have become vulnerable to disease. A new disease might destroy a whole crop within days. We need stronger, disease-resistant crops. An agricultural research center could help develop them.

Finally, a university is a uniquely productive environment for research. A university has great resources for gathering and processing information. In this age of the Internet, a university research center for agriculture could also bring together, online, experts in many different fields of study. Then they could concentrate their attention most effectively on problems in agriculture.

No one denies that business is important. It faces challenges and problems, as agriculture does. Business, however, already has an impressive research capability. Now it is time to give the same capability to agriculture.

Listening ➡

	ANSWER		ANSWER
1	B		Drawing – Featured old buildings, never...
2	A	19	B
3	B	20	D
4	C	21	A
5	D	22	B
6	B	23	*The Sovereign* – Could sail 22 knots
7	C		*The Great Republic* – Burned before being ...
8	A		*The Oriental* – Sailed from Hong Kong to ...
9	A	24	B, D
10	D	25	D
11	A	26	B, D
12	C	27	**Moved to Copenhagen**
13	C		Entered university
14	*Star Wars* – Sound in space		First published his poems
	Star Trek – Faster-than-light travel		Published his first fairy tale
	2001: A Space Odyssey – Artificial gravity		Honored by Denmark in a festival
15	A	28	C
16	B	29	B
17	B, C	30	D
18	Painting – Known for great chiaroscuro		
	Etching – Widely regarded as the best ...		

Structure ➡

	ANSWER		ANSWER
1	A (who)	14	B (in)
2	B (discharges)	15	B
3	C (gorgeous)	16	C (awards)
4	C	17	D
5	B (material from which)	18	D (bankruptcy)
6	B	19	A
7	A (contains)	20	B (other)
8	C	21	D
9	A (is felt)	22	C (domestic industries)
10	B	23	B
11	C (are)	24	C (silver)
12	A	25	C (to support)
13	D (the)		

561

Reading ➡

	ANSWER		ANSWER
1	D	29	D
2	hardly	30	A
3	A	31	C
4	B	32	peripheral
5	Dickinson	33	fixed
6	C	34	C
7	C	35	breakthrough
8	C (them deeply. ■ The standard)	36	B (on Earth. ■ The greatest)
9	B	37	C
10	A	38	cooling-off
11	A	39	C
12	B	40	A
13	essay	41	B
14	D	42	C
15	C	43	C
16	offspring	44	B
17	B	45	D
18	A	46	A (scientific folklore. ■ The idea)
19	specificities	47	intriguing
20	H (to evolution. ■ The essential)	48	C
21	D	49	A
22	C	50	A
23	B	51	collapse
24	D (and adolescence. ■ The classical)	52	D
25	charging displays	53	C
26	B	54	spotted
27	B	55	(bizarre) speculations
28	C		

Writing ➡

Courses in music and art should be required for students in high school. Do you agree or disagree with that proposal? Use specific details to support your view.

Students can benefit greatly from studying art and music in school. A student introduced to music in school may go on to become a famous violinist, pianist, or singer. Requiring all students to take art and music in school, however, is the wrong approach. Courses in art and music should not be required of all students.

Schools do not have enough resources to carry out such a plan. They must teach many essentials such as language and math, and have few resources left over for other subjects. Extra money will be hard to find. So will skilled teachers. This is one practical reason why art and music should not be required for all students. Schools already have enough to do, without giving them more responsibilities.

Then there is the "reaction problem." For every action (Sir Isaac Newton wrote), there is an equal but opposite reaction. That principle applies here. If we force students to study something, most of them will hate it or be indifferent to it. This approach produces exactly the opposite of the desired result. A required subject is hardly ever a popular subject.

Also, good teachers of art and music already exist in large numbers outside the schools. Parents who want their children to learn about art and music can take them to those teachers.

In principle, it would be good if every student took courses in art and music in school. The fact is, however, that such activities are not for everyone. Art and music are best taught as electives, for students who have the desire and ability to study them. Requiring such courses is not the answer.

Listening ➡

	ANSWER		ANSWER
1	B	30	C
2	C	31	D
3	A	32	A
4	C	33	B, D
5	D	34	Vowels were invented.
6	C		Left to right writing began.
7	B		The Greek writing system spread.
8	A		Upper and lower-case letters were ...
9	D	35	C
10	A	36	A
11	D	37	D
12	C	38	B
13	A	39	B
14	B	40	Africa
15	C		Asia
16	C		Europe
17	D		The Americas
18	A	41	D
19	D	42	Paleolithic – Basic stone tools were first ...
20	Geologists – The movement of the Earth's ...		Mesolithic – Warmer weather made ...
	Environmentalists – Changing ice on ...		Neolithic – Agricultural villages started.
	Meteorologists – Atmospheric ...	43	D
21	B	44	B
22	A	45	A, D
23	D	46	A complete sample of DNA obtained
24	C		DNA removed from the egg of another ...
25	Orthographic projection – B		New DNA introduced to the egg of another ...
	Mercator projection – C		Egg inserted into surrogate mother
	Goode's Homolosine projection – A	47	C
26	D	48	C
27	C	49	A
28	C	50	D
29	Radio – Jack Benny		
	Television – *The Waltons*		
	Film – *Star Trek*		

Structure ➡

	ANSWER			ANSWER
1	C (while)	11		C (on)
2	B (ideas)	12		B
3	B (which)	13		A (autobiography)
4	D	14		A
5	C (were put)	15		C (panel papers)
6	C	16		B
7	D (level surface)	17		D (vast)
8	B	18		C
9	A (to find)	19		D (become)
10	D	20		D (feet)

Reading ➡

	ANSWER			ANSWER
1	B	23		B
2	Spain, France, Portugal, Holland	24		C
3	C	25		D
4	D	26		B
5	B	27		H (the planet. ■ In addition)
6	C	28		B
7	B	29		C
8	A	30		C
9	F (lumber, rum. ■ All of)	31		The sun
10	B	32		C
11	American lumber ... lumber, rum.	33		D
12	C	34		C
13	(cultural) phenomena	35		A
14	C	36		C
15	A	37		photography
16	D	38		C
17	B	39		B
18	D	40		A
19	C	41		C
20	C	42		C
21	C (do this. ■ German philosopher)	43		E (open air. ■ But the)
22	B	44		B

Writing ➡

Motion pictures reveal much about the countries where they were made. What can you learn about a country by watching its motion pictures? Use specific examples to explain your answer.

Movies tell us much about the countries where they were made. Let us look at three examples: Japan, Hong Kong, and the United States.

The Japanese see themselves as kind, soft-hearted people in a cruel world. Their movies reflect this self-image. The typical Japanese movie involves a well-meaning, trusting person who wanders into unfamiliar territory and is treated badly. The ending may be happy or sad, but the message remains the same: we are a misunderstood, persecuted people.

Hong Kong movies have fantastic stories. A single swordsman may confront an entire army and win. The message is: China can take on the world. One Chinese is worth a thousand of his enemies. Although Hong Kong cinema is full of violence, it is highly stylized violence, unlikely to be copied in real life. Also, Hong Kong movies have a strong moral element – a noble hero versus an evil villain.

Violence in U.S. movies is different. It is both crude and cruel, and could indeed be copied in real life. U.S. movies also may have no "hero" and "villain," but instead two equally vicious enemies. The "hero" is whoever kills the other first. Brutality, cruelty, and amorality in American films, some would say, reflect the character of American society.

One could extend this list. French and Italian movies are full of romance. Russian movies tend to be serious and formalistic. In almost every case, however, movies are characteristic of the countries where they are made. A Russian could not have made *Star Wars*, nor could a French director have made Kurosawa's *Rashomon*. To a large extent, nationality shapes cinema.

Listening ➡

	ANSWER			ANSWER
1	D		19	B
2	D		20	D
3	A		21	B
4	B		22	Atomic weight – 200.59
5	A			Atomic number – 80
6	C			Density of water – 13 times
7	B		23	Mercury is discovered.
8	A			Mine at Almaden begins operating.
9	C			"Quicksilver galleons" sink.
10	A			Submarines use mercury as ballast.
11	D		24	D
12	D		25	B, C
13	Chuck Yeager – Broke the sound barrier		26	C
	Charles Lindbergh – First to cross the Atlantic ...		27	Ironclads – Hampton Roads
	The Wright brothers – First airplane flight			Pocahontas – Jamestown
14	A, B			Cornwallis – Yorktown
15	B		28	C, D
16	D		29	A
17	René Descartes – Believed animals to be ...		30	C
	Johannes Müller – Devised the doctrine of ...			
	Wilhelm Wundt – Believed psychology ...			
18	B, D			

Structure ➡

	ANSWER			ANSWER
1	D (draining)		14	B
2	C (them)		15	C (they)
3	C (fishing)		16	A
4	B		17	B (be turned)
5	B (any other)		18	C
6	D		19	B (so called)
7	B (which)		20	B
8	B		21	A (arrows)
9	C (but also)		22	B
10	C (accurate)		23	D (flow)
11	C		24	C
12	A (a residue)		25	B (fast)
13	D (daily)			

Reading ➡

	ANSWER		ANSWER
1	B	29	C
2	A	30	A
3	illumination	31	B
4	A (for centuries. ■ Much of)	32	A
5	C	33	C
6	A	34	D
7	B	35	A
8	camphene/(a) substance	36	(the carbon dioxide) concentration
9	D	37	C
10	A	38	A
11	A	39	B
12	B	40	released
13	B	41	B
14	C	42	C
15	B	43	Over the ... relatively constant.
16	cetaceans	44	D (the atmosphere. ■ Some of)
17	C	45	B
18	D	46	narrow
19	H (practically absent. ■ Rather than)	47	C
20	C	48	C
21	B	49	(the) writers
22	C	50	C (enlarging it. ■ By the)
23	A	51	A
24	modest	52	slowly
25	B	53	C
26	E (ground existed. ■ The impact)	54	D
27	D	55	C
28	impact		

Writing ➡

The country is a better place for children to grow up than a large city is. Do you agree or disagree with that statement? Use specific examples and reasons to explain your answer.

Having lived in both the country and the city, I am inclined to favor the city as a place to raise children. Not every city, of course, is equally desirable. Some cities are extremely dangerous, whereas others are relatively safe and pleasant. On the whole, however, I think the advantage rests with the cities, for several reasons.

The city is often criticized for its crime rate, but there is also a certain security in living in a city. If a child gets into trouble, there is often some source of help nearby, such as a police station or a public information desk. Such assistance is not readily available in the country, where one is relatively isolated and must rely on one's own resources when emergencies arise. Here is a hypothetical example. Your small child suddenly falls ill. In which place is medical care more easily available: the country, many kilometers from the nearest hospital or clinic, or a city, where a hospital emergency room may be only a few seconds away? In such a case, the city clearly is preferable.

Urban dangers such as traffic are often emphasized, but it is seldom pointed out that rural areas have their particular dangers too. A child playing beside a lake may fall in and drown. Wild animals present a certain threat as well. In some rural areas, one must be concerned about poisonous snakes, stinging insects, and even large predators such as bears. It is a mistake to think that the country is necessarily safer than the city merely because the dangers in rural areas are more "natural." A threat is a threat, wherever it may occur.

There is of course a wonderful beauty to the countryside, and a child may benefit greatly from it. At the same time, however, the city has beauties of its own. Which would you say is the greater treasure: a view of the Catskill Mountains, or the opportunity to visit the Guggenheim Museum and other galleries in New York City? A child in the country may grow up with an appreciation of birds, flowers, and trees but miss priceless cultural opportunities available in cities. My choice would be the city. It may have its ugly aspects, but on the whole its advantages outweigh them.

Listening ➡

	ANSWER			ANSWER
1	D	32		A
2	B	33		D
3	C	34		Immigration swells New York's ...
4	C			*Evening Post* editor calls for a public ...
5	D			New York City buys land from 59th ...
6	A			A competition is held to find a design ...
7	D	35		Frederick Olmsted – Won the design ...
8	B			Andrew Downing – America's first ...
9	C			William Bryant – Editor of the Evening ...
10	B	36		A
11	D	37		C
12	A	38		B
13	D	39		A
14	A	40		D
15	A	41		Sun clock
16	C			Pendulum clock
17	B			Quartz clock
18	C			Atomic clock
19	D	42		C
20	She moved to Paris.	43		B
	She married Pierre.	44		D
	She discovered 2 radioactive elements.	45		B
	She isolated the element radium.	46		He moved to Italy to study painting.
	She won a Nobel Prize for chemistry.			He became a court painter for a Spanish ...
21	D			He married Isabella Brandt.
22	A			He became a nobleman.
23	D	47		A
24	B, C	48		C
25	D	49		D
26	C	50		D
27	D			
28	B			
29	D			
30	B			
31	A series of earthquakes occurs.			
	Ash begins to emanate from the ...			
	The mountain collapses.			
	A new volcano forms beside Mount ...			

Structure ➡

	ANSWER			ANSWER
1	D (are)		11	B
2	C (mass migration)		12	C (proposed)
3	B (fundamentally)		13	D
4	B		14	C (woven)
5	C (make)		15	C
6	C		16	D (jaw)
7	B (it)		17	A
8	D (it often)		18	B (between)
9	A		19	D
10	C (favorable)		20	D (an hour)

Reading ➡

	ANSWER			ANSWER
1	C		23	D
2	dry		24	culmination
3	B (human occupation. ■ Although there)		25	A
4	A		26	D
5	C		27	emergence
6	D		28	A
7	secondary		29	D (coded messages. ■ Such "eletromechanical")
8	A		30	the electronic computer
9	(the extreme) Southwest		31	D
10	B		32	decipher
11	D		33	D
12	B		34	D
13	C		35	B
14	repeated		36	C
15	A		37	D
16	separated		38	B (for opiates. ■ Such receptors)
17	D		39	C
18	Randall Jones		40	abundant
19	B		41	A
20	B		42	(The) endorphins
21	F (of copies. ■ Gene amplification)		43	C
22	B		44	extremely

Writing ➡

Imagine that the government intends to build a new university. Would your town be a good place to build the university? Why, or why not? Compare the advantages with the disadvantages of having a new university in your town. Use specific examples and reasons to explain your answer.

Most communities probably would be eager to have a new university. My view is just the opposite. I would be reluctant to have a new university built in my community, for several reasons.

A university would attract thousands of students and faculty. The increased population would require municipal services. Someone must pay for those services through increased taxes. If the university's property is tax-exempt, as it most likely would be, then local property owners would have to pay higher taxes.

Students would require housing. The demand for apartments would rise, and so would rents. Prices in general would rise as well, because students have money to spend, and local merchants would raise prices to take advantage of them. Local residents then would have a higher cost of living.

Student behavior is another problem. Students drink heavily. They can be destructive. They make a lot of noise. In short, they are not necessarily assets to a community. They might make their university a liability to that community.

Some people, such as landlords and merchants, would probably benefit from a new university. The rest of the community, however, would not. As for the "cultural opportunities" which a university provides, those same opportunities are available through other sources, such as cable television. In short, the community has little or nothing to gain from a new university, and much to lose.

Listening ➡

	ANSWER		ANSWER
1	C	18	Edison publishes newspaper.
2	D		Edison invents ticker.
3	A		Edison starts his own business.
4	C		Edison conducts research for the navy.
5	B	19	C
6	B	20	C
7	C	21	D
8	D	22	A
9	A	23	D
10	D	24	B
11	A	25	A
12	A	26	Atomic weight – 1
13	Adam Smith – Invented classical ...		Diatomic – 2
	Alfred Marshall – Invented marginal ...		Compound – Water
	John Maynard Keynes – Invented ...	27	Water undergoes electrolysis.
14	A		Hydrogen atoms separate from ...
15	A, D		Hydrogen gas is collected.
16	A		Hydrogen gas burns, forming water.
17	Light bulb – Filament	28	C
	Repeater – Telegraph	29	D
	Ticker – Stock market	30	C

Structure ➡

	ANSWER		ANSWER
1	D (earth's surface)	14	A
2	B (vultures)	15	B (more)
3	D (later)	16	B
4	C (architecture)	17	A (those)
5	C	18	C
6	A (Entering)	19	B (to connect)
7	D	20	D
8	C (that)	21	C (have)
9	B	22	B
10	A (seeing)	23	D (centers)
11	B (relatively small)	24	C
12	D	25	C (dominated by the)
13	C (progressively)		

Reading ➡

	ANSWER		ANSWER
1	C	29	B
2	(Few) Americans	30	B
3	D	31	A potlatch host's
4	B	32	G (the process. ■ Although potlatch)
5	D	33	C
6	A	34	A
7	D (the British. ■ After the)	35	C
8	D	36	B
9	C	37	D
10	D	38	C
11	A	39	A
12	B	40	A
13	D	41	B
14	C	42	D (withstand waves. ■ Kelps found)
15	A (of glaciation. ■ During the)	43	seaweeds
16	B	44	C
17	C	45	B
18	A	46	C
19	the Great Lakes	47	(the) public
20	D	48	B (Polynesian tribe. ■ Once established)
21	D	49	C
22	A	50	D
23	C	51	B
24	C	52	A
25	amassed	53	D
26	D	54	C
27	C	55	C
28	goods		

Writing ➡

One can make decisions quickly, or after thinking long and carefully. Some people say it is always wrong to make a decision quickly. Do you agree or disagree with that view? Use specific examples and reasons to support your answer.

Decisions made quickly are not always wrong, but decisions made after careful thought are usually better. A quick decision does not allow enough time to consider all the important factors in a situation. That is why it is always advisable, if time allows, to think calmly and carefully when making a decision. A minute spent thinking before a decision may save much time and difficulty later. Here is a hypothetical example.

Imagine you are the head of a company which is losing money. The situation is very bad. You must lay off part of the work force. About 100 workers will lose their jobs. Should you give them one month's notice? That would make things easier for the employees, but the company would have to pay them for that month. Also, during that last month, an angry employee might commit sabotage, by damaging the company's computer system, in revenge.

Another approach is to tell them tomorrow that they all have been laid off, and have the security force escort them out of the building the same day. This method may seem cruel, but it would save millions of dollars for the company, at a time when every dollar matters. Also, this way you would avoid the risk of an angry employee committing sabotage before leaving the company. On the other hand, the remaining employees may decide that their jobs are at risk too, and leave. Then you would have to replace them. Either approach has both advantages and disadvantages.

Not every decision is so complicated. Most decisions are comparatively simple, such as what to have for lunch. When a decision affects your life and the lives of others in some important way, however, a cautious, careful decision is best.